MW00833814

¡El Capitán!

The Making of an American Naval Officer

A Memoir

Captain John Frank Gamboa, U. S. Navy (Retired)

**First Mexican-American Naval Surface Warfare Officer to Command
A Major United States Navy Warship**

To Barbara Bahl,

With best wishes!

Frank Gamboa

8/31/2011

FORTIS PUBLISHING

Jacksonville, Florida ♦ Herndon, Virginia

www.Fortis-Publishing.com

¡El Capitán!

The Making of an American Naval Officer

By Captain John Frank Gamboa, U. S. Navy (Retired)

Copyright © 2011. All rights reserved. No part of this book may be reproduced or transmitted in any form or by any means, electronic or mechanical, including photocopying, recording or by any information storage and retrieval system, without written permission from the author, except for brief quotations as would be used in a review.

ISBN 978-0-9846371-7-1 (hardcover)
Library of Congress Control Number: 2011928213

Published by Fortis Publishing
Jacksonville, Florida—Herndon, Virginia
www.Fortis-Publishing.com

Manufactured in the United States of America

All statements of fact, opinion, or analysis expressed are those of the author and do not reflect the official positions or views of the publisher. Nothing in the contents should be construed as asserting or implying authentication of information or endorsement of the author's views. This book and subjects discussed herein are designed to provide the author's opinion about the subject matter covered and is for informational purposes only.

In his heart, a man plans his course, but the Lord determines his steps.

Proverbs 16:9

Table of Contents

Dedication

Para Enriqueta, Teodulo, Chonita y Nacho

For Linda, Jack, Judy, Emma and Loren

For Tina, Bea, Leco, Mosey, Junior and Erlinda

For Emil, Bill, Ruth and Les

For Lone Pine

Acknowledgments

After I left the Navy, Linda and I settled into our new home in northern Virginia and began reinventing our life. Unpacking our household goods, we came across many boxes labeled "Frank's papers and memorabilia." I opened the boxes with the intent of tossing most of the flotsam overboard and just save the most important items in a few 3-ring binders. As I unpacked and organized the stuff, I reflected on the busy, challenging, adventurous and occasionally difficult times that Linda, Jack, Judy and I had experienced during our years in the Navy.

When the task was completed all the boxes were gone, but I had several book shelves filled with binders of official documents, correspondence, personal journals and many photos and news clips. Fearful of nostalgia, I ignored the material for many years and focused instead on our new endeavors, especially our consulting company that Linda and I incorporated in 1994.

In the late 1990s, I began having regular conversations with my mother, mainly by telephone, but also during our visits in California. To give our talks direction, I asked Enriqueta to talk about her life and Dad's life in Mexico and about their families. I recorded most of our conversations, compiling a rich oral history of our ancestors in Mexico and Spain. Mom also discussed her life when she came to America as a six year old and growing up in Ojai and Los Angeles, California. To preserve Mom's priceless recollections, I wrote our family history and shared it with my siblings, who added their own stories about our childhood and youth in Owens Valley. We all deeply appreciate Enriqueta's loving heritage gift to our family's present and future generations.

My enjoyment of the family history project led to my decision to create a memoir about my naval career; a brief and enjoyable pastime while managing our business. I was soon immersed in trying to review and organize the many documents and create a readable text—not a naval technical treatise but rather a narrative that would be even understandable to a non-Navy person.

My quick and easy writing project became considerably more difficult than I had envisioned. So I read several books on how to write about one's life and how to create a memoir. Our business occupied most of my time so it took many months to achieve minimal progress. Not until we closed our company at the end of 2006 was I able to devote adequate time to my research and writing.

Linda, Jack and Judy provided their own remembrances of our adventures in America and foreign lands, and family life during my frequent, extended absences. They urged me to include the "sea stories" we had laughed over so many times, especially with our Navy friends, over the dinner table. Jack and Judy are both well read and talented writers and their ideas about topics to include and the right level of detail were indispensable in my selection and framing of events and issues, and organizing text.

I was most fortunate to be assisted by good friends. In the spring of 2008, the manuscript was reviewed by Admiral Chuck Larson, Dr. Franz Wiedemann, Rear Admiral Ben Montoya, Marine Corps Lieutenant General Terry Cooper, Navy Captains Jack Dittrick, Vern Von Sydow, and Jeff Dennis, and my brother-in-law, Jean Clary. Their encouragement further motivated me. I incorporated their many excellent suggestions and their consensus recommendation to shorten the narrative.

After cutting, condensing and rewriting much text, I had the new manuscript reviewed by Rear Admiral Dick Pittenger, Marine Corps Colonel Art Athens, Marine Corps Lieutenant Colonel Orson Swindle, Joe McCain, and Dr. Juan Hernandez. Susan Cuadrado showed me how to break up the narrative's linearity for better readability. Everyone's comments were most helpful in my "polishing" of the narrative; Joe also helped on the chapter themes and technical content.

Kerry Christenson Powell, my Lone Pine kindergarten-through-12th grade classmate, fact-checked my Owens Valley description. Charles Cervantes provided suggestions on my discussion of ethnicity and culture. Tom Barnett did his naval surface warfare officer look see at my junior officer chapter. Taylor Kiland and Regan Wilson read the manuscript in advance of our hour-long interview about my memoir on their Radio America's "Veterans Chronicles" program.

Senator John McCain refreshed my memory on forgotten episodes from our fun days together in Mother Bancroft with our roommates Keith Bunting and Jack Dittrick. I am deeply grateful to John for his personal foreword to my memoir. I hereby completely forgive him. I have buried in the depths of oblivion, never to be recalled, my memories of all the weekend extra duty he caused me to serve—inadvertent collateral damage from our midshipman escapades.

In June 2010, I submitted the manuscript to a publishing firm, but they decided that it needed to be cut by another 40,000 words. I was ready to quit and take up my golf again, but Joe McCain's incisive analysis and no-nonsense recommendations on how to achieve the reduction caused me to reconsider. Then Linda came to my rescue, "Let me have it. If we have to cut it, we'll cut it. We'll work together." And we did.

During his review of the manuscript for his dust jacket comment, my friend Paul Stillwell, a noted naval historian, did an expert editorial review that upgraded the technical and grammatical quality of the memoir, for which I am deeply grateful.

I am forever indebted to my family and to all my friends for their generosity of time, help and support. Linda and I are thankful to Dennis Lowery and his Fortis Publishing firm's superb services that enabled us to reach our publication goal—June 4, 2011, the 53rd anniversary of my graduation from the Naval Academy.

Most of all, I am deeply grateful to Linda for her composition talents, skillful editing, tireless efforts and no end of patience—and for puncturing my pomposity whenever I attempted to transform the mundane into magnificence.

List of Illustrations

Foreword

I first met Frank Gamboa in our plebe year at the Naval Academy. We were members of the class of 1958, but we had traveled very different paths to our posts in Annapolis—I, the son and grandson of an admiral and a future admiral who enjoyed distinguished Navy careers; Frank, the son of Mexican immigrants, the first of his family to attend college and one of only seven Hispanic Americans in our Naval Academy class.

Frank and I chose to be roommates in our Youngster year. Together, we lived and drilled, threw parties and pulled pranks, applied ourselves and hit the books (well, he more than I). I got Frank in more trouble than he deserved during our four years at Annapolis, and he has never held it against me. This was the beginning of a lifelong friendship.

Frank has now drawn on his lifetime of experiences and recollections and produced a first-rate memoir.

¡El Capitán! The Making of an American Naval Officer traces Frank's journey from his struggle to overcome economic and other obstacles as the son of immigrants, to his entrance into the U.S. Naval Academy, to his many years serving with distinction in the U.S. Navy, ultimately becoming the first Mexican-American naval surface warfare line officer ever to command a major U.S. Navy warship. Frank has opened his life, drawing graciously on his own records, journals, and letters to his family and the result is a deeply moving and personal narrative.

This is the story of a Mexican-American boy, whose parents pursued the dream of a better life for themselves and their children in the United States—a dream that Frank realized to the fullest through a life of service to his country in uniform.

This is the story of the making of a Navy officer and his career at sea—not only the pleasures and the pride that are found in serving a cause greater than one's own interests, but also the hardships, the sacrifices, and the long separations from family that this service entails.

In short, this is a quintessentially American story—a story of dreaming and striving, of encountering hardships but overcoming them, of peoples from foreign lands joining the American citizenry and, through their endeavors, enriching the character of our country.

All of this is Frank's story, and I am privileged to be a small part of it.

John McCain

Washington, D.C.

Preface

A smooth sea never made a skilled mariner.
—English proverb

On June 4, 1958, I graduated from the United States Naval Academy and was commissioned an Ensign in the Navy Line. Aboard American warships I sailed the Atlantic, Pacific and Indian oceans—and lots of other blue water—for more than 17 years while operating in our nation's Second and Third Fleets and forward deployed in the Sixth and Seventh Fleets during the Cold War. The ships that I served on never came under hostile fire but they were always prepared for that eventuality.

This is a remembrance of my naval service to our country. Almost two decades after, I looked back at my 16 tours of duty, albeit through the imperfect filters of time, distance and memory. In due course, I decided to write about that period of my life and recount my quest to enter the academy and my unforgettable days in the Brigade of Midshipmen. Adding a multicultural and ethnic context, I chronicled my ancestry and my mother and father's respective journey from Mexico to Owens Valley, California, where they married, raised their seven children and achieved the American Dream. In the main, however, the narrative sheds light upon my responsibilities and performance of duty as a line officer in the naval surface warfare profession.

After I took command of the USS *Fort Fisher*, oftentimes my mother would proudly refer to me in Spanish as ¡El Capitán! In loving memory, I chose Enriqueta's words for the title of the memoir.

My sea duty spanned warship billets from division officer to commanding officer and squadron commander, the warship captain and commodore tours being the most interesting, challenging and exciting. But my service ashore was also demanding and enjoyable: staff officer in the US Forces, Korea/United Nations Command headquarters in the Republic of Korea; staff officer in two major communications systems headquarters in Washington, DC; commanding officer of a US naval communications station in Panama; and deputy assistant secretary of defense in the Pentagon.

iv

Although many things have changed since I was a midshipman at Annapolis or a line officer in the fleet, much remains the same; especially the Navy's enduring dedication to the defense, safety and security of our marvelous democratic republic.

The experience, knowledge, skills and wisdom that I acquired in the fullness of time, together with my insights gained through retrospection, reflection and unavoidable nostalgia, portray a very unique enterprise— the making of an American naval officer.

My career far exceeded the dreams and aspirations of a young Mexican American from the small, remote desert town of Lone Pine in Owens Valley. One who began his search for a brighter future with limited prospects, but blessed with the great good fortune to have been born in America.

The intent of *¡El Capitán!* is to illuminate my professional development in fleet and shore stations, particularly in command, and to fathom its transformational impact on my family and me.

I hope that every reader will enjoy this view of the Navy of my era and that my experiences and lessons learned will be of value to midshipmen and naval officers, especially those who aspire to command.

My fondest wish is that young Hispanic-American men and women will be inspired by my voyage and, as they pursue their dreams and shape their goals for a happy and fulfilling future, they will also consider serving our great nation.

Part I

Owens Valley and the Formative Years

Chapter One

We are built for the valley, for the ordinary stuff we are in, and that is where we have to prove our mettle.

—Oswald Chambers

In our childhood and youth, we are imbued by our parents and family with the core values that form our character and personality. But the land where we grow up also shapes our enduring traits and outlook. Geography matters. In my first 18 years, I did not live near seashores nor in the mountains, nor on the Great Plains; neither did I reside on a farm nor in a barrio. Instead, I was born and raised in one of America's most unique regions—Owens Valley.

Oriented on a northwest axis in eastern California, the valley lies about 200 miles inland from the Pacific coast. It is the deepest in the lower 48. Its floor is generally flat at 4000 feet above sea level with a maximum width of about 15 miles below Owens Lake. The drive on highway 395 is about 105 miles from its southern gateway near a place called Little Lake up to its northern access on the Sherwin Grade above Bishop, Owens Valley's largest town.

The majestic Sierra Nevada mountain range forms the valley's western boundary. Spaniards named it la Sierra Nevada the snowy mountains after the range with the same name in southeastern Spain. The fertile San Joaquin valley lies west of the Sierras. In Owens Valley the Sierra's peaks, which average 14,000 feet above sea level, block the Pacific's moisture-laden winds, causing a scarcity of water in the valley and throughout the eastern Sierra region that includes Death Valley and borders the Great Basin of Nevada and Utah.

Two rugged mountain ranges of slightly lesser altitude shape the valley's eastern limits. At its northern end and east of Bishop are the White Mountains where bristle cone pines grow, the oldest living trees on earth—some over 4000 years. South of the White Mountains and east of the town of Lone Pine are the Inyo Mountains. Farther south is the low Coso Mountain range, which forms the valley's southeastern border with the arid Mojave Desert.

¡El Capitán!

The view from my bedroom window was the Sierras' beautiful Mount Whitney, a rugged granite peak—the highest in the lower 48—towering at a height of 14,505 feet. The Whitney Portals, at its base, is the gathering place for hundreds of Whitney hikers in May-October. Between Lone Pine and the Sierras are the Alabama Hills, a seven-mile-stretch of enormous weatherworn granite boulders, piled into spectacular shapes and formations by ancient geological events.

Owens Valley's beauty is enhanced by its stark contrasts—the snow-capped mountains, the picturesque Alabamas, the shifting sand dunes on the shores of Owens Lake, the valley floor's ubiquitous sagebrush. Pink dawns bathe the Sierra peaks, signaling the end of night in the valley. High in the cloudless azure sky a blazing sun characterizes the days. In late afternoons, the Sierra's shadows glide across the valley floor and climb up the eastern mountain ranges, blending golden hues with shades of tan, brown and purple. Framed by the mountains, the black night sky sparkles with spectacular twinkling stars, constellations, and planets.

The valley's four seasons are etched forever in the memories of my youth. Autumn's Indian summer turns the leaves of the cottonwoods and the quaking aspens to bright red, orange and yellow, harbingers of cold winters. Storms blanket the mountains with deep snows from November to April; the rays of the rising and setting sun creating a dazzling iridescence on the snowy peaks. Springtime is heralded by a colorful variety of beautiful desert flowers, including Mariposa poppies, yellow desert dandelions, Red Indian paintbrushes and stands of Blue Lupine on snow-water creek banks. Summer's noonday sun raises the valley's temperature, but the low humidity makes the climate bearable even as the mercury soars over 100.

The valley has archeological signs of human habitation earlier than 3000 BCE. Small tribes of Native American Paiute and Shoshone inhabited the valley for many generations, thriving on wildlife, berries in the meadows and nuts from the Pinyon trees that grow at lower elevations in the Sierras as well as in the White and Inyo mountains. The Indians also grew crops on the fertile soil irrigated by the Owens River.

In 1845, Captain Joe Walker's detachment of the John Fremont expedition explored the valley. The reported agricultural and mineral potential sparked a migration to the valley. Cattlemen from the San Joaquin Valley drove herds of cattle, horses and mules into the valley and sheepherders brought their flocks. Prospectors explored the foothills and

2

mountains for gold and silver. The town of Lone Pine, established in 1861, was named by a gold-mining party for a tall pine growing far below the tree line near their creek side camp. The town became a vibrant supply center for the valley's mines, farms and ranches. It had blacksmith shops, saloons, stores, churches, homes and "sporting houses" (brothels).

The new settlers eventually clashed with the Native Americans, which led to the establishment of a U.S. Army cavalry outpost in the town of Independence, 16 miles north of Lone Pine. The town of Big Pine was established between Independence and Bishop. Inyo County (Inyo is Paiute for "the dwelling space of the great spirit[1]") was established in 1866 with Independence as the county seat.

Access to the valley from the south was by stagecoach, wagon train, mule or horse across the Mojave Desert from Los Angeles, or over Walker Pass near the southern end of the Sierras, and by like transportation from Nevada,.

In 1866 in the Inyo mountains east of Lone Pine and above Keeler, which lies at the base of the mountains, at a site named by the Mexican prospector who discovered it, Cerro Gordo (fat hill) became the richest silver strike in California's history. Los Angeles became the mine's logistics support center, spurring its growth. In Cerro Gordo's heyday in the 1870s, over 100 mule-team wagons maintained the flow of supplies to the mines and hauled their ore to the smelters in Mojave and Los Angeles. (The wagons had 16-18 mules; the 20 mule-team wagons operated in the 1880s mainly to haul borax mineral from Death Valley to Mojave.)

In 1883, the Carson and Colorado Railroad Company constructed a narrow-gauge railroad system from Mound House, Nevada, to Keeler, over 160 miles, primarily to haul ore from the mines. For many years, it was the most efficient transportation system in and out of the valley.

The headwaters of the Owens River originate in Mono County in the Sierras north of Bishop. The river courses through the upper half of the valley and debouches into Owens Lake. The river was a source of irrigation for its surrounding terrain. By the late 1800s, farming and ranching had become prominent in the valley's economy. Manzanar, a large orchard about eight miles north of Lone Pine, produced a variety of fruit—mainly apples—and shipped its harvests to Los Angeles and Nevada.

¡El Capitán!

To meet its great need for an additional water source, in 1904 the city of Los Angeles decided to support the city's rapid growth by diverting the Owens River water to Los Angeles through an aqueduct from Owens Valley to San Fernando Valley in the Los Angeles basin. The city purchased Owens Valley land needed for the 237-mile waterway and to acquire the water rights for pumping additional water into the aqueduct from the valley's aquifer. It ultimately purchased over 95% of the valley's land from Inyo County and valley farmers, ranchers and homeowners. (Some of these events are depicted in the movie *"Chinatown."*) This set the stage for contentious confrontations and extended litigation between the city and the valley for decades to come.

Construction of the aqueduct created the need for efficient means to transport construction materials, supplies and people from Los Angeles and elsewhere to Owens Valley. The Southern Pacific Railway Company responded by constructing a 150-mile broad-gauge railroad (the Jawbone Branch) from Mojave to Owenyo, its terminus three miles north of Lone Pine. And the city of Los Angeles and the state upgraded the main highway from Mojave through the valley to Bishop and beyond.

The aqueduct's arduous excavation and construction were accomplished in blazing hot summers and frigid winters by as many as 3900 workers, including many Mexicans and other immigrant groups. The Tenemaha Reservoir was constructed about five miles south of Big Pine for the aqueduct's intake from the river. In October 1913 at the canal's opening ceremony in San Fernando Valley, as the Sierras' snow-melt water cascaded down the spillway, the City of Los Angeles' Chief Engineer William Mulholland commented tersely to the crowd of spectators, "There it is. Take it!"

The city's aqueduct and extensive water pumping rights cut off water to the valley and Owens Lake, which caused the lake's evaporation and its shores to be deposited with soda ash (anhydrous sodium carbonate) and other minerals. Soda ash manufacturing plants were constructed on the lake's shores at Cartago, Keeler and Bartlett. High winds over Owens Lake carried the dry soda ash throughout the valley, causing significant pollution and air quality degradation. Beginning a clean air project in the valley in 2001, the city of Los Angeles spent more than $400 million dollars putting a small percentage of the water from the aqueduct back into the river and lake, and other measures to mitigate the air pollution.

Captain John Frank Gamboa, U. S. Navy (Retired)

The current phase of the project was completed in 2010, and additional phases are planned.

Owens Valley's scenic terrain has attracted Hollywood filmmakers since 1920. More films (over 400), mostly "B" movies were created on location in the Alabama Hills and vicinity than any other site in the world except Hollywood. Over the years, Lone Pine residents and businesses became accustomed to dealing with many famous movie stars, giving the town a cosmopolitan flair.

During the filming of *Tycoon* in 1947 in the Alabamas, my brother Fredrick (Leco) and I were hired by RKO Theaters at $50 a day as "extras" and issued our social security cards. Dressed as Bolivian peasants, we each led a llama on the main street of a small Bolivian mining town set. John Wayne and Anthony Quinn drove up the dirt street in a Model A Ford; children, dogs and chickens scampered out of their way as Wayne careened around us. The scene is the background for the opening film credits. After our filming was completed, we joined Wayne, Quinn and the film crew for lunch on location. But that was the extent of our Hollywood film careers.

In 1989, my good friend Kerry Christenson Powell, motivated by her desire to display and preserve Lone Pine's unique part in Hollywood's movie film industry history, and to improve the attractiveness of southern Inyo County to tourists, created the concept and developed and coordinated plans for a Lone Pine film festival. She then mobilized her husband Ray, Dorothy Bonnefin, the other town leaders and scores of enthusiastic volunteers to stage the festival in October 1990, celebrating movies filmed in the Alabamas and vicinity. Hollywood film stars, directors, producers and stuntmen participated in movie film production forums.

The four-day festival was an immediate success and became a popular annual Columbus Day event. The festival is attended by thousands of tourists, many in cowboy and fancy-lady movie costumes. In 1993, plans for construction of a Lone Pine film history museum were initiated with the generous support of benefactors Beverly and Jim Rogers. The museum opened in 2008 on the town's main street featuring movies filmed on location in the Alabamas and vicinity, and displaying costumes, set relics and other memorabilia from Lone Pine's proud movie film heritage.

¡El Capitán!

On February 19, 1942, President Franklin Roosevelt ordered the War Department to define military areas in the United States and to "hold anyone therein who might threaten the war effort." In less than two months the Army Corps of Engineers built a War Relocation Center at Manzanar, the first of 10 such facilities throughout the United States where American citizens of Japanese ancestry were incarcerated (my father and grandfather worked at the Manzanar construction site when they were temporarily laid off at the Bartlett soda ash plant after Pearl Harbor). In Bartlett, my sisters, my playmates, and I watched by the highway as the advance group of about 200 Japanese men driving their own cars topped with luggage and personal belongings were convoyed with military armed escorts to Manzanar. Afterwards, over 10,000 Japanese-American detainees were transported by train and busses to the relocation center from Los Angeles, thereby creating the valley's largest population center.

Manzanar was closed in November 1945 and each detainee was given $25 upon departure. In the 1980s, on behalf of the nation, President Ronald Reagan made a formal apology to the detainees and their survivors, and Congress authorized payment of restitution. In 2004, the National Park Service opened the Manzanar Museum, with films, artifacts, building replicas, a guard tower and a roster of the center's detainees.

Owens Valley's geographical barriers seem to embrace and enclose its residents, often creating feelings of isolation. But the Sierras and the mountains and rugged, barren territory bordering the valley to the east also promote close-knit relationships—and even influence the residents' manner of speaking. Motoring to Los Angeles is "going down below;" or driving "over to Death Valley;" or "going up to Reno." If traveling to the Atlantic seaboard, folks are said to be "headed back east." Mary Austin best captured the remoteness of the valley in the preface to her book about the region, *The Land of Little Rain.*[2]

> … You may come into the borders of it from the south by a stage journey that has the effect of involving a great lapse of time, or from the north by rail, dropping out of the overland route at Reno. The best of all ways is over the Sierra passes by pack and trail, seeing and believing. But the real heart and core of the

country are not to be come at in a month's vacation. One must summer and winter with the land and wait its occasions. Pine woods that take two or three seasons to the ripening of cones, roots that lie by in the sand seven years awaiting a growing rain, firs that grow fifty years before flowering—these do not scrape acquaintance....

In 1950, Austin's book was re-published with photos taken in the valley by photographer Ansel Adams. In 1948 when he was in Lone Pine, Adams approached a local resident on Main Street and asked where he could find some Mexican children to photograph. "Just go down to the Gamboas, they have lots of them" was his reply, giving Adams directions to our home.

My youngest brother, Junior (five years old) was playing marbles in our front yard with a playmate. Mom was hanging laundry. Ansel introduced himself and explained his project, "May I take your son's picture?" Mom replied, "Let me wash his face, comb his hair and put some clean clothes on him." Ansel replied, "No, please, I want to photograph him just as he is." He posed Junior inside the family car looking out the door window. Adams included the photo in *Land of Little Rain* and in a book of his most-admired photographs.[3]

My mother, Enriqueta Perez, arrived in Lone Pine from Los Angeles in 1927 at age 17 with her mother, Concepcion ("Chonita") Perez de Barraza, and Ignacio ("Nacho") Herrera de Gamboa, her stepfather. Nacho's cousins Teodulo Gamboa de Herrera and Juan Navar de Herrera accompanied them. Nacho got a job on the Los Angeles aqueduct; Teodulo and Juan went to work on the railroad at Owenyo. My grandmother and mother worked at home providing meals to Mexican laborers who worked on the railroads, in the mines, paving Lone Pine's main street (state highway 395), on the ranches and maintaining the Los Angeles aqueduct.

Enriqueta and Teodulo began dating and her plans to return to Los Angeles spurred him to propose. They were married in the Independence courthouse in December 1928. Teodulo was 24 and Enriqueta was 18. They established their home 20 miles south of Lone Pine in Cartago where he worked at the soda ash plant. They lived in company housing. It was a happy time for the newlyweds; they had many friends and enjoyed going to dances in Keeler and Lone Pine. Later, Nacho got a job at the same plant and he and Chonita became their neighbors.

Enriqueta and Teodulo's first child, Ernestina (Tina) was born in the Lone Pine hospital December 16, 1929. Beatrice (Bea) was born at home in Cartago June 19, 1931, and I was born there August 12, 1933. America was in the depths of the Great Depression. To supplement the family larder, Nacho and Dad would hunt in the nearby fields and Sierra foothills for deer, rabbits, doves and quail. Our family always had plenty to eat even during those bleak economic times.

In late 1933, my father and Nacho got jobs at the new soda ash plant at Bartlett, which was north of Cartago on the southwestern banks of Owens Lake. We lived at Bartlett; the plant's housing community near the plant and eight miles south of Lone Pine.

North from Cartago, highway 395 goes along the base of the Sierra foothills and rises gradually to the crest of a broad hill above Bartlett. A dirt road descended into the community, which had about 20 homes that were surrounded by sagebrush and a few cottonwood and willow trees. Water was piped to the houses from a large wooden tank near the highway, but there was neither electricity nor sidewalks.

The Southern Pacific Railroad divided Bartlett into two sections: about 12 houses above the tracks and a triplex and a duplex below. The houses above the tracks had wood siding and indoor toilets, and several had white picket fences and lawns. The houses below the tracks were built on concrete slabs with concrete walls painted white inside and out. Each had an outhouse with a flush toilet about 20 feet from the back door. The surrounding yards were of hard, barren dirt and sagebrush.

Our home was below the tracks in half of a duplex that included a porch, a kitchen, a living room, and a single bedroom—less than 900 square feet of living space. Nacho and Chonita lived in the other half of the duplex. We also had a garage made of railroad ties and corrugated tin roof. Dad screened the parking space between the two houses and enclosed half of our porch for my sisters' bedroom. I slept on a cot in my grandparents' living room or in the screened carport in the summer. My brothers Frederick (Leco) and William Moses (Mosey) were born in Bartlett March 1, 1937 and September 4, 1940 respectively. They shared a bed in our living room.

Our house had no bathing facilities (until Dad built the outdoor shower stall) so everyone bathed in a large galvanized tin tub in the kitchen after dinner with water heated on the wood-burning stove. My sisters, brothers, and I bathed on Saturday nights. The boys had to go last, and Mom would make sure we had scrubbed well. During the weekdays, everyone washed in the kitchen sink with cold water—but it was heated on the stove during the winter.

We kept about two dozen chickens in a fenced chicken coop behind the garage and a flock of pigeons cooped on its roof. Three hutches on the side of the garage held about a dozen rabbits. On some nights, a pack of coyotes would howl on the banks of the gully near our home, frightening the chickens. For fresh milk, my parents purchased a nanny goat. Soon after, Honey gave birth to one kid. We kept the two goats in a fenced enclosure inside the garage. I was responsible for feeding them and milking Honey each morning. Goat's milk is very rich and creamy but it has a gamey odor and taste. I liked it poured over my breakfast cereal, but it almost made Tina and Bea gag.

During the school year, my sisters and I would walk on a path through the sagebrush to the top of Bartlett hill and wait with the other kids by the highway for the school bus; it was awfully cold in wintertime. At 7:30 a.m., the soda ash plant sounded a steam whistle to signal the start of the day shift. It blasted again at noon to signal the lunch break and at 3:30 p.m. to end the day shift and start the night shift. On summer afternoons when we heard the whistle, my sisters and I would often walk along the tracks to greet Dad and Nacho and carry their lunch buckets home. They always saved a snack or piece of fruit for us.

My playmates and I explored the terrain near Bartlett to search for arrowheads. Sometimes we hiked about a mile up to the aqueduct, which was protected by chain link fencing. Along the way we would search for lizards and horned toads—and watch out for rattlesnakes. From a single-lane bridge over the canal, we tossed small sticks into the water to see how fast ours would float out of sight. It was fascinating to see so much cool, clear, rushing, swirling snow water flowing in that vast, arid expanse of sand and sagebrush.

It was often windy in the afternoons so we flew kites that we made from wooden fruit crates, old newspapers, flour and water paste, and rag tails. We played marbles and we made slingshots from willow branches and strips of worn-out inner tubes and discarded shoe leather, and we had contests shooting stones at discarded cans and bottles.

¡El Capitán!

In the spring, clouds of dust to the south signaled that a flock of sheep was being herded from Bakersfield to pastures near Bishop. There were usually two sheepherders with several sheep dogs and a chuck wagon hauled by two burros. My sisters, playmates and I would gather above the highway to watch them pass. Once Tina called out, "Can you please give us a lamb?" They said "No" as they walked past with their flock. So she said, "Can we have a dog?" To our surprise, one herder turned and replied, "I'll bring you a puppy next year!" The next spring when we spotted the familiar dust cloud, we ran up the hill and eagerly awaited the flock's arrival. As he had promised, the chief herder had a puppy for Tina and she happily carried it home. Dad named him *Sarjento*, Sergeant, and said he was in charge of us. *Sarjento* stayed close by when we were outdoors, and slept next to Tina's bed.

Our kitchens had a wood-burning stove so we always kept firewood in boxes beside the kitchen door. Keeping grandmother's and ours filled was one of my daily chores. Every few weeks Nacho would take a playmate and me on a wood-gathering excursion to the *resacas,* Cottonwood Creek's dry washes that were a few miles south of Bartlett. They were littered with pine trees and broken branches carried down from the Sierras by storms and cloudbursts. Nacho would saw, split, and chop while we explored, and then we helped load the truck. Chonita always packed a delicious lunch: *burritos* and *empanadas de calabasas*, pumpkin turnovers. We quenched our thirst with cool water from the wet canvas canteen that Nacho hung on the car radiator.

The Southern Pacific train passed through Bartlett once a week in the morning on its northward journey to Owenyo, and then in the evening on its return to Mojave, stopping at the soda plant to hook up boxcars loaded with sacks of soda ash. A huge, noisy, rumbling monstrosity with clanging bell and loud whistle, the black steam engine spewed clouds of smoke and hissing steam—a marvelous, frightening sight. My siblings, playmates and I would run near the tracks and wave to the engineers. Sometimes they would acknowledge our greetings with short blasts on the engine's steam whistle that was so loud we had to cover our ears. My playmate Moe Mojarro and I would often place large nails on the tracks so the engine's wheels could smash them flat. After several nail-flattening attempts, we made the good ones into play knives.

One evening the train crew said they had hit a cow on the tracks about a mile north of Bartlett in open stock range. Dad, Nacho, and the other fathers quickly gathered up laundry tubs, knives and flashlights, walked along the tracks and located the carcass. My playmates and I eagerly tagged along. The men butchered the cow and filled the tubs with fresh beef. The women divided the meat among all the families. Having no refrigeration, Mom and Grandma sliced their share of the meat into long, thin strips, marinated them, and then hung them to dry on lines strung inside the screened porch. The dried beef made delicious stews and *burritos*. My playmates and I enjoyed our beef jerky snacks.

In summertime, our great-grandparents Andrea and Caco would drive over 200 miles from Ojai, California, in their ancient delivery truck. Behind its cab was a roofed wooden frame with shelves and canvas sides that rolled up like window shades. The shelves would be filled with crates of fresh fruits and vegetables, including *nopales* cactus leaves, *tunas* cactus pears, oranges, apples, grapes, and melons, as well as *carnitas* cooked pork, *chorizo* sausage, *pan dulce* Mexican pastries, and delicious Mexican candy. We proudly shared the abundance with our neighbors.

Andrea and Caco's visits were like a grand feast with lots of talking, laughing and happy feelings among our family. Mom deeply loved Andrea, which was fully reciprocated. Caco always brought his toolbox and went about fixing anything in need of repair—with Mom's supervision. Andrea had a loving personality and a sweet smile. After breakfast, she would read to my siblings and me in Spanish from her Bible. We enjoyed her company and listening to her soft sonorous voice.

Because of the financial contrasts in Bartlett between the families that lived above the tracks and those who lived below, our family was probably considered poor. But we never felt poor, we never went hungry and we were never on welfare. My siblings and I had good clothes, socks and shoes. In winter, we wore warm coats, caps and gloves that Mom purchased from the Sears catalog or the JC Penney store in Lone Pine. We had a new Ford sedan. But, to be sure, there was little money to spare beyond necessities. We didn't celebrate birthdays with parties, or exchange gifts at Christmas, but the Lone Pine Lions Club staged a town Christmas party and gave each kid a Christmas stocking filled with candy and nuts. Sometimes the train crew would toss us bags of candy at Christmas time.

To earn extra money, Mom cleaned house and did laundry for Mrs. Houghton, wife of the plant chemist, and cooked platters of enchiladas for them. In summertime, Mrs. Houghton would invite me and my playmates into their home to play board games and enjoy delicious cookies and lemonade. I was fascinated by their beautiful furnishings, so different from ours.

Our parents were always improving our standard of living. They bought a gasoline-motor powered washing machine to ease the labor-intensive laundry workload. For perishables like eggs, butter, cheese and milk, Dad built an ingenious water evaporation-cooled box on the porch adjacent to the kitchen. Next to the house, he built an enclosed outdoor shower stall with a 50-gallon drum above it filled with water warmed by the sun. To provide us with a radio, he designed and erected a four-telephone-pole tower (the neighborhood men helped) topped with a windmill-powered charger for the radio batteries (Bartlett was wired for electricity in the late 1940s). Mom purchased the windmill and charger through the Sears catalog and bought the radio and batteries in Lone Pine. We enjoyed listening to programs, especially the joyful sounds of Mariachi music while Mom cooked our breakfast. We were one of the few families in Bartlett that owned a radio. Dad had only an eighth-grade education, but he was blessed with a keen intellect, great common sense and an intuitive ability to solve complex mechanical engineering and construction problems.

On warm summer evenings, my parents would often join Chonita and Nacho on their porch. Neighbors would stop by to visit and have coffee. The men drank port or muscatel wine, beer, or a shot of *tequila.* The kids enjoyed candy, fruit, or *empanadas.* The adults discussed everyday life, but they also spoke of their lives in Mexico and relatives there. They described family struggles to survive during the Mexican Revolution and those who died in the war. They talked about coming to California in search of better lives. Pancho Villa's name was often mentioned as well as other revolutionary leaders. Although at times their voices were tinged with sadness, it comforted my siblings and me to see our parents, grandparents and neighbors relaxing after their day's hard work.

Bartlett was an integrated community, but I was aware of our differences. My siblings and I had black hair, brown eyes and olive complexion, unlike our blond-haired, blue-eyed, fair-skinned Anglo playmates; and my sisters, brothers, and I were bilingual. My family celebrated Thanksgiving with traditional American turkey—and Mexican dishes. My Anglo playmates all loved Mexican food such as *arroz con pollo, caldito, burritos, frijoles, tortillas,* and *empanadas.* We especially enjoyed Chonita's exquisite rice pudding.

But tamales were our favorite. To celebrate the New Year, Mom and grandma and our Mexican women neighbors would team up— *"Vamos hacer una tamalada"* we will have a tamale-making! They would labor for two days, first shopping for beef, pork, corn, corn husks, lard, and lye (used in boiling water to soften the dry corn) and then prepare the ingredients in our kitchen. To grind the softened kernels for the *masa* dough, my sisters and I would help turn the handle on the grinder. The delicious smell of tamales cooking on the wood stove kept my siblings, playmates and me nearby.

Throughout the *tamalada*, the women laughed, gossiped, and enjoyed themselves. The finished tamales would be equally divided by the women. Everyone especially enjoyed the sweet ones for dessert. The happy family atmosphere and sounds of contentment resonating in our kitchen—and the aroma—during a *tamalada* are among my most treasured childhood remembrances.

On New Year's Eve, Tina and Bea helped Enriqueta and Chonita make *buneulos,* a tortilla-like fried pastry served with warm honey at midnight. For New Year's morning, Mom would prepare a tasty dish called *menudo,* a traditional Mexican beef tripe stew with white hominy, red chili and spices garnished with cilantro, chopped scallions, and fresh lime juice. Dad claimed it was the only sure cure for a hangover.

Our home was bilingual. Mom could speak, read and write in English as well as in Spanish, but Dad, Chonita and Nacho spoke and read only in Spanish, so Spanish was Tina and Bea's first language (and mine). They learned English in school and by associating with their Anglo playmates. When Tina completed kindergarten, her English was considered inadequate for first grade, so she had to repeat kindergarten. Mother and Dad were very upset and Mom protested, to no avail.

Because the school held Tina back, thereafter Mom spoke to her children mostly in English. I was only three years old and just learning to speak Spanish. Consequently, I became much more fluent in English than Spanish by the time I entered kindergarten. But my learning to read in English was problematic, through no fault of my own.

¡El Capitán!

In 1989, at a metro bus stop near our condominium in Alexandria, Virginia, I struck up a conversation with a neighbor. When I mentioned that I grew up in Lone Pine, she said that her aunt, June White, taught school there in 1940. I laughed, "She was my first-grade teacher and her husband Bob was my grammar school principal!" She wrote to her aunt and about two weeks later she showed me a letter from June. Her first job was teaching my first grade class in Lone Pine. School policy mandated that Mexican-American children in first grade would not be given their readers until several weeks after their Anglo classmates, assuming that they would not comprehend the material, but after several weeks of hearing their Anglo classmates reading in class, the Mexican-American children would be better able to cope with the intellectual challenge.

Despite her great misgivings, June felt she had to implement the policy. Soon she noticed that I was learning to read by looking onto my classmates' books. She also noted that the other kids were comfortable with me reading in class. She therefore decided to give me my reader much sooner than the school policy allowed. I was soon reading as well as my classmates. Thereafter, June said she ignored school policy and gave all her students their first reader at the same time regardless of their ethnicity.

I can only imagine the negative, hurtful impact to all schoolchildren from this disparate and biased policy. (In Orange County, California, Mexican-American public school students were segregated until the late 1940s.)

Mom's decision to speak in English to her children had an unintended consequence—it created a language barrier between me and my father. Tina and Bea had spoken Spanish longer than I had, so they understood him well (Bea remembers that he taught her and Tina their bedtime prayers in Spanish), but I often couldn't understand him. It made Dad angry when I didn't promptly do as I was told. His reaction frightened me, so I tried to avoid him as much as possible, adversely affecting our relationship.

Even so, not all of my relationship difficulties with my father were caused by language. He was emotionally distant to me compared to my sisters and my younger brothers, reflecting Mexican cultural notions concerning first sons—they are expected to be responsible, set an example and be leaders—*tienes que ser un hombre* you must be a man.

14

Captain John Frank Gamboa, U. S. Navy (Retired)

Dad's loneliness for his many siblings and relatives in his home village in Durango affected his morale His cousin and closest friend Juan Navar returned there after Teodulo and Enriqueta were married. "He has you now, he doesn't need me anymore!" Juan poignantly told Mom upon his leave-taking.

Dad must have realized that he was never going to return to Mexico to live again among his family and friends. A very private person with great dignity and self-discipline, he would not express his feelings to his children about his longing for his homeland and relatives but Mom knew that he deeply missed his family and Mexico. And he was undoubtedly affected by his responsibilities in raising a large family during those very trying times—in a land and language that were foreign to him. The Mexican Revolution and the Great Depression also took an emotional toll on both of my parents and grandparents.

We were living in Bartlett when the Japanese bombed Pearl Harbor. I was eight years old and did not understand the event, but felt that something very bad happened because all the grown-ups were so upset. Production at the soda ash plant slowed considerably for a period and many workers were laid off. Dad got a new job at the marble quarry near Keeler. We left Bartlett and moved into the small Dolomite quarry housing community. Chonita and Nacho remained in Bartlett. When Dad was rehired at the soda ash plant two months later, we didn't return to company housing. We moved to Lone Pine.

In the early 1960s, the soda ash plant ceased operation—its loud steam whistle silenced forever. The plant's buildings, brine tanks and equipment are still in place, but are deteriorating as the years go by. Bartlett was vacated when the plant closed, so Chonita and Nacho moved into a small cottage that my parents purchased and moved onto the lot next to our home in Lone Pine. The Bartlett houses were demolished and the debris hauled away. About the same time, in Owenyo the narrow-gauge railroad was sold, dismantled and trucked away by its new owners. A decade later, economic activity in the valley no longer sustained its railroad's profitability so Southern Pacific closed the broad-gauge train's operation and removed its tracks. Only the rail beds of these two vital transportation systems remain, now overgrown by sagebrush.

¡El Capitán!

The concrete slab of the house where we lived is still there, but it is disintegrating and will disappear in time. All the structures that Dad built are gone. Of the four telephone poles that he used to construct a tower for the windmill battery charger, only one stump remains, visible just above the ground's surface. On my office shelf, a jagged piece of wood that I removed from it lies next to a shard of wall concrete that I retrieved near the slab.

In that small, remote desert village, I learned to speak Spanish and English. It is the place and time where I began my assimilation into American culture.

Driving on 395 to visit friends in Lone Pine, when I arrive at the crest of Bartlett hill I exit the highway and drive onto the barely visible dirt road leading down to where Bartlett used to be. I cross over the trackless rail bed and go to where we lived below the tracks, stopping near what remains of our former home.

Standing on its concrete slab, I gaze once more at the scenes of my childhood. Looking to the south, I listen for the plant's piercing steam whistle. I walk a short distance on the rail bed expecting to feel the train's vibrations. I walk a few steps on the path to the highway where we caught the school bus. Other memories well up. My lungs fill with the warm dry air.

I recall the days when this was my whole world—a happy, carefree time with my playmates and my siblings and the loving care of my parents and my grandparents. I am unable to linger but a brief time.

Our first home in Lone Pine was "the Bill Harry House," a large barn-red clapboard structure near the center of town on a corner one block south of Main Street (highway 395). It had been a brothel in the 1920s, which accounted for its large parlor and many small bedrooms with a connecting hallway. And during the Prohibition era, the town's bootleggers had made whiskey there—all part of Lone Pine's colorful past.

We enjoyed the abundant living space with bedrooms for everyone, a large kitchen, a spacious parlor and dining area, even an indoor bathroom with a beautiful white porcelain ball-and-claw-foot bathtub. No more tin tub baths in the kitchen or showers with sun-heated water. The house had electricity so we put away our kerosene lamps, ending our weekly chore of filling the lamps, cleaning their glass chimneys and trimming wicks.

Our school bus days were over; we walked to school one block away, and we could walk to the movie theatre nearby. There were sidewalks and streetlights. The streets were paved and cars drove by day and night. And we spoke to our neighbors in English.

The town's business section was about ten blocks long with stores, auto garages and gas stations on both sides of Main Street. There were about six restaurants and eleven saloons, a carry-over from the town's frontier days as a logistical support and entertainment center. It also had eleven churches of various denominations and Mamie's and Helen's "sporting houses" were about three miles to the north and to the south of town respectively.

In 1942, Lone Pine had about 1500 residents. After America's entry into the war, the valley's economy increased significantly. All the mines were in operation, as were the soda ash plants, the talc mine, the marble quarry, the railroads and the Los Angeles aqueduct—there was full employment. The establishment of the War Relocation Center at Manzanar had a positive economic impact; the valley provided logistical support for the center and for the Army garrison stationed there.

A Civilian Pilot Training Program was established at Lone Pine High, a precursor course for Army and Navy flight schools. The cadets lived in tents next to the football field and marched into town for meals at a vacant store converted into a mess hall. They marched to the airport a mile south of the school and learned to fly Piper Cubs; some with women pilot instructors. Cadet Jim Ellis, who became a Marine Corps fighter pilot, later returned to marry Juanita Ruiz, a Lone Pine beauty.

As in other towns and cities across America, many of Lone Pine's young men enlisted in the armed forces right after Pearl Harbor, or were drafted into the Army as soon as they graduated from high school. The town's Turner Barnes VFW Post is named for the first Lone Pine serviceman to die in the war. After the war, Navy Lieutenant Bill Bauer resumed his job as High School Principal, District Superintendent, and football and baseball coach. Navy Pilot Lieutenant Roy Joseph, his lovely wife Josephine and his brother Don, an Army B-17 bomber gunner, resumed management of their father's Josephs Market, the town's largest grocery store. Marine Corps Captain Jim Ellis returned to run the Ford dealership. Many other war veterans became prominent members of the community.

¡El Capitán!

When we arrived in Lone Pine, my parents had no money to spare, and the war created uncertainty, but they were determined to improve our standard of living. Enriqueta got a job at the Dow Hotel cleaning guest rooms. Over time, she worked in several other motels and the commercial laundry, walking to and from these jobs in every kind of weather. And she catered to town residents, preparing Mexican food dishes at home, assisted by Tina and Bea.

A firm believer that everyone should earn their way in life, Mom soon got babysitting jobs for my sisters and me. Later, Tina went to work in the Lone Pine hospital as a nurse's aide and Bea at the drug store soda fountain. Mom got me a job stocking drugstore shelves at 40 cents an hour. On Saturdays, I worked at the Chalfant Press melting down the used lead linotype strips in a blazing furnace and pouring the molten lead into steel molds for the ingots used by the linotype machine, a huge, noisy contraption with many moving parts. On Sundays, I would clean the doctor's office mopping and waxing the floors, cleaning the bathrooms and polishing the furniture.

Although we would rather have been hanging out with our friends, Tina, Bea and I learned to work in a structured environment and to perform responsibly in a job. Mom allowed us to keep enough money for school clothes and expenses, but we all contributed to the family budget. We were still a growing family. Theodore (Junior) and Erlinda (Linda) were born December 18, 1943, and November 4, 1945, respectively.

In the summer of 1944, our parents purchased a small house in Lone Pine, achieving the American Dream. They also leased the large adjacent lot. Living conditions were crowded in our new home, so in the spring of 1945, they also purchased two old condemned houses to dismantle for the lumber they needed to remodel our home. Each day when Dad got home from work, he and I would hitch our two-wheeled trailer to the car, gather up our hammers, saws, crowbars and nail-pullers and work until dark removing roof shingles, sideboards, floorboards and studs. We loaded the lumber into the trailer, hauled it home and stacked it in sorted piles. Only the large central room in each house was left intact. One day in May 1945, Dad and I were on the roof removing shingles when we noticed the high school students parading their cars up and down Main Street, honking their car horns, shouting and cheering. Germany had surrendered. It was VE Day. I was 11 years old.

Captain John Frank Gamboa, U. S. Navy (Retired)

Once the two houses were dismantled, we had a house-moving company transport the two remaining central rooms to our lot, an amazing evolution. My sisters slept in one "cabin" and my brothers and I slept in the other. During the house remodeling the following spring, we dismantled one cabin for lumber and moved the other onto the back corner of our adjacent lot, placed it on a concrete foundation, installed a full bathroom, plumbing and electricity and used it as a rental for single men.

In spring of 1946, my parents hired a local contractor to repair the main house foundation, build a new roof, add a front porch, remodel the kitchen, and build three new bedrooms, a second full bathroom and a connecting hallway, all with our salvaged lumber. Prior to the start of construction, Dad and I had to remove two large cottonwood trees near the house, an arduous job that required many hours of digging and chopping to remove the two stumps after cutting the trees down.

We all got involved in the house interior design and followed the contractor's progress with keen interest. Dad and I did the daily cleanup of construction debris. By late summer it was finished, a beautiful, comfortable home, the best Mexican-American house in Lone Pine, even better than many of the Anglo homes. Then we pooled our money to purchase new furnishings (Bea paid for our beautiful yellow kitchen table with cushioned chairs and we all contributed to the beautiful new living room furniture). We felt a great sense of accomplishment—and pride.

To pay off her bank home remodeling loan, Mom went into business in 1947 managing the Nogales Café, a Mexican restaurant on Main Street adjoining the Nogales pool hall. Its counter seats and tables accommodated about 25 patrons. Mom cooked Mexican and several traditional American dishes. Tina and Bea waited on customers after school and on weekends, and every day after school and on weekends, I washed dishes, pots and pans and picked up the daily groceries and supplies. Hollywood movie filming companies would reserve the entire restaurant for dinner parties and they tipped lavishly. We all learned to deal with the public and Mom especially enjoyed interacting with her customers and the other town businessmen and women.

Enriqueta's successful business venture established her reputation in Lone Pine as a superb cook and an astute businesswoman. Although it was very hard work, we were proud to have our own business. About two years later, she moved her business to the Spanish Garden bar and restaurant one block down the street. She paid off the bank loan before it was due.

Lone Pine's population was approximately five percent Mexican-American and Mexican. Our parents and grandparents were born in Mexico, and our ancestors are of Spanish, French, Mexican and Mexican Yaqui Indian origin. My maternal great-great-grandmother Patricia was born in Burgos, Spain about 1830. At age 16, she married a Spaniard named Juan Santellanes. About 1847, they sailed across the Atlantic Ocean to the new world and establish their home in the mining town of Parral in Chihuahua, Mexico, where her husband owned property. About ten years later, Patricia was widowed with seven young children when her husband died in a smallpox epidemic. Not long after, she married his brother, but he also died of smallpox about a year later.

Patricia sold her hacienda and livestock and moved with her children to Guanacevi, Durango. Being an excellent cook and baker, she opened a *Fonda* coffee shop offering pastries, coffee, chocolate, *atole* a popular Mexican punch, and liquor. Most of her clientele were men who worked in the mines. To house her large family, she built a home and hired indigenous workers to help run her household.

About a year later, Ignacio Rivera arrived in Guanacevi from Spain. He and Patricia fell in love and married. Soon after there was a gold strike in Parral, so they moved there and built a hacienda. About two years later, they returned to Spain for an extended family visit and to have their own children (Spanish children born in Spain were considered to be of higher social rank than Spanish children born in New Spain). Their daughter Felicita and son Policarpio were born in Burgos. Their second daughter, Maria Anna Andrea Rivera de Santellanes—my great-grandmother Andrea—was born in Madrid, a *Madrilena*, in the 1860s.

When Andrea was an infant, the family returned to Parral where she, Felicita and Policarpio grew up and were educated. Both daughters were beautiful; Andrea had bright green eyes and reddish-brown hair—*castanio*. When they were old enough to help, the girls worked with their mother in their *Fonda*, where they learned to cook and bake.

When she was about 17, Andrea married a young miner, Porfirio Barraza, the son of Jose Maria Barraza, a Spaniard, and Benita, a Sonora Yaqui Indian. The newlyweds established their home in Parral and had ten children, six of whom survived, including their oldest, my grandmother Concepcion (Chonita). They were raised and educated in Parral.

My maternal grandfather Juan Perez was born in Guanacevi, Durango, the only child of Maximo Barrios Perez de Bustamante, a Spaniard, and Pomposa Brion, who was French. When he was a young man, Juan went to work in the mines of Parral and became expert at explosives. He and my grandmother Chonita attended the same church. They were married in 1904. Their first two children died in infancy. Their third—my mother Enriqueta—was born on October 26, 1910, in Santa Barbara, Chihuahua, a mining town not far from Parral.

Less than one month later on November 20, the Mexican Revolution erupted. The American-owned mining companies in Chihuahua, and many others, closed and my grandparents moved to the city of Chihuahua where Juan obtained a job in a chocolate factory and Chonita worked as a cook in a surgeon's home. My great grandfather Porfirio died soon after arriving in Chihuahua and Andrea moved in with Chonita and Enriqueta along with her daughter, three sons and a grandson.

Revolutionary general Pancho Villa learned that my grandfather was an explosives expert and recruited him to blow up trains and bridges for his army. In return, Juan and his family were provided a large, comfortable house in the city (probably the property of a wealthy family who had fled to America). Because of Villa's frequent campaigns, my grandfather was away from home for extended periods so Enriqueta saw very little of her father.

Prior to the Revolution, Andrea's sister Felicita, a bilingual college graduate, worked at a mine and married an American mining engineer whose surname was Johnson. When the mine closed, they moved to San Francisco, California, where the company headquarters was located. They had a close friendship with one of the mine owners named Thacher, who lived in Ojai. Sometime later, Johnson fell ill and died. Felicita remained in California and purchased a house in southwest Los Angeles (now Watts). Later, Thacher contacted Felicita and asked her to come to his ranch to help him care for his wife, an invalid and to help manage his household. She rented out her house and moved to the Thacher Ranch.

In April 1916, Villa led a raid on Columbus, New Mexico. My grandfather took the opportunity to desert—together with many other *Villistas*—and he eventually settled in California. He was never reunited with Chonita and Enriqueta. Because of his desertion, my grandmother and mother lost their home and financial support from Villa. Greatly concerned for their safety, Felicita arranged for Andrea, Chonita and their children to come to California. They entered the United States at El Paso as documented war refugees, traveled by train to Los Angeles, and soon after moved into a house on the Thacher Ranch in Ojai.

A top family priority was to get jobs. Chonita's brothers Federico and Vicente went to work in a chalk quarry at Lompoc, not far from Ojai. Later, Chonita went there to cook and keep house for them. She established a boarding house and met Ignacio "Nacho" Herrera de Gamboa, who worked as a muleskinner (handler) at the quarry.

Enriqueta remained at the Thacher Ranch with Andrea. She attended school and learned to speak, read and write in English—spurred by the need to serve as the family's interpreter and translator. Mom often told me and my siblings that attending school in Ojai and living with her grandmother Andrea were the happiest years of her childhood. After about two years on the Thacher Ranch, Andrea rented a house in Ojai near the citrus orchards. Federico and Vicente left the chalk quarry, got jobs at the orchard, and moved in with Andrea. Their foreman was a Spaniard named Jose Maria Carrasco (Caco). Caco and Andrea became acquainted, fell in love and were married about 1920.

Pursuing a business opportunity, Chonita moved to Los Angeles and rented a furnished boarding house. Enriqueta remained with Andrea in Ojai, attending school. There was great demand for Mexican workers in Los Angeles; they needed room and board. Nacho soon followed Chonita to Los Angeles and moved into her boarding house. They established a relationship that lasted the rest of their lives, but were never married because she could not obtain a divorce—she had no idea of Juan's whereabouts.

Not long after—despite Andrea's and Enriqueta's strenuous objections—Chonita brought Enriqueta to Los Angeles and enrolled her in a school with other immigrant children. After school and on weekends, she helped Chonita. By 1923, Chonita had about 12 boarders and needed more help so she removed Enriqueta from school to work full time in the boarding house. Chonita and Nacho also felt that Enriqueta had had enough education. To her everlasting resentment, Mom's formal education ended in the eighth grade.

Captain John Frank Gamboa, U. S. Navy (Retired)

My father, Teodulo Gamboa de Herrera, was born in February 1904 in the village of San Jose de la Boca, Durango, Mexico. His father Ignacio Gamboa, a Spaniard, was educated in the Catholic Church educational system, was a college graduate and the magistrate for San Jose de la Boca and the adjoining villages. My grandfather and my grandmother Manuela Herrera had a large hacienda, raised crops and livestock, and had ten surviving children—seven sons and three daughters. My father was the youngest. I am named after one of his brothers and Bea after a sister.

In 1924 at the age of 20, Teodulo went to California in search of work. He located his cousin Ignacio Herrera in Los Angeles, who helped him find a job and Chonita rented him a room in her boarding house. That is where he met Enriqueta.

Teodulo was tall and handsome with a charming, gregarious personality. Enriqueta was a pretty young teenager with a strong personality and fiery temperament. He was affectionate with her and liked to tease her, calling her *chaparita,* short. He frequently told her that he was going to marry her when she grew up. Her immediate and unequivocal response to him was, "*Nunca! Primero te quemas en el infierno!* Never! You'll burn in Hell first!"

Reflecting on my forebears, I marvel at their pioneering spirit, courage, endurance and perseverance. My parents, grandparents and great-grandparents lived through President Porfirio Diaz' corrupt, repressive regime and the nationwide upheaval that destroyed it—a seven-year civil war that affected every region of Mexico with devastating effect on its people, its infrastructure and its economy.

Like thousands of other Mexicans, to secure their personal safety my mother, grandmother and great-grandmother left their homeland and came to America. Before leaving Chihuahua, Andrea and Chonita disposed of their household goods and possessions, including their heirlooms, at significant financial loss.

They arrived in America with only their luggage and the clothes they were wearing. But they had things of great value—ambition, ability, determination and hope. Through dedicated perseverance and hard work, they overcame daunting challenges, established their homes in California and created their new lives.

¡El Capitán!

Their formal education was foreshortened by circumstances, but Enriqueta and Teodulo never stopped learning or becoming. Their fierce desire to improve our lives shaped our family's standard of living and our destiny. Enriqueta was the driving force in all our endeavors. Her indomitable spirit was in the tradition of her courageous maternal lineage. To achieve her dreams, Enriqueta turned to her culinary knowledge and skills passed down through three generations of strong, talented women who were excellent cooks. Her family recipes were not written down; they were learned by preparing excellent meals with her mother and grandmother in home kitchens and later in her commercial enterprises.

Our parents overcame great challenges and taught my siblings and me that real achievement in life requires great effort and dedication. Meeting our family's needs in Bartlett and Lone Pine, our parents also taught us self-reliance. The construction of our home and the establishment of our restaurant were the seminal events in our family's history in Owens Valley.

The Gamboas were not in the uppermost socio-economic levels in Lone Pine, but our parents and grandparents were well respected and on excellent terms with school officials and teachers, community leaders and our neighbors. They participated in school and community activities and supported town events. Their reputation as responsible parents was a major factor in our social status.

Our brother Leco was one of the best athletes ever to graduate from Lone Pine High, He was the varsity football team quarterback, basketball team point guard and baseball team shortstop. He was captain of all three sports teams. His two years in the Army as a draftee were served primarily as a baseball player.

Dad was hard working and lovingly dedicated to his family. A very handsome man with a charming smile, he had a distinguished demeanor and was always well turned out. An instinctively courteous person with impeccable manners, my father always wore a hat into town, which he doffed to women when greeting them. He had natural leadership abilities, a great sense of humor and many friends. And he loved to gamble. Dad was a skilled poker player and was often the Nogales Club's house dealer.

Captain John Frank Gamboa, U. S. Navy (Retired)

Accepting nothing less than our best efforts, my parents and grandparents instilled in my brothers, sisters and me the belief that we could improve our lives if we were willing to expend the required effort.

And they imbued us with a core belief that America's promises would not be denied to us because we were born of Mexican parents. They taught us that in America, we were free to dream, to choose, to strive, and to achieve.

My parents stipulated that my siblings and I would complete high school and behave ourselves. We also understood that beyond high school, our future was our responsibility.

In September 1947, I entered the 9th grade in Lone Pine Union High School as a member of the Class of 1951.

Years later, Tina and her husband Jim established their own real estate company in Norwalk, California, and Leco and his wife Evelyn created Gamboa Trucklines Company in Corona, California, after he graduated from Fullerton State College.

Our parents and grandparents chose to remain in the United States to provide a better life for my brothers, my sisters and me. But they retained their cherished Spanish and Mexican cultures, traditions and values—their precious heritage—which they bequeathed to my generation.

Enriqueta proudly became a U.S. citizen in 1960. Teodulo never did. He felt that America was his children's country. He deeply appreciated the opportunities that it provided him and his family, but because of his love for his homeland and cherished birthright, he could never abandon his Mexican citizenship.

Chonita passed in 1966, Teodulo in 1972 and Nacho a few months after. Following Dad's death, Enriqueta moved to La Mirada in southern California and lived in her lovely home purchased and completely furnished by her children, not far from Tina, Bea, Leco and Mosey and their spouses and children. (Leco planted seven beautiful rose bushes in her front yard, one for each of her children.)

Enriqueta became the center of gravity for her extended family, greatly enjoying frequent family gatherings with her children and their spouses, her 17 grandchildren, 23 great-grandchildren and 7 great-great-grandchildren, enriching their lives with her vibrant personality, strong temperament, enthusiasm for life, and her great sense of humor. She was a loyal member and secretary of her widely traveled senior citizens' club, enthusiastically supporting all its activities.

¡El Capitán!

Mom lavished our families with her delicious cooking and unrestrained love.

Enriqueta died in September 2007 at age 96. Her funeral service in Lone Pine lasted almost two hours because so many of her over 60 family members present delivered their heart-felt personal remembrances.

Enriqueta and Teodulo lie side by side in the Lone Pine cemetery together with their youngest son, Theodore Junior, their infant grandson, William Moses, Junior, and Chonita and Nacho.

All are at rest in the beautiful evening shadows of Mount Whitney.

Tina, me and Bea at Bartlett, spring 1934. (Personal collection)

Bartlett boy, fall 1938. (Personal collection)

¡El Capitán!

Lone Pine Kindergarten Class 1938-39. Back row: Kerry Christenson third from left, me fifth from left. Howard Hopkins front row, right. Teacher Ruby Branson. (Personal collection)

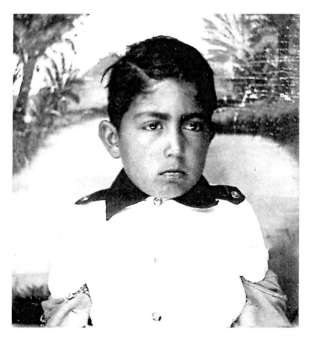

Panchito, Bartlett 1939. (Personal collection)

Brothers, a playmate and our dog Lucky, Lone Pine 1946. (Personal collection)

Mom, Dad, Tina, Bea and me, Lone Pine 1947. (Personal collection)

Part II

Journey to the Naval Academy and Life as a Midshipman

Chapter Two

★★★★★★★

Do what you can, with what you have, where you are.
—Theodore Roosevelt

I began my junior year in Lone Pine High in September 1949. I enjoyed school, hanging out with my friends, playing on the varsity football team and, after school practice and our football games, stocking shelves and bagging customer groceries at Josephs Market, earning enough to meet my clothing needs and expenses.

I had a full schedule of classes, study hall and sports. My English class was taught by Ruth Stevens, the school's most respected—and feared—teacher. (On the first day that we entered her room, Ruth firmly directed Richard Ericson, Dick Gallagher, Howard Hopkins and me to our seating assignments—one in each corner of the seating area. Grinning, we asked her why. She stared fiercely at us, "I know you! I will not tolerate any trouble from you!)

She demanded serious study and hard work from all her students regardless of their extracurricular activities or their intentions about college. She made me participate and do every homework assignment.

After several weeks of work in her class (under iron discipline), I discovered that I enjoyed learning and working on my lessons. My attitude about school and my approach to academics was transformed—I began participating and studying in my other classes as well. Over the school year, my academic record improved dramatically.

In May 1950, Ruth walked into Principal Bill Bauer's office and told him in her most direct and forceful manner that I was the best male student in the junior class. She said, "You have to select Frank for Boys State!" She also told him that it was time for a Mexican American to get the prize—it had never been awarded to a minority student. Bill was aware of my improved performance, and after checking with my other teachers, I became Lone Pine's first Mexican-American student to be selected for Boys State.

California Boys State is a prestigious American Legion-sponsored weeklong convention at the state capitol in Sacramento featuring educational activities about democracy, politics and governance. There were about 500 high school juniors in our July 1950 convention, including a handful of Mexican Americans. At first, I felt a bit uncomfortable and did not have a good feeling of belonging, but I adapted quickly and learned a great deal. I thoroughly enjoyed the program.

Even so, I quickly realized that I was not at the same level of achievement in school as everyone else, but I also felt that I could change my status if I wanted to. I talked with many students about their plans and learned that most were going to college, preferably the one their mom or dad—or both— had graduated from (like UCLA, USC, Stanford). This made a big impression on me.

When I returned to Lone Pine, I told my parents, siblings and friends about my experiences. Everyone was very complimentary, giving me a huge boost in self-confidence. As summer passed, I realized that Boys State had changed my expectations. I could not revert to the indifferent attitude and performance of my first two years of high school in which I did not take any college prep courses and studied just enough to pass each course,

In September, I began my senior year. My intention was to work hard at my studies, but I still had no specific goals, especially no decision about going to college. My classmates elected me class president; I was also a member of the student body council. These responsibilities added to my workload, but I enjoyed my leadership roles and having a say in school activities.

Then one September day in my civics class, our teacher, Emil Neeme, announced that Lone Pine's Congressman Clair Engle was soliciting applications for his appointments to the U.S. Naval Academy. After reading Engle's letter to us, Neeme said, "The academy offers an excellent education in exchange for four years of service after graduation. And there is no tuition! In fact, you get paid as a midshipman!" I listened perfunctorily. After class as I was walking out of the room, Neeme called out, "Frank, I want to see you a minute." I replied, "Sure, coach!" Puzzled, I approached his desk feeling a bit nervous.

Neeme was the assistant football coach and the varsity basketball coach, a good athlete who had played tight end on the Butler College football team. He had served as a Navy lieutenant aboard a heavy cruiser in the Pacific Fleet in WW II. A handsome Armenian American with a friendly smile and an engaging personality, Neeme was popular with the students.

As I stood in front of his desk, the coach said, "Frank, did you listen to my announcement concerning the Naval Academy appointment?" Wide-eyed, I responded, "Yes sir!" He asked, "Are you interested?" Surprised, I quickly replied, "No, not really!"

He stared at me in stony silence long enough to make me uncomfortable. Suddenly—in his typical coaching manner—Neeme leaned right into my face and said, "Gamboa, I think you are coasting through school. You have the brains to do better. The academy offers you an opportunity to get a free education. Your parents can't afford it. You owe it to them and yourself to think about this great opportunity!"

I was so taken aback that I was almost speechless, but I managed to blurt out, "Okay coach, I'll think about it!" He replied, "Good, I want you to!" I walked out of the classroom almost in a state of shock. I hurried down the hall and joined my friends. They asked if I was in trouble. "No, coach just wanted to make sure I got the homework assignment." I didn't mention our conversation. But it was hard for me to suppress a new feeling—excitement.

Lester Hewitt, a 1946 Lone Pine High graduate, had entered the Naval Academy in 1948, the first high school graduate in Owens Valley to gain admission to a service academy; he would graduate in 1952. Les was highly admired in our hometown, which is how I came to know about the academy. But for me Annapolis seemed so distant, so unreachable in every way. Furthermore, if I were to talk about following in Lester's footsteps, the reaction from my friends and teachers would have been incredulous laughter. Les was a star! So it was scary to think about what Neeme said to me.

In the days following, the coach kept encouraging me whenever he had an opportunity—after class, or on the football field. This was something very new to me. Ruth Stevens was the only teacher who had encouraged me to go to college. I had never been scheduled for college prep courses—I was not on a college track.

Flattered by Neeme's interest in me, I did some research in the library on the academy's admission requirements and discovered that the entrance exams included subjects I had never studied and were not in my senior schedule. I was woefully unprepared for college, even less so for the academy. I felt like I was in a no-win situation.

Captain John Frank Gamboa, U. S. Navy (Retired)

After mulling it over for a week or so, I talked to Neeme about my poor overall academic record, my unpreparedness for the academy and the futility of the whole notion.

With considerable emotion, I told him directly, "Coach, why do you believe I should think about going to the academy? I am not a good student or a great athlete! I don't even know if I want to go to college!"

He looked at me with a big smile and replied "Frank, I believe you are intelligent and could be an outstanding student! You also have leadership ability and excellent social skills. As for your academic deficiencies, you can start now by working hard in each class. You still have time to prepare for the academy's entrance exams!"

After several more days of worry and soul-searching, I told Emil that I just wasn't scholastically or emotionally ready to try for the Naval Academy, a radical commitment for me, and I didn't know if I could ever take such a momentous step into the unknown. Nevertheless, he kept leaning on me.

I also felt that, before I could seriously contemplate going to college—and especially the academy—I first had to find out if I was smart enough to succeed in college-prep courses. Just having Neeme tell me I was intelligent and capable wasn't enough; I had to prove it to myself.

I began by evaluating my academic record. As I reviewed my performance in school since the 9th grade—and my basic attitude about study and learning, I discovered that I harbored some deep-seated feelings of inadequacy and inferiority about studying and getting an education. Due to our family's busy lives—mom and dad in their jobs and working to improve our home with our help, and I had a part-time job—it was not customary for my family to spend quiet evenings at home reading books and studying.

Furthermore, my parents had only completed 8th grade; my father could only read and write in Spanish and my grandparents not at all. My sisters had finished high school but had not gone to college. These realities created serious doubt in my mind that I could succeed in college prep courses and college.

And for the first time in my life, I started focusing on, and thinking about, my ethnicity and its relevance to my getting an education. These profoundly personal issues were critically important to my self-esteem.

¡El Capitán!

Sometimes I felt socially inadequate and even inferior to some of my Anglo classmates, especially those whose parents were Lone Pine's business owners and community leaders. A contributing factor in my perceptions of my social environment was the absence of any Mexican-American schoolteachers or Mexican-American college role models in Lone Pine.

With respect to our town's social strata and the relative social positions of Anglos and Mexican Americans, I felt intuitively that these were based on jobs, income, living standards and lifestyles rather than ethnic differences. Nonetheless, the differences in financial and social status among Lone Pine residents influenced the attitudes and relationships among the high school students. Another factor was that some Mexican-American students did not speak English fluently, or had an accent, especially those with parents who spoke only Spanish.

These circumstances created an attitude among some in our community that Mexican Americans were socially and perhaps even intellectually inferior.

Even so, there was great harmony, integration and social unity in Lone Pine since its founding days in the mid-19th century; there were many Mexican pioneers in the valley and marriage between Anglos and Mexicans and Mexican Americans was not uncommon.

My siblings and I did not sense any overt ethnic bias or discrimination towards us or our parents or grandparents. We were equally comfortable socializing with both our Anglo or Mexican-American friends.

Nonetheless, I thought about how I would be treated beyond Lone Pine—especially if I went to the academy. I felt that my ethnicity might be an issue there. This led me to dwell on the overall impact of my Hispanic origins, and how I viewed myself, my family and friends, causing me considerable emotional turmoil. Was I doomed to second-class status in America simply because my parents were born in Mexico? Very quickly, I concluded that such a notion was morally, intellectually and emotionally unacceptable to me—and to my family.

Even so, I knew that, before I could embark on a quest to enter the academy, I had to come to terms with my being a first-generation Mexican American.

But I didn't have anyone with whom I could discuss my feelings about my ethnicity. Certainly not with my friends, we never talked about serious personal issues, especially such complex matters as our families' financial status, our ethnicity or prejudice. Instinctively, it also seemed to me that, because no one talked about them, these were taboo subjects.

Approaching Mom was out of the question. She was so fiercely proud of her Mexican roots and heritage, so sensitive to prejudice, and so volatile about discrimination that I felt she could not clarify things for me. But it was a moot point—intimate talks about personal issues were not customary in our family. I concluded that I would just have to resolve my concerns by myself.

After thinking as much as I could stand about this issue, I simply accepted my Mexican-American ethnicity as a fact. I was who I was. If I entered the academy, I would just have to deal with any issues about my ethnicity if and when they came into my life.

Meanwhile, despite my lack of self-confidence in my scholastic abilities and my concerns about my ethnicity, because of Coach Neeme's sustained encouragement I was getting very excited and motivated. I renewed my studying efforts at home like in my junior year under Ruth Stevens, and started getting top grades again.

But I didn't tell anyone—not my parents or my sisters and especially not my friends—why I had a new interest in my school work. Only Coach Neeme—who by this time had become my confidant and mentor—had any idea of the transformation going on within me—a fundamental change in my attitude about getting an education. And something else, a developing vision and sense of hope about my future.

I had only the vaguest idea about the application process or admission requirements for the academy. I talked with Myrnadel Hewitt (Lester's sister), class of '50, my good friend Dave Guzman's girlfriend, about my interest in the academy and that I wanted to talk to Les. In December 1950, while he was home on Christmas leave she arranged our meeting.

I told Les that I was considering applying for the Naval Academy and asked him for advice. We discussed my academic record and he told me straight out that I would not be able to pass the entrance exams. He recommended that I attend junior college for one year and study math and science, and that I should apply for admission by the college certificate method by which good college grades on the entrance exam subjects can be accepted in lieu of taking the examinations.

¡El Capitán!

Lester also told me that my first step was to obtain Bill Bauer's support for a congressional appointment from Congressman Clair Engle. Without Bauer's backing, I had no chance. Les wished me luck and promised to stay in touch. Later, he sent me a booklet on the academic requirements for admission that included sample entrance examination questions. I could answer some, but I could not solve a single math problem. I was scared and very disappointed.

Since my initial conversation with Neeme in September, I had been thinking for weeks about the Naval Academy from every possible angle and working hard in my classes. Time was passing quickly, and after my meeting with Les, I felt a great sense of urgency.

Accordingly, despite my lack of academic qualifications, and with very serious doubts about my overall prospects, in January 1951, I made the first major decision of my life—to apply for admission to the Naval Academy. I did not know how I was going to do it, and I felt that the odds were heavily against me, but I was going to try.

With the school counselor's help I determined which courses I should schedule in my remaining semester in order to take the academy entrance examinations, but there was simply not enough time to take all the math and science I needed. Les was right. I would have to attend junior college for at least one year to study the entrance exam subjects, and others that I had not taken during my previous years in high school.

Admission to a service academy requires an appointment from a U.S. congressional representative or a senator. Appointments are awarded to applicants based on merit as determined by high school academic performance and extracurricular activities. Character traits and leadership abilities have considerable weight. Participation in varsity sports is important. Letters of recommendation from the high school principals, teachers, and community leaders are required. And applicants must pass a competitive civil service examination and a thorough military physical examination.

Per Les' advice, I needed to ask Principal Bauer for his help and backing. Bill was of German ancestry, a rather stern but good-natured person. Over six feet tall and very athletic, he had excelled in college academics and football, playing for Coach Elmer Layden, one of the famed Irish Four Horsemen. After graduation, he played center on the Chicago Cardinals semi-pro football team while working as a cub reporter for the Chicago Tribune. He then served in the Navy as an enlisted man from 1928 to 1932, attending flight school for an enlisted pilot rating (the program was cancelled a week prior to his completion, negating his wings of gold; he became a boatswain's mate "a right arm rate" but spent much of his time playing on fleet football teams). After leaving the Navy, he taught school in Santa Paula, California, and then became the Principal of Lone Pine High and District Superintendent in the late 1930's.

In 1943, Bill was recalled by the Navy as an officer and served with distinction as a beachmaster in Admiral Nimitz' Central Pacific Amphibious Forces during WW II.

He returned to Lone Pine after the war and resumed his job. As the football and baseball coach, Bill knew all the athletes and was very popular with them. I was not a great athlete and my conduct record was not above reproach. (In my sophomore year, I had been summoned to his office for a warning about my conduct.)

Taking a deep breath, I walked into the admin office and asked Bill's secretary, Mrs. Jean Rodgers, for a meeting with Bauer. She asked me why. I said, "It's personal!" With her head tilted forward just enough to look over the top of her reading glasses—her most disapproving look—she scheduled my meeting.

I arrived on time looking my best. Jean had me wait in an office next to Bill's. A few minutes later, he summoned me and I stood uncomfortably silent in front of his desk. After a pregnant pause, the silence was shattered by his very direct question, "Well, Frank, what do you want to talk about?" I blurted out something about the Naval Academy and wanting his help in getting a congressional appointment—a very dry mouthful.

Bill looked at me for a few moments with a slight frown on his face—he was not going to make it easy—and asked, "Why do you want to go to the academy?" I replied, "I want to get a college education and I think I want to be a naval officer." More silence. "Jean, please bring me Frank's file!" Without a word, she handed him a folder, much like passing my death sentence.

Bauer went over each page ever so slowly. Then he leaned back in his chair with his arms folded across his chest and looked directly at me. "Well young man, you are doing much better, but you are certainly not ready to enter the Naval Academy!" More silence. And then he said, "I think it's very admirable to have such high aspirations, but in view of your overall academic record, I can't recommend you for an appointment!" He paused, letting his words sink in. My hopes vanished.

Again, Bill leaned back in his chair. Then he started rubbing his nose with his right index finger, his trademark mannerism when he was negotiating. A sly grin spread across his face—the expression people get when they think they have you right where they want you. "But I will make a deal with you, Frank. If you graduate with top grades, enroll in junior college, and make the dean's list in the first semester, then I will write a letter to Congressman Engle and recommend you for an appointment!"

In a heartbeat I replied, "Yes sir!" He got out of his chair, came around his desk and we shook hands. "Good!" His left hand firmly gripping my shoulder, he said, "Keep up the good work!" I departed his office, went immediately to Coach Neeme, and told him what had transpired. He congratulated me, but I did not feel very elated because I had no idea where or how I would go to junior college, where I would live, or how I could afford it. I saw Ruth Stevens, who was also very positive and encouraging. Walking to work after school, I worried about what lay ahead and had second thoughts about my deal with Bauer—a bad case of buyer's remorse.

Even so, over the next few days I let my close friends—Bob "Moe" Mojarro, Dale Watterson, Joe Ruiz, Dave Guzman, Howard Hopkins, Arnold Osuna and Myrnadel know that I was going to try to get into the Naval Academy. They were supportive and encouraging, but actually, we did not talk much about it. My admission—if I made it—was at least two years down the road and a lot could happen in that time. They wished me well, but probably doubted—justifiably—that I could pull it off.

It was time to tell my parents. I had never discussed my future, or any other serious topic, with them. Regardless, family protocol on personal issues was to first discuss the matter with Mom. If she deemed it appropriate, when the time was right she would approach Dad.

I said, "Mom, I need to talk to you and Dad about my plans. I am going to try to get into the Naval Academy!" I was startled when she replied, "Oh, I know all about it! I asked how? Smiling, she replied, "a little bird told me!" (My siblings and I could never keep anything important from that little bird or Mom; she kept in touch with all our teachers—and all the town gossips.)

Captain John Frank Gamboa, U. S. Navy (Retired)

A few days later, Mom, Dad and I had an impromptu meeting in the living room, standing around the heater. Speaking to them in Spanish I explained how I had been encouraged in school to try for the Naval Academy and how I had been preparing. I explained how difficult it was, but it would be a free education and a great opportunity for an officer career in the Navy. I told them how Les, Neeme, Bauer and Stevens were helping me, and that they all agreed that I needed to go to junior college to complete my academic preparations for the congressional appointment and entrance examinations.

With her innate political astuteness, Mom set the tone for our discussion by congratulating me saying that she and Dad were very happy that I wanted to go to the academy and wished me well.

But Dad's reaction was just the opposite. He said he was not in favor. He did not want me going into the military because they caused wars and great human suffering, as he and his family and friends had endured in the Mexican Revolution.

Instead, he wanted me to study business so I could earn a good living and have a better life than he had been able to give us.

I was totally surprised. It was the first time my father had ever expressed his opinion to me about my future—my first clue about what he expected of me after high school.

Mom forcefully challenged him, "If he can get into the Naval Academy, Panchito (my family nickname) will get a free college education; he can do whatever he wants afterwards, including going into business! We can't help him financially so the academy is his best opportunity. And he is getting help from some very important people!"

After a period of silence, Dad looked directly at me and said *"Pues, tienes que trabajar muy duro!"* Well, you have to work very hard! Breathing again, I replied, *"Si senor!"*

About a week later I approached Mom, "I have no idea where or how I am going to go to junior college!" In her typical business-like manner, she immediately picked up the telephone and called our Uncle Carlos and Aunt Sandra Martin who lived in East Los Angeles. She told them that I was going to go to college and asked if I could live with them. They agreed enthusiastically and told her that East Los Angeles Junior College, an excellent school, was near their home and I could get there on their local bus line. My concerns vanished and my enthusiasm was restored.

41

¡El Capitán!

My senior year passed very quickly. I was a motivated, busy student. In addition to my full academic load and my job after school, I played varsity football, basketball and baseball. I worked hard at my studies, achieved good grades and was selected to the California Scholarship Federation. I graduated on June 8, 1951, standing third academically among my 24 classmates.

In May 1951, our little brother Junior underwent an appendectomy at the Lone Pine hospital. He returned home a few days later, but he was hospitalized again about two weeks after with severe leg pains. He insisted on attending my graduation so our family physician, Doctor Shultz, relented and let him go in a wheelchair. Soon after, his condition was diagnosed as acute leukemia.

Mom tearfully explained to us, "Junior is very sick." Over the next few days, his condition worsened and it was decided to send him to Children's Hospital in Hollywood. As our parents departed the house to join Junior and a family friend in his van and drive to Hollywood, Leco, Mosey, Erlinda and I watched tearfully. Dad paused, turned to us with tear-filled eyes and a heart-broken visage, "*Pienso que Dios se va llevar a mijo*, I think God is going to take my son."

Dad came home a week later. Mom stayed at the hospital with Junior throughout his illness. Tina and Bea, who were living in North Hollywood, visited with them frequently and were with Junior and Mom when he died in late July 1951.

A bright, beautiful boy, full of love and exuberance, Theodore Gamboa, Junior, was eight years old when God took him from us. Mom brought him home for his funeral service in the Catholic Church, which was crowded with friends, family and many of his Third-Grade classmates. His death had a devastating effect on our family.

Les was home on summer leave from the academy and drove me to East Los Angeles Junior College (ELAJC) and helped me register for a full academic program with classes in algebra, chemistry and English.

At the end of August, I quit my Josephs job and said goodbye to my family and friends.

With all my worldly possessions packed in a cardboard box and a borrowed suitcase, I departed for Los Angeles on the Greyhound bus. As we drove out of Owens Valley, I was almost overwhelmed by feelings of loneliness and separation. Grieving for my brother, I felt a profound sadness for my heartbroken parents, grandparents and siblings.

The bus exited the valley, passed through Red Rock Canyon and crossed the hot, dry Mojave Desert. Then we descended "down below" into the Los Angeles basin.

Thankfully, the journey's five-hour duration and the changing landscapes provided a soothing mental and psychological passage. I got a grip on my emotions.

As we neared the bus terminal, the salt-laden sea breezes flowing inland from the Pacific Ocean filled my lungs with sweet fresh air, lifting my spirits. My optimism welled up.

For the first time in many days, I felt something akin to exhilaration about my new life—and the launching of my quest for admission to the Naval Academy.

Chapter Three

Life is not measured by the number of breaths we take, but by the moments that take our breath away.

—Hilary Cooper

My aunt and uncle warmly welcomed me into their home. Montebello's stores had signs and window advertisements in Spanish. The policemen, firemen, mailmen, and people on the sidewalks were Mexican Americans, as were our neighbors. Living in a Hispanic community was a new experience for me; for the first time in my life, I experienced culture shock. Nonetheless, I enjoyed my new situation.

Making my way around the East LA JC campus was a bit confusing on my first day, but I got to all my classes. My Algebra I classroom was crowded with about 40 students—standing room only. The professor entered, announced that the class had been overbooked; he had to cut some students. He handed out a basic algebra test.

As I studied the problems, I might as well have been trying to read a coded message without the key—I knew nothing about algebraic symbolism or equations. After staring at the problems almost to the point of nausea, I handed my blank test to the professor. Silently, he handed me a registration card for a basic mathematics course, which he also taught. I filled it out and handed it back. He smiled and shook my hand, "I will see you in class tomorrow morning, Mr. Gamboa!"

I worried for the rest of the day and had an almost sleepless night. If I could not learn algebra—moreover, if I did not excel in all my courses—I would have to give up my dream and go back to Lone Pine and an indefinite future.

I arrived early for class the next morning knowing that I had to get an "A." Determined to hear every word the professor spoke and see everything he wrote on the chalkboard, I took the center seat in the front row of the class. I wanted no distractions.

I quickly settled into a daily routine of classes and study. And no social activities. I was courteous to my classmates; however, I was not there to make friends. Besides, I had no car, and money only for necessities. My singular goal was to prepare for the academy's entrance examinations.

The professor loved mathematics (we used his draft textbook) and he had a flair for teaching. He inspired me to work hard and complete every homework assignment. For the first time in my life, I comprehended math and learned to solve math problems. I worked just as hard in all my other classes, adjusting to the heavy homework load; I earned an A in my math class and As and Bs in my other courses. I made the dean's list.

I went home to Lone Pine during the semester break and proudly presented the list to Bill Bauer. He congratulated me, and promptly wrote a letter to Congressman Engle and California Senators Knowland and Nixon, recommending me for an appointment to the Naval Academy. I got letters of recommendation from Irving Joseph, Josephs Market owner; Phillip Sharr, General Manager of Pittsburgh Plate Glass Soda Ash Company at Bartlett; George Shultz, our town doctor; Ruth Stevens; and Bill.

My sisters, Tina and Bea, were living in North Hollywood. Bea shared an apartment with a girl she worked with at Bank of America. Tina lived alone in the same building and worked in a downtown Los Angeles bank. Between semesters, I moved in with Tina. I rode two different streetcar lines and a bus to school so I did a lot of reading enroute. I then discovered that Los Angeles City College (LACC) was only two miles from where Tina and I lived so I visited the school and decided that, if it was necessary for me to attend a second year of junior college, I would transfer there.

I lived on an austere budget. I packed a lunch for school and Tina paid the rent and our living expenses. When my savings were gone, Tina and Bea continued to support me. They also treated me occasionally to movies or we would go to the Hollywood Palladium to dance to famous swing bands such as Tommy Dorsey and Glenn Miller.

In March, I received letters from Congressman Engle and Senators Knowland and Nixon informing me that they had no vacancies for the Naval Academy class entering in June 1952. I was very disappointed and I had to make a decision. The Korean War was ongoing and the universal draft was in effect. I had a student deferment and would not be drafted as long as I remained in college. After talking it over with my parents and Bauer, Neeme and Stevens, I decided to attend a second year of junior college and try for the Academy again in 1953. I went back to work at Josephs during the summer, saving most of my pay for school.

I was considerably discouraged about facing another year of uncertainty. I needed to shore up my morale and sustain my motivation. I began to mentally visualize academy scenarios with myself as a midshipman. This was scary at times because I had no "feel" or comfort about being there. But visualization helped me think about the challenges I would face and great changes that would happen in my life if I entered the academy. I learned that this technique helped me focus on my goals and sustain my motivation. It would be even more valuable to me later on.

I also reflected on my first year of college. My enjoyment of learning together with an almost insatiable thirst for knowledge made my college time a great intellectual adventure. I could almost feel my mind growing and expanding. Making the dean's list in both semesters made me feel confident of my intelligence and scholastic abilities. (I also took several intelligence and aptitude tests and was pleasantly surprised with the good results.) In my first year of college I had proven to myself that my scholastic ability was good enough to succeed in a college curriculum; and felt confident that I could perform well in the Naval Academy's academic program. I had overcome my feelings of inadequacy about my innate intelligence and scholastic abilities, issues that had plagued me in high school.

I also thought about my ethnic culture. Growing up in our close-knit family, I had become very aware of my parents' and grandparents' Hispanic values, mores and traditions. They were very proud of their Spanish and Mexican cultural heritage.

In my mind, a specific ethnic group's culture can be thought of as the group's composite norms for their language, food, music, art, family values, behavior, and religion in particular. The behavior of adults and children within the group reflects cultural influences. Culture strengthens family bonds and enriches the group members' enjoyment of life. And it is difficult and even painful for group members to distance themselves from their culture, either intentionally or as an unintended consequence of their life choices.

As a child and teenager, I felt comfortable within my Hispanic culture. Even so, when I entered East LAJC, I soon became aware that I did not have nearly the same level of Hispanic cultural orientation as did my Mexican-American college student cohorts.

I concluded that my growing up in friendly, open and integrated communities in Bartlett and Lone Pine was quite different than it would have been had I lived in East Los Angeles or any other predominantly Hispanic community.

I also became aware that, being in college and pursuing my Naval Academy goal, I was inadvertently distancing myself from my Hispanic culture, which created feelings of increasing separation between me and my Hispanic friends. This caused me considerable emotional turmoil about who I was becoming.

And I discovered that, despite living with my sisters, more often than not I was lonely. My lack of socializing in college—developing friends and dating—a direct result of my goal focus and meager finances—often undermined my morale and degraded my motivation. I kept telling myself that I would make up for all my lack of fun when I entered Annapolis. But mostly, I just tried hard not to think about my lack of an enjoyable social life.

An unintended consequence of my new behavior pattern was my creation of an emotional barrier to strangers, much like a firewall. Sadly, I did not make a single friend in either junior college during my two years in Los Angeles. I had only intended to stay focused on my goal and live within my means, not to become a loner and to distance myself from people.

Happily, I dismantled my self-imposed social isolation behavior pattern when I entered the Academy, but not completely. Despite my efforts to relate to people—I am naturally gregarious—vestiges of this painful behavior pattern have persisted in my life.

In September, I moved back in with Tina. I transferred to LACC and enrolled in more math and science courses and other subjects that would improve my academic record from high school. City College was near enough that I walked there most of the time for exercise, stress relief, and to save money. It felt good to be back in college and working toward my goal.

In February 1953, the two senators again informed me that they had no vacancies for the Naval Academy, but they would keep me on their lists for appointments to the class entering in June 1954.

¡El Capitán!

Fortunately, Congressman Engle had a vacancy and he directed me to take a physical examination at the Naval Ordnance Test Station, China Lake, about 70 miles south of Lone Pine. I failed the exam because of dental cavities in all my molars. Engle told me that I was not eligible for an appointment, but if I corrected my cavities, he would consider me for the class entering in 1954. I gritted my imperfect teeth and continued my studies at City College, again making the dean's list.

While on one of my weekend visits to Lone Pine, I walked out of the Spanish Garden—Mom's restaurant—and encountered Bill Bauer on the sidewalk. After a brief discussion about my school status, Bill put his hand on my shoulder, looked me in the eye and told me "Frank, this community needs to have a Mexican kid graduate from college. The town needs it, the school needs it, and I need it. Don't let me down!" I replied, "Sir, I will do my best" as we shook hands.

When the semester ended, I returned to Lone Pine and my job at Josephs Market. I met with our dentist and he recommended gold crowns for the two molars on each side in my upper and lower jaws, a total of eight. It would take about two months and cost $800.

I was shocked. I told him that I didn't have the money. I would just have to give up my attempts to enter the academy. Having served in the Navy as an officer, the dentist was enthusiastic about my goal—he loved the Navy and said that I would also. He assured me that his work would meet the academy's standards and urged me to get my teeth fixed and pursue the appointment. I said that I would think about it, but I knew that I had no way to get that much money. My quest had come to a dead end.

And then, in a great stroke of luck, Josephs Market transferred me to their butcher shop, a job that paid over $500 a month. I could afford to fix my teeth and save money for college. (I have often wondered if the dentist talked behind my back to Roy Joseph, the store manager and WW II Navy fighter pilot; he and his wife Ethelyn were enthusiastic about my trying to get into the academy. It was Roy who placed me in the butcher shop,)

I worked with Jack McElroy, Johnny Morris and Elmer Schroeder. They taught me how to carve an entire side of beef, and other butcher skills. They were great friends and constantly encouraged me, as did all the Josephs employees and owner.

I decided to go with the dentist's recommendation, temporarily drop out of college, and return to LACC in January 1954. In July, I began my weekly visits to the dentist, spending over two hours at a time in the dental chair for drilling and gold crown work. My jaws ached all summer.

While I was undergoing my dental repair work, Engle and the senators directed me to take a competitive Civil Service examination at Edwards Air Force Base, California. I made a score of 81 and they informed me that 95% of candidates with scores of 80 or higher were admitted to the academy. Knowland told me I was number five on his list of candidates for a principal appointment in 1954. That was not encouraging; I would continue striving for an appointment from Engle.

I notified the college that I was skipping the fall semester but I would enroll again in January 1954. About two weeks later, I was shocked to receive a letter from the Inyo County Universal Draft Board informing me that, because I had dropped out of the fall college semester, I had jeopardized my student deferment. If I did not return to college promptly, I would be drafted into the Army. I quickly explained my situation and assured the board that I would return to college next January. They granted me another deferment, but warned me that if I dropped out of college again I would immediately be drafted.

My dental work was finished in mid-September and the dentist wrote to Engle that all my dental cavities had been restored and that I could pass the academy's physical examination. In response, Engle directed me to undergo another complete physical exam in October at Edwards Air Force Base near Mojave, which I passed.

In January 1954, with my mouth full of bright new gold, I moved back in with Tina and resumed my studies at LACC. I soon discovered that I had much less enthusiasm and drive than during my first two years of college. Over two and a half years had passed since my high school graduation. Another year and I would be almost too old to enter the academy; the age limit was 22; I would be 21 in August '54.

I also thought about the fact that, if I was able to get into the academy and pursued a naval career, I would indefinitely have to endure many long separations from my family. The thought pained me very much. One afternoon as I was studying in the college library, I could not stop thinking about it and just broke down and cried. Unable to study, I left the library and walked around the campus for an hour to get a grip on my emotions.

¡El Capitán!

I decided that, if I didn't receive an appointment this time, I would give up my dream, get a part-time job, choose a different career, transfer to UCLA and complete my college degree.

Walking to and from school on Santa Monica Boulevard, I passed by a Catholic church. On the way home in the evening (I would do all my homework assignments in the library and leave only reading to do at home) and before dinner with Tina, I often stopped there and sat in one of the pews near the alter to pray and contemplate. These periods of reflection in quiet solitude helped me keep my emotions on an even keel and deal with bouts of loneliness and uncertainty regarding my future.

One day while I sat in my regular pew, an elderly gentleman approached me. I had seen him often and thought perhaps he was a church official. He greeted me with a warm smile, shook my hand and said, "I have seen you here many times. I don't know what it is you are seeking, but I can assure you that you will receive it!"

I smiled and replied that I was trying to get into the Naval Academy. He smiled warmly at me and said "God will reward you with your wish!" I thanked him, departed the church and walked home.

On February 13, 1954, Mom phoned to read me a telegram from Congressman Engle, "Am pleased to inform you of first alternate appointment to Naval Academy at Annapolis. Naval authority will contact you shortly regarding entrance examination scheduled March 24. I wish you every success."

I was thrilled and went home for the weekend with my friend Dale Watterson, a student at UCLA. Bill Bauer greeted me with a huge bear hug. He showed me his copy of Engel's letter with a hand-written note "Bill, this is an outstanding lad and we will get him in if he stays with it. All good wishes, Clair." I saw Ruth and Coach Neeme, who were very happy for me. And my parents, grandparents, siblings and friends were very happy and proud of me.

But on the way back to North Hollywood, I couldn't help feeling that, despite almost three years of effort, my entrance to the Naval Academy was still a long shot. Only a limited number of alternates get in.

Two weeks later, I received a letter from Richard Nixon, who had kept me on his list when he became Ike's Vice President in 1952. He awarded me a second alternate appointment.

Captain John Frank Gamboa, U. S. Navy (Retired)

On March 2, Mom called to read me another telegram, "I am pleased to advise you that I have designated you as my principal appointment to the United States Naval Academy for entry July 1954. The Department of the Navy will contact you further giving complete details. Best Regards, William F. Knowland, United States Senator."

I was shocked and breathless. I had been fifth on his list! I could hardly believe my luck! That night I celebrated with Tina, Bea and her new husband, Al Fisher. We were pretty excited and happy.

My appointments were big news in Lone Pine and Owens Valley and the town paper ran a front-page story. Even *La Opinion,* the leading Spanish-language newspaper in Los Angeles, ran an article about my appointments by the Senate Majority Leader, the Vice President and Engle.

I immediately wrote to Les Hewitt, who was by then an Air Force first lieutenant at Osan Air Force Base in South Korea flying F-86 Sabre jets. Les wrote back, "Drop out of college, go home, party and enjoy yourself because you're in for a very tough freshman year at the academy—and you'll be locked up for the next four years!"

Les also told me to contact his sister Myrnadel and her husband Dave Guzman; they were holding a $100 check from Les to pay for my initial uniforms deposit when I was sworn in.

I promptly withdrew from City College, packed my suitcase; thanked Tina and Bea for all their loving support, and caught a bus back to Lone Pine.

Two weeks later I received a less pleasant surprise: a draft board notice to report within one week at the Los Angeles Army Induction Center; I had broken my student deferment for the second time.

I immediately contacted Bauer, who called Engle, who spoke with the California Selective Service director, who said that I had broken my student deferment twice so according to the rules I had been immediately drafted. The director agreed to delay my induction into the Army long enough for me to take the Naval Academy aptitude test in March at Los Angeles City Hall. He told Engle that, if the Academy accepted me, I would be discharged from the Army. But I was going do some soldiering before I became a Sailor.

On April 7, 1954, I reported to the Army recruit induction center in downtown Los Angeles, passed my physical and was sworn into the Army. I boarded a train to Fort Ord, California with several hundred other draftees for 16 weeks of marching and drilling in Army boot camp. We learned basic infantry tactics, how to fire weapons, and in general how to be a soldier. Getting up at 4 a.m. each morning and crashing onto my bunk at 11 p.m., I fell asleep totally exhausted—not my idea of fun and parties in Lone Pine.

In May, I received orders from the Naval Academy to report to Balboa Naval Hospital in San Diego for a physical examination. About halfway through I underwent a very extensive vision examination and missed one letter. The doctor told me I had flunked. He said I could drop out of the rest of the examination and end all consideration for my admittance to the Academy.

Or, I could sign a request for a vision re-examination at the Naval Academy and complete the rest of the Balboa examination. I signed the request and successfully completed the rest of the exam. The academy would notify me when to report for a vision re-examination.

On the flight back to Fort Ord, I had a sinking feeling that my chances of passing a re-exam were slim. Even so, I felt I had no choice but to see the matter through. I was not going to abandon my quest without a final decision by the academy.

In May, I received a letter from the academy informing me that I had been accepted academically for admission with the Class of 1958. All my hard work in junior college had paid off.

I completed basic infantry training in mid-June and received orders to Camp Irwin, near Barstow, California, for 16 weeks of advanced infantry training, and two weeks leave before reporting. I also received a letter from the Naval Academy instructing me to report to the academy's clinic in Bancroft Hall on Monday morning June 28 for my vision re-examination.

I went home, borrowed a friend's car, drove about 150 miles to Camp Irwin, and reported to the Battalion Adjutant, who happened to be a West Pointer. I explained my situation to him, showed him my orders, and asked for leave for my re-exam. He asked, "Why didn't you go to West Point?" Before I could answer, he smiled, granted me two weeks of leave and wished me luck.

Bill Bauer contacted Moffett Field Naval Air Station near San Francisco and learned that I could catch a military hop on "space available" to get back east. Jim Ellis then arranged for Bob White, an expert pilot who operated the Lone Pine Airport, to fly me to Moffett.

Captain John Frank Gamboa, U. S. Navy (Retired)

On the morning of June 24, at his request, I met Jim, who was President of the Lions Club, in front of Josephs. He handed me $100. "This is a gift from the Lions Club to help you with your expenses. We wish you the best of luck." I thanked him. We shook hands and embraced.

Mom and Dad drove me to the Lone Pine airport. I hugged them as they wished me luck and said they would keep me in their prayers. Bob loaded my duffle bag and several large yellow blocks of salt in the luggage space of his small single-engine airplane. With a lump in my throat, I got into the plane's back seat and waved farewell to my parents.

The view of lakes, streams and meadows in the beautiful Sierra backcountry was spectacular. Bob skillfully landed on a grass strip between tall pine trees at Tunnel Air Camp in Monache Meadows and we off-loaded the blocks of salt for the horses and cattle grazing in the meadows. Then we flew over the vast agricultural fields of San Joaquin valley.

We landed at Moffett and made our way to base operations where I was assigned to a Navy flight to Westover, Massachusetts. Later that day, I boarded a Navy four-engine transport aircraft and enjoyed my first flight across America. At Westover, I caught another Navy hop to Anacostia Naval Air Station in Washington, DC, arriving there about 9 a.m., took a taxi to a hotel in DC and went to bed. I slept until late afternoon, and then went sight-seeing the rest of that day and the next, visiting the Lincoln Memorial and the museums on the National Mall, to my great enjoyment.

On Saturday afternoon, I boarded a bus to Annapolis and on Les' advice checked in at a private home that rented rooms to academy candidates. I introduced myself to three young men who had already been accepted for admission. I told them about my eye exam on Monday morning and one of them thoughtfully loaned me his dark glasses to rest my eyes from the bright sunshine. Then I walked to the King George Street home of the parents of Les' lovely wife Loretta, right outside the Academy wall near Gate Two. Loretta was staying there while Les was in Korea.

On Sunday morning, I walked down Maryland Avenue with the three other candidates and entered Gate Three to the Naval Academy Yard. We paused there to take in the beautiful scene: stately oak, maple and chestnut trees; soft, filtered sunlight; expansive lawns bordered with beautiful flower beds; long, curving sidewalks of worn red bricks connecting the academic buildings to Tecumseh Court; marble and granite monuments, benches and large, oxidized sailing warship cannons bordering the walkways. In the distance, the Severn River marked the limits of the Yard.

I had seen this view many times in books, but as I stood in the Yard for the first time and took it all in, I felt the beautiful scene had entered my soul.

We walked by the Administrative Building, pausing to read a large bronze plaque mounted on a granite block in front of the building:

Mission of the United States Naval Academy

Through study and practical instruction, to provide the midshipmen with a basic education and knowledge of the naval profession; to develop them morally, mentally, and physically; and by precept and example to indoctrinate them with the highest ideals of duty, honor and loyalty; in order that the naval service may be provided with graduates who are capable junior officers in whom have been developed the capacity and foundation for future development in mind and character leading toward a readiness to assume the highest responsibilities of citizenship and government.

Two huge black sailing ship anchors framed the entrance to the chapel, its massive, ornate bronze doors hinged on Doric columns. From this vantage point, Buchanan House, the superintendent's residence, came into view, as did Dahlgren and Ward Halls. Then we walked to Tecumseh Court, eager to see Bancroft Hall, our home for the next four years. We stood between the two cannons guarding the entrance to the courtyard and gazed at the world's largest college dormitory, a majestic building of grey granite with two enormous bronze doors at the center entrance. Despite its imposing size, Bancroft Hall did not seem intimidating. (It is affectionately called "Mother B" by the midshipmen.) It appeared empty; the brigade was away on their summer training cruise to Europe.

We entered the rotunda, walked up the stairway and entered Memorial Hall; our eyes were drawn to a large framed flag bearing the words "Don't Give up the Ship". We viewed the other historic battle flags and paintings and proceeded to the main office to buy meal tickets for dinner in the mess hall that evening.

Leaving Bancroft Hall, we walked down to Santee Basin to look at the first boats, sailboats and yachts I had ever seen. From there we could see the Chesapeake Bay, crowded with sailboats of every shape and size. That evening we returned for dinner in the mess hall with many other candidates and we talked about what we had seen and about what lay ahead of us.

This was the place where I was meant to be. I was happy and felt confident as we walked out of Gate One.

On Monday morning, June 28, I reported to the administration building and handed my orders to a Navy lieutenant, who directed me to Bancroft Hall for my vision re-examination. As I walked across the Yard I saw a large crowd of young men gathering in Tecumseh Court; they would be sworn in as midshipmen that day.

Pausing to look at the group, I saw naval officers and other distinguished looking men dressed in suits and women wearing hats and gloves. Everyone looked so well off. But I did not see a single Hispanic among them. A frightening thought flashed through my mind—I might not fit in.

I continued up the steps to Bancroft Hall, passed through the huge doorway and went to the main office. The midshipman officer of the watch assigned a midshipman to escort me to sickbay, where I handed my orders to a hospital corpsman.

A few minutes later, a Navy captain came out of his office and instructed me to stand at a line marked on the floor, cover my left eye, and read a line of letters on a chart on the opposite wall. Perfect. Then he had me cover my right eye and read the same line with my left eye. Correct. He jotted some notes in my file and then he looked up at me and said, "Okay, Mr. Gamboa, you passed. You are in."

For the longest moment, I just stood there, unable to breathe or move. Finally, I managed to say, "Is that it? Is that all there is to the exam?" The Captain nodded and replied, "The dumb bastards in San Diego should never have flunked you!"

Unable to speak as my eyes filled with tears, I walked toward the doctor and we shook hands, smiling. He signed my physical examination form indicating that I met all physical requirements for the academy, and then he sent me back to the administration building. The officials congratulated me and told me that they would get me discharged from the Army as soon as possible. I was directed to stay in the visiting team dormitory, take all my meals in Bancroft Hall with the new Plebes, the Class of 1958, and wear my Army uniform. When discharged from the Army, I would be sworn in as a midshipman.

I walked out Gate Three, went directly to Western Union and sent identical telegrams to my parents and to Bill Bauer, "I have passed the exam and will enter academy as soon as discharge from Army comes through. Will write later. Love and best wishes, Frank."

My quest to enter the academy had required more than three years of study and hard work. I had never imagined that it would take so long or that it would be so difficult. Overcoming my lack of confidence; surmounting my ethnic and cultural barriers; learning to excel in high school; earning my academic credentials in junior college; enduring the long wait for an appointment in a life of genteel poverty; repairing my teeth; passing the civil service exam, being drafted and getting through Army boot camp; flunking the eye exam and then passing the re-exam— these challenges simply made me more determined. The academy might reject me, but I would never give up on my own.

My determination and perseverance came from the lessons I learned at home. And reading and thinking about the academy, I bought into the idea so deeply that it became virtually impossible to give up.

Through intense study in my senior year at Lone Pine High and my two years in junior college, I learned how to think, to study, to focus and to write. But it required many days and weeks of effort to develop my scholastic abilities, catch up academically and gain self-confidence. Perhaps I could not have done it in less time.

I could never have entered the academy but for the inspirational help of Emil Neeme, Bill Bauer, Ruth Stevens, Les Hewitt, my endorsers, and my Lone Pine friends. The loving support from my family, especially from Tina and Bea and my Aunt Sandra and Uncle Carlos, was critical to my success. I am eternally grateful to all of them.

In my heart I felt that my admission to the academy was very much a tribute to Enriqueta, Teodulo, Chonita and Nacho—and God's reward to them for their years of hard work and countless sacrifices for my brothers and sisters and me.

My success affirmed their belief that, in America, you could go as far as your abilities, ambition and hard work could carry you.

When I departed home for college, and especially when I left for the academy, my relationship with my father changed forever. Our distant attitude and demeanor toward one another melted into feelings of love, warmth and affection.

Even though I never overcame my difficulty in communicating as fluently with Dad as I had so wanted, and we never achieved the level of camaraderie that I yearned for, I had earned my father's respect and admiration. That was more than enough.

For the first time in my life, I was completely happy.

Chapter Four

★ ★ ★ ★ ★ ★ ★

Four years together by the bay where Severn joins the tide,
then by the service called away, we're scattered far and wide
—Navy Blue and Gold

On the morning of July 12, 1954, I was seated in Memorial Hall with about 50 other candidates. We listened to the Commandant of Midshipmen explain the oath of office that we were about to take. "Are there any questions? Good. Please stand, raise your right hand and repeat after me:"

> I, John Frank Gamboa, having been appointed a midshipman in the United States Navy, do solemnly swear that I will support and defend the Constitution of the United States against all enemies, foreign and domestic; that I will bear true faith and allegiance to the same; that I take this obligation freely, without any mental reservation or purpose of evasion; and that I will well and faithfully discharge the duties of the office on which I am about to enter: So help me God.

With a big smile, the Commandant said, "Congratulations gentlemen! Welcome aboard!" I smiled joyfully with tear-filled eyes.

There were 1237 midshipmen in the Class of 1958, including one each from Nicaragua, Peru and the Philippines. About 45 classmates were "Navy juniors," those with fathers, and some with grandfathers as well, who were alumni. Including '58, the Brigade of Midshipmen numbered about 3600 mids, all residing in Bancroft Hall.

Bancroft's dormitory rooms were very austere. Each had metal bunk beds, a dull-green metal desk, a thinly cushioned metal chair, a tall metal wardrobe locker and metal waste paper cans for each occupant. The rooms were lighted by large fluorescent light fixtures. They had one or two sinks and a shower. The community restrooms were located in the main corridors. Each room had large windows kept open in warm temperatures for ventilation and cooling, but had no screens to keep out the mosquitoes, flies, birds and pigeons. In wintertime, the rooms were heated by steam radiators. The deck (floor) tiling was an unattractive dark brown. The bulkheads (walls) were light green, as were all the corridors.

Plebes were not allowed to have pictures, art, radios or phonographs, and only one personal photograph could be displayed inside a plebe's locker. But despite our Spartan accommodations, after a few days "Mother B" began to feel like home. (Bancroft Hall was completely remodeled in the 1990s with air-conditioned two-person rooms; attractive wooden furnishings, computers and telephones, and the staff offices were upgraded and modernized.)

After paying the required $100 deposit for my uniforms and getting my haircut, I carried to my room bundles of newly-issued bedding, clothing and uniforms, including four pairs of shoes plus a pair of gym shoes, more footwear than I had ever owned at one time in my life. I spent the rest of the day stenciling my new wardrobe with my name and laundry number. Then I placed everything in my locker precisely as specified in the locker stowage diagram issued to all midshipmen.

That night I had trouble falling asleep. I felt very happy, but apprehensive. What if I couldn't measure up to the academic demands and military discipline? If I flunked out how could I face my family and friends? These thoughts almost paralyzed me with fear. To get a grip on my anxiety I resolved that failure was not an option for me.

The next morning I began my plebe indoctrination into the academy's fast-paced daily routine that was planned to the minute from the 06:15 a.m. ring of the reveille bell to the lights-out bell at 10:15 pm (0615 and 2215 in the military 24-hour time system that is used at the academy). We had to double-time (run) to every military formation, which was the prelude to each event. Officers inspected us in ranks for correct uniform, clean shave, proper haircut and shined shoes. We marched to all events, including Sunday morning chapel.

About twice a week, the academy band played stirring marches in their gazebo (and during our weekly afternoon dress parades in the fall and spring on Worden Field) as we filed past. Throughout plebe summer I was in a happy, almost euphoric state, feeling so grateful that I was a midshipman in the Naval Academy. The band's joyful music then and in my next four years often moved me to tears. (During June Week, my father told me that he cried the first time he and Mom witnessed the Brigade parade.)

¡El Capitán!

A cadre of new '54 ensigns conducted our plebe summer indoctrination and training. We learned how to march in parade formation on Worden field in preparation for the brigade dress parades every Wednesday during the spring and fall academic terms. We trained at the academy's rifle range, learning to shoot a carbine, an M-1 rifle and a .45-caliber pistol. Thanks to Army boot camp training, my first Navy medals were for expert rifle and pistol marksmanship. In an indoor pool we had swimming lessons and abandon-ship drills in working uniform (without shoes), and learned how to rescue a swimmer in distress. We also learned to row pulling whaleboats—an arduous task—and to sail a 26-foot single-mast sailboat (knockabout) with a mainsail and a jib on the Severn River.

We took all our meals together in the mess hall, a huge three-winged facility with seating space for the entire brigade. We got acquainted and laughed about our daily experiences and concerns, bonding with each other and initiating the creation of our class identity. On August 12, my tablemates sang happy birthday to me. At 21, I was one of the oldest members in '58; three-fourths of my classmates had entered the academy directly from high school at age 17 or 18. The remainder came from other colleges or the armed services. But regardless of how we became midshipmen, plebe year was a great leveler; after a few days, we were all just plebes. Age and origin were irrelevant.

Stash Wiklinski, a tall, charming, muscular Polish guy from Ohio, and Dick Beam, an ex-soldier like me, were my roommates. At night, we relaxed, shined our shoes, and studied our "Reef Points," a small book filled with Naval Academy facts and trivia, Navy customs and traditions, fleet data and other subjects. We had to memorize the contents, plus the words and tunes to the Navy sports "fight songs," plus the fight song for each opposing college's football team. But our favorite pastime was reading our mail and writing to family and friends.

We were learning how to become officers and gentlemen, so meticulous table manners and proper etiquette were stressed at meals. We were given a diagram of the correct place setting of china, crystal and silverware and the correct use of each item. We learned to tear a slice of bread into quarters before buttering, to place our knife on the side of our plate, blade inward, while eating, and across the top of the plate blade inward when we had finished. We turned our cup upside down on the saucer if we did not want coffee. Talking with food in one's mouth and chewing food with an open mouth were verboten. And we learned to eat with one hand while placing the other on our lap, except when cutting or buttering.

Ethical conduct is the moral foundation of an officer's career; character and integrity are key virtues—an officer's word is his bond. A Navy captain instructed us on the midshipman honor concept, which is based on the premise that a midshipman does not lie, cheat, or steal. The honor concept is not just a matter of behavior. Unethical conduct—such as lying or hedging in combat—can cost lives and lose battles. An honor violation, the most serious conduct offense by a midshipman, usually resulted in expulsion from the academy. We were instructed on how to avoid compromising situations.

We were not allowed outside the Yard during our summer indoctrination period. The ensigns enjoyed telling us that the Yard's high grey-brick perimeter wall was intended to keep the girls out, not to lock us in; our first "liberty" would be Parents' Weekend in late August, the end of our plebe summer indoctrination and training that prepared us to join the brigade.

Mail from home and friends is critical to a midshipman's morale. I was upset with Mom. Despite my weekly letters to her, I had received only one reply. My father and my grandparents couldn't write so I never expected letters from them. My brothers and Erlinda were too young, and Tina and Bea were married and busy raising children.

I complained. Mom replied that she was not comfortable writing to me because she only had an eighth-grade education; she was embarrassed about her grammar, spelling, and penmanship. She wished that she could go to school and improve her writing in order to better express herself. (Years later as secretary of her senior citizens' club, she enrolled in a college course in English to better write her minutes.) And she feared that her letters might embarrass me or cause me to think less of her.

I reassured her that her letters mattered a great deal to me. I needed to explain my new life to her. I told her that her grammar and spelling were fine and that I enjoyed her writing style. (When she wanted to make a particular point or to better express her emotions, she would switch to Spanish, which felt more intimate.) Mom reached a level of comfort in her letters to me. She was my most important correspondent. I told her about the great times and those that just had to be endured. I held nothing back.

¡El Capitán!

The three upper classes returned from summer leave the Friday before Labor Day and '58 was integrated with the brigade, which was composed of two regiments. Each regiment had three battalions of four companies. The 24 companies averaged about 150 Mids. Plebe rooms were interspersed with upper-classmen's rooms. I was assigned to 17th Company, Fifth Battalion, and Second Regiment with four roommates. We had no choice in selecting our roommates until our second year. For mentoring, each plebe was assigned to a first classman (firstie, a senior).

Our plebe academic year included algebra, English, history, seamanship and navigation, and a foreign language. Even though I could speak conversational Spanish, I had never studied the language. Hoping for a relatively easy course, I signed up for basic Spanish. When the professor at registration saw my name he asked, *"Habla Espanol?"* I instinctively replied, *"Si senor!"* He lined out basic Spanish and wrote in advanced Spanish. It was my toughest course; however, because I had studied most of our other subjects in college, my end of year academic standing was in the upper half of the class.

Mids attended classes or study periods all day, Monday through Friday, and until noon on Saturdays, with about 15 midshipmen in each one-hour class (two hours for a lab or exams). "Gentlemen, man the boards and draw slips!" Each slip of paper had a problem to be solved or a sentence to be written in a foreign language on the chalkboard for the entire class to critique as directed by the professor. Each class ended with a 10-minute quiz. About every four weeks, we had a full-period examination, called a "P-Work" (Practical Work). Grades were posted every Thursday afternoon in the main corridors of Bancroft Hall. If we fell behind or flunked a quiz or a P-Work, we were given extra instruction after the last class of the day, which took precedence over athletics. The faculty made every effort to ensure our academic success.

Dr. Langdon, who taught "Bull" (English, History, and Government), was my favorite professor. He relished teaching and had a wonderful sense of humor. And he liked to single me out. One day as we entered his classroom and took our seats, he announced, "Gentlemen, let me quickly ask Mr. Gamboa a question before he falls asleep!" He then asked me something really off-the-wall that neither I nor anyone else could answer. Smiling, he said, "Don't sell your books, Mr. Gamboa!" provoking loud class laughter. I studied hard in his courses and we developed a good relationship. When I was struggling in youngster (sophomore) year with a personal issue, he provided good counseling.

On weekdays after last class, all midshipmen, except those who were on the binnacle list (ill), on watch, or officially excused for other reasons, participated in organized sports at the company, battalion, junior varsity or varsity level. Fall intramural sports included football, flag football, field ball, wrestling, boxing, handball, squash. In springtime, the sports were softball, tennis, soccer, cross country, and lacrosse. We competed for the Color Company—the best all-around company—so the games were spirited, hard-fought contests, great fun and good stress relievers. Teams included plebes, youngsters (sophomores), segundos (juniors); firsties (seniors) were team managers or officials. My firstie coached the battalion tackle football team and recruited me. I played right guard on offense and middle linebacker on defense. The teams included many drops from the varsity, JV and plebe football teams so the skill level was high, and it was the roughest team sport; more mids were injured playing battalion football than in any other sport.

Our fall and spring schedule included a brigade parade in dress uniform on Worden Field every Wednesday afternoon; they were reviewed by visiting dignitaries. The stands were filled with tourists taking pictures. The Queen Mother of England and the Sheik of Saudi Arabia each reviewed one in my youngster year. By tradition, they were permitted to grant amnesty to all midshipmen on restriction or "serving extra duty" (marching off demerits).

Each Saturday we were inspected during the noon meal formation, usually by our company officer, sometimes the battalion commander, even the commandant on rare occasions. Midshipmen who had missed a haircut, were not properly shaved, did not have mirror-bright shined shoes, or did not have a spotless, pressed khaki or well-brushed blues uniform were "placed on report."

After inspection, we were allowed to skip noon meal and go on liberty, but we could not go beyond "the 7-mile limit" from the chapel dome, or ride in automobiles. We ate in local restaurants, went to a movie, or just walked around Annapolis ("Crab town") looking over the girls being escorted by upperclassmen. Plebe liberty expired at evening meal formation on Saturday (1800). We could not leave the Yard on Sundays or weekdays.

¡El Capitán!

I enjoyed my plebe year roommates, but one day I was alone with one of them in our room as we studied. Suddenly, he stood up and asked, "What are you doing here, Gamboa?" Puzzled, I asked what he meant. Sneering at me, he replied, "You are a Mexican. You don't belong here!" Standing up, I looked him right in the eye and replied, "You are wrong, mister. I belong here. You don't!" Per his request, several weeks later he was moved out to another plebe room in our company. He eventually resigned.

I never related our confrontation to my other roommates, or to anyone else. It was the only overtly discriminatory remark ever made to me in the Academy. (I don't know if Richard Cordova, one of my four roommates and a Mexican-American from Los Angeles, received the same treatment.)

There is great exaggeration among Naval Academy alumni about the rigors of their plebe year; every alumnus declares, "Ours was the last class to have a real plebe year!" As my nephew, Mark Bradley, USNA '77, put it, "They take away all of your personal rights and then you have to earn them back, very slowly, over the next four years as privileges." The segundos were in charge of plebe indoctrination, under the supervision of the firsties, who ran the brigade. Happy to have their own plebe year behind them, the youngsters just enjoyed their new privileges, helped the plebes adjust, and didn't "run" us.

Our plebe year was generally good-natured with a great deal of humor, but with a serious purpose: to test the mettle of the new midshipmen and find out what we were made of.

Midshipmen have interesting backgrounds, and most have impressive records of accomplishments in high school or college, but as prospective officers, they must be able function as part of a team and to lead, the core organizing principles in the Naval Academy and the Navy.

Therefore, the upperclassmen want to know who you are. Despite any personal reticence, your character and personality traits will be found out.

Our indoctrination occurred mainly in Bancroft Hall and the mess hall. We were required to walk in the center of all hallways and double-time up and down all ladders (stairways), giving way to all upperclassmen. When outside our room we had to be in complete uniform or athletic attire during sports. At meals, we were integrated with the upperclassmen at 12-man tables with two firsties, two segundos, four youngsters, and four plebes.

Plebes were required to sit on the front 3" of our chair, braced straight-backed at attention, with "Eyes in the boat, mister!" (Looking straight ahead).

Our meals were served family style. Plebes passed the food to the firsties, and then to segundos, followed by youngsters, and last to themselves. The food was abundant and tasty. Ice cream was the favorite dessert, a product of the academy's own dairy farm.

To ensure that the upperclassmen got acquainted with each plebe in our company, we were rotated to a different table every month. The plebe mix was also changed so we got to know each other. Our main fear was to be seated at a tough table with a bunch of "hard asses." We preferred upperclassmen that were "big and easy." Regardless, we quickly learned that teamwork and mutual support were the best way to survive our indoctrination.

Plebes were not permitted to speak during meals except to answer an upper classman's question. There were five acceptable answers: the factual information requested, usually something out of Reef Points or naval history, considered a "professional question," but the subject matter was limited only by an upperclassman's imagination. The other permitted responses were "Yes sir," "No sir," "I will find out, sir" and the ubiquitous "No excuse, sir!" Plebes could never say, "I don't know, sir."

If per chance one did utter that forbidden phrase, the result was a "come-around," an order to report to the upperclassman's room at an appointed time for further indoctrination—usually between supper and evening study period (or at reveille)—to provide the correct answer, or correct the errant behavior, or receive punishment for some misdeed.

A come-around usually involved good-natured fun at the expense of the plebe. "Running the plebes" included activities such as uniform races (changing into a completely different uniform as quickly as possible in competition with another plebe), or "swimming to Baltimore" (exercising inside the come-around room's dry shower stall in gym gear until covered with sweat), or singing Navy fight songs.

But a come-around could be a very serious and hazardous confrontation with an upperclassman. Because most of the brigade ate lunch in town on weekends, only one wing of the mess hall was open Saturday noon through Sunday noon so you never knew who you would be dining with. During one Saturday noon meal, a firstie at my table was "running" a plebe and my classmate was not doing well. The firstie noticed me smiling. He asked, "What's your name, mister, and what's so funny?" I replied, "Gamboa; nothing, sir!" He said, "Then wipe that smile off your face (I did so immediately with my right hand). You seem to enjoy "bilging" (putting down) a classmate. Come around to my room Sunday evening and explain why!"

The firstie was a striper (midshipman officer) from 10th Company in the Third Battalion, which had a well-deserved reputation as the toughest company in the brigade, "a bunch of hard-asses!" I agonized all weekend about what I had gotten myself into. After Sunday dinner, I reported to the firstie's room. While I stood at my best brace-up wearing spotless, well-brushed uniform and gleaming shoes, he proceeded to instruct me on the fine points of loyalty to a classmate. After about a ten-minute ordeal, he dismissed me. I never saw him again. I never forgot the lesson.

If a firstie or a segundo got on your case because of your attitude, or some aspect of your behavior or uniform appearance, the result could be even more pressure on you, and you could even be "fried" (placed officially on report with a Form 2), resulting in an "award" of demerits.

Every five demerits (the minimum for an offense) required an hour of serving extra duty – marching in infantry gear, with a rifle, on one of Bancroft Hall's several redbrick terraces on Saturday afternoons during liberty hours. Plebes who exceeded 300 demerits were subject to expulsion from the academy. The limit on demerits decreased by 50 each year in the second, third and fourth years, with 150 demerits the limit for expulsion of seniors, who were placed "in hack" (restricted to their rooms on weekends) in lieu of marching.

I spent many a Saturday afternoon my plebe, youngster and segundo years marching on the terrace, and several weekends on restriction as a firstie. I received over 100 demerits in each of my four years. During plebe year, Mom asked why I was getting so many demerits. I explained that it was not deliberate.

Plebes frequently engaged in a battle of wits with the firsties and segundos, who often challenged us on our responses to their questions: "Do you bet your ass on that, mister?" Meaning, are you confident enough to wager a swat on your butt with your large, heavy atlas? If you accepted the bet and won, then the tables were turned and you got to swat the upperclassman with his atlas in a public ceremony outside his room prior to study hour. But this occurrence was very rare because they would not issue the challenge unless they were certain that you were factually incorrect. If you refused to bet, you were accused of "not having any hair on your ass" (lacking courage, boldness or self-confidence), which led to confidence-building come-arounds. Either way, the bet was a losing proposition for plebes.

In our time on Severn's shores, some outsiders considered the Naval Academy to be an overly expensive government institution, even an extravagance. Many years before our class arrived on Severn's shores, a congressman inserted his acerbic remarks about the academy into the Congressional Record—with a comment that the Naval Academy was "nothing but a school for the spoiled and pampered pets of Uncle Sam!" The Brigade promptly immortalized his sarcastic phrase in one of its fight songs, which to this day the mids proudly sing–with great glee.

Well, we did not feel privileged, spoiled or pampered. We lived not in luxury but in austere facilities, and worked hard for meager pay (our plebe monthly stipend was $2 cash; the rest of our $111 was withdrawn to pay for our uniforms, textbooks, school supplies, etc.).

The academics were very demanding and we endured a 24/7 regimen of strict military discipline. We earned our keep, and after graduation, we paid Uncle Sam back with four years of obligated military service (now five years).

More accurately, in my time the academy was a boys' school in every sense. Many in the brigade believed that midshipmen's boisterous behavior in Bancroft Hall was attributable to their high testosterone level. We joked that, to moderate our spirits, the academy added saltpeter to our food. Saltpeter, or sodium nitrate, is a constituent of gunpowder and has long been feared by boys in boarding schools as a chemical added secretly to their food to reduce their libido. It was, and is, of course a myth.

Our behavior could more accurately be characterized as stress relief and playful macho rowdiness. For example, plebes—or any speaker—who couldn't be heard by the mids was exhorted to "knock 'em together!" (exercise a part of our anatomy) to increase the volume of our voice.

A favorite antic during breakfast, just for the hell of it, was to dispatch a plebe to a neighboring table to shout, "Sir, does anyone have any extra cereal (or rolls, oranges, bananas, etc.)?" Immediately, everyone in hearing distance stood up and threw their individual boxes of cereal, or whatever, at the targeted table, forcing the occupants to dive for cover. This unprovoked attack always caused retaliation in kind. One morning this led to a full-fledged food fight in one entire wing that was ultimately suppressed by the officer of the day, who ordered the offending regiment to march out, skipping breakfast.

One brigade hallowed custom called for the recipient of a "Dear John" letter to post it in the corridor next to his door with a comment sheet for readers. The letters had a common theme: "You are destined to be a great naval officer, but I am not cut out to be a Navy wife;" or, "I'm sorry, but I just don't love you anymore;" or, "I didn't mean for this to happen. I met him by chance;" or, "He is very much like you; you would like him." The recipient's emotional wound was thus "cauterized." The letters and ribald comments contributed substantially to the brigade's *macho* humor.

Plebes had to know the score of every Navy varsity game each weekend, and to attend at least one varsity sports activity in the Yard. For home football games, rousing pep rallies were held after evening meal in Tecumseh Court on Friday nights. Plebes made posters to decorate Bancroft Hall and fire up brigade spirit. When Navy won, plebes were allowed to "carry on" (no bracing up to eat, and talking was allowed at meals) from the end of the game until evening meal on Sunday.

The entire brigade went to the Army-Navy football game in Philadelphia and the Notre Dame-Navy football games in Baltimore, by bus and train. After beating Army our plebe year, Navy went to the Sugar Bowl, beat heavily favored Ole Miss 21-0 (the SEC champion), and was ranked among the top five in the nation.

Plebes were not allowed to date at the academy or in town, but we could attend the occasional Saturday afternoon tea dances ("Tea Fights") at Carvel Hall Hotel in Annapolis with coeds brought in from nearby colleges. The Brigade Hop (dance) Committee also organized an occasional tea dance for plebes in Dahlgren Hall on Sunday afternoons with girls from the same colleges.

The brigade-attended away football games gave us a chance to participate in post-game parties or enjoy a night of liberty on the town. On my first brigade trip to Baltimore for a Navy-Notre Dame game, I joined a group of 17th Company classmates at a post-game party in a private home with girls from Goucher College. I met and danced with an attractive, witty and personable girl. Making small talk, I asked, "Sally, did you have a good seat during the football game?" Her girlfriend quickly interjected, "She certainly did!" Sally blushed and said, "I sat in Governor McKeldin's box." She was the governor's niece. I was somewhat intimidated by this information, but when the party ended we agreed to correspond and even get together whenever she visited her cousin Clara in the governor's mansion in downtown Annapolis.

My 17th Company classmate, Ron Fisher, a tall, lanky and brilliant Tennessean, joined me one afternoon on my date with Sally. When we arrived at the governor's mansion, the butler led us to a drawing room to wait for the girls. Unexpectedly, Governor McKeldin walked in, introduced himself and talked with us for a few minutes. Afterwards, Ron and I spent an enjoyable afternoon with Sally and Clara, playing Ping-Pong, watching TV, snacking, and dancing to records.

One Saturday, Ron and I were invited to a luncheon with Mrs. McKeldin and the girls in an ornate Governor's mansion dining room at a table set with fine china, silver ware and sparkling crystal glasses. After dessert and coffee, the servers placed a bowl of clear liquid with a floating slice of lemon at each place setting.

Our Academy place-setting diagram had not shown anything like this. Ron and I looked at each other, wondering what to do. Deciding it was soup, I picked up my unused soupspoon. Sally quickly caught my eye and dipped her fingers into her dish—demonstrating the proper use of a finger bowl. She smiled playfully, knowing she had just saved Ron and me from a *faux pas* with Maryland's First Lady.

As much as I was enjoying being at the academy, plebe year was a challenge for me, as reflected in my November 1954 letter to Mom:

> The daily life here is very rigorous at times. I cannot help but get discouraged....My grades are good but they could use improvement. It is so hard to get too much accomplished....Our day is just too short. But then, the Academy has to be tough if its graduates are going to be competent men. The Navy can't put a dope in charge of a destroyer or an aircraft carrier. I hope I can meet the standards. God knows I will try hard enough. Don't be surprised if you receive some very mixed-up letters from me,

Mom. It is very easy to get confused here and down in morale. But don't worry about me. You can help me best by writing to me as often as you can. You have no idea how much contact with the outside world means to midshipmen. We are really shut-in here; we lead a 24-hour a day Navy life!

At times, I was homesick:

> It seems like a very long time ago that I waved goodbye to you and Dad at the airport this summer. I had quite a few mixed emotions and fears…. I suddenly realized that this goal of mine is going to be a very demanding one and will separate us for many years to come. It makes me sad when I think of it; you and Dad have been the most wonderful parents in the world to me and my brothers and sisters…. I hope to God that my accomplishments have brought you both a measure of happiness and pride. If they have not, then I have been a complete failure; my sole purpose in everything I have ever done is to please you both and try to show you in some way my love for you and my deep appreciation to you for all the hardships and tribulations that you have endured for my beloved brothers and sisters and me.

I became good friends with my 17th Company classmate, Jack Dittrick, who invited me to his home in Elizabeth, New Jersey for our first Christmas leave. We received warm, loving hospitality from his wonderful parents, Dorothy and John, who sent us off to New York City, with dates arranged by Dorothy, to see the famed Rockettes at Radio City Music Hall, and a Broadway show. I met Bill McCutchen, Jack's close friend from grammar school days, and we went to dances in Elizabeth. One spring break a group of us were at Jack's and there was a surprise snowfall. We had no overcoats to wear into New York City so Dorothy promptly borrowed seven from neighbors, even two from her pastor. Jack's parents treated me like a son; they were among the nicest, most decent people I have ever known.

Returning to Mother B after Christmas, we experienced a time referred to by mids for decades most appropriately as "the dark ages," a time at the academy characterized by a pervasive gloom throughout the Yard due to frequently overcast skies and shortened daylight time. This bleak winter period has to be endured in order to comprehend its emotional impact.

In the first two weeks back from the holidays, we faced final exams—frightening academic trials that lowered brigade spirit to the pits of despair. (Final exams are now conducted prior to Christmas leave, resulting in better midshipman grades and higher morale.)

From January to March, the temperature in Annapolis hovers near freezing during the day and below freezing at night. Blasts of cold wind off the Chesapeake Bay made marching to and from classes miserable. And raingear didn't protect our faces from the cold rain and snow. Mids came down with colds or the flu, but sickbay dispensed only APCs (all-purpose capsules, mostly aspirin) that did little to alleviate suffering. There were no football games to attend and few sports victories to cheer about. Outdoor company sports were either cancelled, or were played in cold, damp, miserable conditions.

During this time of trial, I often felt lonely or depressed, even to the point of harboring doubts about my commitment to the academy. But midshipmen's spirits can never be permanently dampened—youthful vigor and spirited optimism got us through those miserable days. We learned to laugh and enjoy ourselves despite the gloom, developing valuable coping skills. The sheer joy of interacting with my roommates and company mates and the pace of our daily routine prevented me from dwelling on dark thoughts, which is one reason academy classmates bond so deeply.

Looking back, I believe my feelings and outlook during the dark ages, or whenever I felt down, were just part of my adjustment to the academy's demanding academics and its strict discipline and military regimen. Fatigue was also a factor. I had been continuously striving for an education and self-improvement beginning in my high school senior year. In junior college, I learned that prayer helped to strengthen my resolve and steady my emotions when I had doubts about my goal. Then I realized that I had stopped praying and seeking God's help after I entered the academy. As I struggled to keep my morale positive and cope with occasional low spirits, I came to the realization that I simply could not bear my burdens alone. I started praying again and seeking God's help, and never ceased.

I was baptized and confirmed in the Catholic Church and throughout high school, I attended Catholic mass. But I am not a devoutly religious person, rarely read the bible, and I am irregular about attending church. Nonetheless, I do believe in God, having concluded long ago that the human race, our universe and nature are simply too complex, awesome and marvelous to be happy accidents or an evolutionary quirk.

My religious attitude is more a belief in the fundamental spirituality of man and our purpose in life, more than in any particular religious doctrine. In January 1961, President John F. Kennedy concluded his inaugural address with a passage that well-characterizes my outlook on life. "With a good conscience our only sure reward, with history the final judge of our deeds, let us go forth to lead the land we love, asking His blessing and His help, but knowing that here on earth God's work must truly be our own."

In late March 1955, all the plebes in the Fifth Battalion (Companies 17-20) were assembled in a 6th wing basement in Bancroft Hall. We were addressed by a segundo member of the brigade hop committee, the prestigious midshipman organization responsible for planning the brigade's formal dances. Hops were major social events at the Academy. Mids wore their dress uniforms, and the girls wore formals.

The segundo said we had to elect our battalion's plebe representative to the committee; he described the requirements: leadership, organizational ability, social graces, diplomatic skills, and being comfortable with the protocol for dealing with senior officers and their wives.

Fearful of being selected, my classmates and I actually tried to hide behind each other. The 18th Company nominated John Poindexter and 19th and 20th Companies each nominated one of their members. Without warning, Ron Fisher shouted in a loud Tennessee drawl, "Frank Gamboa is dating Governor McKeldin's niece, he's a frequent guest in the governor's mansion, has had conversations with the governor and dined with the first lady of Maryland! He knows all about protocol, social graces, and diplomacy!"

That night I learned about mob behavior. 17th Company cheered and yelled for me, greatly relieved that someone else would "take the bullet." When the votes were tallied, I had won over Poindexter by the landslide margin of one vote. Despite slaps on my back and congratulations from my company mates, I spent a sleepless night worrying about a fearful responsibility that I knew absolutely nothing about, one that seemed fraught with peril.

Even though it required much extra time and effort (sneaking down to the basement to study after taps), I enjoyed working on the hop committee, planning and organizing dances. I developed great friendships among the committee members, including Jesse Hernandez, a Spanish-American from California, Wes Phenegar, and John Wandell. I became adept at the protocol for escorting a hostess, usually an academy senior officer's wife, preceded by dinner at their quarters in the Yard.

My duty was to escort her to the dance, stand with her in the receiving line and introduce her to each midshipmen and his date, who were required to greet the hostess. We supervised the hop and ensured that mids behaved like gentlemen and that the girls were "lady like." After the hop, I would escort the hostess back to her quarters. I was on the hop committee all four years and in our first class year, the committee elected Jesse as chairman and me as vice.

One Sunday afternoon in my senior year, I was in charge of the hop committee's first academic-year Fifth Battalion plebe tea dance. Attendance was mandatory and the plebes were unenthusiastic, much preferring to "rack out" (sleep). My committee assistants and I matched up each girl with a plebe and directed the couple to the receiving line and onto the dance floor.

I soon noticed that the group of plebes was dwindling faster than the group of girls. I walked around the hall and then checked the men's head (restroom), where I discovered 15-20 plebes hiding out. I rounded them up and led them to the remaining group of waiting girls. I placed my hand on the shoulder of the nearest plebe and directed him, "Mister, I want you to go dance with that girl! I will be watching!" Despite his nervousness, they danced. I continued in this manner until all the plebes were on the dance floor.

Later, one of the plebes approached me with a big smile, "Sir, thank you very much for getting me on the dance floor. I had a great time. That girl was a lot of fun. She has a great convertible and she invited me to her home in Baltimore during the Christmas holidays!" Sometimes a midshipman's luck is like that. I should have cut in.

Near the end of plebe year, we chose our roommates for youngster year. Jack Dittrick, John McCain and I quickly agreed to room together.

¡El Capitán!

We knew that Keith Bunting was the smartest guy in our company so we promptly asked him to join us, much like drafting a top NFL quarterback. With a loud sigh and slight frown—and then a warm smile, the "Rab" agreed. Our future academic success was in the bag.

We had very different backgrounds. Jack was an only child of German ancestry from Elizabeth, New Jersey; Keith was of English heritage from East Rockaway, New York and had two sisters. I was a first-generation Mexican American from California with two brothers and three sisters. Jack, Keith and I had no military background—we were the first in our respective families to serve in the armed forces.

Conversely, John was the third-generation member of his family to attend the Naval Academy; he had a sister and a brother. His father, Captain John S. "Jack" McCain, Jr., Class of 1931, was a highly-decorated submariner who served in the Atlantic and Pacific theaters during WW II, sinking many Japanese ships. He was stationed in Washington, D.C., serving on the chief of naval operations' staff as chief of legislative affairs. John's grandfather, Vice Admiral John S. "Slew" McCain, Class of 1906, was an aviator who commanded the Pacific Fleet's Fast Carrier Task Force 38, which fired the last shot in combat against Japan in WW II. (The McCains were the first father-son four-star admirals in Navy history.)

Our Plebe Year ended with June Week (now called Commissioning Week) which concludes with graduation for the firsties. My first year had been as arduous as I had expected, but I was treated fairly by the upperclassmen. I got through relatively unscathed. I accumulated over 100 demerits, but no serious offenses. Many plebes had a much rougher time than I did, and we lost over one hundred classmates for academic, conduct or personal reasons.

My class academic standing was in the upper-half. I did well in military aptitude ("grease"), achieving the midshipman rank of lieutenant junior grade and designation as a platoon commander.

I dated a girl I had met in Elizabeth, escorting her for three days including the Farewell Ball. Jack's parents drove our dates to Annapolis, and even prepared a picnic to launch our festivities. In my last letter to my parents as a plebe I wrote, "It's been a great year!"

Captain John Frank Gamboa, U. S. Navy (Retired)

At 0400 the day after '55's graduation, my classmates and I—the new third classmen—and the new firsties (Class of '56) embarked on a midshipman practice cruise task group. Anchored in the Chesapeake Bay, the ships were an awesome sight: Two battleships, three cruisers and ten destroyers. I was assigned to the USS *Des Moines*, a heavy cruiser with teakwood decks and triple turrets of twin eight-inch semi-automatic guns. We got underway for Norfolk to anchor and embark NROTC midshipmen. The next morning the task group sortied for a two-month cruise to Spain, England, Cuba and back to Annapolis.

Our workday began at 0600 and our first task (before breakfast) was a fresh-water wash-down of the main deck and bulkheads and polishing all brass fittings on the lifelines and elsewhere under the watchful supervision and instruction of the boatswain's mates. On Fridays after breakfast, we "holy stoned" (scrubbed) the decks with salt water and bricks pushed by mop sticks, a physically arduous task that made the teak boards gleam white in the sunshine.

We stood watches on the bridge, signal bridge, combat information center, and engineering main control. It was exciting to see the ships in our task force sailing in formation day and night and maneuvering alongside the oiler to refuel. It felt great to be away from plebe indoctrination, the academics, and the pressures of daily life in the academy.

Des Moines was well led and managed with a smooth-running ship's company organizational structure and daily routine. Her crew was proud and spirited, and kept her looking clean, sharp and shipshape. I understood my division roles and duties and I adapted easily and enthusiastically to shipboard life. I thoroughly enjoyed the teamwork with my classmates and the enlisted men on watch and at our work stations.

My love of the sea began on that cruise. I was enchanted by the sight of the deep blue ocean, the beauty of sunrises and sunsets, cloud formations and distant rainsqualls, and sighting flying fish, dolphins and whales. At night, it was exciting to identify navigational stars, planets and constellations. Inhaling the salt air felt pure and healthy. I was fascinated by the entire scene, so vastly different from Owens Valley's mountain-locked desert terrain.

We sailed for 15 days across the Atlantic, through the Straits of Gibraltar and into the Mediterranean, where the task group called at several Spanish ports; Des Moines visited Malaga. We enjoyed city tours and an exciting train ride to Madrid for four days of sightseeing. The task force then sailed into the English Channel for an eight-day visit to Plymouth and other ports in England. The mids and crewmembers had a four-day tour of London. Our return voyage home included a four-day stop for live gunnery training with the U.S. Fleet Training Group at Guantanamo Bay, Cuba, known as GITMO.

Youngster cruise was a great introduction to life at sea in a warship and I made many new friends. We were happy to sight the chapel dome on our return to Annapolis, which completed our transformation into youngsters. We disembarked and departed for home on summer leave.

I was very happy to see my family, visiting with all my friends and going to lots of parties. Everyone wanted to know all about my life as a midshipman. It was the most enjoyable summer I had ever spent in my hometown. But all too soon, I was flying back to Annapolis for my second year at the Academy.

The academics were more difficult, but my life was immensely more relaxed and enjoyable than plebe year. I quickly settled into a routine with my new "wives" (roommates). In October 1955, I wrote to Mom:

> There are many things that I have not told you about my life here … my roommates are the most interesting people that I have ever met. Jack is tall and handsome with a warm and friendly smile and a gregarious personality … one of the most personable and popular classmates in our company and great fun to be around because of his intelligence, outgoing manner, sharp wit, and great sense of humor. I told you about him in my earlier letters when I spent Christmas leave at his home. He is a great friend …
>
> Keith and I are in the advanced Spanish class and talk a lot of Spanish to each other. He speaks Spanish excellently, although his New Yorker accent makes his pronunciation sound a little foreign. Like me, he was class president and attended Boys State. We both play battalion football; he is second string quarterback … has a large forehead, a Roman nose, and blue eyes (his grandparents are from England). Keith will make a good officer because he likes responsibility, has ability, is a gentleman, and gets along well with

people. He is very modest and is always willing to help a fellow out with studies, or anything else for that matter.

John is very sincere with a very dynamic personality. He has an excellent knowledge of history and likes to read history books and novels, especially Hemingway. He has prematurely grey hair, due mostly to his nervousness and constant state of tension. His eyes are deep blue that remind you of cold steel (pardon the melodramatic analogy). He has a sharp wit and an excellent sense of humor, though the latter borders on good-natured sarcasm most of the time. He does not brag or put on airs; he dislikes life here but likes the Academy. He has very good athletic ability and likes boxing and wrestling. He is pretty well known and has quite a number of friends in the brigade. In his tastes, he likes things plain and unaffected. His favorite pastime is partying, like all midshipmen.

Our daily routine consisted of classes, athletics and study. To keep our uniforms clean and pressed, we studied in our skivvies (under shorts and t-shirts).

One October evening, the four of us were studying when John got up from his desk, got to the washbasin and suddenly started dousing us with glassfuls of water. We quickly retaliated, and soon everyone was soaking wet.

And there were two sharp knocks on our door, the brigade-wide signal that a firstie or an officer was entering the room. We bolted to attention. Frozen in place with my back to the door, I heard a stern, authoritative voice, "Carry on, gentlemen!" This order was followed by "This is a gross room!" and then, "Goddammit, Johnny! No wonder you're flunking! Get dressed and come down to the Rotunda!"

Turning around, I came face to face with a naval officer with gold braid seemingly up to his elbows. Captain John S. "Jack" McCain, Jr, John's father, introduced himself to Keith, Jack and me and politely chatted with us while John got out of his wet skivvies and into a dry uniform. Then the captain departed to await John in the rotunda.

Despite the captain's cordial tone and friendly demeanor, we were scared out of our wits. After they departed, we cleaned up the room, got into dry pajamas, and hit the books hard for the remainder of study hour. John soon rejoined us in a chastened mood.

¡El Capitán!

The next day when we returned from classes, we discovered that our room had been inspected by none other than the commandant of midshipman. The person in-charge-of-room (ICOR) was on report for "room in gross disorder" (it was my turn). Since the commandant rarely, if ever, inspected a midshipman's room, we figured that his good friend Captain McCain had requested that the commandant honor us with his personal attention.

On the following Saturday afternoon, I spent two hours marching on the terrace. I also had time to think about how my life would be living with John McCain. I came to the conclusion that it would always be interesting and fun, but at times hazardous.

My 17th company classmates and I also learned that McCain would not hesitate to "fight the system," especially if he thought rules were unfairly enforced. He was strongly opposed to any mistreatment of a fellow human being.

One Saturday, John and I both had duty so after noon formation inspection we went to have lunch in the mess hall. We found seats at a table with mids we didn't know and sat down next to each other. We soon noticed that the lone firstie at our table was berating and harassing the Filipino steward who was serving our table. The firstie had told him to bring seconds of some menu item, but the steward said there was none ('ain no mo!). The firstie reacted in a very harsh manner, berating and belittling the steward, who looked frightened. I sensed John tensing up.

Suddenly, with a tight jaw, John said to the firstie, "Why don't you pick on someone your own size?" Stunned by McCain's audacity, the firstie growled, "What did you say, mister?" John replied, "That steward is doing the best he can. Why are you picking on him?" The firstie glared at John and in a most threatening tone and said, "What's your name, mister?" John shot back, "McCain, what's yours?"

Flabbergasted by the temerity of an underclassman's challenge to a senior, the firstie stared angrily at John for a few moments in stony silence. Then with no further word, the firstie abruptly left the table and the mess hall.

I was dumbfounded. A few moments later, John got up and walked out. I quickly followed him. As is his style when he is angry, John walked at a very brisk pace, swinging his left arm in an exaggerated manner, just like his father. I had to practically run to keep up with him.

Captain John Frank Gamboa, U. S. Navy (Retired)

He slowly cooled off. As we walked to our room, he said in an angry tone of voice, "It really pisses me off to see someone use his power to mistreat a subordinate!"

McCain had reacted instinctively, with total disregard of the possibly dire consequences to himself. He could have been severely reprimanded, even expelled for insubordination, but nothing happened. We never saw the bullying first classman again.

Another time during youngster year, we returned from morning classes to find that our room had been inspected by our company officer, a Marine Corps captain. He had pulled John's bedding off the mattress and piled it in the middle of his rack.

McCain slammed his books down on his desk, stormed out of the room, burst into the captain's office, stood at attention in front of his desk and said, "Sir, if you do not like the way my bed is made up, place me on report. Don't tear it up. I only have time to make it up once a day!"

Then he turned on his heels, stomped out of the office and returned to our room. He told us what he had done. Stunned, we waited for the dreaded repercussion, but the captain did not retaliate (but over time, it became obvious to us that he did not forget).

At warp speed, these incidents and others became legend in our class. We were amazed at John's courage and bravery. He was fearless. McCain gained our respect and admiration. He became true north on our moral compass.

A huge morale factor in our new status was a treasured privilege: dating. Our weekend liberty as youngsters was extended to Saturday evenings and Sunday afternoons after mandatory chapel service. We all got right into the spirit of dating, which was called "dragging" and our dates were "drags" because the mids were always rushing to or from an event and literally dragging their dates along, or so it seemed to the girls.

They stayed at "drag houses," private residences in Annapolis that rented spare bedrooms to girls dating mids. Due to the mids' meager allowance ($7 per month for youngsters), the girls usually paid for their own transportation, room, and sometimes even their meals. My letter to Mom in the spring of '56 portrayed a typical dragging weekend.

> This Saturday I have to help decorate Dahlgren Hall for the
> hop, which will take up all my spare time. I also have to

coordinate the entertainment for the hop this week with guys elsewhere in Bancroft Hall, which will take more time that I don't have. Also, a friend is going to teach me some square-dance steps. (The dance theme is a Farmers' Ball in costume!) After I finish decorating, I will run back to my room, shower & change uniforms, then go out in town and meet my date. We will go to a gymnastics meet and then a swimming meet all against Army so we have to cheer Navy on, then scramble back to the drag house and leave my date there. I come back to evening formation, then back to the drag house and out to dinner, then back to the drag house for my date to dress for the hop, then hurry to the hop, then hurry back to the drag house, then run all the way back to Bancroft Hall so I am not late, up to my room and fall into bed, exhausted. But right now I have to polish my shoes, fold laundry and God knows what else. Mom, life is hell here sometimes!

A midshipman who had a steady girlfriend was often requested by his roommates or other classmates to get them a date. "Can you fix me up for the weekend?" A midshipman's girlfriend was the usual instigator, looking out for her friend. "She's been out of circulation." Or, "She is over her break-up and needs to go out!" These situations required delicate maneuvering, strategizing and sizing up by everyone concerned.

It was our most challenging and perilous social task. If a blind date was successful, you were a hero. If, for whatever reason, it turned out badly, the friendships all around underwent a severe test. Regardless, the outcome of weekend dates was a favorite discussion topic at Sunday-night dinner in the mess hall, and matchmaking episodes provided the brigade a mother lode of anecdotes, gossip and *macho* humor.

An unsuccessful match could have dire social consequences. If a mid's date was judged by his peers to not "have even a good personality," the hapless mid was subjected to a raucous Sunday-night ritual—a "bricking party" organized by classmates, which began with the company plebes dressed in pajamas and bathrobes parading in the company corridors and noisily banging their "klacks" (wooden shower shoes) to attract spectators, coming to a halt in front of the unfortunate mid's room.

The traditional protocol required that the honored mid stand in his room doorway and receive a brick on a pillow, presented like a sacred object. Then he had to listen while a plebe read the "brick award" proclamation, which described the attributes of his date in lurid detail, written by the recipient's own roommate(s). He had to respond appropriately and place the brick in the transom over his nameplate for all to see. It remained there until the next mid in the company accomplished an equally or more notorious dating feat. Each company had their own brick and organized their own bricking parties. Another example of the Mids' occasional rowdy behavior.

Regardless of our enjoyable new social life, the strain of being a midshipman was always present. "Mom, I had a typical day at Navy: four classes and four tests. Only went to sleep in one class, Spanish. Boy will I be glad to see the end of these "dark ages." This is the most miserable period of the year at the academy. I have never felt so lifeless, blue, frustrated, defeated, and just plain disgusted in many a day. Wasn't so bad plebe year because it was all so new, but this year—ugh! But hurrah! The end is in sight. Only 17 days until spring leave!"

For spring break, John invited Jack, Keith and me plus several other classmates to his parents' home on Capitol Hill in Washington, D.C. Having attended Episcopal School in Alexandria, John had many friends and lined up several great parties.

Captain Jack McCain and his wife Roberta had a large, elegant home and were gracious hosts; we became frequent guests. The captain would always meet with us in his study and inquire about our status. Often a congressman would be visiting and the captain would introduce us as "the future leaders of our Navy and our country," proudly extolling the virtues of the Naval Academy and the Navy. He would talk about how great it was going to be to serve our country as naval officers. When we expressed concern about the long family separations endured by naval officers on sea duty, he replied, "Gentlemen, absence makes the heart grow fonder!" John's younger brother, Joe (his middle name is Pinckney; his father called him Joe Pink), often joined us. We called Captain McCain's inspiring pep talks "our shot of Blue and Gold!"

Jack, Keith and I learned a great deal about the Navy's culture, etiquette and protocol in the McCain household and developed great admiration and affection for the captain and Roberta, who always treated us like sons. Their guidance inspired us and gave us confidence.

When I was a lieutenant, I talked with Roberta about becoming a career naval officer. She advised me, "Honey, (her name for all of us) if you want to be successful in the Navy, then you have to pick the hard jobs. That's what Jack did!"

Jack McCain was the most inspirational naval officer I ever met. I called on him whenever I had the opportunity throughout my career. I always came away walking taller and with renewed enthusiasm for the Navy.

My youngster year passed even faster than plebe year; my academic standing was again in the middle of the class. We all plunged enthusiastically into the June Week festivities. Several of us rented a house in nearby Sherwood Forest and invited girls down for the week— they stayed at the house and we stayed in Bancroft Hall. I dated Sally and escorted her to our youngster hop. I also dated Patricia from the Australian Embassy in D.C. (my 17th company good friend Dick Pittenger "fixed me up," a friend of the girl he was dating.)

My parents sent me money. I responded, "Thank you! Your telegram was most welcome. It feels wonderful to have two stripes of gold and to be half-way through the academy. I only hope that the next two years are as crammed full of excitement, adventure, experience, hard work, play, and pure enjoyment as these past two years. They have truly been the greatest years of my life!"

After '56's graduation, '58 boarded amphibious ships in the Chesapeake Bay and got underway for two weeks of amphibious warfare training at Little Creek, Virginia, with the Marines. As a company commander, I was very busy. Our shipboard training focused on amphibious assault on a hostile beach, climbing over the ships' sides on nets down into floating landing craft, and conducting an amphibious landing. The Class of '58 stormed the beach, like the Marines during WWII—but no live fire. Our social life included receptions, mixers, dances and other activities almost every evening and weekend, hosted by the amphibious naval base commander.

After amphibious training, we boarded the aircraft carrier USS *Tarawa* (CVS 40) for a two-week cruise to Nova Scotia. We received aviation training, making carrier take-offs and landings in anti-submarine warfare aircraft. Our six-day port visit in Halifax featured a dance aboard ship in the hangar bay with girls from Halifax, and receptions and sightseeing with Canadian girls. In August, we went home on 30 days leave.

Captain John Frank Gamboa, U. S. Navy (Retired)

Returning to the Yard, we discovered that the dire warnings were true. Second class year was the toughest we would face at the academy. A heavy academic load combined with plebe indoctrination responsibilities made for long days, but we enjoyed higher status in the brigade and we got along well with '57, the new firsties.

I wrote to Mom, "Being a second classman does change my outlook a little. I find this life a little different looking at it from an upperclassman's point of view. Running plebes is quite a novelty; the poor creatures are scared to death of us. I haven't made any of them bleed, but I am a little meaner than I thought I would be!" But I also told her that Bunting, Dittrick, McCain and I were considered to be "hard but fair!"

> Just returned from evening meal so I have a few minutes before the plebes start falling in our doorway for a half-hour of 'discipline.' Running plebes is quite an experience, folks. They are a source of entertainment and work, mostly the former. We— my wives and I—give them quite a going over. I'm beginning to remember all of the little irksome things that I had to do as a plebe so it gives me a big kick to put them through the same routine. Guess you can call it revenge. Last night we had a choice group around singing Navy songs for us. I doubt that any of them could carry a tune in a bucket, but we got a big laugh out of their horrible attempts. We have the group coming back again tonight at the end of study hour for a repeat performance!

In October, Air Force Captain Les Hewitt and his wife Jean visited her parents in Annapolis and I invited Les to dinner in the mess hall. It was his first time at the academy since his graduation. I felt proud to have my friend and mentor from Lone Pine as my guest. But on his departure, a tinge of homesickness surfaced in my letter to Mom, "I sure wish I was going back to California with them.... The next two years can't go by fast enough for me. For four years now, I have been studying constantly and striving for an education and self-improvement. I want to get out of here and live a little—a whole lot in fact!"

That fall, '58 passed a significant milestone: we selected our class rings, to be received the following April. Keith was a member of the committee that designed our class crest, which we began wearing on our neckties youngster year, and pinning them on our OAO (one and only). Our class ring features our crest on one side and the academy crest on the other.

Beginning in my high school junior year, I had been subordinating practically all of my social life to studies and schooling. My priorities changed when I became a midshipman. One weekend in the fall of 1956, Sarah, the girlfriend of my classmate Walt Ryan, fixed me up on a blind date with Betsy, an attractive girl from Women's College in North Carolina. She had a friendly, outgoing personality and Southern charm. She fit in very well within my group of friends and could hold her own in a battle of wits, even with McCain, who was notorious for his sarcastic wit and "running" our drags at a hop, "My, those are lovely elbow-length gloves. Are they the latest style in Kansas?"

Betsy and I dated several times that football season, including the Army-Navy game. At a party afterwards, we agreed to get "pinned," that is, she would wear my class crest, a higher level of commitment, but far short of a formal engagement. Nonetheless, after our initial blush of happiness reality set in during the dark ages. Betsy's school was a long distance away and she couldn't afford to travel to Annapolis every weekend. Neither of us was content to spend weekends alone. We both began to have second thoughts.

I turned to my "wives" for advice, and each had an opinion, especially McCain, who was considered the subject-matter expert on all personal problems, especially lovelorn issues. Because he had slightly grey hair, we regarded him as worldly and wise in the ways of women.

John reviewed my letters to Betsy—whether I asked him to or not— and advised me on revisions he thought necessary. All took note of my distress and advised me that I was taking matters too seriously, and to "cool it." I agreed that I was causing myself too much emotional turmoil over the matter. And my grades were beginning to deteriorate. Then Mom wrote, "You better pick up your ass and quit trying to be a playboy or you will finish last!"

Betsy's parents invited me to their home in Amelia, Virginia, for spring leave. I was very apprehensive about meeting her family, so my roommates coached me, and even Dorothy Dittrick offered motherly advice on how to behave and what to say in Betsy's home, especially to her mother.

Captain John Frank Gamboa, U. S. Navy (Retired)

During my visit, Betsy paraded me before their neighbors at evening socials, giving me a taste of Virginia hospitality and culture. We took walks down country roads and talked about the Navy, her college, and our respective career plans. I didn't plan to get married until I had been in the fleet for at least a couple of years and had launched my career. At the end of my visit, we decided that I would take back my class crest, but we would continue to correspond and see each other whenever possible.

A major underlying discomfort in my relationships with both Sally and Betsy were my feelings about my family's status compared to theirs. Sally's father was a college graduate and a wealthy Baltimore developer, and her uncle was the governor of Maryland. Betsy's father was a graduate of Virginia Tech and owned his own dairy business. The disparities in educational, social and economic status between our respective families were so enormous that, enjoyable as they were, I never felt that I could reach the long-term level of comfort that I sought in our relationships.

My ethnicity was also an issue for me in my relationships with Betsy and Sally. I was not yet totally comfortable with my own identity or my minority status. The vast majority of midshipmen were Caucasian. My black hair, brown eyes and olive complexion made me look different. And we all had nicknames: Jack's was "the Deacon," John's was "John Wayne," Keith's was "Bunny" or "Rab." One of my nicknames was "the Mex."

I didn't mind being called the Mex at all, because my friends always used it affectionately and in good humor, but the fact remained that my ethnicity did not go unnoticed. Though our ethnic differences caused me some inner turmoil in my relationships with the opposite sex, I felt totally comfortable in the brigade and the academy.

But I was not totally comfortable with my minority status with respect to Betsy and Sally. Even so, my feelings about my ethnicity were not a barrier to our respective mutual attraction.

There were three other Mexican Americans in Class of '58: Ben Montoya, Richard Cordova and John Pinto. Our other Hispanic classmates were Jesse Hernandez, a Spanish American, and two Puerto Ricans, Carlos Hernandez and Mark Alvarez. We also had one African American, George Fennel. And Francis Hasegawa in 17th company was

85

of Japanese and Hawaiian descent, and Irv Goto was a Japanese American.

One day in February 1957, I returned to our room after last class. McCain said, "Frank, I have to meet Dad in front of the officers' club at 1800. Admiral Burke, the Chief of Naval Operations, wants to meet me. I am not doing this alone. You have to come with me!" John's father was on Burke's staff and a member of the Naval Institute Board of Directors. They were attending a board meeting.

We posted in front of the O'Club. A Navy captain came out, approached us and asked, "Are you Midshipman McCain?" John replied, "Yes sir!" and introduced me. The captain went back into the club and soon returned with a group of naval officers, including Rear Admiral Smedberg, the academy superintendent, and Captain Shinn, the commandant. John's father introduced John and me to Admiral Burke and about four other admirals. John and I were surrounded by more gold braid than I had ever seen close up.

Radiating his beautiful smile, Admiral Burke asked, "How are you young fellows doing?" Before we could answer, the Supe interjected, "They could be doing better, Admiral." The commandant quickly added, "They could do much better, Admiral." Everyone laughed as we grinned sheepishly.

Looking directly at us, Admiral Burke said, "Gentlemen, you are not going to make much money serving our wonderful country as naval officers, but you are going to have an exciting, challenging and honorable career, and you will make the best friends of your life!" Each of the admirals and the commandant shook our hands and wished us well. I was to learn that Admiral Burke was right on all counts.

The end of my second class year was rapidly approaching. In April 1957, we received our rings, the largest ever made for an academy class at that time. I wrote to Mom:

> I will be bursting with pride and emotion when I finally put on my class ring for keeps. I have been wearing it in my room since I got it (as has every other segundo!) and I never tire of looking at it. There is so much behind it and so many wonderful memories— and equally unforgettable heartaches—that it is the biggest thing in my life next to the day that I graduate. Gosh, it seems so long

ago that I was a scared plebe and now here I am one year from being an officer. The time has gone by awfully fast, mainly because we have been so busy, but it is the only way to get through this place. Just work like hell and never feel sorry for yourself (as I am wont to do!) …. There is so much of this place that is in me that I doubt if I will ever be able to leave the Navy. But I will cross that bridge when I come to it!

My last month as a segundo was extremely busy with final exams and final preparations for the Ring Dance (I was the committee chair). I explained my relatively low academic standing to Mom, "This was an awful year, but last month was absolutely the worst of my entire life! I never want another one like it, believe me. I successfully made it through all my exams. I am not too proud of my final class standing, but in view of all the circumstances it was the best that I could do!"

June Week was a very happy time. I invited Betsy to the Ring Dance and we had a great week together. Each drag dipped her '58 mid's new class ring in a binnacle traditionally filled with water from the seven seas, then each couple kissed within the giant replica of our ring. It is the only time that a midshipman may kiss a girl in public at the academy except for the Color Company parade ceremony when the company commander kisses the Color Girl (his date).

The morning after June Week ended, we boarded our midshipman practice squadron in Chesapeake Bay for a two-month training cruise to Rio de Janeiro, Brazil. I served in USS *Iowa* (BB-61) as a division officer, a junior officer's role, and conned (maneuvered) the ship during bridge watches. I also stood watches in engineering main control and combat information center.

The cruise featured a traditional "crossing the line" ceremony in which we transitioned from lowly pollywogs to trusty shellbacks, a memorable event. Our eight-day port visit to Rio and the girls from Ipanema were up to our expectations. Our homeward-bound cruise again featured live gunnery training at the Fleet Training Group in Guantanamo Bay, Cuba (GITMO), Iowa and her sister ship Wisconsin firing nine-gun broadsides from their 16-inch guns.

Upon our return from summer leave, '58 took charge of the brigade. My good friend Chuck Larson's natural leadership abilities and high academic standing earned him the top spot as brigade commander and '58 elected him as our class president, a rare double achievement. Keith was elected class treasurer.

I was being interviewed by our company officer for the position of company commander when he told me that he had a problem with the fact that I hung around with a group he referred to as "the back room boys." With a stern look he said, "Mr. Gamboa, if I were to select you as company commander, would you discontinue your association with that group?" I replied, "Sir, I intend to maintain all my friendships as long as I am a midshipman." The interview ended on that note, but I did get two stripes as a platoon commander. Keith was selected 17th company commander for the winter set.

Being a firstie was an unmitigated pleasure. The tension that I had endured for three years evaporated. Academics were still a challenge and required a great deal of our time, but with the end only ten months away and our graduation and commissioning on our horizon, our morale was at an all-time high. Our "clutch factor" was reduced practically to zero and we didn't "sweat the program." We just "maintained an even strain."

I had developed a wide circle of '58 friends. Many were members of a social group self-proclaimed as "the bad bunch" due to our very spirited and enjoyable parties that pushed the edge of the social envelope in Annapolis, D.C., and elsewhere. Our leaders were McCain and Larson. They cut a wide swath with very attractive drags, which further enhanced their cool reputations. Chuck even dated Miss America.

McCain had great charisma and a flair for creating excitement in a group just by his presence. His intelligence, natural leadership abilities, sharp wit and his exceptional social skills came to the fore in our parties, enhancing his John Wayne image (years later, we had a hearty laugh when I told him that, even though he had been our group's moral compass, occasionally his gimbals would tumble. Gimbals keep a compass level and properly oriented.)

John continued to challenge "the system" during first class year. He was a boxer and liked to watch the Friday night fights on TV. So McCain convinced Dittrick and three other 17th Company classmates to join with him in purchasing a TV set—strictly forbidden to mids in Bancroft Hall. But John persuaded the group and they hid the small black and white set in a plumbing pipe access locker near our room—another forbidden act.

They set it up in John's alcove during study hours on Friday nights for boxing matches and on Sunday nights to watch *Maverick.*

These events quickly drew an ever-increasing crowd. Eventually the company officer got wind of it, searched for and found the prized TV. He directed Dittrick, who happened to be alone in our room when the captain found the set, that one name be provided to him for the misconduct report (the dreaded Form 2).

In keeping with brigade custom, the owners "shook around" with a "hup, hup, ho," (rock, paper, scissors) to determine who would take the hit. Due to John's high number of accumulated demerits, he would have exceeded the expulsion limit had he won, so his teammates tried to exclude him from the shake, but he would not allow it. The tension was palpable. But good fortune prevailed. Hank Vargo, who had zero demerits, took the bullet.

Despite his reputation for toughness and his rollicking sense of humor, McCain was keenly sensitive about another person's feelings. One afternoon I returned to our room from class and John was there alone. I guess I had a down look on my face because he thought something was troubling me. He asked me what was wrong. I can't recall what was on my mind, but I replied that it was not important.

John put his arm around my shoulder and said, "Look pal, I apologize for giving you a hard time and calling you 'Mex' and stuff like that. You know I don't mean any disrespect. But I know that when we get out of here, others in the fleet might not treat you as well, and I want you to be able to handle it."

I replied that I didn't mind him "running" me; we all gave as well as we got. I looked at him and smiled, "Thanks for your concern, John. I really appreciate it. I think I will be treated just fine!" His thoughtfulness about my future in the Navy and how I would be treated touched me deeply.

The firsties' major issue was our individual service selection and community—Navy Line, Navy Staff Corps, or the Marine Corps. Because the first Air Force Academy class would not graduate until 1959, we could also go Air Force, either to fly or Air Force Ground. In December, I passed my commissioning physical examination but did not qualify for aviation training because I had less than 20-20 vision. I had no interest in flying.

¡El Capitán!

One reason that Les Hewitt had gone into the Air Force was to avoid Navy's long deployments, which caused family hardship. Les encouraged me to consider the Air Force. I knew that I did not want to be a Marine, so my decision came down to a choice between Navy Line in ships and Air Force Ground.

Beginning in our Revolutionary Navy, naval officers of the line have protected our national interests and security and safeguarded our trade lanes. The term "officer of the line" evolved in the British Navy in their sea battles with other navies. The signal "Form Battle Line!" assembled the British battleships in a line ahead 100 yards apart, concentrating their cannon firepower in a "broadside." Officers in command of a ship of the line were called officers of the line.

The U.S. Navy's line officers evolved into three separate professional warfare communities: surface, submarine and air. Line officers commanded ships, submarines, aircraft, task forces, fleets, and the Navy. (In the '70s, the Navy created the Surface Warfare Officer (SWO) community, designator 1110, for line officers eligible for ship command.)

I had entered the Naval Academy intending to be a naval officer. During my four years as midshipman, I had been imbued with the academy's traditions and nautical heritage so prevalent in the Yard and buildings, especially the quotes by famous naval officers displayed in Sampson Hall: "I have not yet begun to fight!" "I will find a way or make one!" "Give me a fast ship for I intend to sail in harm's way!"

Memorial Hall, with its historic battle flags and the numerous plaques depicting the heroic deeds of those who had gone before me had a big emotional impact, as did the sublime beauty of the chapel and the powerful solemnity of John Paul Jones' crypt.

Key to our senior year indoctrination were our evening lectures by distinguished flag and general officers. They inspired us with their talks about duty and service. (One salty Admiral commented in his opening remarks, "You men have a much tougher academic program than my class did. When we were here, the motto was 'get 'em young, treat 'em rough, and teach 'em nothing!'")

I enjoyed shipboard life and going to sea in warships, felt confident about my leadership and seamanship abilities, and was comfortable with the notion of being a line officer. And although the thought of commanding a warship seemed very daunting, the prospect interested me.

Captain John Frank Gamboa, U. S. Navy (Retired)

And Captain McCain and Roberta's inspirational treatment of us were major factors in my esteem for naval officers and the Navy. The fact that my roommates and other close friends were going to select Navy line was also a major consideration. Naturally, I wrote to Mom:

> By the time I graduate, I will have had six years in college. I have had to overcome a lot of obstacles and in general give up quite a bit in order to gain what I have now. And I do not feel one bit sorry for having done so. But I am anxious to get as much out of life as possible; not material benefits—money I have never had and doubt that I ever will—but a rewarding life with plenty of experiences and variety. And to have such a life I will have to make the right choice of a career. I will not go into the Navy if I find that I will not be happiest there; I could not give it my best if I did. I will write to you a lot on this subject, Mom. But please don't worry if I seem to be depressed. I just have to try to think objectively and soberly about this matter!

In February, I selected Navy Line and duty in ships. I would be a "blackshoe" (ship drivers wore black shoes; naval aviators' wore brown). Keith also selected Navy line, surface. Jack and John selected Navy line as aviators. 187 of my classmates chose Air Force and 70 went into the Marine Corps. I wrote to mom about my decision:

> After giving many factors as much thought as I could, I have decided to go into the Navy in ships as a line officer. I am happy that I gave the Air Force some thought because it made me all the more sure that I want to go into the Navy. The reasons I gave you for considering the Air Force were not enough.... I will just have to find things in the Navy to compensate. If I can't, then I guess I will get out ... but right now, I feel that I will probably make a career of it.

Soon, ship selection night was upon us, determined by drawing lots based on class standing. In coordination with my company mates Dick Pittenger, Ron Fisher, Keith Bunting and John Ruth, we selected destroyers in Destroyer Squadron Twenty Two (Desron 22) out of Norfolk, Virginia. It was deploying to the Mediterranean in early

91

¡El Capitán!

September '58 for six months. We all wanted to "hit the decks running" and get our naval careers off to a fast start in the most intense operational environment available. And we were ready to see the world! I drew a good number and selected USS *Putnam* (DD 757).

In the 1950s, academy graduates got sixty days of leave before reporting to their first duty station. I had other ideas. In December 1957, the seamanship and navigation department announced that it would select 16 new '58 ensigns in the spring to be plebe summer sailing instructors for the new class of midshipmen. The officers would report to the academy three weeks after graduation for two months of temporary duty until the end of August.

The ensigns' principal responsibility would be to spend about six hours a day, five days a week instructing the new plebes in sailing knockabouts and dinghies, and, if qualified, yachts and yawls. This sounded liked a lot of fun. I had co-captained the 17th company knockabout sailing team with Ron Fisher, chalking up some hair-raising victories in sailing competition. I was confident of my sailing skills.

After discussing the matter with Lieutenant Foley, the head of sailing division in the Seamanship and Navigation department, I applied for the duty. Then I convinced my friends Dick Pittenger and Pete Wiedemann to do the same. We lobbied Foley hard throughout January and February. In March, he called us into his office and said, "I feel like I am making a big mistake, but I have selected the three of you. You will report for duty the last week in June. Now get out of my office!"

Jubilantly, we made plans to rent a house near the Academy. Pete had a car so our transportation problems were solved. We would receive an allowance for quarters of about $85 each per month over and above our monthly base pay of $222, so we could pay the rent, buy groceries and essentials (beer). Chuck Larson was selected for the executive department to administer the plebe class summer training so we convinced him to join us. He, in turn, persuaded an academy math professor to rent us his fully furnished home in Wardour, Annapolis, for the summer while he was away on sabbatical. Our plans for a great summer were complete.

A cherished tradition at the Naval Academy is for roommates to write a short biographical sketch about each other to accompany their formal graduation picture in *Lucky Bag,* the brigade yearbook.

Captain John Frank Gamboa, U. S. Navy (Retired)

With the exception of a few brushes with both the Dago Department and those Penn coeds, "The Deacon" crashed through his four years on the Severn at flank speed. Believing that everyone should have a good time, he had a friendly manner and humor that could brighten any occasion. While not a star man, his academic standing was well above reproach and gave him much more time to devise bigger and better parties. Jack has great potential to do what he wants to do. His big desire is to fly for Navy.

"Bunny" came to Navy Tech complete with a golf bag packed with slide rules, a star-studded black book, and "Rules of Contract Bridge." Here was a fellow who never sweated the books. When the going got rough, he would just derive his own formula and chalk up another 4.0. His success with the academics gave him ample time for distinguishing himself as a rugged intramural competitor as well as charming the femmes. A loyal friend in any situation, Keith parlayed a sense of humor and a great ability and understanding into many lasting friends.

John, better known as Navy's "*John Wayne*," was always reputed to be one of our most colorful characters. Following his family forebears to our sacred shores, he thought the Navy was the only way. A sturdy conversationalist and party man, John's quick wit and clever sarcasm made him a welcome man at any gathering. His bouts with the Academic and Executive departments contributed much to the stockpile of legends within the hall. His prowess as an athlete was almost above reproach; that is, if he could resist the temptations offered by the blue dragon. John looks forward to a long and successful career in the Navy. He is a natural and will not need the luck we wish him.

After a sneaky, moonlit swim across the Rio Grande and a period of Army boot training in California, "the Mex" found a home in Mother Bancroft's open arms. Certainly not to be outdone in the more pleasurable aspects of Academy life, he repeatedly internationalized the Hops in Dahlgren Hall with his many attractive drags. A lover of hard work, he was always in the middle of things, which ranged from the Class Hop Committee to the battalion football team. Perhaps he gained this worldly manner in traveling the tortuous path to his home in Lone Pine. Frank's ambition, personality, and drive will be invaluable assets in his career in the Navy.

My class standing was 679 among 900 graduates. Keith finished 17th, Jack stood in the 300s, and John, by his own design, was 895, falling short of his goal of being the '58 anchorman (last in our class). Bruce McCandless stood 1st academically, but John Poindexter stood 1st overall. (He beat Bruce out on "grease.") Only our graduation and commissioning remained before we departed the Yard.

It is traditional that Company Officers host a dinner in their home for their company's firsties during the last month before June Week. Our officer and his wife invited each set of roommates to their home for an elegant dinner in their dining room. John, Keith, Jack and I were the last to be hosted. We were determined to be on our best, smiling most gentlemanly and officer-like behavior.

When we arrived, the captain led us not inside his house but to his back yard, where he grilled hot dogs and then served them to us on paper plates at a picnic table. So much for the three-course dinner with lovely china, crystal and silver that our company mates had told us to expect. We were not at all surprised.

In April, Mom informed me that she and Dad had decided not to attend June Week. They didn't have suitable wardrobes and felt they would not "fit in" at the academy's social functions because they didn't know Navy protocol. She didn't want to embarrass herself, Dad or me in front of my friends.

I told Mom if they did not come to my graduation, I would resign and not graduate. I notified my sister Tina, and she immediately brought them down to Los Angeles and they selected suitable wardrobes. Accompanied by my brother Mosey, Mom and Dad participated in all June Week events. My roommates and I rented a house near Annapolis for all our parents. Mom and Dad were very sociable and comfortable. They quickly made friends with the Dittricks, McCains, Buntings and other parents. Mom and Dad were in great form, enjoyed June Week and were happier than I had ever seen them.

Betsy attended the first three days of June Week. After she departed, I escorted two other girls to hops. I asked Mom what she thought of my dates. She was very complimentary, but added, "They are very thin!" With his beautiful smile, Dad said, *"Mijo*, we want you to concentrate on your career. When the time comes, I will take you to Mexico and find you a good wife." Mom punched him playfully. It was my most enjoyable week at the academy, and my happiest time ever with my parents.

On the morning of June 4, we gathered in our final class assembly in Halsey Field House for our graduation and commissioning. It was filled with excited parents and friends and an air of anticipation, but we were relaxed and content, seated by companies.

President Eisenhower delivered the commencement address and presented diplomas to the top 100 members of our class. The CNO commissioned the naval officers and the Marine Corps Commandant commissioned the Marines.

At the end of our traditional "Three cheers for those we leave behind," I heaved my midshipman cap in the air with all my strength and exuberance. After hugging my roommates, diploma in hand, I found my parents and brother in the huge crowd of people.

Mom and Dad attached my new ensign shoulder boards onto my uniform, an exquisite moment. My graduation gift from my parents, grandparents and siblings was my naval officer dress sword, which I proudly wore on formal occasions throughout my career.

After the graduation ceremony, Dad, Mosey and I were sitting together in the field house lobby waiting for Mom. People were everywhere, talking, laughing, all very excited and happy. I was holding my diploma. A very dignified lady walked up to us and said, "Please forgive me for intruding on your privacy, but I just couldn't help noticing how happy and content you all look. It made me feel happy just watching you!"

Enriched by my cherished '58 classmate friendships and the joyful remembrances of our days together in the brigade, I departed the Yard with a feeling of gratitude, a sense of obligation, and a desire to serve my country.

¡El Capitán!

Boy's State Sacramento, CA, 1950. Top row third from left. (Personal collection)

Dad and his soldier son, Lone Pine, June 1954. (Personal collection)

Captain John Frank Gamboa, U. S. Navy (Retired)

Naval Academy Plebe, Bancroft Hall terrace, October 1954. (Personal collection)

Youngster with Mom, Dad, Grandma and Grandpa, Lone Pine 1955. (Personal collection)

17th Company Century Athletic Club. McCain, Dittrick and me in front row. Dark Ages, Bancroft Hall 1957. (Personal collection)

Naval Academy 17th Company First Class Stripers, spring 1958. (USNA photo)

Captain John Frank Gamboa, U. S. Navy (Retired)

Annapolis graduate, June 1958.

Naval Academy 17th Company graduates and officers, June 1958. I am top row, left. (USNA photo)

Part III

Officer of the Line

Learning the Trade

Chapter Five

★ ★ ★ ★ ★ ★ ★

Captains are made, not born.

—Napoleon

The day after graduation, I was best man for my company classmate Hank Vargo and his fiancée Jo Ann at their wedding in Annapolis. The next day, McCain, Dittrick, Bunting and I were at Fort Myer, Virginia, with Larson and four other ushers in our company classmate Jim Hamrick's marriage to Virginia (VG), Then John, Jack and I drove to Walt Ryan and Sarah's wedding in south Virginia; I was best man and McCain and Dittrick were ushers along with several other classmates.

It was a very fast-paced social schedule that taxed our endurance, but we were equal to the challenge. Then I went home for a great two weeks in Lone Pine where I enjoyed another round of parties. I was beginning to think that my life as a naval officer would be a never-ending, fun social whirl. I was to learn otherwise, but not that summer.

On June 26, I reported to the Naval Academy with my classmates, Ensigns Chuck Larson, Dick Pittenger and Pete (Franz) Wiedemann. We joyfully established our "snake ranch" in the professor's home, which was located in a prestigious neighborhood that included Navy captains and retired flag officers.

Even though the professor's wife had expressed serious misgivings about renting their home to four new bachelor ensigns, he persisted. But at the lease signing he said rather wistfully to Chuck, "If I can't trust the brigade commander, who can I trust?"

We plunged into our new life with exuberance. Almost before we unpacked our suitcases, classmates were showing up at our door, including others on plebe summer detail. Some just needed a place to "crash" before reporting to their duty stations. John McCain's group regaled us with tales of their grand tour of Europe. We also celebrated his father's selection to rear admiral.

We contacted several girls we knew in Annapolis, starting with Alice Trone, Carol Thompson and Grace McColl from St. Mary's College, who were staying in Carol's parents' home while they were on summer travel. We began having parties at our place and theirs, which we dubbed "the

101

palace;" when the ranch hands or the palace queens ran out of money, the others would provide food and beer. Pete and Alice quickly fell in love and were engaged. We all got into the excitement of planning their wedding in the Academy main chapel.

At the sea wall, we turned to each workday. Dick, Pete and I would arrive at Dewey Basin at 0730, organize our plebes into five–man crews, and spend the day sailing on the Severn River training the mids how to sail a knockabout. We conducted sail-rigging contests to see which crews could properly rig and hoist the jib and mainsail and be first underway, and competed in man-overboard drills—using a life ring, not a plebe. We enjoyed teaching sailing to the class of '62.

Because it was no longer our home, the Yard felt different to us as we relished our great feeling of liberation from the academy's strict regimen and regulations that had governed our lives for four years; we had total control of our free time.

But our transition to being officers and gentlemen was not entirely smooth. Our nightlife soon overtaxed our stamina and we began arriving late for work, with the other knockabout crews underway and our plebes waiting for us on the sea wall. Lieutenant Foley summoned Pete (who was senior, not the tardiest) to his office and spoke directly, "I realize you guys are enjoying your new social life, but if you don't show up for work on time, I'll fire your asses and send you to the fleet with fitness reports that reflect!" Thereafter, we arrived early.

Despite our best efforts to hold down the volume on the music and our reverie, the ranch evening socials eventually exceeded our neighbors' tolerance. In late August, the professor telephoned us to say that they were returning early from Maine. He directed us to vacate his premises and join him there to inspect the house after they arrived. The ranch hands agreed to face the music together. On the appointed date, we would meet at the academy officers' club after work and then proceed to our reckoning.

Chuck, Dick and Pete seemed very relaxed when I met them at the bar so I joined them for a beer and lighthearted banter. And then I said, "Well guys, let's go face the good professor!" Pete replied, straight-faced, "Oh, Frank, we got off work early and we've already been over to the house. The professor wasn't there so we just retrieved our belongings." I asked them, "Did you get mine?" All replied, "No. We left your stuff there!" With a long stare at their grinning faces, I said, "Thanks guys!" and departed on my suicide mission—alone.

As soon as I knocked, the door flew open and the professor grabbed my arm and hauled me into the foyer. "Where are the rest of them?!" I replied, "Sir, they have the duty!" Scowling knowingly, he growled, "They should be here too!" as he led me from room to room, pausing frequently to point out discrepancies. I nodded silently at his exclamations. In one well-appointed bedroom, he reached up to the bed canopy, grabbed something and flung it onto the bed, "Look at this!" I stared wide-eyed and speechless at a pair of pink panties. It was a thorough inspection. We settled with the professor on the cost to restore some minor collateral damage to his furnishings.

Our summer ended with Pete and Alice's beautiful wedding on August 31st, but not without a near disaster.

Two nights prior, after Pete's bachelor party, he, Dick, Bob Fuller and Bill Bauer were ambushed by a gang of "townies" on Main Street, Annapolis. Pittenger got his capped front tooth knocked out, Bauer got a black eye, and Fuller was knocked unconscious in the middle of the street. Pete was backing his car down the street to rescue Fuller just as the police arrived; they arrested Pete and jailed him for driving the wrong direction on the one-way street.

Chuck borrowed funds from the midshipmen's welfare fund and bailed Pete out of jail just in time for the wedding rehearsal (Pete repaid the loan), and Pittenger went back and found his tooth cap on the sidewalk.

At the rehearsal, some of the ushers wore eye patches to show solidarity for Bauer's "shiner." (The gang of townies was subsequently rounded up by the Annapolis police, charged and convicted of assault; they had been attacking mids for some time.)

The day after the wedding, Chuck departed for *Pensacola*, Dick headed to his destroyer in Norfolk by way of sonar school at Key West, and Pete and Alice honeymooned along their way to his destroyer in San Diego, detouring for a party stop at Pensacola with McCain, who was in flight training.

On September 2 at Annapolis, I boarded a bus to Norfolk. During the long ride there, I missed my fellow ranch hands and the palace queens, but I also I had time to think about what lay ahead of me. As a midshipman, I had sailed on a cruiser, an aircraft carrier and a battleship, very stable and comfortable platforms with lots of spit and polish and formality. I knew practically nothing about destroyers. I had chosen one for my first sea duty assignment because I wanted to experience their reputed dashing, independent style and informality. Together with three other 17th company classmates, I had selected Destroyer Squadron Twenty Two because it was deploying right away to the Sixth Fleet in the Mediterranean. We were eager to hit the decks running, experience life in the operating fleet and see the Med.

I thought about what the wardroom and the captain would be like. How would I perform in shiphandling and as a bridge watch officer? How would I do as a division officer? How would I like shipboard life? I was full of anticipation—and a little anxiety. I was stepping into my new life.

Despite my concerns, I was resolved to work hard, enjoy myself and get through the next four years as best I could. I would decide about pursuing a Navy career when I had completed my four years of obligated service.

Arriving in Norfolk late that evening, I hailed a taxi to the destroyer-submarine piers. *Putnam* was moored outboard in a nest of four destroyers alongside a tender (a large repair ship). In a rather undignified manner, I struggled with my large, cumbersome footlocker and heavy suitcase down the dark pier and up the tender's long, steep accommodation ladder to her quarterdeck. Mercifully, the officer of the deck (OOD) directed his messenger to assist me to my ship.

At 2230, I stepped onto *Putnam*'s quarterdeck, proudly saluted the OOD and handed him a copy of my orders, "Ensign Gamboa reporting for duty, sir!" He directed his messenger to escort me to the wardroom and assist with my luggage. I was welcomed by a lieutenant, who was the operations officer and the command duty officer.

Glancing at my baggage, he said, "The academy should remind its graduates that there is no room for footlockers in a destroyer." After small talk over a cup of burnt coffee, he showed me to my stateroom in forward officers' country. I unpacked, put in a wake-up call to the quarterdeck and climbed wearily into my bunk.

Putnam was a 14-year-old WW II 2200-ton Sumner class manned by 18 officers and 300 enlisted men. She was 365 feet in length with a 40-foot beam and 14-foot draft. Powered by two main engines, four boilers and twin screws, she had a top speed of 36 knots. Her armament included three twin 5-inch gun turrets, four 40-millimeter twin gun mounts, five torpedo tubes, and depth-charge racks on the main deck aft, port (left) and starboard (right) sides. She was equipped with surface and air search radars and sonar.

On her bridge wings, *Putnam* displayed three rows of WW II battle ribbons earned in the Pacific theatre, and the squadron "E" (for excellence, top ship). Her voice radio call sign was "cabin boy," her nickname "steaming Pete" and her motto "We've been there!"

Her officers, chiefs, and crew were proud that "steaming Pete has never missed an operational commitment!" In July, Commander, Destroyer Squadron 22 (Desron 22), had shifted his flag pennant from *Putnam* to USS *DuPont* (the Navy's newest destroyer class), and in August, *Putnam* had received a new commanding officer.

The next morning at breakfast in the wardroom, I met the captain, the executive officer (XO, Exec; second in command), and most of the other officers. The XO told me I would be his administrative assistant for two weeks and then I would be assigned to deck department as the 2nd division officer. I asked, "Sir, what is my special sea and anchor detail assignment?" (my designated station for leaving or entering port.) He replied, "Just go up to the bridge and try to stay out of the way!" I took station between the bridge and the signal bridge.

At 0800, Desron 22 got underway for seven months in the Mediterranean with the Sixth Fleet. The sortie (departure) seemed chaotic: one long and three short blasts from each ship's steam whistle to signal engines backing; tug horns sounding; bridge radios blaring tactical messages; signal flags flying on every halyard. But soon the eight-ship squadron was formed into a column behind the flagship and stood out to sea, joined up with an oiler, and shaped course for the Straits of Gibraltar.

Beyond the sea buoy, we encountered 30-knot winds and rough seas. *Putnam* began pitching, rolling, and taking green water over the bow. I struggled to get my sea legs, adhering to a timeless Sailor's rule—one hand for your ship and one hand for yourself. Soon I was nauseated, with a slight headache and a strong desire to just lie down in my bunk and sleep—I was seasick for the first time in my life. Unable to eat, I nibbled saltine crackers all day trying to settle my stomach and ease my hunger pangs.

¡El Capitán!

That evening I tried to eat dinner before going on watch. Quickly exiting the wardroom, I learned another timeless rule of the sea—when you throw up over the side, be sure you are in the lee. I returned to my stateroom, showered and put on a clean uniform. Not the most elegant way for a new line officer to begin his first sea duty.

I reported to the bridge as Junior Officer of the Watch (JOOW), a training and indoctrination billet on the bridge watch team. The OOD looked disparagingly at me and sent me to the signal bridge for a bucket and told me to keep it handy so I wouldn't mess up the bridge if I threw up again (I didn't).

The squadron was steaming in a screen formation with the oiler as the guide. Soon after I assumed the watch, a maneuvering signal from the commodore directed all ships to form a column, with *Putnam* in the van. The OOD announced to the bridge watch team, "Our station is at the end of the column!"

Having accomplished the signaled column formation many times in academy patrol craft on the Chesapeake Bay, I said, "Sir, I believe the van is the lead station!" The lieutenant grumbled in disagreement, but called combat information center (CIC) for their recommendation. CIC responded, "We are assigned to station one, the van station. We are the lead ship!" The junior officer of the deck (JOOD), laughed and complimented me, but the OOD sneered and said loudly, "Just another smart-ass Annapolis grad!"

My first tasking by the XO was to get all the previous month's neglected in-port watch logs written. He directed the wardroom to submit their logs to me for typing by the yeoman. But the officers still delayed, and let me know in colorful terms that log writing was a pain in the ass, mainly because they were too busy with watch-standing and other work.

Nonetheless, I persisted—even waking up officers who rated "late sleepers." I was soon getting results; the logs were being written and typed up.

A few days later as I entered the wardroom for dinner, the operations officer (third senior) commented in his loud, abrasive New Yorker manner, "Gamboa, you've been aboard one week and in that time you've managed to piss off every officer in *Putnam*! Well Done!" Everyone laughed.

But the XO retorted, "Gentlemen, he is simply carrying out my orders. Keep up the good work, Mr. Gamboa!"

Desron 22 passed through the Straits of Gibraltar and "chopped" (changed operational control) to Sixth Fleet from Second Fleet. By then I had gotten my sea legs and adjusted to the daily routine of watch standing, ship's work, meals, and trying to get enough sleep.

I completed my tasks for the XO, reported to the deck department head, and assumed my duties as the second division officer, one of the first leadership responsibilities assigned to a warship junior officer. It had about 15 non-rated enlisted men, two third class petty officers and a first class boatswain's mate who was the leading petty officer (LPO).

At the Naval Academy, I had been immersed in leadership training in the classroom. As a firstie I had served in leadership roles. But leadership within the orderly, pristine confines of the academy is one thing; it is quite another matter on the decks of a rolling, pitching fleet destroyer.

Walking from officers' call to my division for the first time, I intended to deliver inspiring remarks to my men and establish my leadership role, but I felt cold in the chilly morning sea air, slightly nauseous and a bit nervous.

The LPO, the division's senior enlisted—a big, salty first class boatswain's mate with a gruff, no-nonsense demeanor—saluted me and said to the men, "This is Mr. Gamboa, your new division officer." Standing before my men and looking them in the eye, unexpectedly I was speechless.

After a few moments of awkward silence, the LPO growled, "Well? Do you want to say anything?" I blurted out, "I am proud to be in *Putnam* and I am proud to be your leader!" Then I passed on information from officers' call, told the LPO to take charge, exchanged salutes, and departed. And so much for my inspirational remarks.

In the fall of 1962, when I was a student at the Naval Postgraduate School in Monterey, California, the Navy's chief of information, Rear Admiral Jack McCain, visited the school. Known throughout the Navy as "Mr. Sea Power," the admiral delivered his famed presentation to the assembled student body.

As was his custom, McCain paced back and forth on the stage as he talked, gesturing with his ever-present but unlit cigar. He complimented us on being at postgraduate school and learning about the Navy's newest technology, especially the amazing "computer."

Suddenly, the admiral stopped in his tracks, pointed his cigar at us and in a gruff voice said, "But the best and fastest computer you will ever see is when you stand in front of your bluejackets (Sailors). They will size you up and figure you out faster and better than any fancy computers. So goddamit, remember that when you return to the fleet and you will do just fine!" (Another of the admiral's nicknames was "Goddammit McCain.") We responded with knowing laughter and hearty applause. And I wished I had received his gem of wisdom prior to assuming my division officer duties.

Second division's assigned spaces extended from amidships aft to the fantail, and from the main deck up to the top deck of the superstructure, including the number two smoke stack. Busy standing watches, I had about two hours a day to manage my division and inspect my spaces. The LPO assigned the division's daily work and supervised very capably— with an iron hand. He kept our spaces in a high standard of cleanliness and maintenance and our division's gear ready. He treated me with mild disdain at first, but we soon established a good working relationship and mutual respect.

The keys to leading a group of Navy men are to set a good example; treat them with courtesy and respect; maintain good order and discipline, make everyone perform their duties,look after their welfare and morale; be loyal and keep your word. Use the chain of command to establish unit standards of work, conduct and appearance. Leave the details of execution to the chiefs and petty officers, and hold everyone accountable, especially yourself.

I worked hard and learned each of my men's name, background, skills, performance, potential and aspirations. Applying the principles that I was taught at the academy, through attention to duty, application, hard work and by trial and error, in time I learned the rudiments of "deck-plate" leadership.

I also had to learn to do my collateral duties of postal officer and voting officer assigned to me by the XO. But my main professional duty was standing bridge watches at sea and quarterdeck watches in port.

Captain John Frank Gamboa, U. S. Navy (Retired)

My primary goal as a bridge watch officer was to qualify as an OOD, the principal deck watch officer in a warship. Underscoring my desire was the wardroom's (ship's officers) need to have a large pool of qualified deck watch officers in order to spread the watch workload and allow officers more time for their respective administrative duties.

The OOD reports directly to the commanding officer (CO), and is legally in charge of the ship, acting on the CO's behalf and conning the ship (maneuvering by orders to the helm and the main engines) under the CO's supervision.

The watch workload is divided between the OOD and his principal assistant, the Junior Officer of the Deck (JOOD), usually an ensign. When operating at sea in routine situations, the OOD "has the deck," legally in charge of the ship, and the JOOD "has the conn," legally responsible for orders to the main engines throttle (the engine order telegraph) and the helm.

My first step in the OOD qualification process was to become qualified as a combat information center (CIC) watch officer. CIC is the ship's operations center that collects and displays the status of all weapon systems, surface and air search radars and sonar; plots all radar and sonar contacts; and assists the bridge team in navigating and maneuvering the ship.

I was not in the engineering department so I stood several orientation watches in main control, the ship's propulsion control center.

A basic, important step in my watch officer qualification process was to learn the ship's many systems, including damage control, internal and external communications, propulsion, weapons and sensors, which required many hours of inspection, system tracing and study during my off-watch "spare time."

Two scenarios governed my bridge watch officer qualification process: "independent steaming," (sailing alone) and "formation steaming" (sailing in company with other ships in a specific formation and station). Formation steaming poses ship-maneuvering situations that are more complex and more hazardous. I would first have to qualify for independent steaming.

I soon learned that a bridge watch calls for total situational awareness and a rapid grasp of the "big picture." This required thorough preparation, attention to detail and rapid assimilation of a great deal of essential information.

¡El Capitán!

Before relieving (taking over) the watch, I had to understand the ship's overall readiness posture including status of the propulsion plant; radars, sonar and weapon systems; tactical and ship-shore-ship communications systems in use; machinery casualties that degraded ship's readiness; the ship's tactical situation including other ships in company; navigation track, current position and intended movement (PIM); and current and predicted weather and sea conditions.

The OOD's principal responsibility is to maintain the safety and security of the ship. His team must keep a vigilant watch for other ships on the high seas. He is assisted by three lookouts (one each on the port and starboard bridge-wing and one on the stern/fantail); the signal bridge watch also acts as lookout.

The closest point of approach (CPA) of all shipping in the ship's vicinity was monitored on the bridge and in CIC, which maintained radar plots on all contacts within 12 miles (generally the distance to the horizon from the ship is based on own ship bridge height above sea level; the higher the bridge, the more distant the horizon).

I had to learn the international nautical rules of the road, which specify which ship has right-of-way in ship meeting, crossing, and overtaking situations. In these situations, the ship having the right of way is the privileged vessel, and the ship having to maneuver in accordance with the rules of the road is the burdened vessel.

An approaching ship's bearing, heading and relative motion with respect to own ship are determined visually and by radar; at night by also observing the other ship's masthead, range and running lights. The most dreaded situation is an oncoming ship with "constant bearing, decreasing range" (CBDR), which usually requires one or both ships to maneuver to avoid collision.

Prior to sailing, the captain and navigator together chart the ship's intended movement and navigation track. A ship's safe passage is based on expert navigation, avoiding hazards such as shoal water, channel buoys, breakwaters, etc. The OOD is directly involved in the ship's safe navigation, adjusting her course and speed to stay on the track that has been approved by the captain.

Safe navigation requires an accurate surface radar and visual navigation plot well-coordinated by the bridge and CIC navigation teams. The OOD executes all base course and speed changes with the captain's approval and frequently checks the ship's navigation track. If necessary, he calls the navigator to the bridge to "fix" (determine) the ship's position.

The captain's night orders to the OOD are kept in a notebook on the bridge, to be read by all the bridge and CIC watch officers.

The officer watch team must know all unexecuted orders and tactical signals and read all radio messages received over the Naval Communications System or by signal light from the officer in tactical command (OTC), informing the captain of any urgent operational messages.

In a warship, the captain directs combat actions through the OOD, especially the firing of weapons, which are controlled from the bridge or CIC, depending on the ship's battle doctrine and the combat situation. During our deployment, *Putnam* conducted gun-firing exercises at sea with a surface target towed by a tug or a canvas sleeve towed by an aircraft. We also practiced shore bombardment gunnery at Filfla Rock, near Malta. There was always spirited competition between *Putnam*'s gun mounts for most hits on target.

Ships steaming in a designated formation are assigned to a numbered station relative to the ship designated as the formation guide. The officer watch team must know the ship and radio voice call sign of the officer in tactical command of the formation (OTC) and the radio voice call signs for all other ships in the formation.

The bridge and CIC watch officers must keep track of the formation guide ship and their own ship's station that is based on a true bearing and range to the guide. The range to the guide is checked by radar; the bearing is checked both by radar and visually with an alidade (a bearing circle marked in degrees and used on top of compass repeaters in the pilothouse and bridge wings).

As required, I learned to keep the ship on its assigned station within plus or minus1.5 degree tolerance by adding or removing turns on the screw shafts to increase or decrease the ship's speed, and to maintain the required range within plus or minus 100 yards to the guide by adjusting the ship's heading by one or two degrees to port or starboard. I also learned that station-keeping in foul weather is a more demanding task.

The bridge watch team must know what to do in the event of a collision at sea or a fire aboard ship, two emergencies that can have disastrous consequences. In the event of a man overboard, the ship is turned smartly to create a "slick" (a calm sea space) in the ship's lee, where the lifeboat is quickly and safely launched, and after the rescue, the maneuver is repeated and the lifeboat is recovered in the slick. If it has a helicopter, the ship is maneuvered into the wind for launch and recovery in helicopter man-overboard rescues with a ready lifeboat as backup.

After the watch has ended and before leaving the bridge, all key events that occurred are recorded in the ship's log and signed by the OOD (usually written by the JOOD). The data for the log entry is compiled from the quartermaster's notebook, in which all navigation and maneuvering data during the watch has been recorded.

To perform well, watch officers need to be healthy, well rested, physically fit and in a clear frame of mind, unburdened by personal problems or other concerns. Bridge watch officers also require good physical stamina; they are on their feet throughout their watch.

Although all watch officers prefer having a quiet, uneventful watch, this rarely happens. A warship at sea is dynamic and operational, conducting myriad activities. The watch team has to be prepared for the unexpected and ready to react promptly and effectively to new situations and emergencies.

At sea, the captain spends most of his waking hours on the bridge. There is a CO's chair on each side of the pilothouse, and on each of the bridge wings. He sleeps in his sea cabin just a few steps away (his more commodious captain's cabin is used in port). At sea, the bridge watch officers are usually under his direct observation and supervision. In many situations, the captain conducts JO training by personal instruction, especially in shiphandling.

Depending on the captain's character, personality and the training situation, his style can vary—a calm word of advice; a slight frown; a stern tone of voice or an intense tongue-lashing for unsatisfactory performance.

According to the Navy's immortal John Paul Jones—"I have not yet begun to fight!"—a naval officer "… should be quick and unfailing to distinguish error from malice, thoughtlessness from incompetency, and well-meant shortcoming from heedless and stupid blunder!"

Putnam's junior officers (JOs) helped each other prepare for bridge watches;— they passed on information about the captain's moods and how he interacted with the watch officers. We especially wanted to know when—and how—an officer or the watch team had screwed up and received a chewing out from the Skipper. The most colorful watch officer's screw-ups and captain's reprimands instantly became part of wardroom lore.

Despite the need to come on watch well rested and with a clear mind, in reality I occasionally assumed the watch not having had enough sleep and with much on my mind. I soon learned to put my concerns aside and focus on the bridge watch demands, but it required many days and weeks at sea to develop the mental discipline and emotional self-control necessary to stand an effective bridge watch.

In his OOD, JOOD and CIC watches, a naval surface warfare officer begins to comprehend what it means to command a warship. I soon discovered that standing a good watch was a very satisfying feeling; it was the most enjoyable part of my shipboard life. I felt in charge when conning the ship. The duty was interesting, frequently exciting, and always challenging—hours of quiet routine punctuated by moments of intense activity.

My goal was to qualify in all aspects of bridge watch standing and shiphandling as quickly as possible—to become a fleet OOD. But after several weeks aboard *Putnam*, I realized that it would be a difficult undertaking requiring months of study, training and performance under the captain's close supervision.

To coordinate their daily shipboard routine and events, Navy ships are equipped with an audio broadcast announcing system—the One MC (Main Circuit), with a speaker in each living compartment and workspace. The One MC is controlled on the bridge at sea and on the quarterdeck in port.

The major events in the ship, as scheduled in the Plan of the Day, or in an emergency, are announced over the system by the boatswain's mate of the watch, as directed by the OOD. "Now, relieve the standing watch. On deck section one!" The bos'n first alerts the crew by the trilling of his boatswain's pipe, which varies according to the type of announcement (in earlier times, WWII, the announcements were preceded with the phrase, "Now hear this!").

A Navy ship's daily 24-hour watch cycle underway and in port is composed of six 4-hour watches, each with distinctive activities, pace and rhythm. The new watch cycle begins with the mid-watch (0000 to 0400), a normally a quiet, serene time as the crew sleeps. Only communication drills by the signal bridge and CIC are conducted.

The morning watch (0400 to 0800), Homer's "rosy-fingered dawn," begins the ship's workday. The OOD awakens the captain at the time specified in his night orders and then briefs him on the weather, the ship's status, and the major events of the morning. The boatswain's mate of the watch sounds reveille at 0600. By 0630, the crew is at breakfast. Throughout the day, the bos'n announces all ship evolutions indicated in the ship's Plan of the Day, as directed by the OOD.

The forenoon watch (0800-1200) and the afternoon watch (1200-1600) are similarly busy times. The captain usually arrives on the bridge after breakfast in his cabin, "the captain is on the bridge!". Major ship or task group events, such as underway replenishment, are scheduled in the forenoon or afternoon watches. If the ship is scheduled to enter port, navigation and piloting are primary concerns. "Now station the special sea and anchor detail. Make all preparations for entering port. The ship will moor port-side-to pier three at 1500."

The evening watch (1600-2000) is "dogged" (divided into two 2-hour watches; first dog, second dog), so the watch teams will rotate to different watches each new cycle. Join-ups with the task group for night steaming usually occur in this period, requiring ship's coordination with the OTC for information concerning the designated formation, base course and speed, own ship station assignment, and that of all other ships in the formation.

The night watch is from 2000 to 2400. "Now lay before the mast all eight o'clock reports. Reports will be taken by the executive officer at 1915 in the passageway outside his cabin." Department heads assemble and report the status of their departments. The XO ensures the next day's Plan of the Day (POD) is understood, and passes out other information such as the next scheduled mail delivery to the ship and the need to conserve fresh water. He then goes to the bridge and reports on the condition of the ship to the captain, beginning with the traditional phrase, "All secure, sir!"

"Movie call!" The night watch is intended to be uneventful. Movies are normally shown at sea on the crew's mess decks, in the chiefs' mess and in the wardroom at eight bells. The captain often joins the officers for the movie, and to relax and socialize, bringing to a close another busy day at sea.

In my time the Sixth Fleet was organized in a decimal numbering system: Task Force (TF 60), Task Group (TG 60.1), Task Unit (TU 60.1.1), and Task Element (TE 60.1.1.1). Each had a specific mission. Task forces and task groups usually steamed in ship formations that dated back to WW II, such as circular air defense formations employed in the Pacific Theater to provide collective protection against attacks by Japanese dive-bombers and torpedo planes. Destroyer task units were usually arranged in an anti-submarine screen formation positioned three to four thousand yards ahead of a "main body" of larger combatants such as aircraft carriers, battleships and cruisers.

Soon after joining Sixth Fleet, *Putnam* participated in task group anti-air, anti-submarine, and anti-surface ship exercises. We spent many hours at general quarters (battle stations). Then *Putnam* was detached to proceed to Naples, Italy, for a six-day port visit. With several other officers, I enjoyed a three-day tour of Rome, visiting St. Peter's Basilica, the Sistine Chapel, the Catacombs, the Colosseum, and other fascinating sights in the Eternal City. We saw the Pope at Castel Gandolfo, his summer residence. We also walked the city streets and enjoyed delicious Italian cuisine. (Fortunately, I did not have officer shore patrol duty.) As the Navy advertised, I was seeing the world!

Returning to sea, *Putnam* was assigned to operate with the aircraft carrier USS *Forrestal* along with our squadron sister ship *Henley* to provide anti-submarine screen protection and plane guard.

We reported for duty "with a bone in our teeth" (at high speed) as expected of destroyers, also known throughout the fleet as "small boys" or "tin cans," nicknames from WW II.

Forrestal stationed *Henley* broad (45 degrees) on the carrier's starboard bow and our station was broad on the carrier's port, both ships at 1500 yards range from the carrier. For flight operations, *Henley* would maneuver to a station 1000 yards astern of the carrier in its wake as plane guard to recover pilots in the event of downed aircraft during launch or recovery. *Putnam* would remain on its port bow station to provide a horizon reference (especially important at night) for catapulted aircraft.

A carrier task unit maneuvers at high speed to create sufficient wind over the flight deck that helps generate the lift required for aircraft launches and recoveries. *Forrestal* maneuvered at speeds up to 30 knots heading directly into the prevailing wind, holding steady on course for 30 minutes or longer until all planes were either launched or recovered. Then she would resume her base course and speed (12 knots).

On *Putnam*'s bridge, we kept our eyes on the carrier, especially when she was turning, either into the wind or a retiring course. Sometimes she would commence turning and increasing her speed before she signaled her intentions, leaving the DDs scrambling to regain station. When the carrier completed its flight operations, both destroyers would maneuver smartly to resume their respective screening stations. A carrier unit needed lots of sea room to conduct flight operations.

Operating with a carrier involved a great deal of tactical signaling, maneuvering and speed changes, putting maximum stress on the captain, the bridge team, CIC, and the engines and boilers. There was little room for error, especially during night operations. Some of the Navy's most horrific collisions have occurred during carrier flight operations.

On April 26, 1952, on a dark Atlantic night, the destroyer USS *Hobson* was plane guarding for the carrier USS *Wasp* and attempted to change stations by crossing ahead of the carrier's bow during flight operations. The *Wasp* sliced the *Hobson* in half, sinking the destroyer, and many crewmembers lost their lives. The destroyer's captain went down with his ship.

With all four boilers on line during flight operations, the destroyers burned their fuel oil at a high rate, so we refueled from the carrier about every third day. "Now station the refueling detail. The ship will receive fuel from *Forrestal*, port-side-to. Mail and movies will be transferred!"

When the carrier's helicopter was available, it delivered mail and movies to the destroyers. If the destroyers responded promptly and safely to changing operational situations in a smart, seamanlike manner—and especially if a destroyer recovered a pilot from the sea—the carrier would show appreciation by sending five-gallon containers of ice cream to the ship by helo, delivered when we were detached to "Proceed on duty assigned!" Operating with a carrier (which we called "the bird farm") was exhilarating—and fatiguing. It was our most challenging assignment.

In late October, *Putnam* and two other destroyers—one was the commodore's flagship—went to Golfe Juan, France, for a port visit. As *Putnam* was anchoring, she suffered a casualty to her starboard engine; the high-speed pinion gear shattered with a loud, grating, metallic noise.

Captain John Frank Gamboa, U. S. Navy (Retired)

The commodore came aboard and conducted an investigation, including an "open and inspect" of the damaged main engine. He concluded that the cause was material failure and that the engine required repairs in a Navy shipyard.

A few days later, the fleet commander directed *Putnam* to lock her starboard shaft, return to Norfolk, and then proceed to the Philadelphia Naval Shipyard in December 1958 for repairs. We were very disappointed to have our cruise abruptly ended just as we were getting comfortable with Sixth Fleet operations.

We remained anchored in Golfe Juan for two weeks while we waited to join up with a destroyer squadron that was returning to Newport, Rhode Island. I enjoyed my first visit to France, going sightseeing and enjoying French cuisine and wines. I also purchased a new Volkswagen Beetle, to be delivered in Norfolk. We then sailed to Gibraltar to join the destroyer squadron and an oiler for our voyage home.

Our transit across the North Atlantic in November was not a pleasure cruise. We encountered gale after gale with sheets of cold rain, wind speed up to 40 knots, and 20-30 foot waves—lots of green water over the bow and spray on the bridge. It made me seasick to do paperwork and the pitching and rolling made cooking almost impossible—we ate lots of peanut butter and jelly sandwiches.

To counteract the port screw's right-torque action on the hull, we had to carry a constant 10 degrees of left rudder, which made shiphandling for refueling alongside the oiler even more challenging.

The gales finally ended and the sun broke out the day before we arrived at Norfolk, a weary and hungry crew. We entered the Philadelphia Naval Shipyard in December, completed repairs in January 1959 and then returned to Norfolk. Our squadron returned from deployment in February.

Despite our fore-shortened deployment with the Sixth Fleet, I had achieved JOOD and CIC watch officer qualifications, making good progress toward my OOD qualification. Our Mediterranean cruise acquainted me with destroyer duty and the pace of Sixth Fleet operations. I looked forward to our next deployment, scheduled for January 1960.

While overseas, our operational tempo caused the captain to spend most of his time on the bridge so I was around him a good bit of time while on watch. Because of his personality and mannerisms, I was not

117

comfortable in his company, but I was too busy to dwell on the matter. But in Norfolk, we were exposed to his total persona.

Our commanding officer had no command presence, lacked self-confidence, and wore a dour facial expression. His high-pitched, southern-accented voice had a dissonant tone. And he stuttered whenever he was stressed or in an angry mood, which was his usual disposition.

He was very argumentative. When meeting with an officer on an issue, the captain became confrontational, stifling discussion of the matter at hand. His command and leadership style demoralized the officers; we tried to stay away from him as much as possible.

In port, he kept an ordinary seaman on messenger duty outside his cabin door, periodically ordering him to "go and fetch mistah (named officer)!" The messenger wore a broad, white military belt. The ensigns kept a logbook of white belt "fetches," and recorded the captain's memorable outbursts.

Periodically—for our entertainment—we gathered in after-officers' country lounge to read the log to each other; "Mistah Gamboa, I could not be moa suprahsd if the sun came up in the west, ah say, ah say!" I held the record—three "fetches" in one day.

The captain had many idiosyncrasies. He insisted on personally signing all requisitions for ship supplies and spare parts (the normal procedure is for the supply officer to sign them within the captain's guidelines, speeding up the process). When he received a batch of requisitions, pre-screened by the supply officer and XO, the captain would often summon the originating officers to his cabin and challenge them on their requests. One morning I stood at attention in his cabin as he reviewed my requisitions. "Why do yo'all need paint scrapahs? They doan wea out! Ah believe yoah men just throw them ova the side!"

The captain had no concern for crew morale. In port, he conducted below-decks inspections on Friday morning followed by a ship's company personnel inspection that afternoon. The other squadron ships conducted theirs on Thursday afternoon and Friday morning respectively and then granted weekend liberty at Friday noon.

Their wardrooms took note, "You guys must be really screwed up to have to work on Friday afternoons. We're going on a long weekend!"

The captain had a loud, excitable manner on the bridge, and he was known throughout the squadron as "Shaky Jake." He was a poor shiphandler and our sister ships' crews took every opportunity to poke fun at us. One afternoon when we were returning from sea and preparing to moor alongside a squadron sister ship, they actually sounded their collision alarm, with several officers and Sailors on deck laughing and gesturing. (Destroyer crews are spiritedly competitive within their squadron.)

In June, we sailed up to Annapolis with Desron 22 and embarked 20 academy youngsters and firsties for a two-month summer training cruise on the Great Lakes and the official opening of the St. Lawrence Seaway. I was responsible for coordinating the midshipmen's shipboard training. Several of the mids had received knockabout instruction from me during their plebe summer so it was fun to reminisce. We had a very enjoyable cruise with interesting port visits in the Great Lakes.

After the cruise, we anchored at Annapolis and disembarked the mids. I had arranged with my department head and the XO to depart the ship there to get my car from a girl I dated and drive it back to Norfolk. Just as I was getting into the whaleboat to go ashore, the OOD told me that the captain wanted to see me in his cabin. I was fetched again.

He proceeded to chew me out about a postal matter, which I had already resolved with the XO, so he brought up other matters that clearly were not urgent—and some not even in my area of responsibility.

I lost my cool. "Sir, you always bear down on me more than any other ensign. Why?" He glared at me and then replied, "Because yoah an academy graduate and ah expect moah from you!" I felt like it was plebe year de ja vu all over again.

The next week I submitted my application for submarine duty. I did not want to leave destroyers, but the captain had exceeded my tolerance.

After my physical examination at Portsmouth Naval Hospital, I went to Bupers to talk to the submarine detailer about orders to sub school, but there were questions about my vision and he wanted a re-exam. I returned to the ship feeling very discouraged.

But the XO urged me to stay with *Putnam*, assuring me that I would be a key member of the wardroom during the ship's deployment in January. He also said that there were rumors the commodore intended to replace the captain before we deployed. I withdrew my sub school application.

In the fall of 1959, Desron 22 spent several weeks conducting underway training and working up for our Med cruise. My main professional challenge was being a good division officer and accomplishing all my "other duties as assigned." I explained to Mom.

> Here I find myself very busy most of the time. There is always something to be done and a lot more to learn. But I look forward to each day with hopes that I can do everything possible to be a good officer and a credit to the ship. Many times, I get quite discouraged because the responsibilities come faster than one has time to prepare for them. I make many mistakes, but just the same I learn and I just try not to make the same mistake twice.
>
> And it is quite difficult for me to be in charge of so many men. I am an easy-going person, but I think I can get the most out of my men by appealing to their better nature. If this soft approach doesn't work, though, I will not hesitate to toughen up. I do have your Perez blood in me you know!

On December 4, 1959, I was promoted to lieutenant junior grade. I welcomed the pay raise (my base pay as an Ensign was $222.40 and my subsistence allowance was $47.88; married officers received an additional $85 quarters allowance). Soon after, I was transferred to the operations department and assumed duties as the combat information officer and operations division officer.

As rumored, the commodore shortened Shaky Jake's tour and a change of command was scheduled for December 31. The XO had already granted me two weeks leave over the holidays and I flew to California. But a few days later, the Ops boss phoned me and said the CO had cancelled my leave; he wanted all officers on board for his change of command. My last fetch. I returned to the ship the day after Christmas.

Shaky Jake had a terrible impact on the wardroom. None of the other ensigns remained in the Navy and one department head that had planned to make the Navy his career resigned when his tour was up. The CO did not command again nor was he promoted to the rank of captain.

I never served with another naval officer like him. In retrospect, I realize that every organized human enterprise can be burdened with toxic people. Job selection and promotion systems are imperfect in any profession and some can rise to a level of responsibility that they are clearly not suited for (the Peter Principle).

Captain John Frank Gamboa, U. S. Navy (Retired)

The lasting value of my experience with my first commanding officer was my sacred oath to myself—if I were ever fortunate enough to command a warship, I would be his opposite.

In January 1960, the new commanding officer designated me as a fleet OOD (all ship watch officers are so designated by the CO after the subject officer has met all qualification requirements). The squadron departed Norfolk for the Med in late January.

My initial OOD watch occurred on the first night of our deployment, a pitch-black, moonless mid-watch. The squadron was steaming in screen formation with the oiler as guide.

After I assumed the watch, the commodore signaled an alteration of the formation base course to starboard to conform to the navigation track, requiring a reorientation of the screen axis to the new course. *Putnam* had a new station. I informed the captain, who was asleep in his sea cabin, and told him my maneuvering intentions, expecting him to say, "I'll be right out." Instead, he replied, "Very well, let me know when the signal is executed, and when you are on our new station."

Just like that, I was on my own. Milestones come very quickly in a naval career, seemingly, before you feel completely ready, but you just have to suck it up.

Upon execution of the signal, I increased ship's speed, turned smartly to starboard, "making a bold move," and maneuvered *Putnam* safely into our new station, a relatively uncomplicated change. After informing the captain, I relaxed and enjoyed my first cup of mid-watch coffee—with a sigh of relief. The rest of the watch was uneventful steady steaming.

After a busy transit, well to the south to avoid winter gales, our squadron passed through the Straits of Gibraltar, entered the Mediterranean, chopped to Sixth Fleet from Second Fleet and joined our designated task group. For the next two weeks, we participated in anti-air and anti-submarine exercises, carrier operations, gunnery exercises and underway replenishments. It felt like we had never left the Med.

And our commodore liked to sharpen his destroyers' shiphandling as often as possible. "Stanford Indians, this is Empress Dorothy. Stand by for an hour of tactics before the movie!" We did tactical maneuvers at 25 knots, 1000 yards between ships.

Unlike Shaky Jake, our new captain would employ whichever OOD and JOOD were on watch, giving the watch officers great training opportunities. This was just what made a line officer's life at sea exciting. I wrote to Mom, "Our new captain is a splendid naval officer and he has completely restored my faith in the Navy. He is a top-notch shiphandler and a leader of men. He has a great deal of patience; he is never unpleasant when you make a mistake—rather he tries to instruct so that we learn what we did wrong, and believe me I have made my share of mistakes!"

The Navy takes great pride in its ability to "keep the sea," operating its task forces 24 hours a day for weeks on end. The fleet's ability to conduct sustained "blue water" operations is based on replenishment of ships (fuel, ammunition, spare parts and provisions) at sea using techniques developed during WW II.

Underway replenishment (UNREP) evolved with new technology, such as replenishment by helicopter. UNREPs are the preferred method of replenishing ships in the deployed fleets; by helo is faster and generally safer than alongside, but all ships maintain their readiness to be replenished by either method.

Alongside UNREPS are normally scheduled in good weather during daylight hours, at night only if necessary, and rarely in high seas or strong winds. Helo unrep operations are normally not conducted at night or in limited visibility. Safety is always paramount in peacetime.

In the Sixth Fleet, the strike group (carriers, cruisers, and destroyers) would rendezvous at first light with the UNREP task group, a formation consisting of two oilers, two provisions ships, and one or two ammunition ships. The high-speed join-up was a tense, hair-raising tactical maneuver called "opening the fly."

When range to the UNREP ships was approximately 15 miles, the two groups would align head-on for join up; with their projected tracks offset about three miles. The strike group would increase speed to 18 knots; the replenishment group was on base replenishment course and speed (12 knots).

When the formations were close to abeam, with about six thousand yards separation between the closest ships in each formation, the strike force would execute a formation turn towards the UNREP group and release the ships—like a billiards ball break—to proceed independently to their first assigned replenishment stations. It was a very aggressive tactic—not for the faint of heart, especially at night. Welcome to Sixth Fleet, the best in the world!

Ship underway replenishment alongside is a complex evolution. On a DD, it is an all hands effort. "Now station the replenishment detail. The ship will receive provisions fore and aft, starboard-side-to! Muster the all-hands working party on the fantail and amidships to strike (carry) provisions below!"

All hands not on watch would unload received cargo pallets and then quickly get the fresh, chilled and frozen provisions to the proper storerooms, refrigerators and freezers by "daisy chain" (hand-to-hand in line). Hard work, but the crew enjoyed the prospects of fresh vegetables, fruit, and steaks.

On the bridge, the XO coordinated the hooking-up and un-hooking of the various rigs and the cargo transfer, keeping the OOD and the captain informed on the status of the replenishment.

The Ops boss kept tabs on the TG's replenishment status. Receiving ships would be alongside a replenishment ship for 60 to 90 minutes, and then proceed to their next designated waiting station until signaled to proceed alongside. These UNREPS took a full day, even longer in inclement weather.

Because of the Cold War, Soviet Navy trawlers constantly shadowed Sixth Fleet task groups. These "spy ships" had extensive communications monitoring and intercept capabilities.

As a security countermeasure, UNREPs were conducted in "silent" mode using signal flag and flashing-light communications rather than radios. Our ships had to maintain alert bridges and signal bridges and know when communications were being directed to them by the officer in tactical command.

In our first underway replenishment, the captain directed me to take *Putnam* alongside our initial station, an oiler's port side. He designated the other three fleet OODs to take her alongside the two provisions ships and the ammunition ship respectively, all under the CO's watchful eye.

With the oiler steady on replenishment course and speed, I maneuvered *Putnam* into standby station 300 yards astern of the oiler, in its wake. Concurrently, all our stations reported ready to the XO on the bridge.

¡El Capitán!

When the oiler was ready to receive us alongside, she hoisted her international signal flag "Romeo" (R) on her signal bridge port yardarm. Immediately, I had our signalmen hoist a Romeo flag on our starboard signal bridge yardarm ("two-block Romeo!"), increased speed to 19 knots, seven higher than the base replenishment speed; steered to port out of the oiler's wake; steadied on the replenishment course about 150 feet abeam the oiler's wake; and began my approach to our station alongside.

At a distance of about one and a half of our ship's length from the oiler's stern, I reduced speed to 12 knots. The trick is to do this at just the right moment so your ship will decelerate and steady up in the alongside station with zero fore and aft relative movement between the two ships. It takes lots of practice and skill to accomplish this maneuver "smartly."

As I neared the oiler's stern, I had the word passed "Now standby to receive shot lines fore and aft, starboard side!" A special rifle was used by the providing ship to fire a metal rod with a plastic bulb tip to the receiving ship. The bulb contained string attached to the sending ship.

Once our deck sailors had the string in hand, they hauled it in, and several lines were passed between ships: a small-sized messenger line (rope) attached to a distance line marked with small, square numeral flags at 10-foot intervals to indicate the distance between the two ships, and a phone line for voice communication between the ships. A separate messenger line was attached to the fuel hose wire rope.

After the wire rope was hauled in and hooked securely above our fueling station, we hauled in the fuel hose, which rode on trolleys along the wire rope.

When we signaled that the hose was connected to our fuel intake pipe on the main deck bulkhead and we were ready, the oiler could begin pumping oil into our tanks at about 90 lbs. pressure. This evolution took 15 to 20 minutes if done well.

While alongside, I maintained the distance between ships at about 120 feet, and zero fore and aft relative motion. This required constant attention and frequent changes to the rudder angle by 1-2 degrees and to the engines by adding and taking off 2-3 turns on both shafts. Refueling took about an hour.

When our tanks were topped off, the oiler stopped pumping, air-blew the fuel line clear of oil, and then the fueling rig hook-up sequence was reversed.

For training, we usually executed a rapid-sequence disengagement—a simulated emergency breakaway—which all ships must be prepared to accomplish. To add flair to our "breakaway," we departed our station at 20 knots while playing loud music over the One MC.

UNREPs are inherently risky so, besides the captain and XO, only the ship's most senior and experienced OODs conn the ship alongside. *Putnam* would train watch officers for alongside replenishment by teaming up with another destroyer for several hours of approaches on each other in turn, called "leap-frogs," with the watch officers taking turns under the captain's supervision.

Putnam made port calls at Athens, Trieste, Iskenderun, and Beirut. Then we transited the Suez Canal and the Red Sea, making port calls for fuel and liberty at Djibouti in French Somaliland and Aden en route to the Persian Gulf. In each port, the ship's company enjoyed going on tours, sightseeing and dining on local cuisine. Along with the other officers, I was assigned shore patrol duty in some of the port visits, coordinating with local police, keeping an eye on our sailors and ensuring that they did not get in trouble, or assisting those who did.

We spent six weeks on patrol in the Gulf, monitoring its considerable oil-tanker traffic. During port visits, we would rig a canvas awning on the ship's forecastle and host receptions for the American Ambassador, U.S. businessmen, and local dignitaries—Arab men in their ghutras and flowing white thobes (head dress and robes).

I continued to develop my shiphandling and seamanship skills throughout the cruise. With lots of procedural review and coordination with the navigator and the first lieutenant, I learned to anchor the ship with reasonable precision, and learned even more from the captain's critique.

I also learned how to moor a ship to a pier with the assistance of tugs and a pilot, and the procedure for putting over the mooring lines to the pier: number one on the bow, forward spring, breast, after spring, and stern line And then doubling them up. To get under way, the mooring lines are first singled up (a single strand between the ship and the pier) and then they are taken in from stern to bow sequentially with number one line last.

¡El Capitán!

Returning to the Med, *Putnam* joined up with the Sixth Fleet strike group for two weeks of exercises and plane-guarding with the bird farm. Our port visits included Rapallo and Leghorn in Italy, Cannes and Marseille in France.

Putnam also visited Tarragona, Spain, with *DuPont*, our squadron flagship. (During my youngster cruise I became the first direct descendent of my Spanish maternal great-great grandmother Patricia and my maternal great-grandmother Andrea to set foot on their native Spain since Patricia and her husband sailed from their homeland to La Nueva Espania about 118 years earlier.)

On our first evening in port, the commodore held a reception for the mayor and other city dignitaries and their ladies on his flagship. All *Putnam* and *DuPont* wardrooms were included in the reception on the torpedo deck. The commodore did not speak Spanish so I was assigned as his interpreter.

Meanwhile, my *Putnam* shipmates were enjoying getting acquainted with several beautiful Spanish girls. After the reception, two sisters invited me and two of our other officers to their home. We joined their parents for dinner at about 2200, the customary Spanish time for dinner.

Their father, who was a naval historian, asked me if I knew anything about the Spanish Navy Gamboas. I did not. He invited me into his study and showed me several Spanish naval relics including an ornately carved desk from one of the Spanish Armada's surviving flagships.

And then he told me about Pedro Sarmiento de Gamboa, a noted 16th century navigator/explorer who discovered and mapped a new, safer route through the Straits of Magellan and was on the voyage of discovery that named the Solomon Islands in the South Pacific. He also wrote a history of the Incas while serving the Viceroy of Peru. The Spanish consider Gamboa an equal to England's Drake in abilities and achievements. Our host told me that he had christened the Spanish Navy destroyer Sarmiento de Gamboa.

After my visit, the historian had the Director of the Spanish Maritime Institute in Madrid send me a copy of *Vida y Viajes de Pedro Sarmiento de Gamboa*, Life and Voyages of Pedro Sarmiento de Gamboa, a treasured memento.

I have never tried to find out if I am his descendent, but I know the Gamboas are from the northwestern region of Spain near Portugal. Traditionally, many are mariners.

126

Captain John Frank Gamboa, U. S. Navy (Retired)

Together with several other officers, I traveled to Barcelona by train for an overnight in that beautiful city. We enjoyed the sights, cuisine and wine and watching beautiful Spanish women in the restaurants and sidewalks. We even took in a bullfight. And attempted unsuccessfully to imitate Hemingway's drinking of red wine from a *bota*, but we did stain our shirts.

Our squadron successfully completed its deployment and arrived at Norfolk the end of August. Shortly thereafter, I received orders transferring me to the staff of Commander, Destroyer Squadron Two in Norfolk for duty as communications officer. I detached from *Putnam* on October 10, sad to leave Steaming Pete's wardroom, but excited to join a destroyer squadron staff (although my *Putnam* buddies joked that I was going to be a "staff puke," feigning a low opinion of staff officers).

I had successfully completed my first tour of sea duty, experiencing 25 months of thorough shipboard and fleet indoctrination—many weeks of blue water ops. I had achieved the basic line officer qualifications the Navy expected of a line officer of my rank and time in service.

Wearing my first promotion insignia on my shirt collar, I felt ready for greater responsibilities, new challenges and more adventure.

A key factor in a naval officer's career progression is an annual performance evaluation by his commanding officer, called a fitness report or fitrep. Ensigns are evaluated every six months. The report, generally two pages long, assesses an officer's overall performance and fitness for increased responsibilities and promotion in comparison with his professional community peers of the same rank and time in service.

The report format covers an officer's every dimension and trait except shoe size—performance, personality and character. For a surface warfare officer, the key categories are leadership, shiphandling and command potential. Category grades range from "outstanding" to "not qualified." Many commanding officers, in their initial fitness report on an ensign, rank the officer in the middle of the pack in order to show progress in professional development on follow-on fitreps. The final section provides the CO's summary evaluation comments.

Although the report was the single most important document in one's official record, in my era as a JO it was not customary for officers to be shown their fitreps prior to submission to Bupers, unless it was adverse, which required a statement by the subject officer. To see their reports, officers had to go to the bureau.

In the early 1970s when he was chief of naval operations, Admiral Elmo Zumwalt made major changes in the fitness report content and format and mandated that the reporting senior show the subject officer his fitness report before it was submitted. Additionally, to assist in the development of a complete, objective and fair evaluation, officers were encouraged to submit their own list of accomplishments ("brag sheet") to their reporting senior. My fitness reports in *Putnam* were drafted by my department heads, reviewed by the XO and signed by the captain.

I drove to Bupers and reviewed my reports. I was happy to see that I was rated "particularly desire to have" and "outstanding" in all categories, and not rated "not qualified" in any. In comparison to my peers, I was ranked in the upper quarter. Here are excerpts from my ensign and my first Lt.j.g. fitreps CO summary evaluation comments:

> Ensign Gamboa has exhibited excellent potential by performing all duties assigned him enthusiastically and efficiently ... accepts responsibilities readily ... frequently chosen to do minor but important jobs because of his capacity to get them done well ... a very aggressive and competent young officer ... most courteous and always presents a very neat and pleasing appearance. His ability to grasp situations and to accomplish a difficult task is well above average ... attitude is always healthy ... cheerful personality makes him a credit to the ship ... recommended for promotion when due.

> Lt.j.g. Gamboa is an effective officer who performs his assigned duties well. While ASW officer he did a particularly fine job ... reliable and confident under stress ... eager to assume new duties and broaden his professional experience ... industrious, friendly and adept at dealing with the public; has done an excellent job as CIC officer and has considerably improved the state of training, and particularly the attitude, of the personnel assigned to CIC. A most personable and effective young officer. His excellent performance of duties as an underway officer of the deck and *Putnam*'s CIC Officer contributed to the ship's successful completion of an extended deployment with the Sixth Fleet.... He is an outstanding team worker. Although he has a tendency to be

forgetful, it is believed that, with further experience and accompanying maturity, he will develop more self-confidence and reach his full potential. He presents an outstanding military appearance ... recommended for promotion when due.

I took note of the comments about forgetfulness and self-confidence, which came as a complete surprise to me. The source was undoubtedly my immediate superior, the operations officer, a very demanding academy graduate ('52). He multi-tasked his subordinates so perhaps some things "slipped through the crack." Neither had he, the XO nor the CO discussed this comment with me.

I resolved to make more complete notes in my "wheel book," a green-covered pocket memo pad carried by many officers.

On November 4, 1960, I reported to Commander, Destroyer Squadron Two in Norfolk, Virginia, and plunged right into my new duties. The commodore's staff consisted of a chief staff officer who was also the squadron material officer; an operations officer; a communications officer and an electronic warfare officer. The enlisted included a chief yeoman and third class yeoman, a master chief signalman, a master chief radioman and a third class radioman, and a steward (now culinary specialist).

Because we were a small staff, my new job required even more initiative and flexibility. I coordinated squadron communications requirements with our eight ships. My primary responsibility at sea was watch standing and assisting the ops boss in planning and executing squadron operations; and I was the staff secretary. The commodore told me that I was also, unofficially, his aide. My plate was full.

The commodore was embarked in USS *Barton* (DD 722). A week after I reported aboard, our squadron went to sea for anti-submarine and convoying exercises. The commodore was OTC. I assisted the ops boss in planning operations and ship formations, tactical maneuvers and corresponding tactical signals (voice radio or flag hoist). I stood watches in charge of the task group and executed formation maneuvers, a dramatic change from being a fleet OOD.

In port, I visited our ships to coordinate with my counterparts. As staff secretary, I also coordinated the embarkation of the staff when it became necessary to temporarily shift the commodore's flagship to another squadron ship, calling on the XO and providing him with our staff support requirements.

I would also call on the captain if it was his policy to see all staff officers visiting his ship, a wise decision since we also served as the commodore's eyes and ears and reported to him on our ship-visit impressions. From the moment I stepped on the quarterdeck until I departed, I looked for indicators of the ship's readiness, smartness and morale—assessing her command climate.

Desron Two, motto "Second to None," was scheduled to deploy to the Sixth Fleet in September 1961. In February, the squadron entered the Norfolk Naval Shipyard for a five-month overhaul, primarily for underwater hull preservation, painting, and repair of propulsion machinery and electronics equipment.

The commodore and the staff moved into a shipyard office where we planned the squadron's training and work-up for deployment and conducted ship administrative inspections. Our ships completed overhaul in June. Each ship was scheduled for three weeks of refresher training (Reftra) at the Fleet Training Center in Guantanamo, Cuba (Gitmo).

Normally the commodore and staff would have remained in Norfolk while our ships were in Reftra, but a military coup and accompanying civil unrest occurred in the Dominican Republic. Due to concern for the safety of American embassy personnel, American residents and tourists, a large Navy contingency task force was positioned offshore for possible evacuation of Americans.

Desron Two was assigned to the task force. Public order was soon restored and the crisis abated. About a week later, Desron Two was detached to proceed to Gitmo for Reftra, but the commodore and staff remained on stand-by at Gitmo to evacuate Americans should the need arise. We moved ashore to the fleet training group headquarters offices while the ships conducted their training.

During my first two years of sea duty, I had enjoyed an enjoyable but modest social life in port within my very limited budget, going to parties in Norfolk with my fellow wardroom bachelor junior officers or to the officers' club. I dated girls who I met at parties, and also one in Annapolis and one in D.C. who I knew from my academy days.

They all disliked the amount of time Navy men were away at sea. I often had to defend my being a naval officer. I therefore resolved that I would remain a bachelor until I completed my initial four years of sea duty. But this was not a difficult decision—I had no romantic prospects.

I had plans to spend Christmas with Jack Dittrick's parents in Elizabeth, New Jersey. He was on a Med cruise and his parents were lonely. My classmate Ron Fisher and my shipmate Lou Wislocki, a Navy doctor, invited me to a Christmas Eve party at their apartment in Norfolk. I agreed to drop by before heading for New Jersey.

As I entered their apartment, I glanced across the room. Standing beside the Christmas tree was the most beautiful girl I had ever seen. My gaze met her bright, lovely hazel-green eyes. Exchanging greetings with friends as I made my way through the crowd, I found it almost impossible to keep my eyes off her, and she was looking at me!

I introduced myself. With a warm smile, she replied, "Hi, I'm Linda." In that instant, I felt that something very powerful and exciting had just happened in my life. My attraction to her was almost overwhelming; however, she was Lou's date. We chatted long enough for me to find out she was a student nurse at DePaul Hospital in Norfolk. Everyone asked me to stay, including Linda, but I left the party a short while later. As I drove to New Jersey, all I could think was "Wow!"

Lou worked nights in the DePaul hospital emergency room where he had met Linda. He was leaving for a month in Panama to study tropical medicine. I gave him a ride to the airport accompanied by Linda and her friend, Scrubby. Afterward, I drove the girls back to DePaul, commenting, "Well, I'll see you later!" Linda smiled and replied, "You'd better!" I tried not to dwell on her remark.

Two days later, I was visiting with my academy roommate, Keith Bunting, his wife Bonnie, and their infant daughter. Keith was serving on a diesel submarine and preparing to attend nuclear power school. They invited me to their New Year's Eve party, but they insisted I had to bring a date. I said I didn't know anybody to invite, but Bonnie persisted.

Finally, I agreed that I would make one phone call, and I called Linda, fully expecting her to be committed for New Year's Eve. To my surprise, after teasing "It took you long enough to call!" she accepted, saying that afterward, we had to attend another party she had been invited to.

We continued seeing each other at every opportunity. We discovered that our family backgrounds were very similar. Her parents had left Finland during WW I because of the turmoil in their country in the aftermath of the Russian Communist revolution, just as my parents left Mexico due to the Mexican revolution. Her mother, Ina, had sailed across the Atlantic and emigrated through Ellis Island with her eight brothers and sisters and their mother in 1916 to join their father, who had gone earlier to Michigan to find a job and home for his family. Linda's father, Martin, and his parents and brother had emigrated via Canada from Finland, established their citizenship there, and then immigrated to New York.

Like mine, Linda's parents met and married in America. She had five siblings and so did I. We were both first-generation Americans and had similar values. Most important, Linda was very impressed that I was a Naval Academy graduate and a naval officer. I was very proud of her being a student nurse and near the top of her class. We socialized at parties with her friends and mine. I felt proud to introduce her to John McCain when we went to a party at his Virginia Beach snake ranch. Linda enjoyed his charm and wit.

Our relationship quickly flourished into a full-blown romance. In March, I proposed to Linda and she accepted. I then said that I was expecting to receive her engagement ring soon—a Naval Academy '58 miniature of my class ring, with diamonds. She was anxious to have it.

She often called me around midnight after she got off evening duty, and one night in April she asked if her engagement ring had arrived. "I have it here now." Laughingly, she said, "Bring it to me!" I was already in bed, but she said, "Meet me in the back of the dorm in 15 minutes." So I climbed out of bed, pulled my trench coat on over my pajamas, slipped the ring box into my pocket, stepped my bare feet into my shoes, walked out to my VW and drove to her dorm. I parked across from the fire exit door at the back of the student nurses' residence. Linda ran out, still in her nurse's uniform, and jumped into the car. I slipped the ring on her finger and we kissed.

Suddenly, a blinding light was shining into the car. I opened the window, "Yes, officer?" He demanded, "What's going on here?" I told him that we had just gotten engaged and that I would be leaving right away. He smiled, "Okay. Take your time!" But Linda had to get back into the dorm—she had propped the exit-door open with a coat hanger—so we kissed again and she ran back to the dorm. I returned to my apartment, thankful that the policeman had not made me get out of the car.

Captain John Frank Gamboa, U. S. Navy (Retired)

The next day Linda phoned her parents from my apartment and told her mother that we were engaged. Her mother said, "I don't want you to marry him!" Linda said, "Why not, Mom!" Ina replied, "Because Mexicans make grand romantic gestures before marriage, but after marriage they beat their wives!"

She was unaware that I was on the extension phone. I laughed and said, "Mrs. Lehtio, don't worry, I'll always wrap her in a blanket so the bruises won't show!" For years after, whenever we visited with her parents, we laughed about the "grand romantic gestures," or "GRGs" and I would comment, "Look at her, Ina—no bruises!"

About a week after our phone call, Linda and I traveled by train to Florida so I could meet her parents in person and formally ask for her hand. Martin and Ina gave us their blessing and we had a great visit. After our return to Norfolk, I wrote to Mom:

> Mom, I am so in love with her. I just didn't think that I could ever find such a wonderful person for a wife. It is such a joy to realize that God in his infinite wisdom always works things out for the best. Her name is Linda Marie Lehtio.... Her parents were both born in Finland and came to the U.S. as children. Linda was born in Ithaca, New York, but grew up in Danville, Virginia, so she has a slight southern accent. As you can see by the pictures (taken at Williamsburg two Sundays ago) she is very beautiful and has the loveliest green eyes you ever saw. She is intelligent, warm hearted, conscientious, understanding, loyal, vivacious, cheerful and very sensible. And she loves the Navy (well, she is getting to love it!) Her parents ... are not wealthy, and they have six children, with Linda the baby and the only unmarried one.

Because of the uncertainty—my squadron was still on stand-by for contingency operations—it became almost impossible to plan a wedding before my departure for a seven-month cruise in the Mediterranean, so on July 14 we were married in a church near her parents' home with her youngest brother, Eino, and sister-in-law, Susan, as our attendants. We returned to Norfolk, rented a furnished apartment and established our home.

The squadron was on its way back to Norfolk and I had only a few days of leave. Our apartment complex was near the naval base. Many other young married junior officers lived there and we enjoyed socializing with them. Linda and several of the other Navy wives established a good mutual-support network when their husbands were out to sea. We tried to enjoy every day together to the fullest. I had never been happier in my life.

In late July, our staff re-embarked in the flagship and commenced final preparations for our deployment. On September 8, we departed for the Mediterranean. We had three staff watch officers: me, the ops boss, and the electronics warfare officer, a limited duty officer with minimal underway watch qualifications. He was assigned to all the mid-watches and the afternoon watches when squadron operational activity was minimal. The ops boss, Lt. Harry Kinsley, stood all the forenoon and night watches and I stood all morning and evening watches. This scheme permitted Harry to deal with operational matters and plan future operations with the commodore during the workday.

I was totally immersed in every aspect of Sixth Fleet operations and worked closely with the commodore. All squadron and task group join ups happened on my watches. During my morning watch (0400 to 0800), we would release our ships for independent exercises or other task group assignments; they would rejoin for night steaming during my evening watch (1600 -2000). It was a very intense, fast-moving operational pace with barely enough time to eat and sleep, and no time for the evening movie. Fatigue was constant.

Our squadron commodore, Captain Walt Stencil, USNA '42, served in WW II on the battleship USS *California* in the battle of Leyte Gulf. All of the squadron COs had combat experience. Their common characteristics were great command presence, mental toughness, and a deep sense of duty and patriotism. They created a lasting impression on me and my academy classmates, imbuing us with a strong sense of mission and dedication to duty.

It was fascinating to witness first-hand the command relationships between the commodore and his commanding officers, whose personalities varied from quiet professionals to "due course" officers and one real SOB. The commodore dealt very directly with his COs when they screwed up or did not measure up to his expectations.

Stencil had a ferocious temper—his face reddened when he was angry—but he was not mean-spirited. He was a master of sarcastic humor to make a point. Conversely, he was generous in his praise of excellence. A polished officer, especially in relating to flag officers, he instinctively observed the nuances of Navy protocol. I liked to observe him in action and learned how senior naval officers think, perform, and behave at sea.

It's a boy! One of the happiest and most exciting events in my life occurred during the cruise—the birth of our son, John Frank, Jr., "Johnny." Linda's mother was there to help her adjust to motherhood, but Ina shortened her stay because another grandchild had arrived. In fact, three of her grandsons were born within one month, and she was there to welcome each one. When the squadron arrived back in Norfolk in March I quickly adjusted to the joy of fatherhood.

In May 1962, I received orders to the Naval Post Graduate School in Monterey, California, for a degree program in communications engineering, a good career-enhancing assignment. I was not eager to go back to college, especially in a technical program, but after four years of intensive fleet operations, three overseas deployments and a Great Lakes cruise, I was ready for shore duty and time to enjoy our family life. In June, I was promoted to lieutenant and detached from the staff. My fitness report was very gratifying. "Lieutenant Gamboa has performed in a variety of tasks with distinction ... he demonstrates a keen feeling of confidence and a quick grasp of the situation.... He developed and administered one of the best communications divisions in the Sixth Fleet ... handled destroyer formations involving such evolutions as high-speed join-ups for replenishment ... effectively displaying foresight and a keen sense of responsibility above that normally expected.... He expresses himself exceptionally well; his thoughts are concise and to the point ... recommended for promotion when due."

My sea duty in destroyers had lived up to my expectations. I liked being a warship line officer. I enjoyed being in the salted element. Most important, I was motivated to excel and ready for more challenges. Nonetheless, I was happy to be going ashore and looked forward with great anticipation to two years with Linda and Johnny.

An exciting aspect of Navy life is the change of duty station about every two years. My permanent change of station (PCS) orders usually required travel to a new location, interesting and exciting journeys with sightseeing along the way—especially after Admiral Zumwalt's Z-Gram mandated 30 days leave between duty stations. We used this quality time to discuss our future as we drove to Jacksonville for a visit with her parents. Our journey to Monterey (guided by our trusty AAA TripTik map booklets and state guidebooks) took us through a marvelous variety of geography and scenery across the south and southwest; we were especially amazed at the great expanse and vistas of the rugged terrain in New Mexico and Arizona. We stopped in Ft. Hood, Texas, to visit Linda's sister, Judy, and her husband, Phil (an Army captain helo pilot), and Bill and Bob, their two little boys.

We arrived in Anaheim to a boisterous reunion at my sister Bea's and her husband Al's home. Tina and Jim, and Leco and Evelyn and their kids soon joined us and we spent several days catching up—I had not seen them in over two years—the first of many happy family gatherings. Then Linda, Johnny and I headed for Lone Pine. My parents and grandparents greeted us with great love and warmth, welcoming Linda and our son into the family.

The next day I walked Linda up one side of Main Street and down the other, stopping at each store to introduce her and visit with friends. "So, Linda, you're from back East!"

We rented an apartment in Pacific Grove, about 20 minutes from the college, overlooking the Monterey Bay and Steinbeck's famous Cannery Row. My two-year academic program was a demanding curriculum with a heavy concentration on math, electronics and radio communications theory. Even so, we took time to enjoy seeing our son begin to walk and talk. Throwing breadcrumbs to the ducks in the city park pond was his favorite pastime. Linda would prepare picnics for us to enjoy, surrounded by flowering ice plant (the "magic carpet") along the cliffs overlooking the bay.

We had many friends among the '58ers and my curriculum classmates and their wives. We also exchanged visits with Pete and Alice Wiedemann, who were in San Francisco for his nuclear submarine's overhaul at Mare Island.

Our daughter, Judith Ann, was born in August at Fort Ord Army Hospital near Monterey. At the viewing window, I quickly identified her among the several newborns on display in bassinets—she was, of course, the most beautiful one, with lots of curly black hair. And we qualified for three-bedroom Navy housing closer to the campus; we moved there in September.

On the morning of November 22, I was sitting in class when a professor suddenly opened the door and announced, "The President has been shot!" Stunned, everyone gathered their papers and books, walked out of the classroom and went home to await news of his condition. The Wiedemanns were visiting for the weekend, and we had planned a class of '58 party at our home. Our guests were as stunned by the tragedy as we were. We learned that JFK had not survived. The shock and sadness we felt was near overwhelming.

There were 116 of my academy classmates attending postgraduate school with me. Al Carretta, Newt Moore, John Rorbaugh, George Jenkins, Tom Buell and many others created a '58 chapter and I was elected chapter president. We organized class social activities, including monthly luncheons. It was great to catch up and swap sea stories about our experiences since being "scattered far and wide."

Under George Jenkins' spirited leadership, we staged our first five-year reunion in June '63 (a similar event was held at Annapolis by the large number of classmates on duty at the academy and in the D.C. area). We then created a class association and constitution and Chuck Larson was again elected class president.

I graduated on June 1, 1964 with a Bachelor of Science degree in communications engineering. I had received orders in April to the newly converted guided missile cruiser USS *Columbus* (CG 12), homeported in San Diego, for duty as communications officer. She was scheduled to deploy on August 5 for a seven-month cruise with Seventh Fleet. Linda and I decided she and the children would stay with her parents at Buckroe Beach in Hampton, Virginia, during my deployment. In the meantime, we drove to San Diego, rented a temporary apartment and I reported to the ship. It felt good to be back in the fleet and serving in a warship.

Columbus was flagship for Cruiser-Destroyer Flotilla 11 with a rear admiral and staff embarked. I was assigned additional duty as the assistant staff communications officer. I had a staff of four officers: assistant communications officer, radio officer, signal officer, and registered publications custodian; and a radio division and a signal division. I had a significant management role, coordinating communications matters with the captain, executive officer, heads of department and the embarked staff.

On the night of August 4, I was watching television in the *Columbus* wardroom lounge when the program was interrupted by President Lyndon Johnson. He informed the nation that, in response to an unprovoked attack on two Seventh Fleet destroyers by North Vietnamese torpedo boats in the Tonkin Gulf, he had ordered U.S. Navy carrier aircraft attacks on the torpedo boat base in Haiphong harbor. The announcement triggered a flood of messages to *Columbus* and our flotilla commander. Pre-dawn, the USS *Ranger* (CVA 61) and four guided missile destroyers from our flotilla got underway and headed to the Far East at "best speed."

On August 5, *Columbus*, six destroyers and an oiler sortied from San Diego and sailed to Pearl Harbor, beginning my first Seventh Fleet deployment, a "Westpac." The fact that we were facing the possibility of engaging in combat created a new attitude in the wardroom and crew—we might be headed for war. We exercised at general quarters almost every day, even at night, and had frequent gun target practice with our 5-inch batteries. Everyone performed their jobs with a spring in their step and an increased sense of responsibility.

A few days later, we learned that Lt.j.g. Everett Alvarez, an A-4C pilot from USS *Constellation*, had been shot down during the raid on Hon Gai harbor torpedo boat base north of Haiphong on the afternoon of August 5 when his plane was hit by ground fire during his low-level attack with his flight leader.

Alvarez, a California Mexican American like me, was the first U. S. pilot shot down and captured by the North Vietnamese. He spent the next eight and a half years as a prisoner of war, heroically resisting torture and enduring abject living conditions and physical and mental abuse, the longest-held military prisoner in U.S. history. (In 1985, Linda and I became good friends with Ev and his wife Tammy when he was the deputy administrator of the Veterans Administration and Linda worked there as a political appointee under President Reagan.)

Our task group made a brief port-call at Pearl Harbor to victual, re-supply, and refuel. We then resumed our fast transit to the Philippines. I was amazed by the Pacific Ocean's calm vastness and inspired by the beauty of the sunrises and sunsets.

Captain John Frank Gamboa, U. S. Navy (Retired)

With twin screws and twin rudders, *Columbus* sailed very much like a destroyer, but her high superstructure gave her a tendency to roll in high winds and heavy seas. The flag bridge was beneath the ship's bridge.

She was armed with twin Talos missile launchers forward and aft on the main deck with large radar guidance antennas above the launchers, and Tartar missile systems on her port and starboard sides just aft of the bridge wings.

The wardroom included about 75 officers and embarked staff and the crew numbered about 800 enlisted. A very habitable ship, *Columbus* was a far cry from the austere living conditions I had experienced in destroyers. I shared a stateroom with Lieutenant David Chigos. (After leaving active duty as a Lt. Cdr., David earned a Ph.D. and went on to create National University in San Diego, the third largest private university in California.)

In addition to standing regular OOD watches, I was the general quarters OOD so I spent many hours on the bridge. As the senior watch officer, I created the officer underway watch bills for the bridge and CIC, and organized and conducted a training and qualification program for the JOs.

Meanwhile, the U.S. Congress had passed the Tonkin Gulf Resolution, which eventually led to the escalation of hostilities and the Vietnam War.

When we arrived at Subic in late August, the port was crowded with Seventh Fleet ships. President Johnson's strong response to the North Vietnamese torpedo-boat attack on our destroyers and the Congressional Tonkin Gulf resolution had created much excitement within the fleet.

On our first night in port, the officers' club was filled wall-to-wall; it seemed as if all my classmates serving in Seventh Fleet were there. The enthusiasm and energy were palpable; it was nearly impossible to elbow up to the bar.

All ships faced an increased op-tempo; we fully expected that our deployments would be extended. No one really wanted war, but if our ships were attacked again, we were ready and willing to fight back.

We soon got word that our task group would proceed to a sea navigation point called Yankee Station in the South China Sea, the fleet's carrier operating area off the coast of South Vietnam. We would join up with the USS *Constellation*, the attack carrier that had launched the air strikes on the torpedo boat base.

¡El Capitán!

In early September, *Columbus* and several destroyers sortied from Subic Bay and proceeded to Yankee Station. The national command authorities had decided to send two of our destroyers into the Tonkin Gulf. The carrier would provide air cover and our mission was to provide air defense and anti-submarine warfare protection for the Connie and a direct communications link from the flagship to the destroyers.

Columbus took station 40 miles northwest of the carrier strike group and about 100 miles southeast from the entrance to the gulf. I was very busy resolving urgent communications issues and flew by helo to the Connie to coordinate task group radio circuits.

On the scheduled date and time, our two destroyers, with a captain unit commander embarked, proceeded into the Tonkin Gulf. About 2300 as I was awakened to go on watch, the comm watch officer phoned me, "Sir, we are getting flash-precedence messages from the destroyers. It looks like all hell is breaking loose in Tonkin Gulf!" I rushed to the comm center. It appeared that the destroyers were under attack by torpedo boats. About ten minutes later, several attack aircraft launched by the carrier passed overhead en-route. I assumed the OOD watch and continued to monitor the situation, but no other messages were received from the destroyers. We were very concerned about the situation and our destroyers' status.

We finally made contact late in the afternoon of the second day. The destroyers had been on four boilers and operating at high speeds almost continuously since the torpedo boat attacks, and were low on fuel. They were directed to depart the gulf and rendezvous with *Columbus*.

We joined up 40 miles south of the gulf at 2200 and topped them off. The commodore passed a canvas bag by light-line to *Columbus* filled with over 50 high-precedence message teletype tapes that the destroyers had been unable to transmit. Our communications center rapidly processed the messages into the Naval Telecommunications System, providing our admiral, the fleet commanders and the national command authorities their first details of the destroyers' engagement in the Tonkin Gulf.

The DDs then proceeded to Subic Bay and *Columbus* remained at Yankee Station another week, but there were no other clashes with the North Vietnamese. We returned to Subic Bay for two weeks of upkeep.

During the next four months, we made port calls at Manila Bay, Yokohama, Kobe and Sasebo. I enjoyed my first visit to the Far East. In

Sasebo for the Christmas holidays, we were suddenly ordered to "Sortie when ready for sea; proceed at best speed to Yankee Station."

We conducted an emergency crew recall and got underway at 0100. I was the OOD. After steaming for two days at 27 knots, our urgent mission was cancelled and we were diverted to Hong Kong just in time for New Year's Eve, a happy turn of events.

We departed Hong Kong several days later and spent an uneventful week on Yankee Station with two carriers. Then we sailed to Sasebo, conducted a turnover with the cruiser USS *Canberra* and her task group and departed for San Diego on January 28.

In February, soon after our chop back to Third Fleet, President Johnson ordered the commencement of Operation Rolling Thunder, the U. S. bombing of North Vietnam. *Columbus* arrived in San Diego the last week in February 1965.

Linda, Jack and Judy flew to San Diego the next week (During their stay with Linda's parents, Johnny's grandfather nicknamed him "Jack"). We rented a house in Claremont and resumed our life together.

For the rest of the year, *Columbus* conducted routine operations and a brief overhaul at Hunters Point naval shipyard in San Francisco. The ship was notified that, after the Christmas holidays; its homeport would be changed to Norfolk, swapping with the nuclear-powered cruiser *Long Beach*. Linda, Jack and Judy again stayed with her parents in Buckroe Beach during the ship's two-month operations and transit to Norfolk.

We rented our third home in two years, a townhouse in a new development along with lots of other *Columbus* families. I was expecting orders for shore duty in July and had requested assignment to the chief of naval operations staff (OPNAV), feeling that it was career essential. My Bupers detailer had told me informally that my chances "looked good."

On a Saturday morning about a week later, the phone rang; it was my detailer. Anxious for Linda to hear the good news, I said, "Honey, it's my detailer, get on the extension!"

The detailer said, "I am sending you message orders assigning you to the Communications division in the United Nations Command/United States Forces Korea."

Stunned, I asked, "The U.N.? In New York?" He replied, "No. Not in New York. In Korea." I then said, "How long?" He replied, "13 months."

Linda asked, "Is this an accompanied tour?" He said, "No ma'am, I'm afraid not." She slammed the phone down.

The detailer lamely commented, "I know this is not what you were expecting." I listened to his explanations about "urgent, high-priority assignment," said thanks, and hung up.

I went upstairs to face Linda. She had locked the door to our bedroom and refused to open it. I could hear her crying. After about ten minutes, she unlocked the door and with tear-stained eyes told me, "Except for PG School, where I saw the back of your head for two years, all I've had with you is sea duty and now I get an unaccompanied tour!"

A week later, she was watering the lawn in front of our townhouse. A new neighbor walked up to introduce herself. Linda replied, "You don't need to get to know me. We're leaving. My husband has orders to Korea, unaccompanied, and I'm moving in with my parents again!" The woman replied, "My husband is an Army officer and had an unaccompanied tour in Korea, but I went along anyway." Linda said, "Tell me how you did it!"

When I came home that evening, Linda was very excited. She said, "The kids and I are going with you to Korea!" They would fly at our expense to Korea on a 30-day tourist visa. Once in country, she would apply for a job with the Army. They were always in need of American typists who could get security clearances. Once she was employed, she would be granted an extended visa and the Army would pay her way back to America with me; the kids could fly home with us, space-available.

Linda vowed she would "live in a tent for a year rather than be separated again." But there were minor complications. She had never had a job, didn't even have a social security number, and couldn't type. Brimming with confidence, she said, "I can learn to type! I can be a secretary!"

Despite her optimism and determination, I had great misgivings about taking my family to Korea without government sponsorship, but after much discussion, we decided that we would rather take the risks than endure a 13-month separation. We would just consider it an adventure in foreign travel. Judy was almost three and Jack was four and a half so their schooling was not an issue.

We would gather as much information as we could about living and working conditions in South Korea, obtain a loan from our credit union (Navy Federal) for airfares and related expenses, get our passports, and put our household goods into storage. If things didn't work out, Linda,

Jack and Judy would fly back to Buckroe Beach and stay with her folks (Plan B).

The Bureau issued my orders: "When relieved detached duty; proceed Commander in Chief, United Nations Command, Commander U. S. Forces, Korea, duty Joint Staff. Report to port of embarkation not later than 10 August 1966. Dependents not authorized."

My tour in *Columbus* reinforced my conviction that fleet communications is the most dynamic function in the Navy—a demanding 24/7 task. Supervising four junior officers and all the bridge watch standers, I had transitioned to shipboard middle management. I had thoroughly enjoyed conning a heavy combatant. Departing *Columbus*, I felt ready to serve as a destroyer department head or even as an executive officer. My fitness reports supported my confidence.

> LT Gamboa is aggressive, well-motivated, and dedicated.... he maintained flagship communications performance at a high level of effectiveness ... a professional, productive officer who works long hours in untiring style ... extremely versatile, being equally at home on the bridge or serving as a communications officer, as advance liaison officer for foreign port visits or as a mentor and liaison officer to midshipmen embarked for summer training. LT Gamboa works best under pressure, remaining in high-tempo operations cool and level-headed ... skilled, alert fleet OOD who has contributed extensively to the training of deck watch officers ... Respected and trusted by seniors and subordinates, LT Gamboa is fully qualified for promotion ... strongly recommended for duty as destroyer executive officer.... An officer of high command potential ... quite capable of filling a billet normally occupied by an officer one grade senior.

Linda, Jack, Judy and I enjoyed our cross-country drive to California, sightseeing along the way, including a visit to the Air Force Academy and horseback riding at a ranch in Colorado (Judy, not yet three years old, argued for her own horse rather than riding double like Jack). I flew to Korea from McChord Air Force Base in Washington State, but Linda and children had to delay their travel when Jack and Judy came down with chicken pox. They stayed with my sister Tina until they departed for Korea. Before leaving, Linda sold our car.

¡El Capitán!

The U.S. Forces Korea headquarters and the U.N. command were located at Eighth Army headquarters in Yongsan, a suburb of Seoul. I got a room at the BOQ and after assuming my duties, began my search for housing. Our J-6 division secretary, Billie, had a network of friends and soon found a temporary single room in Army bachelor women officers' barracks with a nearby mess hall at an Army engineering facility about 30-minutes from Yongsan. It wasn't ideal, but I was ready for my family to fly to South Korea.

In the third week of August, Linda, Jack and Judy arrived late at night. They had just two suitcases of clothing. It was nearly midnight when we got into the taxi. There was a curfew from midnight to 0500 as a security measure to prevent North Korean infiltrators from entering and committing acts of sabotage in the Republic of Korea (ROK).

On the ten-mile drive from Kimpo Airport to Seoul, we were stopped at several fortified checkpoints by helmeted ROK soldiers armed with machine guns, who sternly questioned the driver, looked us over, and checked our passports before opening the barbed-wire barricades and letting us pass on to the next check point.

The whole scene was frightening. Jack and Judy seemed fascinated, but Linda looked worried. I had a fleeting thought "I have brought my family into a war zone!"

Our room had two single beds, with a small table in between, a simple wooden chair, and a dresser. The bathroom was down the hall; the mess hall was in another building (since it was a women's BOQ, Linda stood guard outside the door when I used the restroom or the shower). The entryway to the building was covered with a concrete slab, which rainwater slowly seeped through and had created stalactites.

It certainly wasn't five-star, but we were happy to be together and we even had a party in our tiny room to celebrate Judy's third birthday. The Korean civilian cooks and staff in the mess hall "adopted" Jack and Judy, giving them special snacks and anything they wanted to eat. I rode an Army bus to work. Linda, Jack and Judy would often get on the bus and ride the circuit, sightseeing—and to pass the time of day.

The U. N. Village apartment and housing complex, located about 20 minutes from Yongsan, housed many U.S. citizens. In October, we succeeded in obtaining a temporary apartment with a bedroom (two double beds), a bathroom, and a closet that had been converted into a tiny kitchen. We used the entry foyer as a dining room. After our first night in our new home, I brought Army blankets from my BOQ room to hang over the bare windows at night so the roving security guards couldn't shine their flashlights on us while we slept.

We went to the commissary in a taxi to buy groceries and we prepared our first home-cooked meal in over three months. We had steaks, feeling good about establishing ourselves "on the economy" in Korea. During our celebratory dinner, Jack commented, "We sure are poor, huh Dad!" getting a good laugh from Linda and me. We never felt richer.

After dinner, still feeling great about our progress, we asked Jack why he thought we were poor. He said that he opened a drawer on his side of our "dining room table" just as we sat down to eat, and cockroaches scampered around the inside; he just quickly shut the drawer but said nothing to us. Our next purchase was bug spray.

Linda went to the Army civilian personnel office and applied for a job. To qualify, she had to pass a typing test. I brought home a rugged Army manual field typewriter from the office and lots of paper. The typewriter required good hand strength to operate and Linda's fingers would ache after a day of practice. She flunked her first two attempts, complaining that it was so cold in the Quonset hut test room (it was November and snowing) that her fingers wouldn't limber up. But she passed on her third attempt and was hired as a GS-2 clerk typist, the lowest grade in the civil service system, but it was a job, and that was all we needed.

A few days later, she went to work for a colonel in charge of the Army's Korea Military Advisory Group. Her office was across the parade field from mine. We breathed a sigh of relief.

While living at the women's barracks we began attending the American Lutheran Church and met Deanna Yu, an American who lived in U.N. Village with her Korean husband, Kunchoon Yu, a U.S.-educated engineer. They helped us make our life as comfortable as possible. When we were finally able to rent a larger home in U.N. Village, they helped us shop for furnishings: cushioned sofa, chairs, coffee table, end tables, dining room table, six chairs (all hand-made and black-lacquered; and delivered by bicycle), and they helped us find a housemaid, Ajumoni, to care for Jack and Judy while we were at work.

Ajumoni became a key member of our family. She taught Judy to sing Korean songs; she cleaned house, did laundry and cooked for us, including Korean dishes such as kimchee, a pungent, spicy cabbage dish. Jack and Judy became very fond of her "sticky rice."

We were able to enroll Jack in the Eight Army dependents' Kindergarten and he rode in an Army taxi to and from school each day. He loved school and excelled. Judy stayed at home with Ajumoni.

I was the chief of operations branch, J-6 communications division, a commander's billet. Colonel Hugh Foster, a West Point graduate and the Eighth Army signals officer, was the division chief. Lt. Col. Horace "Doc" Moody, USAF, a fighter pilot, was his J-6 deputy and my boss, and together with our very able secretary, Billie, we ran the joint side of the communications staff. I coordinated communications policy issues within the joint staff; maintained war plans; and monitored U.S. and ROK communications projects in South Korea. Liaison with the ROK armed forces was conducted by Foster and Moody; I was often included in their meetings.

President Johnson was eager to obtain additional support in South Vietnam from our allies. The ROK government agreed to provide more combat forces in South Vietnam under the operational control of U.S. forces in country. Vice President Hubert Humphrey visited the ROK and announced that, in support of South Korea's commitment of troops to South Vietnam, the U.S. would increase its ROK military and economic developmental aid. He also met with US armed forces families at the American embassy and Linda, Jack, Judy and I were included. As Humphrey made his way through the crowd, he took Judy from my arms and kissed her on the cheek, a great photo op.

A U.S. Navy Seventh Fleet destroyer was assigned to patrol the Sea of Japan during the Vice President's visit. The destroyer was under operational control of Rear Admiral Irvine, the U.S. Navy component commander in the ROK. He telephoned Colonel Foster to ask if he could provide a direct, secure communications link between his Navy headquarters and the destroyer. Foster summoned me and explained the admiral's request. He asked me how Navy ships communicated. I replied, "By HF radio, sir." "So does the Army" said Foster, "but my Army staff tells me that we can't do this—it's never been done in Korea. The Army and Navy were able to communicate with each other during WW II. I can't believe we have lost that capability. Make it happen!"

Over the next few days, I learned all about Army mobile HF communications vans and the intricacies of HF communications on land.

Captain John Frank Gamboa, U. S. Navy (Retired)

Together with the admiral's staff and our army staff, I developed and coordinated a plan for the Eighth Army signal command to provide HF comm vans and necessary operating frequencies. We sited the vans and antennas on a hill near Navy headquarters with a jeep driven courier system for message delivery. The secure channel worked reliably throughout the ship's patrol in the Sea of Japan.

Afterwards, the admiral wrote to Lt. Gen. Benjamin O. Davis, our chief of staff. "During special surveillance operations conducted by units of the U.S. Navy and ROK Navy ... Commander, Naval Forces, Korea, for the first time was able to establish and maintain direct, secure communications between his headquarters in Seoul and U.S. Navy ships at sea. This could not have been accomplished without the assistance of Commander, U.S. Forces-Korea, especially the help of LT Gamboa ...." Davis wrote, "I add my personal congratulations for a job well done!"

Foster and Moody then tasked me as the action officer on a long-standing request by the ROK Joint Chiefs of Staff (JCS) for a communications system linking the ROK Army headquarters in Korea with ROK Army units in South Vietnam. The request required high-powered HF radio transmitters, receivers, antennas and ancillary equipment for both the ROK JCS headquarters and ROK Army headquarters in South Vietnam. The request had been stalled in the Eighth Army staff for almost one year and was becoming a contentious issue between the ROK JCS and U.S. Forces Korea headquarters.

I read several thick files of messages and correspondence, and then created my first-ever staff study. I concluded that the ROK JCS request was operationally valid and should be fulfilled by the U.S., but it was also a political issue in the U.S. Army. Moody and Foster agreed with my recommendation to approve the ROK JCS request; however, Foster put it on hold pending further guidance from higher authority.

A couple of weeks after the Vice President's visit, the U.S. Ambassador to the ROK directed that all U.S. Forces headquarters and components in the ROK "should be more forthcoming" in dealing with ROK aid requests, particularly those related to ROK armed forces in South Vietnam. The ROK JCS' request for a communications system met the Ambassador's new aid criteria and Colonel Foster directed us to fulfill the request. I coordinated with all the staff divisions, component commands, Commander in Chief, Pacific (CINCPAC) and the ambassador's deputy chief of mission, who was coordinating all U.S. aid

147

to the ROK. It necessitated several weeks of occasionally contentious staffing to line up unanimous support.

Foster, Moody and I met with Lt. Gen. Davis (the famous black West Point graduate who had commanded the Tuskegee Airmen in the European Theater during WW II). Davis exuded inspirational leadership, command presence, and had great charm and charisma. After talking on the phone with the U.S. embassy chief of mission while we listened, Davis approved our recommendations. Successful resolution of this complex, sensitive international project with a close ally established my action-officer credentials within our headquarters, the component commands, and the ROK Joint Chiefs of Staff.

Linda and I were included in all the Navy component command social events. The admiral's wife was very proud of Linda for having the gumption to come to the ROK on her own (the first Navy wife to do so). In November, Col. Foster and Linda's boss, Col. Batt, were both selected for brigadier general. We celebrated with them in their joint "wetting down" party.

In November 1966, I was selected for lieutenant commander. This critical career milestone ended my days as a junior line officer and marked my transition into executive middle management in the Navy. I was promoted in May 1967 and Linda was promoted to GS-4, so we had our joint wetting-down party at the officers' club attended by many friends. In July, Foster was relieved by Col. Jack Cole, and in August, Moody was relieved by Lt. Col. John "Hamp" Hamparian, an Air Force communicator, making me the "old hand" in J-6.

In August, Linda, Jack, Judy and I traveled space-available aboard a U.S. Sea Transportation Service troop ship from Busan, Korea, to Sasebo, Japan, to visit with her brother Eino, an Air Force master sergeant. Eino and his wife Susan and their wonderful boys Marty, William and Jacob were stationed at Itazuki Air Force Base. They took us on tours of the area, including the Hiroshima war museum.

When we returned home, my orders were on my desk, "When relieved detached duty joint staff; proceed Washington, D.C., Report Manager, National Communications Systems, Arlington, Virginia."

In late October, Linda and I were at home listening to Armed Forces Radio as we fixed dinner. A news bulletin announced that "Lt. Cdr. John

McCain, son of the commander in chief, Pacific," had been shot down over Hanoi on October 26, 1967, but it was not known if he was dead or alive. Tearfully, Linda asked me what I thought. Hugging her I replied, "We just have to pray he's alive!" Several days later, Armed Forces Radio announced that McCain was a prisoner of the North Vietnamese. Linda asked me what would happen to him. I said, "If they don't deliberately kill him, he will survive!" They nearly did. John was in our prayers for the next five and a half years.

The POWs were released in stages, commencing in February 1973. McCain was released on March 14th. Only then did America and the rest of the world learn of the brutal torture, abusive treatment and inhumane living conditions that McCain and his fellow prisoners had endured in the infamous Hanoi Hilton and other North Vietnamese prisoner of war camps. The incredibly brave and heroic resistance to their captors exhibited by John and his fellow POWs continues to inspire all Americans.

Our life as a family in "the land of morning calm" under trying circumstances had been made endurable and even enjoyable by Linda's courage and indomitable spirit, overcoming daunting challenges with intelligence, grace, understanding, care and a wonderful sense of humor. Despite our hardships, she kept a loving hearth and home and sustained our morale. Now our tour was rapidly winding down. We were eagerly looking forward to our departure—longing to see our families and our homeland. Our flight to America was scheduled for January 25, 1968, "only four days and a wake-up!"

Late in the night of January 21, 1968, 31 North Korean commandos crossed the demilitarized zone (DMZ) that divides North and South Korea, made their way into Seoul, and in an assassination attempt on President Park Chung Hee, directed rocket grenade and small-arms fire at Blue House, the presidential residence. We could hear the gunfire and explosions as the Blue House guards repulsed the commandos, killing or capturing all of them.

The next day several North Korean Navy ships conducted an unprovoked attack on the USS *Pueblo*, a Seventh Fleet intelligence-gathering ship operating in the Sea of Japan. *Pueblo* was in international waters outside the 12-mile territorial limit near the DMZ's seaward extension.

¡El Capitán!

The North Korean Navy ships illegally forced the *Pueblo*—under fire—into a North Korean port and took its officers and crew into custody, the first U.S. Navy ship captured on the high seas since the War of 1812.

The U.S. quickly reacted. Air Force fighter squadrons deployed to South Korea from Japan and Okinawa and the Seventh Fleet dispatched a carrier task force at best speed to the Sea of Japan.

All U.S. forces in South Korea and the ROK armed forces were put on a wartime alert. Operational holds were placed on all U.S. military personnel scheduled to depart the ROK. It was a frightening time for me and Linda.

In our Eighth Army transient quarters, we separated our luggage in case I would not be able leave with them. Fortunately, my replacement was in country and had already relieved me of all duties, so the next day Col. Cole detached me.

With a huge sigh of relief, Linda, Jack, Judy and I departed Korea as scheduled on a chartered Northwest Airlines flight—the big red tail—to McChord AFB in Washington. There were many empty seats on the plane.

BG Foster wrote in my fitness report, "LCDR Gamboa has continually proven himself to be a truly outstanding officer. His ability to maintain close and effective relations with the ROK counterparts during some highly sensitive military/political staff maneuvering, and to adhere to established staff positions in the face of mounting pressure to the contrary, is particularly noteworthy…. If my sons should have to go into combat I would be particularly pleased, confident and reassured to have Gamboa as their commander and leader."

The Navy component commander, RADM Irvine, added his endorsement, "LCDR Gamboa demonstrated outstanding initiative, professional ability, industry and imagination by initiating and carrying through to successful conclusion several communications projects in support of my command…. None of these projects were easy; they were particularly difficult to accomplish here in Korea … involving detailed technical … and operational knowledge coupled with real executive ability … he should be considered for accelerated promotion."

Col. Cole wrote, "LCDR Gamboa is the most outstanding staff officer of his grade that I have ever had work for me from all services … consistently and repeatedly demonstrated to the highest degree, qualities of competence and devotion to duty which make him an outstanding officer. He has exceptional abilities in leadership and executive management."

The ROK JCS presented me with a beautiful certificate of appreciation for establishing their multi-channel HF single side band system to Vietnam. And Commander, U.S. Forces Korea/United Nations Command awarded me a Joint Service Commendation Medal.

My nine years of naval service as a junior line officer had been characterized by intense operational warship duty in each of the Navy's four numbered fleets, tough joint staff duty in a foreign station, and challenging post-graduate school. Putting on my Lieutenant Commander shoulder boards, I felt proud of my accomplishments.

And I knew what lay ahead of me as a surface warfare officer—a destroyer department head assignment and then duty as an executive officer in destroyers. I also knew that I would face stiff competition for these billets. I was therefore mentally ready to work hard in my forthcoming Navy tour to earn these assignments.

But instead of duty in the CNO staff as I had requested, Bupers had ordered me to another communications staff assignment ashore—a consecutive joint tour. I would be away from the Navy for another two years.

I was not happy with the orders and felt very concerned about my new duty station and its career impact.

Chapter Six

★ ★ ★ ★ ★ ★ ★

There are old fuds, young studs, and lieutenant commanders.

—R. G. Voge, Lt. Cdr., USN (Ret,)

The National Communications System (NCS) was created by President Kennedy in the aftermath of the Cuban missile crisis so that the major federal agencies could coordinate their communications needs and systems development and ensure reliable support for the President during national security emergencies. The secretary of defense was assigned the system management task, and the director of the Defense Communications Agency was "double-hatted" as NCS manager with a staff of about 15 senior civil service employees, three military officers, and representatives from each NCS member agency. I was the plans officer.

My principal task was to develop a long-range NCS program plan to guide the development of systems interconnects and interoperability. I soon discovered that my working relationships with my counterparts in other NCS agencies were problematic. They feared that NCS communication systems interconnections would adversely affect their budgets so there was minimal cooperation on the plan development. I learned all about bureaucratic turf battles, but I persevered.

Linda and I bought a house under construction in Alexandria, Virginia, about a 30-minute commute from my office. Linda, Jack and Judy stayed with her parents again during construction and I rented a room in the bachelor officers' quarters at Fort Myer. We moved into our house in June.

Building on her Korea job credentials, Linda got a job at the Defense Communications Engineering Office as a division chief's secretary in the building complex where I worked; we commuted together. We enrolled Judy in kindergarten and Jack in first grade in a private school near our home, dropping them off in the morning and picking them up on our way home.

We made new friends in our neighborhood, and thoroughly enjoyed owning our first home in the suburbs with a community swimming pool and many other children for Jack and Judy to play with. We also lived near Linda's sister Judy and her husband Phil for the first time; we were happy to be able to spend more time with them.

The NCS was my fifth consecutive communications assignment. I felt that the Navy was pigeonholing me in my warfare sub-specialty. I had enjoyed my shipboard communications tours and my U.S. Forces Korea billet, but I had no desire to be a career communicator.

Linda and I discussed the issue at length and decided that a master's degree would broaden my expertise and add value to my NCS tour. Understanding how our government and nation relate to others countries has always interested me, so in January 1969, I enrolled in a University of Maryland night school international relations program, an intellectually challenging curriculum that absorbed most of my off-duty time. Linda helped with research and typed my term papers.

My tour was scheduled to end in February 1970, but I wouldn't complete my Master's degree until August so I visited Bupers to request an extension. My detailer felt that I should return to sea duty as scheduled; however, I argued for the delay. He was not persuaded so I submitted an official request with a strong endorsement signed by our rear admiral deputy manager. My detailer changed my tour rotation date to September, but ominously implied that I would not be returning to destroyers.

In July 1970, I received orders to an amphibious warfare ship, USS *Pensacola* (LSD 38), as Operations officer, third senior officer in the ship. She was under construction at the General Dynamics shipyard in Quincy, Massachusetts. Although I had requested duty in a destroyer, I reluctantly concluded that amphibious warfare might broaden my surface warfare knowledge and skills. I had finished my master's degree and was happy to be returning to the fleet. And Linda was glad that I wouldn't be deploying right away.

In September, we traveled to Massachusetts and rented a beautiful house on Little Harbor in Cohasset, a picturesque New England town. Our home was an easy walk to the Atlantic Ocean and a short drive to the Quincy shipyard.

I departed the NCS with a laudatory fitness report and my second Joint Service Commendation medal. "LCDR Gamboa consistently demonstrated initiative, dedication to duty ... and persuasive leadership in dealing with difficult and complex problems.... His actions were necessarily original, since no precedent existed.... The new NCS plan will ... shape programs of the agencies which provide communications to the federal government...."

In early October, I reported to the Supervisor of Shipbuilding, Conversion and Repair (Supships), at the General Dynamics shipyard in Quincy, the Navy's representative that oversees the shipbuilder's contractual performance and ensures that Navy ships are built in compliance with Navy specifications.

After checking in, I walked to a three-story brick building and selected office space for our unit. The prospective commanding officer had arrived in Quincy but had not yet reported for duty. I introduced myself by phone and let him know that I had established our offices and selected our parking spaces. We agreed to meet at the shipyard the following week. Then I walked to the waterfront to get my first look at *Pensacola*.

Standing on the quay wall, I was awe-struck by her huge size and graceful lines. Her bow was much larger and her freeboard significantly higher than a destroyer's. She had 50-ton lift cranes amidships on each side of her main deck and a helicopter flight deck one-third the length of the ship. But her most prominent feature was her cavernous dock—the well deck—two thirds the length of the ship.

Pensacola's weather decks and superstructure were rigged with scaffolding; electrical cables, high-pressure air lines and steam hoses strewn all over her topsides. Helmeted shipyard workers were everywhere on her decks. I was eager to explore her from stem to stern and bridge to engine rooms, but I deferred to Navy custom; the prospective commanding officer should be the first to step aboard his new ship.

LSDs were designed, constructed and operated during WW II for transporting troops, armor, artillery and other materiel. These ships were called "wet wells".

Pensacola was the third ship in the Anchorage landing ship dock (LSD) class, with a crew of 19 officers and 295 enlisted, and berthing compartments for 304 troops. The ships were 562 feet long with an 84-foot beam, and a full-load displacement of 13,700 tons. They were powered by steam propulsion with two boilers and twin engines with a maximum speed of 22 knots. They had twin rudders, twin screws and a large fuel capacity ("long legs".)

Pensacola had a mezzanine deck over the forward third of the dock to stow light vehicles, howitzers and palletized cargo. She had a large metal vehicle ramp from the well deck to the mezzanine deck and another from the mezzanine to the flight deck. These ramps facilitated movement of vehicles, weapons and cargo between the flight deck and the well deck. LSDs had their own landing craft, medium (LCM-6), a landing craft, vehicle personnel (LCVP), and a gig (captain's boat) used to lead boat waves to the beach from the anchored ships.

The LSD dock had a system of seawater ballast tanks beneath the well deck and along both sides of the dock (called wing walls). To take landing craft into her dock, LSDs would ballast down and flood the dock by lowering the stern gate and opening the sea valves in the ballast tanks in a controlled sequence. It took about thirty minutes to ballast down to the desired depth of water at the stern gate.

The landing craft entered the dock to load troops, weapons, vehicles and cargo, called wet well operations. When these "wet well ops" were completed, the ballast tanks were blown free of seawater by high-pressure air compressors. Water in the dock was discharged through drain valves in the well deck and the open stern gate; de-ballasting took about thirty minutes.

Construction of a naval ship is a very complex industrial process. Most ship construction requires about two years from keel laying to commissioning (five for carriers). *Pensacola*'s keel was laid on March 12, 1969. She was christened and launched in 1970 when the ship was 80% complete. When I arrived, much "finish" work remained to be done, including the installation of her combat systems and connecting all the equipment-operating controls.

To facilitate our ship familiarization, the captain and I visited her sister ship, USS *Portland* (LSD 37), which had immediately preceded us in construction at Quincy. She was moored at Boston Naval Shipyard for fitting out and commissioning. We met with her captain and XO and toured their ship. She was clean, ship-shape, twice the size of a destroyer and far more complex—ballasting like a submarine, carrying troops like a transport, hauling cargo like a logistics ship, and operating helos like a carrier. Compared to the cramped, Spartan living conditions in a destroyer, LSDs had excellent habitability. By the time we completed our tour, my disappointment in not returning to destroyers had vanished.

Pensacola's commissioning crew was split into two components: about 40 officers and senior enlisted in a nucleus crew located at the building site; and the remainder, called the balance crew, at the Amphibious Base in Little Creek, Virginia. The XO headed the balance crew, directed the creation of the ship's administrative structure—regulations, directives and bills—and sent personnel to damage control and firefighting schools.

The nucleus crew's mission was to assist Supships in overseeing the final stages of construction; coordinate *Pensacola*'s fitting out after acceptance by the Navy; and assist in her commissioning. In addition to me and the commanding officer, we had the supply officer, chief engineer, main propulsion assistant, damage control assistant, electrical officer, electronics materiel officer and about 30 enlisted personnel. I was responsible for all operations department spaces and equipment and I was the unit's acting executive officer.

A new-construction U.S. Navy ship's initial crewmembers are called "plank owners." As first to report, I was plank owner number one. The remainder of our nucleus crew reported a month after my arrival. I established our organization and daily work routine, with weekly tours of *Pensacola* by the captain and the officers. We were Supships' eyes and ears for monitoring her construction. I drafted and coordinated the bi-weekly progress reports submitted by the captain to the CNO, copy to Supships.

A Navy ship's personnel complement—its crew--is headed by the commanding officer. The executive officer is second in command and is responsible for coordinating the command's administration and management. The crew is organized into a ship's company, which has two tiers below the captain.

The ship's company first tier is composed of departments, each with a unique functional purpose. Heads of department coordinate with the XO and report to the captain.

The XO functions as second in command and head of the executive department, which includes the captain's office, admin office, personnel office, master at arms office, public affairs and other ship's company support offices. The medical organization on ships with no doctor assigned is included in the executive department.

The ship's company second tier is made up of divisions within the departments, each led by a junior officer. Each enlisted person is assigned to a division, such as boilermen to B division and electricians to E division. Deck department divisions are designated by number such as first division and second division. Each division has one or more work centers.

To operate the ship in normal conditions in port and at sea as well as during combat operations, the ship's company is further organized into bills, which are specific functional teams such as the general quarters or battle bill; the watch, quarter and station bill; the abandon ship bill; and the repel boarders bill.

The company is also organized by detail, such as the special sea and anchor detail, the replenishment detail, the rescue and assistance detail. And by party, such as the boarding party for going aboard a merchant ship to inspect for contraband; beach party, to establish a liberty-boat loading/unloading point in a foreign port; shore patrol party to maintain crew good order ashore; and various working parties for loading ship supplies, provisions and cargo.

Finally, the entire ship's company is organized into duty sections for the ship's routine operations underway and in port. The XO coordinates with department heads on the assignment of all personnel to these teams. The ship's senior bridge-watch-standing officer, called the senior watch officer (SWO), is the XO's principal assistant for assignment of personnel to the ship's duty sections.

Pensacola's ship's company was created by the bureau of naval personnel for the Anchorage class, but we had to create the ship's administrative framework—the controlling directives and regulations. This was the XO's primary task, but each department head was responsible for developing their respective internal directives. To avoid "reinventing the wheel," we obtained copies of directives from the *Anchorage* and *Portland* and adapted them to *Pensacola*.

My priority task was to ensure that each watch station had qualified personnel who were prepared to operate the ship in port and underway when she was commissioned.

Normally, a ship's in-port organization consists of four duty sections headed by the senior officer in the section as the principal assistant for organizing, manning and training duty section personnel. Each section is assigned in-port duty in successive section daily rotation. If the ship's company is organized into four sections, duty is assigned every fourth day or "one-in-four."

In port, a ship is under the control of a command duty officer (CDO), who reports directly to the CO and is the principal assistant to the XO. The CDO is qualified to get the ship underway in an emergency, such as a hurricane evasion, aiding a ship in distress at sea, or a combat situation.

Anyone who has seen a movie about old Navy sailing-ship sea battles knows that the ship's quarterdeck is where the swashbuckling captain, sword and pistol in hand, directs his men's valiant efforts to fight his ship and vanquish the enemy alongside.

The 21st century quarterdeck is absent the cannon shot of old and the blood and gore of dead and wounded. In today's Navy, the quarterdeck has a more prosaic function: to direct and control the ship's in-port activities. The officer of the deck executes the ship's plan of the day (POD), which schedules the daily routine and all major shipboard events, such as working parties to load provisions and supplies; major ship repairs; material or personnel inspections; training events; meetings; and ship visitors. The One MC on the quarterdeck is used to make event announcements to the crew and render honors to flag and other officers on ceremonial occasions.

Although the modern ship's quarterdeck lacks the glory of bygone eras, its importance remains. On this watch station a naval surface warfare officer will experience the burdens of responsibility for the operation, safety and security of the ship. His countless hours spent on the quarterdeck will serve the line officer well in preparation for command at sea. But Hollywood notwithstanding, the quarterdeck officer—the OOD—now wears his sword only for ceremonial events— and cake cutting.

Pensacola's construction was completed during one of the coldest winters in New England's history. We endured below-freezing weather in the Boston area for a record sixty consecutive days as well as a record number of inches of snowfall.

Our home had a spacious living room with a large fireplace and beautiful view of Little Harbor. The house was owned by a retired Navy captain—the former CEO of the Quincy shipyard. When they relocated to

Chicago, he and his wife decided to rent their home, fully furnished, during their children's school year, and return for the summer. Luckily, they would be gone the same nine months we planned to live in Cohasset. Our realtor had shown us the property in passing, not expecting us to rent it because of the cost. We loved it and were thrilled when our low offer was accepted.

We quickly learned to enjoy the winter climate and ice-skating on a nearby frozen pond. Linda, Jack and Judy made it look very easy and graceful. They laughed at my unintended acrobatics, especially when Ginger, our year-old golden retriever, ran circles around us and leaped on me in excitement. Jack became skilled at sledding down the long hill near our home, careening onto our snow-covered driveway and onto our narrow pier on the harbor's banks.

In warmer weather, we enjoyed walks along the beach, with Ginger plunging into the chilly ocean to retrieve sticks. One spring day while Jack was exploring in the woods near our house, he found some old bottles, so he got library books on the subject and went on to gather an impressive collection.

The house had an art studio where Linda enjoyed oil painting. Judy took ballet lessons. Ice hockey was very popular in the area and all the boys tried to imitate Boston Bruin's hero Bobby Orr. Jack joined a hockey team and in addition to practicing on the frozen pond, he and I would get up at 4 a.m. for his team's 5 a.m. scheduled practice in the local ice rink ("ice time"); his efforts paid off when his team won their league championship.

We visited the Boston area's historic sites: North Church, the USS *Constitution* and Plymouth Rock. And we enjoyed a visit by my parents for *Pensacola*'s commissioning. We have many fond memories of our time in Cohasset.

Following successful pier-side testing of all systems and the engineering plant light-off (fire in the boilers generating steam for the main engines and generators, producing the ship's electricity), *Pensacola* was ready for her initial sea trials.

On a cold, dark morning in February 1971, with shipyard and Supships personnel and all the officers in the nucleus crew embarked, *Pensacola* got underway for the first time.

¡El Capitán!

On the bridge, the captain and I felt the ship's decks come alive with vibrations as she backed away from the quay wall and sailed down the Quincy River, through Boston Harbor and out to sea under the civilian master's expert conning. The captain and I observed how she rode in the seaway, how she felt and handled at different speeds, how she turned, and how she sailed. It felt great to be on a ship at sea again.

The shipyard personnel put *Pensacola* through her paces, observing and recording data on her performance. She was maneuvered at various speeds ahead and astern to test her engines and throttles, and her watertight integrity. Her helm, rudders, and steering systems were tested from the bridge and at her alternate steering station, deep in the ship's stern. Her speed was increased to full throttle—22 knots—for two hours, then abruptly reversed full astern, a "crash back," severely testing the main engines, boilers and rudders.

And then we anchored in Boston harbor, opened the stern gate, flooded the dock and tested the ballasting/de-ballasting system.

In March 1971, the Navy Board of Inspection and Survey boarded to observe *Pensacola*'s acceptance trials with the nucleus crew and other officers and key enlisted personnel from the balance crew embarked.

After successful sea trials, *Pensacola* returned to port and moored at the Boston Naval Shipyard. In the wardroom the board briefed General Dynamics and Supships on the results, handed the shipbuilder a list of discrepancies to be corrected, and stated that the Navy would accept *Pensacola*. Supships handed a General Dynamics representative a substantial check, and signed a document assigning security of *Pensacola* to the prospective commanding officer.

We immediately posted the in-port duty section and *Pensacola*'s initial quarterdeck watch. A ship's working party loaded damage control equipment, mattresses and bedding, and prepared berthing for the duty section. The next day we commenced loading provisions.

The captain directed the Exec to execute the movement order and bring the balance crew to the ship from Little Creek; they arrived two days later and the nucleus and balance crews merged into the ship's company.

The captain is the catalyst for the ship's company, blending its different personalities and talents into a unified team. His character, personality and leadership style have a huge influence on his crew. By precept and example, he sets the performance standards and the tone and tenor for his command, creating its corporate personality—its "command climate."

His control and influence over his subordinates are unequalled in any other organizations, civilian or military. His power and prestige are exemplified by the fact that he is literally referred to by his ship's name. When the captain arrives at, or departs from his ship, the OOD directs the sounding of four bells over the ship's One MC and announces, "*Pensacola* Arriving!" or "*Pensacola* Departing!"

In the business world, an organization's top management is known collectively as the board of directors. In the Navy, the wardroom officers are the key leadership unit. A major difference is that board members are simply hired and can depart at any time, while naval officers hold a commission from the President of the United States to support and defend our Constitution and serve for obligated periods.

Each member of the wardroom has a distinctive character, personality, intelligence, education, ethnicity, religion, regional background, experience level—and leadership style. Some officers are on their second or third sea tour, and some are newly commissioned.

By their key roles and seniority, the XO and department heads significantly affect the wardroom's character. Through their sheer numbers, the junior and warrant officers have a major influence on wardroom's spirit.

The officers' wives also contribute to the wardroom's personality. Many junior officers' wives are unfamiliar with the Navy; it makes a big difference if a young couple have children or are expecting their first child—especially when the ship is scheduled for an extended overseas deployment.

While it is ultimately the captain's responsibility, the XO maintains harmony in the wardroom. But regardless of the circumstances, officers are legally bound to execute their responsibilities to the best of their abilities.

Like George Washington's "band of brothers" (his revolutionary war staff), the officers must stand and work together, even though personality clashes may occur. In top-performing ships—winners of the battle efficiency "E" for excellence—the wardroom and the chiefs' mess have a pervasive spirit of synergistic teamwork oriented toward successful mission accomplishment. They strive to excel.

¡El Capitán!

Each ship's company department was responsible for its own fitting out with spare parts and material, such as portable test equipment, special equipment, tools, instruments and consumables, such as office supplies, navigation charts for the bridge and CIC, paint, and lubricants. Since she was the third ship of her class to be delivered to the Navy, *Pensacola*'s allowance of material and spare parts had been standardized and pre-positioned at the Boston Naval Shipyard supply center. Working parties loaded and stowed each item securely in its designated place. We topped off the ship's fuel tanks. Each day we increased *Pensacola*'s readiness for sea.

As the operations officer, I was responsible for coordinating with the department heads, the XO, the CO and the Atlantic Fleet Amphibious Force Commander's staff to develop our annual employment schedule, accounting for each ship-day in port and at sea. The ship's company planning board for training, headed by the XO with all heads of department, is the principal shipboard organization for coordinating the schedule development and implementation.

After fitting-out, our employment schedule included commissioning in Boston Naval Shipyard, ammunition load-out in New Jersey, and two weeks of upkeep in Little Creek, our homeport.

Pensacola was commissioned on March 27, 1971, with many blanketed guests seated on her flight deck in near-freezing temperatures, including my parents. It was their first time on a Navy ship.

Commissioning marked the commencement of *Pensacola*'s service with the Navy's operating forces as a unit of Amphibious Squadron Four in the Atlantic Fleet. The Secretary of the Navy's order placing a ship on active service is symbolized by its commissioning pennant. The pennant is blue at the hoist with a union of seven white stars and the fly is composed of two horizontal red and white stripes. At the moment of breaking the pennant (hoisting it on the ship's mast), the ship becomes the responsibility of the commanding officer. Traditionally, the commissioning pennant is replaced with a new one at each change of command, and the outgoing CO is presented with the pennant that was flown during his tour.

When a squadron commander or an admiral is embarked, the commissioning pennant is replaced by a commodore's broad command pennant or the admiral's star flag respectively, signifying that it is his flagship.

Captain John Frank Gamboa, U. S. Navy (Retired)

The pennant is believed to date from the 17th century when the Dutch were at war with the English, and the Dutch admiral hoisted a broom to his flagship's masthead to indicate his intentions of sweep the English from the sea. This gesture was answered by the British admiral, who hoisted a horsewhip, signaling his intention to subdue the Dutch. The British were victorious and ever since, the narrow "coach whip" pennant has been used as the distinctive pennant of a commissioned ship in the British and American navies.

In early April, *Pensacola* sailed out of Boston Harbor, proceeded to an ammunition depot in New Jersey to fill its magazines, and then continued on to Little Creek. It was exhilarating to be operating our brand new ship and working together as her first crew.

Two weeks later, we got underway for our "shakedown cruise" and sailed down the east coast and around Florida to the city of Pensacola to participate in its annual Gasparilla Festival, celebrating the city's sovereignty under five flags since its founding in the 17th century (Spain, France, England, U.S., and our civil war confederacy).

In a wardroom ceremony, the mayor and city officials presented *Pensacola* with a commemorative silver service, which we proudly displayed in a wardroom showcase. Many visitors toured the ship, and the crew enjoyed the city.

All private-sector companies have a product, either a manufactured item or a service. So does a Navy ship's company—its product is readiness, a measure of its preparedness to accomplish its mission. A Navy ship's readiness is evaluated daily by the CO and periodically by outside independent organizations, and reported to higher authority. Evaluations include material and systems conditions and crew performance in shipboard tasks, drills and exercises from the small-unit team level to performance and complexity at the highest levels of engagement. My job was to coordinate the attainment of *Pensacola*'s required level of readiness.

As a newly commissioned naval ship, we needed to be trained to work as various teams in every facet of *Pensacola*'s capabilities as soon as possible. This is the fundamental purpose of "shakedown" training for a new ship. Our shakedown would consist of six weeks of training.

Because of crew rotation and before she deploys overseas, a ship also undergoes 2-3 weeks of refresher training called Reftra.

Upon the ship's return to Little Creek, we prepared *Pensacola* for shakedown. We assigned the crew to the watch, quarter and station bill and Condition III watch sections in which each section has personnel sufficient to operate approximately one third of the ship's weapon systems. Condition III is set when a ship is in a high-threat area, but not facing imminent combat, enabling the ship to respond rapidly to emerging threats while allowing for routine crew work and rest, facilitating the ship's rapid transition to battle stations if necessary.

The general quarters (GQ) bill, also called the battle bill, is implemented when the ship expects to engage in combat action or to respond to a major emergency such as a shipboard fire, a collision with another ship, or grounding. When a ship is at GQ, she is fully manned with all weapon and sensor systems ready for action and repair parties prepared to conduct damage control. There is no rotation on stations during GQ; it is the crew's most physically demanding readiness posture. "Now, General Quarters, General Quarters! All hands man your battle stations! Set condition Zebra!"

Guantanamo Bay (Gitmo) is a large harbor on the east coast of Cuba. Its size, depth and unrestricted offshore sea areas make it an ideal training site for the fleet. The U.S. Navy leased the bay and surrounding territorial sea area from Cuba in the early 20th century and established there a fleet training group (FTG) to conduct underway training for Navy ships in the Atlantic Fleet (the Pacific FTG is in San Diego). It is not a Sailor's favorite port of call; in fact, the chorus of an old fleet barroom ballad goes like this:

> "So, hurrah for old Gitmo on Cuba's fair shore,
> The home of the cockroach, the flea and the whore,
> We'll sing of her praises and pray for the day
> We'll get the hell out of Guantanamo Bay."

My first visit to Gitmo was in the summer of '55 as a youngster on board the heavy cruiser *Des Moines*. The days were hot, humid, and uncomfortable, especially during training exercises. Almost 16 years later, I found that nothing had changed.

After *Pensacola* anchored, a large contingent of FTG trainers—"ship riders"—(mostly senior enlisted personnel) arrived by launch to drill the ship's general quarters teams. Waiting in the wardroom were our officers, chiefs, and leading petty officers. The FTG team leader briefed us on how the training would be conducted, the number of required drills for each department, and our overall schedule. And then the ship sounded GQ and we commenced our first "walk-through" drills, at anchor under supervision of the riders.

For the next six weeks we trained in every facet of *Pensacola*'s capabilities, including gun firing, alongside replenishment, personnel transfer by highline, towing another ship, being towed, engineering casualty control, defending against ship and aircraft attacks, suppressing fires, control of flooding, and providing first aid to wounded personnel. "Sir, the helmsman has a sucking chest wound!"

During GQ, we conducted battle messing consisting of box lunches and fruit-flavored punch ("bug juice") at battle stations, provided by "runners" to each GQ station.

Each department had to successfully accomplish a standard set of training exercises. Our typical training day started at 0600. By 0730, the ship was at special sea and anchor detail ready to get underway, and at short stay (the anchor chain hauled in, tending up and down and the anchor flukes ready to break ground).

GQ was sounded as soon as the FTG ship riders were on station. We got underway for a full day of drills at sea, returning to our anchorage in the evening after a long day of intense training. Each rider, accompanied by a ship's team leader, went to the bridge and briefed the captain on the type of drills conducted, team deficiencies and strengths, and the corrective actions required before the next "ride."

The captain's reactions were consistent: we will do better next time—an expectation and an order. We were all tired, hungry and beaten down—and glad to see the riders depart each day. But we analyzed their written critiques to determine what went wrong. We made changes in our teams and procedures and resolved to get the drills right the next time. But during our first four weeks at Gitmo, it seemed like there was no light at the end of the tunnel.

I tracked our progress, compiled all the drill results at the end of each training day and submitted a message summary to the FTG. Then I coordinated the next-day's drill schedule and riders; and the services, such as aircraft for radar tracking or a ship for towing. I was up at dawn and fell into my bunk long after taps.

Our "graduation exercise" consisted of a full-scale battle problem at sea, defending ourselves against air and surface attacks, restoring battle damage, controlling flooding and fires, and providing aid to our wounded. Six weeks after our arrival, we completed our shakedown with a grade of "excellent."

We arrived at Little Creek three days later, happy to be reunited with our families. After two weeks in port, we returned to sea for two weeks of amphibious training, learning how to execute our primary control ship (PCS) mission. We trained offshore at Little Creek, with our weekends in homeport, so the pace was much less arduous than at Gitmo. We completed all our training requirements with top grades.

The last two major events in *Pensacola*'s development into a warship fully ready for fleet operations were her final contract sea trials and shipyard availability at the Norfolk Naval Shipyard in Portsmouth to correct all material deficiencies and install the latest equipment upgrades and alterations. The sea trials, conducted by the board of inspection and survey, were our last opportunity to identify equipment problems that were the shipbuilder's responsibility to correct. The shipyard period was also a most welcome opportunity for crew rest, attending to family matters, and much-needed personnel time off.

Fourteen months after I reported to her building site, *Pensacola* was ready for fleet amphibious operations. It had been an intense period of hard work with little time for personal matters, families, recreation, and socializing.

The end of my tour was on the horizon and I began thinking about my next tour of duty. In order to achieve a warship command, I knew I could not spend the next two years ashore. I needed a "split-tour" (two consecutive sea duty assignments) and to "cross-deck" (transfer to another ship) to an XO billet in an amphibious ship, preferably LSD.

In December 1971, I contacted my detailer, a classmate and good friend, Cdr. Ray Williams, and explained my desires. Ray was supportive, but said that XO slots on LSDs were commander billets, and I wouldn't be in the zone for selection to commander until the following year. But he agreed that I was fully qualified and that a split tour would enhance my career. He would have a look see and get back to me.

About a week later, Ray called and said that a commander XO billet had unexpectedly opened up in an amphibious landing platform dock ship (LPD), very similar to an LSD, and a relief was urgently required.

If I agreed, Ray would cut my orders. I enthusiastically accepted and asked if it was homeported in San Diego. Laughing, Ray said, "Oh, it's much further west than that, Frank. It's in the Persian Gulf!"

On December 27, 1971, I received orders to USS *La Salle* (LPD 3) for duty as executive officer. She was being re-designated as flagship (AGF) for commander, Middle East Force. Her new homeport was Bahrain, an Arabian island in the Persian Gulf.

Linda and I had an exciting dinnertime discussion with Jack and Judy about our new duty station, our forthcoming travel, and our future adventures in the Middle East. We opened our atlas and discovered that our new home was half-way around the world from Little Creek. I knew that *La Salle* would be of far greater significance to me than all my previous sea tours—she could be a precursor to a warship command.

In March 1972, I departed *Pensacola*. The commanding officer's evaluation of my fitness was gratifying.

> LCDR Gamboa's careful attention to every detail throughout the many ship evolutions ... demonstrated an outstanding management capability, both in personnel and materiel ... a hard-working, intelligent officer who leaves nothing to chance and is always completely in control of the situation.... Despite his rank, LCDR Gamboa was required to stand OOD watches underway throughout most of his tour.... He demonstrated that his seamanship ability matched his outstanding administrative ability. LCDR Gamboa, with his wife, is a credit to Pensacola and the Navy. He is highly recommended for command, and promotion to next higher rank.

My *Pensacola* tour was a major turning point in my development as a naval surface warfare officer. I learned the basics of naval ship construction, how to crew a ship, how to fit out and prepare a new ship to join the fleet, and how to train a ship's crew. I rounded out my knowledge of ship's company organization, management, and administration.

Pensacola marked my transition to the amphibious force from the destroyer force. I learned the LSD's role in an amphibious assault and commenced the development of my expertise in amphibious warfare. Most important, I came away with the knowledge and skills required to achieve and maintain a high level of ship's readiness.

On the morning of May 26, 1972, with keen anticipation I drove to Norfolk Naval Base where *La Salle* was berthed. At the head of her pier was the first indicator of my new status: next to the captain's was my parking sign: PXO (prospective executive officer) *La Salle*. Gone forever were my frantic searches for waterfront parking.

She looked impressive in her glaring white paint—a unique requirement to help keep her internal temperature cool in the extreme Arabian heat.

As I climbed the accommodation ladder, two loud bells sounded over the ship's One MC. "Lieutenant Commander, United States Navy, Arriving!" I saluted the colors (American flag) and stepped proudly onto the quarterdeck. Returning the OOD's smart salute, I handed him a copy of my orders, "Reporting for duty, sir!" The OOD replied, "Welcome aboard, Commander. Messenger, escort Mr. Gamboa to the executive officer's cabin."

I had been an officer of the line for 14 years—more than eight years at sea in four different ships. I knew my new billet. Four days later, I relieved the incumbent and assumed duties as *La Salle*'s executive officer.

La Salle was the third LPD built and the first configured as an amphibious flagship. Her length was 520 feet (40 feet shorter than *Pensacola*) with an 84-foot beam, a displacement of 13,900 tons, and a top speed of 21 knots. She was similar to the LSD Class, but with a larger helo deck (two landing spots) and berthing spaces for 800 troops. She had one crane on her main deck on the starboard side forward of the flight deck. Her flag bridge and flag plot were beneath the ship's bridge. Her dock was about two-thirds the length of *Pensacola*'s, and had no mezzanine deck. Instead, she had a large two-deck vehicle and cargo storage area forward of the dock. Fitted on the dock's overhead were six manned mobile crane cars for loading and unloading cargo in amphibious landing craft.

During *La Salle*'s five-month shipyard availability, a helicopter hangar was erected on the port side forward of the fight deck. A large pipe framework was constructed alongside the hangar, over the forward helo spot, and rigged with a white canvas awning to provide a ceremonial area shielded from the sun. The ship's air conditioning capacity had been doubled, a two-chair dental facility was installed, and the external satellite communications systems were upgraded.

She was fitted with a complete TV broadcasting studio and a closed-circuit TV system throughout the ship. Part of the troop berthing space was converted into a large ship's store. Her flag staff offices, ship's work centers and crew berthing spaces were refurbished. And to prepare for their future homeport, the crew and their families were screened to ensure they were healthy and emotionally stable for conditions in Bahrain.

Captain Jim Morin, a naval aviator, was *La Salle*'s CO. He was an outstanding leader and a very personable individual with several aviation commands under his belt, but this was his first ship command. (Amphibious ship COs included aviators and diesel submariners as well as surface warfare officers. Those who had no amphibious shipboard experience were paired with XOs who did.)

Our priority task was to prepare for the ship and families' departure for Bahrain. Wives and children had to obtain passports, get inoculations, and arrange air travel to Bahrain. Household goods and automobiles would be transported in our dock, saving Navy travel funds.

Families were encouraged to purchase non-perishable food and household items that would not be available or costly on the island. Their purchases would be shipped along with their household goods.

Linda planned and purchased one year of groceries in case lots at the base commissary. They were labeled, palletized, and delivered directly to the ship. We also had to go over our wardrobes to be sure we had sufficient clothing for our year in Bahrain. There was no Navy exchange or commissary and shopping "on the economy" would not meet our needs or budget.

We had a new Ford station wagon. For some obscure political reason, neither Fords, Coca Cola, nor Frank Sinatra records were permitted in Bahrain. We sold our car at a loss and special-ordered a new Chevy Malibu sedan with a "stick-shift," as recommended. We chose a white interior to reflect the heat and an appropriate exterior color—oasis green. Once more, a loan from our trusty Navy Federal Credit Union got us through all these extra expenses.

Throughout our preparations for Bahrain, Linda and I kept in touch with our families, about our pending departure. One evening I phoned

Mom and Dad. When Dad got on the phone he asked, *"Es la despedida?"* Is this farewell? I replied, *"No, Papa, toda via no!"* No, Dad, not yet.

Two weeks later, just as we were walking into our kitchen from an evening shopping trip, the phone rang. It was my sister Tina—Dad had suffered a fatal heart attack. I hung up the phone and turned tearfully to Linda, "I had so many things I wanted to tell him!"

The next day I flew to Los Angeles and accompanied Mom and my brothers, sisters, their spouses and children to Lone Pine for Teodulo's funeral. On a beautiful Sunday afternoon on June 17, 1972 at his graveside, I delivered Dad's eulogy. It was Father's Day.

Duty in *La Salle* was designated a hardship tour (13 months) and a call was issued Navy-wide for volunteers. This created significant crew turnover; we needed two weeks of refresher training at Gitmo. On June 23, *La Salle* departed Norfolk and shaped course for Cuba. After a busy two-week Reftra at Gitmo, we sailed for Dakar, Senegal, our first stop on a seven-week voyage across the Atlantic, around Africa, through the Indian Ocean to our new homeport.

A ship's readiness and morale depend in part on stability and predictability within its working environment. I was responsible for directing the daily routine and work to be scheduled, performed and supervised. The large number of daily matters requiring my attention necessitated a prioritized to-do list and delegating effectively to my subordinates; I found it enjoyable to empower people. My staff and I and the department heads worked hard to create a ship's routine with an efficient flow of work and activities.

My top management function was developing and coordinating the ship's plan of the day with the daily schedule of events, notices and announcements. I depended on timely input from department heads and my own staff. The ship's secretary, Warrant Officer Birkumshaw—a big, burly former submariner who loved riding his Harley—drafted the POD, coordinating with me and the other departments throughout the day to get the latest word.

I met with members of my staff and others frequently throughout the day, focusing on matters requiring the captain's personal attention and items with deadlines.

Captain John Frank Gamboa, U. S. Navy (Retired)

I inspected the crew's berthing and messing spaces at 1030 every weekday, accompanied by a yeoman and the chief master at arms, with the division officers and/or LPOs standing by in their respective spaces.

A good berthing and messing inspection is vital to the ship's cleanliness, sanitation, and crew morale. Are the urinals and toilets in good working condition, scrubbed clean, and odor-free? Shower curtains in good condition, free of soap scum? Any plumbing problems? Do berthing compartment and heads have sufficient supplies?

Is the crew sleeping on clean sheets and pillow cases, and are the Sailors properly making up their bunks? Ship's laundry doing a good job? Decks clean, scuff-free, waxed and buffed? Any problems with the air conditioning or heating? Is any damage control equipment missing or not functional?

These daily inspections provided me reliable assessments of command efficiency. Through my daily rounds, I also learned if the LPOs, the chiefs, the division officers and the department head were looking after their people. And I obtained good "deck-plate" intelligence about the crew's concerns. If I asked the right questions in a straightforward manner, our Sailors would tell me everything I needed to know, thereby gaining a reliable indication of *La Salle*'s morale.

My daily inspections and look see about the ship had a greater lasting value to my effectiveness than a lot of my paper pushing.

I also enjoyed inspecting the crews' mess, evaluating the health, grooming and cleanliness of the mess men and the cleanliness and sanitation of the food preparation and serving areas. Occasionally, I sampled the food on the serving line, even though I assigned a junior officer to sample the crew's meals daily and submit an evaluation sheet to the commissary officer.

Our supply officer, Lt. Cdr. Lew Bryan, USNA '61—a personable Georgian—knew that I liked chili, and one day it was on the menu. In anticipation, Lew instructed his mess chief to set a full bowl aside, garnished with cheese and onions just the way I liked it, but to keep it out of sight for a surprise at the end of my inspection.

Well, I was on a tear that morning, being very thorough and rather grumpy. I even got down on my hands and knees to inspect underneath the steam tables with my flashlight.

"Ah ha! You found the dumb dirt out on the open areas, but you missed the smart dirt hiding under here in the dark!" Everyone reacted with shock, dismay and embarrassment, especially the chief. I concluded my inspection with a frown and departed the mess decks feeling self-satisfied, even a bit smug. "They can't fool the XO!"

That afternoon Lew dropped by my cabin to inform me that all the "smart dirt" had been removed from the mess decks. And then, grinning widely and with great delight, he described how his chief had quietly slid my surprise bowl of chili out of sight, and had dumped it down the garbage grinder when I departed. There is a lot of spirited give and take in running a Navy ship.

A Navy ship's crew averages less than 20 years of age among the first-term enlisted; many energetic, inexperienced Sailors—every day is a new adventure. The Navy's goal is to have each crewmember develop professionally, mature and be a better Sailor by the time he completes his tour; their shipmates should regret his leaving rather than feel that "losing him is like gaining two!"

But youth and exuberance leads inevitably to some missteps, which must be dealt with quickly and fairly ("justice delayed is justice denied"). Bi-weekly adjudication of regulation infractions was conducted in my cabin (XO's screening mast). I reviewed misconduct report "chits" (forms) submitted by a petty officer, chief, or officer. The offenses varied: late returning from liberty, poor military grooming, worn and tattered uniform, etc. More serious offenses included failing to carry out a lawful order, dereliction of duty, possession or use of illegal substances, intoxication, disorderly conduct, fighting, assault, theft, absent without leave, and missing ship's movement.

Assembled in my cabin would be the person "on report" (the accused), his division officer, division chief, LPO, witnesses, and the accuser. I would hear testimony, ask questions, and evaluate the facts and circumstances. If I deemed the report valid in all respects, I would refer the case to a captain's mast (a non-judicial hearing). In some instances, I would recommend to the commanding officer that the case be tried by a summary courts martial. I also had authority to dismiss the offense—a rare occurrence. Although time-consuming, my screening masts provided me another vital insight on the state of crew morale and our command climate.

Captain John Frank Gamboa, U. S. Navy (Retired)

Captain's mast required the presence of the chain of command of the individual on report, plus the accused, the witnesses, the chief master at arms, me and the commanding officer. Punishment "awarded" at mast ranged from restriction to the limits of the ship, a monetary fine, a reduction in rate, or any combination thereof. Sometimes the accused was sent to the brig for up to three days on "reduced rations" (bread and water—or as the Sailors called it, "piss and punk"). Sometimes the captain suspended the punishment for up to six months, depending on good behavior.

In very rare instances, the case was dismissed. This felicitous outcome required a very creative yet credible story by the accused. Some Sailors are very skilled in this regard. Mast results were effective immediately and published in the next plan of the day.

To ensure that all our departments (air, communications, deck, dental, engineering, executive, medical, navigation, operations, and supply) were on the same page, I scheduled a department head meeting each week in my cabin with a coordinated agenda, which was normally limited to one hour. Everyone was pressed for time—a navy ship runs on deadlines.

Our meetings were characterized by friendly, spirited banter and were among my most enjoyable professional interactions. Teamwork had its genesis in these meetings, and the cooperation, harmony and ship's spirit displayed by the department heads reverberated throughout the decks.

The meetings were valuable to me in another way. The quality of the officers' preparation and participation were reliable indicators of their leadership abilities, management style, attention to administrative detail and control of their respective departments. By observing their behavior and performance (and by counseling them in private as necessary), I was able to assist the captain in making balanced judgments about their professional abilities, capabilities and potential (the officers' fitness). I drafted fitness reports on department heads and my executive staff, and I reviewed all other reports.

At sea, a naval ship's bridge is the command's operations center. The captain is on-call 24 hours a day and often deprived of sleep. Yet the administration and management of his command are continuous. Despite his constant burdens of command, the captain cannot permit himself to be bogged down in details or pre-occupy himself with matters that should be handled by the XO or department heads. Proper delegation, and holding the officers accountable, are the most important keys to successful command.

The captain depends on the XO and the department heads to keep him informed in a timely fashion on matters requiring his attention, so they met individually with him after morning quarters (or any time on urgent matters) to discuss action items, first running things by me for a "sanity check."

I met with him on administrative matters, such as preparations for the forthcoming enlisted promotion examinations, which officers' fitness reports were due next, or captain's mast cases. I monitored the issues awaiting the captain's decision. When I felt that he had sufficient information and time to make a decision, I would approach him, "Captain, what are your desires in this matter, sir?"

Going to the bridge also permitted me to gauge the tempo of ship operations, observe the bridge team in action, and relax over a cup of coffee, courtesy of the boatswain's mate of the watch. It was refreshing to gaze for a few moments at the sea and the sky and fill my lungs with fresh sea air. And chatting with the officers and Sailors always lifted my spirits.

The taking of eight o'clock reports was my last meeting of the day with the department heads and my staff. I ensured complete understanding of the new plan of the day, and then I made my report to the captain on the bridge or in his sea cabin, "All secure, sir!"

La Salle had 10 days of smooth sailing across the Atlantic, arriving at Dakar, Senegal, for a brief visit. We then sailed down to Monrovia, Liberia, for another two-day visit and then on to Abidjan, Ivory Coast, for our last port of call on the west coast of Africa.

We crossed the equator at the prime meridian (latitude 00, longitude 00)—a rare occurrence for a U. S. Navy ship. Neptunus Rex, Ruler of the Raging Main, together with Davy Jones, his majesty's scribe, and his royal court, were welcomed aboard by the captain, who requested leniency for his outstanding crew. But King Neptune promptly denied the CO's request and he and his royal court proceeded to initiate all pollywogs—those poor souls who had never crossed the equator—into the solemn mysteries of the ancient order of the deep. Our trusty shellbacks assisted in initiating the "slimy wogs."

Captain John Frank Gamboa, U. S. Navy (Retired)

In all my sea voyages, I was concerned about Linda, Jack and Judy. I thought about their safety and well-being on their flights to Bahrain, their first travel to the Middle East. I sent Linda a telegram, "Hi honey, hope you are all fine and ready to leave for our new home. We are doing fine, except for a boiler problem, which will delay our arrival until the 23rd, but, don't change your plans. Send telegram to Griffin (my classmate on the admiral's staff in Bahrain) giving flight number and date/time of arrival. Send me a telegram when you leave. Have a fun trip see you soon. Love, Frank."

On August 21, I received Linda's reply, "After ticket trouble and re-routing, being stranded in Beirut, and losing our luggage, we are finally in Bahrain. All problems now resolved. We are all fine and happy to be in Bahrain at last. It really looks lovely. Life's beautiful—my cup is full. I love you. See you on the 23rd at noon. Linda."

After we were reunited in Bahrain, I learned the details. Their first planned stop was London for a two-day layover for sight-seeing. Traveling with our cat, they were advised in New York that the cat would be euthanized upon its arrival at London.

Linda proceeded to reschedule their trip with a brief stop at Heathrow airport. The NY officials had her running with the kids and the cat from one office to another, finally agreeing to permit them to board their flight after she signed a statement absolving the airport of responsibility for allowing the cat to go to England. (She was ill advised; when they were changing flights at Heathrow, the lady processing her tickets asked Linda why they weren't touring England for a few days. Linda said, "We wanted to but you will euthanize our cat! With a shocked look, the attendant replied "Oh my good heavens, that is not so!" But it was too late to reschedule.)

With no direct flights to Bahrain, they wound up in Beirut. The American Embassy was under siege, barricaded and encircled with barbed wire. There were no immediate flights to Bahrain so they had to get a hotel room for two days. It had no bed linen or towels, and their luggage had gone elsewhere—but they had the cat.

When they finally got to their hotel in Bahrain, they were each suffering from a stomach ailment. And after we moved into our quarters the cat disappeared. (We got the kids a new kitten-a beautiful black real Persian cat that Judy named Papa Tango for putty tat.)

Navy wives are very special. And a cut above.

¡El Capitán!

After a two-month voyage, *La Salle* arrived at Bahrain and was greeted by our families on Mina Salman pier in 110-degree heat and high humidity. (The daily temperature averaged 135 degrees during the "hot" season.) Rear Admiral Bayne and his staff embarked as soon as the brow was down. The first lieutenant had the automobiles unloaded and for our first two weeks in our new homeport, we were all very busy reuniting with our families and finding housing.

Most of the families stayed in the Dilmun Hotel in Manama while we waited to move into our new homes. Lt. Joe Breslin, the ship's doctor, made daily rounds at the hotel, checking temperatures and dispensing Lomotil, "the miracle pill" to the families, most of whom had fallen ill with a local stomach virus ("the creeping crud.")

Many *La Salle* families simply took over the houses or apartments of our predecessors, from the USS *Valcour*. As soon as homes were available, the ship unloaded the personal household goods and pallets of groceries and delivered them to each family's residence. Linda and I rented one of five houses in Manama in a high-walled compound. Our neighbors were four other Navy families, and a British doctor and his wife.

Linda managed our move-in and unpacking while I ensured that the admiral and his staff were settling comfortably aboard *La Salle*. Linda enrolled Judy and Jack, in 2nd and 3rd grades respectively, in the Defense Overseas Dependent School at Jufair, the former British naval base, taken over by the U.S. Navy.

She also hired a Persian houseboy, Abdul Latif Nasrulla, "Abdullah," father of 11 children, who said his "father had 12, so Abdullah himself must bring one dozen!" He had worked for our predecessors. He and Linda quickly established a great working relationship. He did all the grocery shopping, made sure we always had fresh, filtered water, kept the air conditioners in good working order, and paid our utilities bills.

Linda trusted him completely. She kept a brass bowl on top of the water heater in the kitchen filled with dollars and Abdullah would take what he needed. When the level of cash was low, she replenished it.

Linda did most of the home cooking, but Abdullah would often treat us to his delicious "shrimp najif," a recipe Linda learned from him and still prepares on special occasions. Our landlord, a big affable Arab, Ali Sulman, would drop by in his immaculate flowing white thobe and ghutra, often at dinnertime, so Linda always prepared enough to serve an extra plate, just in case. If she was serving pork, he asked that she just not mention what it was.

Bahrain, an independent sheikdom, was ruled by the emir, Sheikh Isa bin Salman Al Akhalifa. Five days after our arrival in Bahrain, *La Salle*'s wardroom was invited to a royal banquet at the Emir's palace on the occasion of a visit by the deputy supreme allied commander in Europe, a four-star U.S. Air Force general, and his wife. To guide the wardroom in the event, the flag secretary provided a two-page protocol memo.

> Arrive at Rafaa Palace at 1845. The officers will be in Mess Dress and the ladies in long gown with long sleeves.... After crossing the courtyard, you will walk through the large doors and into the main hallway. Directly ahead is the Majlis (a huge room for royal functions).... Walk down the center of the Majlis to where the Emir is seated (he will stand and shake hands), introduce yourself, and your lady (if applicable) including your organization—U.S. Navy. The Emir is addressed as "Your highness" and the ministers as "Your excellency."
>
> Following introductions proceed to the outer edge of the room where there will be rows of chairs.
>
> At 1900, General and Mrs. Burchinal and Rear Admiral and Mrs. Bayne will arrive in the Majlis.... After a short visit, the Emir will rise and escort the Burchinals and the Baynes to dinner. You will fall in behind as they pass.
>
> Before entering the dining room, you will stop briefly to wash your hands in rose water (offered in bowls by attendants). After entering the dining room, you will be motioned to a seat; there will be no seating chart or plan. During dinner, don't be surprised if no one talks to you. Arab custom dictates dinner is for eating, not socializing.
>
> At the conclusion of the dinner, the Emir will rise and escort the general and the admiral and their wives back to the Majlis for coffee.... Incense and rosewater will indicate that the banquet is over and the Emir will shortly be escorting the Burchinals and the Baynes to the door.... As you depart, thank whoever is saying farewell to the guests (either the Emir or his representative).

With slightly nervous anticipation, Linda and I entered the majlis and walked on what seemed like a mile-long long Persian carpet. We paused in front of the emir and introduced ourselves, "Good evening, your highness" as we had rehearsed. We seated ourselves and were served small cups of cardamom tea by dark-visage men in flowing Arabic robes.

After visiting briefly, the emir escorted the official party out of the majlis. We followed along, dipped our hands in the rosewater, and strolled across a courtyard and into a large, beautiful, brightly-lit banquet hall. A long, wide T-shaped banquet table was near overflowing with large platters of Saffron rice and bowls of vegetables, fruit and dates and whole roasted lambs—a scene right out of "Arabian Nights."

There were no Bahraini women at the event—or at any other social events with men while we were in Bahrain. (Our wives socialized with Bahraini women separately at the Sheikha Hessa's royal events).

We were seated at the banquet table, and just as we were wondering what to do next, one of our majlis cardamom tea servers leaned over Linda's shoulder and, in a Bahraini gesture of hospitality, tore hunks of meat off the nearest lamb with his bare hand and tossed them onto our dinner plates, properly initiating us in a feast which Middle East Old Hands call "a goat grab."

The primary mission of the commander, Middle East Force, was to promote goodwill, understanding, mutual respect and acceptance between the American people and people of countries visited by his ships—"showing the flag." *La Salle*'s cleanliness, "spit and polish" and smartness, especially on the quarterdeck, were the order of the day.

When we entered a port for an official visit, the crew manned the rail in sparkling whites. We fired a gun salute and received a reciprocal honor. After we moored at a pier or anchored, the admiral would make a round of calls on the American ambassador and local dignitaries and attend luncheons and dinners in his honor.

The officials would then make return calls on the admiral aboard *La Salle*. We paraded an honor guard (a platoon of enlisted men under arms led by a junior officer with sword), which was inspected by the senior guest. The VIPs then would be taken on a tour of the ship by the captain. Then the admiral hosted a luncheon or a dinner in his roomy, well-fitted cabin.

Our initial visit was to Kharg Island, the Iranian oil depot near the top of the Persian Gulf, my first professional and social encounter with Iranians, who were friendly and gracious hosts. Then we made a five-day visit to Port Victoria in the Seychelles islands to commemorate the 200th anniversary of its British sovereignty. Princess Margaret and her husband Lord Snowden represented the monarchy. *La Salle* had a marching unit in the official parade and Captain Morin and I were seated two rows in front of the royal couple; the captain met them at an evening reception.

Along with many of *La Salle*'s crew, I enjoyed touring the Tsavo game preserve during our visit to Mombasa, Kenya.

In October 1972, I was promoted to commander. Since I was serving in a commander's billet, Captain Morin immediately "frocked" me with three stripes. I could wear the insignia, but I wouldn't receive the pay raise until I "made my number" on the lineal list of officers the following spring.

When *La Salle* was in port, our workweek was Sunday through Thursday, with our weekend on Friday and Saturday consistent with Muslim custom. Linda, Jack, Judy and I adapted to the heat and again learned to live without television or radio. On weekends, we sometimes went on driving tours to explore the island, stopping occasionally among the burial mound ruins for "surface picking"—looking on the ground for artifacts such as pottery shards and beads. (Digging was not permitted.) We often joined other families for a swim in the Jufair pool, or went aboard *La Salle* for the evening movie.

The Emir had a private beach on the western coast of the island and extended *La Salle* families an open invitation. Elsewhere women had to have their arms and legs covered in public. We were at the beach one day when the emir was there entertaining guests in his private tent. One of Judy's friends had been given riding privileges on one of the emir's horses, and Judy wanted to do the same. Jackie said, "Just go ask him!" The next day, the emir sent two young Bahraini boys each leading a horse over to Jackie's house. Judy and Jackie enjoyed riding the spirited Arabians with the boys running alongside to catch them in case they fell off.

We occasionally went to the horse and camel races on Friday afternoons. In the Suq (Arab shopping district), we enjoyed many sights and sounds and the fragrance of exotic spices. The suq's narrow, twisting streets had shops with a variety of exotic offerings, reflecting Bahrain's importance as a trading center. I bought Linda beautiful 22-karat gold jewelry and gulf pearls.

We lived nearby and Jack enjoyed venturing into the Suq with his friends, or even alone, somehow finding his way back, bringing home interesting tales and treasures. Some evenings we stopped on a sidewalk to watch the bread making in outdoor clay ovens. The dough, shaped into discs like big fat tortillas, was tossed up onto the oven's domed ceiling over the flames of a wood fire. The aroma was delicious; customers would be lined up to buy fresh warm bread for their dinner.

At street-vendor stalls, we would purchase deep-fried sanbusaks, triangular buttery, flaky pastry filled with a spicy mix of potatoes and onions—a great snack with a bottle of Orange Crush.

When they departed Bahrain several months after we arrived, Rear Admiral Bayne's wife, Sybil, turned over the keys to her art studio at Jufair to Linda. It was a wonderful gesture, and turned out to be a great get-away for her with a window to the pool. She shared the space with other wives who wanted to paint.

The Jufair chiefs' club discovered Linda's artistic talents and three days before we departed Bahrain, they asked me if I could get her to paint a large seascape mural on a wall in their club. After exclaiming, "No way! I can't! I don't have time. We're getting ready to move!" she took on the arduous but exhilarating project and completed the huge seascape literally hours before we flew out.

Captain Morin's wife was ill and not able accompany him to Bahrain so Linda took on her leadership role among the *La Salle* wives. Together, we planned the wardroom's social activities and Linda managed the officers' wives social events.

Some of the wives traveled on their own while the ship was at sea, shopping and touring in the cities of Isfahan, Shiraz, and Tehran in Iran. In the summer of 1973, Linda, Jack and Judy planned to go with a good friend, another *La Salle* wife, Rosemary Bryan, and her two daughters on a trip to Athens, Greece, but shortly before their trip the Athens airport was bombed by terrorists. At the last minute, they changed their destination to Cyprus, and spent a week at the beach and another at the beautiful Hotel Berengaria high in the mountains. They toured the island including an ancient coliseum, a crusader castle, and a mosque in the armed and barricaded Turkish sector of the island.

Linda, Rosemary, and Dot Watson, the wife of the staff judge advocate, established a Girl Scout troop in Bahrain, each scout earning the rare troops on foreign soil (TOFS) badge. The troop was a first for Navy families in Bahrain. They also negotiated the use of a building at Jufair for the scout meetings, a thrift shop, and a co-op day care. The spaces needed refurbishing. "We need help painting; can the ship provide some Sailors?" I minced no words, "Absolutely not! We are very busy getting ready for our next voyage!" Dinner continued in silence.

The next day Linda and Dot came aboard *La Salle* and posted flyers around the ship enticing our Sailors to volunteer ("help paint an air-conditioned building; enjoy cookies and punch; bring your "boom boxes" and favorite music!"). Dot and Linda stopped by my cabin and cheerfully informed me of the great response—many Sailors had signed up to help! XOs are all-powerful, but they can be outsmarted.

Three days later, the first lieutenant, Bob Hagenbruch, also stopped by my cabin. He told me that most of his ordinary seamen were busy painting the new family community center at Jufair, so the ship's sides wouldn't get painted before we got underway. He could not compete with the cookies and lemonade served in an air-conditioned building.

Bob allowed that the captain would not be pleased that the sides would not look their best. With my sternest look, I replied that I would speak to Linda. Meanwhile, he'd better figure out how to do both, or so inform the captain. And so it came to pass that *La Salle* sailed with no unsightly rust streaks—and the Girl Scouts and wives enjoyed their freshly painted multi-purpose center.

In November, *La Salle* participated in an annual sea exercise called Mid-Link, which required that we visit the Iranian naval base at Bandar Abbas along with ships from Iran, France, the U.K., and Pakistan. The day after exercise ended, the captain had to make a departure-call on the Iranian admiral before our departure, but in order to reach Bahrain in daylight; *La Salle* had to get underway prior to the captain's return. "XO, get her underway and I'll fly back aboard along the ship's track in an hour." The evolution went smoothly. It was the first time I got a ship underway without the captain on board.

In December, Captain Morin went on leave for three weeks, so I was acting commanding officer. We hosted the admiral's change of command, welcoming our new boss, Rear Admiral Robert Hanks. Captain Morin returned the end of December and was relieved in January 1973 by Captain Howard Crosby, an Academy graduate diesel submariner. Soon after, Linda traveled to India and Pakistan with several *La Salle* wives, including the captain's wife, Phyllis Crosby, who had just arrived on the island, leaving Jack and Judy plus the Crosby's three children in the care of Abdullah.

¡El Capitán!

After departing *La Salle*, Jim commanded an aircraft carrier and subsequently was promoted to rear admiral. My fitness report from him said, "CDR Gamboa has performed his duties as executive officer in a completely outstanding manner. He is a tireless worker, dedicated to the betterment of the welfare of the crew.... An extremely organized individual, scheduling his myriad tasks most effectively, keeping always on top of the situation and not missing a step. He is, in the fullest sense, the captain's right arm, anticipating problem areas, using his excellent judgment in all situations. He is recommended for promotion and increasing responsibilities."

In February, *La Salle* got underway to participate in the Imperial Ethiopian Navy Days at Massawa hosted by Emperor Haile Selassie, whose small fleet consisted of several coastal patrol craft. The Lion of Judah (one of the emperor's several titles) invited countries with naval ships operating in the Indian Ocean. *La Salle* joined ships from Iran, India, France, Pakistan, Saudi Arabia, the Soviet Union, the U.K. and Ethiopia. The ships were all moored at the same crowded pier, with the French ship berthed between *La Salle* and the Soviet destroyer, creating a diplomatic buffer between the two Cold War adversaries.

The festivities included reciprocal visits to all the ships by the admirals, sports events among all the ships' teams, a race by boats with oars, and a day at sea (Sea Dog Day) with guests embarked for ship joint maneuvers. Admiral Hanks called on the emperor and each ship, including the Soviets, hosting and attending many luncheons and dinner parties. I hosted a luncheon in *La Salle*'s wardroom with two officer guests from each ship including the Russians, and led them on a tour of the ship.

I suggested to the two Russian officers that, in the spirit of friendship, we conduct tours of our respective ships. They could not make the decision so I said that I would come to their ship and discuss the idea with their XO. They quickly agreed.

That afternoon I went aboard the Soviet destroyer. I was escorted to the starboard side amidships, where the Russian admiral, the captain, the XO and a group of officers and Sailors were at the rail, watching the rowing races. Just as I arrived, the Russian boat crossed the finish line first.

I joined in the cheering by the Russians, and then I introduced myself. The admiral said, "We beat you, what do you think of that?" I replied, "Congratulations, Admiral, your men rowed an excellent race. We will do better next year." He smiled. A big, barrel-chested man with ruddy complexion and a face of good character, the admiral exuded leadership and power.

I offered the admiral tours of *La Salle* for his officers and Sailors and suggested reciprocal tours of his ship for our men. The admiral asked, "How many Sailors?" I replied that we could take 30 or 40 including officers on our ship each day. We looked at the captain, who indicated that 30 would be better for them. The admiral said, "I will show your men everything except our missiles and communications center. Those I can't show you." I replied, "Of course, we understand. And we have no missiles."

With a broad grin the admiral said, "Aren't you afraid to have your Sailors mingle with communists?" I smiled, "No sir, we are all here in friendship. And our Sailors are good Americans. We have no fear of communists!" He grabbed my right arm and then crunched my right hand with his handshake. (I learned later that he had been their naval academy's wrestling champion.)

I returned to *La Salle* and briefed the captain, who immediately informed the admiral. The tours went on for three days, a first for the U.S. and Soviet Navies in Ethiopian Navy Days (and perhaps anywhere else in the world). These historic visits didn't end the Cold War, but we did create a slight thaw in the Indian Ocean.

Emperor Selassie called on the admiral and I joined the captain and the admiral in touring the emperor about the ship. That evening the captain, Lew Bryan, the Ops boss John Momm and I attended a reception on the Russian destroyer, a very crowded affair on the fantail. We were quickly surrounded by several Russian officers, who enthusiastically proposed a friendship toast. Lew grabbed full tumblers from the tray and put one in my hand. Emulating our hosts, we bottomed-up the vodka, which felt like swallowing liquid fire.

As I gasped for air, the Russians quickly supplied us with more lethal glasses. They were enjoying it immensely. Numb and woozy, I got away from the group as quickly as I could and departed the ship. When I woke up the next morning, I felt like my head had been split with a fire axe. I pulled myself together and braced for the day's events, realizing that, if vodka was the weapon of choice, we were going to lose the Cold War.

That morning Great Britain's Princess Anne called on the admiral. After her quarterdeck honors, I joined the official party in the admiral's cabin. When I was introduced, the lovely princess commented, "Oh, you're the one who does all the paperwork!" Captain Crosby interjected that, with all the festivities, we had little time for paperwork. Smiling, the princess said to me, "How grand, but do watch out for the Russians—lots of vodka, you know!" Laughing through my headache, I replied that her warning was too late.

Commercial shipyard availability was scheduled in Singapore to ship-check *La Salle*'s scheduled boiler fuel conversion to an environmentally cleaner oil distillate. As we transited the Straits of Hormuz outbound, Captain Crosby summoned me to his cabin. I could see he was agitated, but he spoke calmly, "I am ready to relieve the navigator for cause (poor performance). I have repeatedly told him how I want our navigation track laid out and the minimum distances to coast lines and shoal water. He again failed to carry out my instructions. I want you to go to the bridge, assess the situation, and give me your recommendation." I took a deep breath as I returned to my cabin and summoned the lieutenant.

On board for only a few months, he had relieved our previous navigator a few weeks earlier. Not the typical hard-charging junior officer, he was very quiet, almost diffident, with an air of uncertainty. From the outset, I knew the captain was not comfortable with the lieutenant's performance as navigator; I had been keeping an eye on the situation.

We sat down in my cabin and I asked him to describe the captain's desires concerning the ship's navigation track. Then we went to the bridge and I examined the navigation charts and listened to his explanation. He had failed to comply—again. I sent him to his room.

I then met alone on the bridge with our chief quartermaster (an enlisted man well trained in navigation), an intelligent and highly competent individual who knew his profession. Advising him that safety of the ship was paramount, I asked the chief for his opinion on the lieutenant's grasp of navigation. He looked me in the eye and did not flinch, "XO, the lieutenant is a very nice guy and I have tried my best to train him, but he will never be a navigator!" I stared hard at him for a few moments. "Very well. Thank you, chief. That will be all."

I returned to the captain's cabin. "Sir, I concur. You should relieve him," thereby ending the lieutenant's career. The captain appointed the operations officer as navigator temporarily until a relief could be provided by the bureau of naval personnel.

The end of my tour was in sight and I was working on my next duty assignment. I wrote to my detailer at Bupers. For the first time, I confidently requested a warship command. But having served on sea duty for three years, I fully expected to go ashore first so I also requested assignment to the CNO staff, or to the National War College. My detailer would only say that I would be assigned to the D.C. area and he assured me it would not be another joint assignment. I could expect orders in late July or early August.

By early August, I had not received any word so I arranged to place a radiotelephone call to my detailer from the Navy communications unit at Jufair. On the appointed day, I drove to the station with Linda, Jack and Judy. They wanted to know as soon as I did where we were going next.

A secretary informed me that my detailer was away from his desk. But she said that she knew my orders and asked, "Would you like to know?" I said, "Please!" She replied, "You are going to be the next commanding officer of the United States Naval Communications Station at Balboa in the Panama Canal Zone. What do you think of that?" In my greatest understatement ever, I replied "That is great news, but totally unexpected!" She said that Balboa's CO had suffered a heart attack and his replacement was urgently required. I had been nominated by the Naval Telecommunications Command.

In a state of shock and excitement, I returned to the car and said. "You will never guess where we are going! Panama!" Linda, Jack and Judy cheered and laughed. Linda said, "Panama! Isn't that just like the Navy, always surprising us?" Yes. The rest of the day, we enjoyed spreading the news to the wardroom. The next day I received message orders to report for duty in October 1973 for a three-year tour in the Canal Zone. My detailer had kept his word—it was not a joint assignment.

Captain Howard Crosby was the best CO I ever served with. Linda and I thoroughly enjoyed our time with him and Phyllis, his lovely, fun wife. They are our most world-traveled and adventure-loving friends. When he read my orders, Howard immediately called me to his cabin. Without the slightest equivocation, he insisted that I had to drive to Panama. Think of it! An adventure on the Pan American Highway! Sightseeing in Mexico and all the countries of Central America! The chance of a lifetime! I couldn't deny my family this traveler's dream!

I was speechless. But Howard was very persuasive; and I was soon caught up in his enthusiasm. I would just have to figure out how to get Linda to agree, and get extra time for the trip. That evening at dinner, I broached the idea.

The kids looked puzzled, but Linda had a read-my-lips response. "Absolutely not; I'm not doing it. Jack and Judy can't miss that much school. You can drive down there by yourself. The kids and I are going to fly to Panama!" We dropped the subject and went on to other matters. Linda would again have to manage all the packing and moving of our household goods and the sale of our car while the ship was cruising to Singapore.

And so, I surreptitiously began developing a plan for the trip, knowing that Jack and Judy would enjoy the sightseeing and would only miss a month of school. I would have to muster all my charm and win Linda over. "*Insha Allah!*" (Arabic, God willing)

When *La Salle* arrived at Singapore, my relief was waiting on the pier. Four days later, I flew back to Bahrain, joined up with Linda, Jack and Judy, and departed the next day for our long flight to D.C. My fitness report reads as follows:

> Commander Gamboa continues to perform ... in outstanding manner.... He possesses to the highest degree all the necessary requisites for command at sea.... He should be assigned his first sea command at this stage of his career ... recommended for promotion and positions of greater responsibility. The Gamboa's have contributed to the community. Mrs. Gamboa was recently commended for organizing and helping run the Girl Scouts, organizing a thrift shop, providing (art) instruction and ... counseling Navy wives in Bahrain. The Gamboa's ... are extremely well suited for any assignment overseas particularly in a situation where it is imperative that the United States be represented in the best possible manner.

Captain John Frank Gamboa, U. S. Navy (Retired)

I would have added that Linda was indispensable to me in every aspect of my job, especially with the wardroom and the crew's families, and keeping our family well cared for in a challenging environment.

I was ready and eager to command my own ship. But first, there was the matter of commanding a naval communications station in the rain forests and jungles of Panama, about as different in every dimension from our small, salt-sand, arid desert island in the Persian Gulf as one can imagine. It was a great career-enhancing opportunity; however, having been given a shore command as a commander, I knew that I might be hard-pressed to get what I really wanted in that rank—a warship command.

By the time we arrived in Washington, Linda had reluctantly agreed to our Pan American Highway adventure and Bupers had granted my request for extra travel time. We spent three weeks in Washington with Linda's sister and brother-in-law, visiting with her parents, buying a new Ford station wagon and obtaining all the necessary visas for each country we would traverse.

I had a happy reunion with John McCain, who was living in Arlington, attending the National War College, and undergoing physical therapy for injuries he had suffered bailing out of his aircraft and being tortured while a North Vietnamese prisoner of war. We embraced and John said, "I thought about you every day, pal!" I replied, "I prayed for you every day!" We celebrated by taking our wives to a Navy football game at Annapolis.

My mother accepted our invitation to join us on our journey to Panama and we drove across country to Buena Park, California, where she lived. Mom was 63 years old and Dad had died a year earlier on the day before they were to leave for an extended vacation in Mexico. Having her with us would be good for her morale—and mine. I wanted her to be present when I assumed my first command. We enjoyed a great family reunion with my siblings and their spouses and children at my sister Tina's home.

With Mom, we drove to Lone Pine for a weekend visit. Friends quickly put a hand-made poster on the post office bulletin board: "Dinner tonight for the Gamboas at the VFW. Everyone is invited. Bring a dish!" The VFW clubhouse was standing room only, including Bill and Thelma Bauer, Ruth and Darrel Stevens and even my former kindergarten teacher, Ruby Branson, who, during the remarks, read my kindergarten report card and presented it to me. Enriquetta announced that her Panchito was "going to command the Panama Canal" (not exactly) and invited everyone to the ceremony. With good wishes and applause ringing in my ears, we returned to Tina's for final preparations.

We waved goodbye to my siblings and headed for the El Paso border crossing. We took a vote on where we would eat our last meal in the USA for the next three years. McDonald's! In Bahrain, when we stopped at the local Wendy's (no McDonald's), we had "lamb burgers (no beef)" and Orange Crush (no Cokes). As we ate, we were already feeling a bit homesick. For the third time in seven years, we were leaving our wonderful country.

At the border crossing, Mom tried to take charge, "Let me do the talking, I know how to handle these Mexicans. Linda, turn your rings around!" Smiling to reassure my wife, and cautioning mother, I grabbed all the passports and car documents and went into the border office to clear customs and immigration. Mom got out of the car to talk with the agents as they inspected our station wagon and luggage. By the time the officials were done, they knew that her son, el capitán (she promoted me on the spot) was on his way to Panama to command the canal. I smiled at Linda, "Honey, only six more border crossings to go!"

On the highway, we drove toward the city of Chihuahua where we would spend the night. As the sun went down, Linda and the kids fell asleep in the back seat and Mom, sitting in front with me, reminisced. In the enveloping dusk, I started thinking about the uncertainty of what lay ahead of us. I realized that I really didn't know what the hell I was doing. And I was putting my family at risk—unnecessarily. We could have flown to Panama in a single day as Linda had insisted. I tightened my grip on the steering wheel and said a silent prayer.

We spent two days in the city of Chihuahua and visited Mom's former home and grammar school. Mom took us to visit Luz Villa, Pancho Villa's widow. Luz showed us her pictures from the revolution and many photos and relics including the bullet-riddled car in which Villa was assassinated; she had it encased in glass in the courtyard. We spent two nights and a day in my father's village, San Jose de la Boca, in the state of Durango, meeting his sister, nephews and nieces, and his cousin and best friend Juan Navar. We toured Dad's family home and the room where he was born, and my aunt gave me the key to the original front door. At Mom's request, I wore my uniform on our last day. She said Dad would have wanted me to. And one of the men saddled up a beautiful black horse and let Judy ride it; Linda and I did not know she had asked when her cousin saw her looking at the horses in a field near my uncle's house.

We also spent a night in the city of Durango and met Juan Navar's brother Alfredo and Dad's sister Trinidad. Alfredo was a big, handsome man with a warm, friendly smile. With a twinkle in his eye, he said that, unlike his blue-eyed brother, Juan, and my light-complexioned father, he and I had brown skin. We would live longer *"porque tememos tierra en la sangre!"* Because we have soil in our blood! He told me stories about growing up with his brother and my father. I liked him immediately. We have the fondest of memories of the affection and hospitality we received from my relatives in Mexico.

Our journey was an exciting adventure through Mexico, Guatemala, Honduras, Nicaragua, El Salvador, Costa Rica and Panama, just as Howard Crosby had predicted. But there were some unexpected challenges, including two uncharted shallow-river crossings—successful, near Dad's village. And a not-so-shallow river almost crossing in Honduras.

Taking the detour around a damaged bridge, I drove into the river, but could not exit on the opposite bank due to the steep gradient and poor traction. I was stuck in the middle of the river and water was coming into the car. A farmer came to our assistance with two huge white oxen.

Underwater in the cool river current as I hooked the oxen's pulling chain onto the LTD's frame, a question came to mind: What in hell is a U.S. Navy commander doing underwater beneath his car in a remote river in Honduras? (But my career did not flash before my eyes.) After a couple of attempts, with the oxen pulling, I backed the heavy station wagon out of the river onto the path I had entered. I stopped on the highway, opened the doors to let the water pour out of the car. I gratefully paid the farmer $20 for his rescue services. Mom, Linda, Jack and Judy got back into the wet car (they had walked across the damaged bridge to wait for me on the opposite bank) and we drove back into town.

At Gringo Jim's Texaco station (he was a retired U.S. Navy chief), we removed all the wet clothes and items from the car's storage well. Then Linda and Mom hung them on nearby shrubs and trees to dry. I put the car on the lift, removed the wheels, air hosed the river sand out of the brake drums, and inspected the undercarriage for damage.

¡El Capitán!

Five hours later, with more accurate directions from Jim, we drove safely across the river on the correct detour and bridge. At my request, the 20 kids who had spread tree branches on the riverbank for traction, shouted encouragement to the beautiful oxen, and helped push the car were lined up on the side of the road waiting for us. I gave a dollar to each one and thanked them in Spanish. Mother beamed and so did Linda and the kids. We have great pictures.

Experience is often the best teacher—if you survive the lesson. But another gem of wisdom rings most true: "Good judgment comes from experience. But some experience comes from bad judgment." As I drove down the highway, I said a silent prayer of thanks for our deliverance.

In late afternoon on Thursday, November 22, we entered the Canal Zone, crossed the Bridge of the Americas, drove through the main gate at Fort Amador and found our quarters—the third house on the left. My XO, Lt. Cdr. Vern Von Sydow, and his wife, Gail, had arranged for our quarters to be temporarily outfitted with Navy furniture, and they had thoughtfully stocked our refrigerator with some basic groceries. They also invited us to join them for Thanksgiving dinner, but we respectfully declined—we were so glad to be in our new home that we did not want to go anywhere.

Linda and Mom prepared our first Thanksgiving dinner in the Canal Zone—delicious American hot dogs.

Chapter Seven

★ ★ ★ ★ ★ ★ ★

The great art of commanding is to take a fair share of the work.

—Noah Porter

In 1904, the United States and the Republic of Panama signed a treaty creating the U.S.-controlled Panama Canal Zone and permitting America to construct a trans-isthmus canal. In the jungles and rain forests, with tons of dynamite, giant steam shovels, and trains to haul away the excavated earth, the newly created U.S. Panama Canal Company (Pan Canal) began digging the waterway, employing thousands of workers. From the White House, President Theodore Roosevelt urged them to "Make the dirt fly!"

In 1908, the U.S. Navy commissioned Radio Station Colon at Panama's Atlantic port city of Colon to provide a wireless ship-shore-ship communication system for canal operations. Radio Colon, Morse code call letters NAX, had three transmitters with 500 watts of transmitting power and a 1500-mile range. It was the Navy's second radio communications facility; Annapolis was the first.

The Panama Canal opened in October 1914. Transiting ships communicated with NAX by radiograms giving their name, flag, type, length, beam, draft, cargo, logistic requirements, and estimated time of arrival at their canal entrance, either Balboa in the Pacific or Colon in the Caribbean. NAX re-transmitted the radiograms to Pan Canal's port captains, who replied with ships' anchorage assignments, transit date and time, pilot information, and tolls. Paid in U.S. cash, the tolls created a need for banking services, leading to the establishment of a large private banking sector in the city of Panama, dubbed "the Switzerland of the Americas."

In October 1914 on the Pacific coast near Balboa, the Navy established Radio Balboa, Morse code call letters NBA. Twelve years later, the Navy commissioned a more powerful radio transmitting facility at Summit, an area near the east bank of the canal and 13 miles north of Balboa. The new facility served both Radio Colon and Radio Balboa. A public coast radio station was also established at Radio Balboa, permitting NBA to re-transmit maritime radiograms to addressees other than Pan Canal.

In 1942, accelerated by the WW II needs for expanded fleet communications capabilities, Navy Radio Receiving Station Farfan was constructed and commissioned near Balboa on the canal's west bank. This event completed Navy Radio Station Colon's 34-year evolution into U.S. Naval Communications Station Balboa.

On December 3, 1973, I assumed command at a ceremony at Farfan. Mom, Linda, Jack and Judy were in the audience, as well as Balboa's officers, enlisted, and civilian personnel and families, and commanders of other military organizations in the Canal Zone. Rear Admiral Kenneth Haynes, deputy Naval Telecommunications was the principal speaker. I read my orders, proudly exchanged salutes with the acting commanding officer and assumed total authority, responsibility and accountability for Balboa's mission and its crew.

Our climate transition from the arid sands of Bahrain to the tropical jungles of Panama was dramatic, particularly during the six-month rainy season. We lived in Navy quarters surrounded by a large lawn with tall palms and huge mango trees. Our comfortable three-bedroom house was across the street from my headquarters building, so I walked to work.

I knew very little about the operation of a naval communications station. To learn about Balboa's operations, facilities, equipment and its organization, I visited the three operating sites and administrative offices and got acquainted with Balboa's 12 officers, 203 enlisted men and women, and 23 U.S. and 43 foreign civilian employees. Its annual budget for fiscal year 1974 was $1,364,200 and its motto was "Serving the Americas."

Balboa was a component of the Naval Telecommunications System, one of 31 stations around the world that supported the Navy fleet and shore establishment. The primary communications medium was high frequency radio (HF), with worldwide broadcasts to fleet ships and direct HF circuits between ships and shore communications stations. The Atlantic and Pacific Fleet headquarters provided operational direction to naval communications stations for fleet support requirements. Commander, Naval Telecommunications Command in Washington, D.C., was responsible for system technical developments and funding.

Captain John Frank Gamboa, U. S. Navy (Retired)

Radio transmitters and receivers and their associated antennas must be physically separated a distance sufficient to avoid radio frequency mutual interference. My three widely separated main communications facilities were interconnected by paved roads, landlines and microwave systems.

The headquarters was located at Fort Amador on the second floor of a very large, bunker-like concrete WW II building. On its ground floor was Balboa's communications center that included a technical control center to coordinate communications operations at Summit and Farfan; a fleet center for communication with naval ships; and a message center for over-the-counter message service for all Canal Zone Navy and Marine Corps commands and several other military agencies.

Summit was north of the headquarters on 710 acres. It had 72 high frequency transmitters and a variety of transmitting antennas and two submarine systems: a very low frequency transmitter with a huge antenna structure consisting of six 600-foot-tall steel towers supporting a horizontal rectangular wire grid "top hat" antenna larger than two football fields, and a low frequency transmitter with an eight-hundred foot steel tower antenna.

Farfan was seven miles west of the headquarters on 760 acres on the canal's western bank. One large building housed all the station's radio receivers, operating and maintenance centers, with a microwave tower on the roof; and Comle, the Pan Canal and public coast radio station operations center.

The Inter-American Naval Telecommunications Network (IANTN) control center, which linked the naval headquarters of 11 countries in South America and the Dominican Republic with the U.S. Chief of Naval Operations, was also at Farfan, together with the IANTN Secretariat, which managed and maintained records for the system and supported periodic inter-American naval communications conferences. Farfan and Summit each had about 100 personnel with a warrant officer in charge.

The naval communications area master station (Navcams) in Norfolk was Navcommsta Balboa's operational boss. Balboa provided circuits to designated U.S. Navy ships and to U.S. Coast Guard cutters operating in the Antarctic for their exclusive use (called a termination), and a separate common circuit to all other ships for their ship to shore message transmission only.

¡El Capitán!

The fleet center also supported Commander, Naval Forces Southern Command, with circuits for the admiral's aircraft when he was on travel in the Caribbean, or Central and South America.

Balboa also provided communications services to designated foreign navy ships. The British destroyer HMS *Jupiter*, which we served with a termination, visited Balboa for several days. During a shipboard reception, the captain and I were standing near the top of the ladder on her bridge when I noticed a young officer standing below. Smiling, he motioned to me for the captain's attention. I said, "Captain, I believe one of your officers would like to speak with you." He excused himself and joined the officer for a brief conversation; when he returned, the captain told me, "That was Prince Charles, our Communications officer." I replied, "Yes, I recognized him!" I did not mention that I had met the prince's sister in Ethiopia.

Balboa was my first time to command civilian and uniformed women. I was several days into my initial site tours to meet my crew when Command Master Chief Bennett came to see me in my office. He asked me, "Sir, may I speak directly?" I replied, "Of course, master chief; what's on your mind?"

He looked me in the eye and said, "When you talk to the women in the headquarters staff, and especially when you talk to the female sailors at the sites, you always have a broad smile, but rarely when you talk to the men—in fact you mostly have a stern expression with them. Everyone is noticing. I don't think you want to signal any favoritism to the women, Commander."

Embarrassed, I thought about it for a minute and then replied, "You're absolutely right, master chief. In the future, I will be careful not to smile inappropriately. Thank you for bringing this matter to my attention!" Then we had a cup of coffee and discussed other command matters.

After our meeting, I walked into the XO's office and told him about my discussion with Bennett. Vern, who had reported to Balboa two months before me, replied, "Sir, I have the same problem!" We had a good laugh. And then we discussed the issue and quickly agreed that it was our problem (a self-inflicted wound). We resolved to interact with all hands in an even-handed manner and smile appropriately. And also frown, look stern or angry or mean or pleased, etc. as the situation called for.

The command master chief had performed a vital but sensitive duty with his customary no-nonsense approach; Bennett had taught the new CO and XO a more professional way to related to the crew.

With a reasonably firm grip on my new situation, I was beginning to feel comfortable in command. We enjoyed our first Christmas and New Year in the Zone, highlighted by a round of holiday parties with our new friends and neighbors. Life was good!

In the first week of January 1974, I was at my desk preparing for travel to Brazil to inspect Navy Communications Unit Rio. Velma, my administrative assistant, passed me a phone call from Navy Supply Center, Charleston, South Carolina. I greeted the caller in my most confident command voice. A woman with a sweet, soft southern accent responded cheerfully. After polite amenities, Mrs. Pinckney said, "I just wanted to be sure you knew that your command has over-obligated its FY 1973 funds and that you are potentially in violation of U.S. Code 3672." I asked her what that meant. She replied sweetly, "Well, your command may have spent money that the Congress did not appropriate, so you could go to prison!"

As a TV commercial says, life comes at you fast. I immediately started taking notes. I learned that Etta, my civilian financial officer, was aware of the situation and knew what to do, but she had not been able to resolve the matter with the supply officer and had vented her frustration to Mrs. Pinckney.

I asked Mrs. Pinckney how much time I had before the issue would be reported to higher authority. "Not much," she replied. I thanked her and promised to call her before departing for Brazil.

I immediately convened a meeting with my Exec and Etta. The Supply and Fiscal department was headed by a supply corps lieutenant, who was on leave in the U.S.

I asked Etta what the hell was going on. She explained that Balboa allocated funds to U.S. Navy Communications Unit Rio and the unit had over-obligated. The funds had not yet been expended so the over-obligation could simply be canceled, but Etta's recommendations to do so were rejected by the supply officer. It became clear that the lieutenant and

Etta had an unsatisfactory working relationship—no mutual trust or teamwork.

Assuming this was probably not the only problem in the department, I initiated a Navy judge advocate general (JAG) investigation. Assisted by a supply corps Lt. Cdr. from the 15th Naval District staff, my XO would take a top-to-bottom look at our supply and fiscal operations and submit findings and recommendations.

I ordered Etta to take immediate action to cancel the over-obligated requisitions, coordinate with Mrs. Pinckney, and keep the XO informed.

The next day I departed for Rio, determined to conduct a thorough inspection and take a very close look at their supply and fiscal operations and procedures. And determine how they had managed to screw up my station finances.

Our Navy's operations and administration are based on integrity and trust. Honest and timely reporting up and down the chain of command are required for its effectiveness. Nonetheless, it is not easy to report bad news to one's boss, especially if it might reflect unfavorably. But one of the surest ways to fail in stewardship is to withhold vital information from an immediate superior just because you "might not look good." On February 1, 1974, I wrote to Rear Admiral Jon Boyes, Commander, Naval Telecommunications Command.

> I would like to [report] on Naval Communication Station Balboa's readiness…. My major problem is in the … Supply department…. I initiated a JAG informal investigation on 7 January on the apparent over-obligation of $3300 in FY 72 funds….The investigation revealed weaknesses in our reconciliation procedures and spending controls…. Due to this station's spending policy … we may get into a critical situation as late charges fall. I am accelerating the review of our FY 73 expenditures to date … and will inform your headquarters promptly if I determine that augmentation of our FY 73 budget is required. I have taken corrective actions to preclude any possible over-obligation of FY 74 funds; however, I am still not satisfied with our spending controls of Rio's budget. I am also concerned about the supply system support … particularly for our new 80-series transmitters. We have over 250 outstanding priority five material requisitions—a few of them over six months old. I have therefore expanded my initial investigation to a

complete look at the operation, management and administration of the Supply department....Very respectfully.

Admiral Boyes promptly replied:

> Your most informative letter of 1 February was a pleasure to read. The staff has briefed me on the good work you are doing down there.... I have gone over your supply department situation with Commander Hamilton and with Admiral Haynes. We are very distressed. However, you are on the right track. My only advice is don't wait too long to get it down on paper and take appropriate action. If you have any doubt as to what to do, I would suggest you get together on the phone with Admiral Haynes. I hope you are planning to come to San Diego in the fall for the IANTN Conference.

Thus began my command relationship with the first admiral I worked for directly. Naval Academy '44, Boyes was a highly intelligent and forceful leader with a background in submarines, where he was known as "Silent Jon." The admiral had a unique assignment in the Navy, serving on the CNO staff as Director, Naval Telecommunications, and as Commander, Naval Telecommunications Command, an echelon II systems command; two different jobs in the Navy simultaneously—a "double hat." He began each workday at the Pentagon, and then drove to headquarters at noon to deal with system issues, returning to the Pentagon at day's end to wrap up.

In February 1974, he sent a six-page memo to his key deputies and staff assistants in both organizations, copied to all communications station commanding officers, explaining how he would accomplish both jobs while maintaining clear and separate lines of authority in each. I studied his memo carefully to determine which issues I should bring to his personal attention.

His guidance was clear. "… Some believe little should be brought to DNT or CNTC's attention because this action might necessarily disturb his busy schedule or bring problems to his mind. I cannot too strongly emphasize the fact that a handwritten note, a short telephone conversation or a quick pop into my office to keep me up-to-date and current on all large or small matters, which will influence my decisions or command responsibilities are a necessary part of my modus operandi. I would encourage you, therefore, to keep me advised, over-advised, if necessary...."

In the nuclear-powered Navy, Admiral Rickover required each commanding officer to write him a personal letter about his command every Friday. I decided to write to Boyes as necessary to address major issues and events at Balboa.

In March, I received a short note from the admiral, "You have been wonderful about keeping me informed.... You ought to plan to come to the headquarters within the next few months to touch base with the staff. We would like to have your ideas on Balboa realignment concepts that the staff is working on. Charge, tiger!"

Opportunities often come disguised as problems. In early February, my Exec handed me his report on the Supply and Fiscal department. After studying it, I concluded that I had inherited a unit—possibly an entire command—that lacked effective working procedures and viable internal communication.

It was also very clear that the Supply and Fiscal department had not received effective oversight, guidance and control; it had been allowed to drift along with the tide of events with minimal leadership or direction— or command attention. It was no mystery to me why Balboa had over-obligated. But even more distressing, we were in danger of over-spending on my watch.

In my first two months at the helm, I had concentrated on learning the operational, technical and area-coordination aspects of my job. I had assumed that Navcommsta Balboa's organization, management and administration were in good shape. Now I knew better. But I also realized that the revelation of a serious problem in my command before I "owned it" was a very lucky break. Even so, I had to find out what other short-fused time bombs lay buried in Balboa.

Because of the command's annual schedule, I had limited time to correct deficiencies and establish command performance standards. I therefore seized the moment and expanded my assessment to the entire command to determine how Balboa was actually being led, managed and administered. But rather than expand the JAG investigation, the XO and I would assess each organizational component in collaboration with the heads of departments.

Captain John Frank Gamboa, U. S. Navy (Retired)

My executive officer, Lt. Cdr. Vern Von Sydow, USNA '63, was a gifted naval officer with great command presence and leadership ability—a helicopter pilot with a friendly smile and gregarious personality. He (related to movie star Max Von Sydow) exuded competence, energy and enthusiasm.

Vern had played first-string right guard on the academy's football team (the class of '63 football players were the only ones to play with both of the academy's Heisman Trophy winners, Joe Bellino and Roger Staubach). Vern was also elected class vice president by his classmates, who had affectionately nicknamed him "the Beast."

We quickly developed complete trust and confidence in each other, and established a balanced approach on Balboa's command issues.

One of our major concerns was the lack of command-centralized management. There were no established regular meetings between me, the XO and the department heads; the three main sites—the Comm Center, Farfan, and Summit—were operating like independent entities.

To find out what was happening, Vern and I had to periodically visit the three sites—not an effective way to run the show. To change the organization's mind-set and impose my own way of doing things, in February 1974, I established a weekly meeting of all officers and chiefs, my leadership team, each Friday at 1000 in the headquarters conference room, which I designated the command management information center (MIC). After some initial grumbling by some of the participants, the meetings soon had excellent involvement and information flow, which reverberated throughout the command.

To further promote and support the station's internal communication, I approved the publication of a station newspaper, entitled *TROPICOMM,* as proposed by three of our female Sailors.

Taking action on the JAG investigation, on February 26, I directed the supply officer to take immediate corrective action on a long list of major deficiencies in his department. I also awarded him a non-punitive letter of caution informing him that his performance of duty was unsatisfactory and his career was at risk. He worked hard to correct the deficiencies the last few months of his tour.

He was relieved in June by Lieutenant Bob Reardon, an outstanding supply corps officer who knew Navy logistics and finance and thrived on challenges—he loved to solve problems. His goal was to create a high-performance department that excelled. In short order, he overhauled the station's spare parts pipeline, coordinating with Naval Supply Center Charleston and repair depots to reduce the shipping time for new radio modules and the turn-around time for repairs, which eliminated our new HF transmitters' spare parts backlog.

The professionalism that Bob instilled in his people reverberated to all other departments and improved our overall readiness and morale. I reported to Boyes, "We are making progress in our 80-series transmitter spare parts problems ... and beginning to receive new and repaired parts. We have identified bottlenecks ... in the requisitioning system ... Very respectfully."

My orders to command Navcommsta Balboa had made no mention of my duties in the IANTN, a system established in the early 1960s linking the ten South American Navy headquarters and the Dominican Navy headquarters to our Chief of Naval Operations. Over the years, the U.S. Navy had provided technical assistance and outdated radio equipment at no cost to our friends.

The network had languished in the backwaters of U.S. Navy concerns. The member stations' periodic requests for upgrades of their IANTN communications equipment and improved technical support were generally ignored.

Beginning in the 1960s, the U.S. and South American chiefs of navy convened a biannual Inter-American Naval Conference (IANC), alternating between South American hosts every two years and the U.S. Navy hosting every six. These periodic navy chiefs' gatherings focused on combined naval operations in support of mutual national security interests, assistance in at-sea emergencies including search and rescue incidents, and technical issues. IANCs were conducted with the highest level of naval protocol and diplomacy and showcased the host's navy, country and culture.

In 1971, CNO Admiral Elmo Zumwalt hosted the VI IANC in Newport, RI. His good friend and Annapolis classmate, the Venezuelan Navy CNO, was a participant. During discussion of the IANTN status, each of the South American Navy Chiefs lambasted Zumwalt for the lack of U.S. support for the network.

The admiral was blindsided. Zumwalt had little knowledge of the IANTN. But the U.S. Navy had been cast in an unfavorable light by his South American peers—and a classmate. Zumwalt was embarrassed and angry. He promised his fellow navy chiefs that he would take a hard look at the network and he pledged his support.

Before Zumwalt's plane landed at Andrews Air Force Base, his staff sent a high-priority message to my predecessor, Commander Bill Burch. The gist: "Admiral Zumwalt wants to know what the hell is wrong with the IANTN! Get your ass up here!" Burch arrived in Washington the next evening. He was aware of the IANTN status and the members' concerns.

After meetings with Director, Naval Communications staff in OPNAV, Commander, Naval Telecommunications Command staff, and Commander, Naval Electronic Systems Command staff, agreement was reached to conduct a site-survey at each of the twelve IANTN stations on an urgent basis and determine what was needed to upgrade the network to U.S. Navy standards. It was a huge undertaking—befitting a CNO mandate.

In September 1971, Burch headed a four-man team of U.S. Navy electronics and communications engineers on a six-week survey of each station and determined their equipment and technical support requirements for three circuits: voice, secure teletype and Morse code consistent with current U.S. Navy standards. The survey resulted in a management engineering plan with specific equipment suites for each station.

The plan also called for the establishment of network and equipment operations and maintenance training programs at Navcommsta Balboa and a ten-person bilingual (Spanish/English) communications assistance team (CAT) of U.S. Navy enlisted electronics technicians, radiomen and a supply chief, headed by a Lt.j.g.

The U.S. Navy would provide equipment to each IANTN station on a five-year no-cost lease, which was renewable. The suite consisted of modern FRT-39 HF transmitters (the U.S. Navy comm stations' workhorse), receivers and test equipment, a two-year spare parts package, and antennas. Member stations would be responsible for providing facilities, site support and installing their equipment, assisted by the IANTN CAT.

The CNO approved the plan in March 1972. The brunt of the project technical implementation and member station personnel training was assigned to Navcommsta Balboa. By late 1972, lease agreements had been concluded with each Navy, except that Brazil opted to purchase the equipment, and Ecuador got hung up in internal political disputes.

¡El Capitán!

Coordinated by the secretariat and CAT, each IANTN station's equipment was delivered by the U.S. Military Airlift Command. The CAT assisted each station with site planning, equipment installation, and initial on-site operational and technical training. The project had been underway for a year when I assumed command.

In January 1974, Vice CNO Admiral Jim Holloway, the CNO-designate, tasked Balboa to provide his delegation's communications support, through the IANTN, for the IANC convening in Mar del Plata, Argentina, in April 1974. Also, a Chiefs of Naval Communications Conference was scheduled for San Diego in September 1974, hosted by Rear Admiral Boyes.

Although Balboa's state of readiness and my on-going command assessment were my main concerns, I had to quickly get a handle on the IANTN's status and issues. I wrote to Boyes, "I have been assigned to the delegation accompanying the Chief of Naval Operations to the VII Inter-American Naval Conference in Argentina in April as assistant for communications." I also informed him of my IANTN station inspections.

> I will visit Chile before the CNOs' conference and the IANTN stations in Brazil, Bolivia, Paraguay, Uruguay, and Peru after ... three countries at a time in order to minimize my absence from Balboa, but get a good look at the stations, discuss problems with my IANTN counterparts and assess their readiness. I plan to have visited all the stations by this summer in order to prepare for the V Inter-American Naval Communications Chiefs Conference in San Diego on 22-28 September 1974.... I depart this evening for an eight-day visit to Quito, Ecuador; Bogotá, Colombia; and Caracas, Venezuela. Very respectfully.

A station visit required two days of travel and two working days in country. I met with the U.S. Military Group chief and our staff counterpart, and then called on the U.S. ambassador. During my station visit, the host director of naval communications and his staff briefed me on their upgrade status and their agenda items for the V Inter-American Naval Communications Chiefs Conference. If he was available, I called on the Chief of Navy as well. In April, I sent my initial assessment to Boyes.

> (My latest trips to South America) included Bogotá, Quito, Caracas, La Paz and Lima. My overall impression is that it is doubtful that we can

complete all station upgrades prior to the Communications Chiefs Conference in September.... Overall, the IANTN is progressing to a modern, reliable communications system ... with command interest at the CNO level in each member country. The two major problems ... are the procurement ... of spare parts for the upgrade packages, and the establishment of the IANTN training facility here at Balboa. I am taking action ... and will keep you informed. I will visit Santiago, Chile on 15-17 April and Buenos Aires 17-20 April. My final visit will be to Paraguay, Uruguay and Brazil in June. I plan to submit a comprehensive report on the IANTN in July ... for the Communications Chiefs Conference. Very respectfully.

As CO of the largest Navy facility in the Canal Zone, I had many social responsibilities. Linda and I entertained Balboa's officers and their wives and Balboa VIP visitors, as well as our neighbors. Linda made our house a home and took care of the family, which now included two dogs, a green macaw, and a Persian cat (Papa Tango) we brought from Bahrain. She kept a busy schedule attending classes at the local college in art and Spanish, participating in officers' wives club activities, organizing and conducting Girl Scout events as co-leader, and planning social activities in our community, from fundraisers to formal balls.

In early June 1974, Lt.j.g. Wayne Beck, a limited duty officer, reported for duty as head of the CAT and assistant IANTN secretary—I served collaterally as the secretary. An ex-enlisted electronics technician, he was expert in communications equipment maintenance and communications station operations.

I immediately dispatched him to the South America stations for orientation, assessment of the network's readiness, and to prepare the secretariat for the Inter-American Naval Communications Chiefs Conference.

An outstanding leader and loyal, dedicated officer, Wayne excelled in management and had a huge capacity for completed staff work. Under his direction, we accelerated completion of the IANTN station upgrades and resolved secretariat operation and member station training issues in a timely manner.

I had additional duties as assistant chief of staff, communications for U.S. Naval Forces Southern Command and the 15th Naval District communications officer for Rear Admiral Robert Blount, who was "double-hatted." Vern attended the admiral's weekly staff meeting and as necessary, I would get on the admiral's calendar. Blount was responsible for maintaining Navy relations with all Central, South American and Caribbean Navies. He traveled to each country to meet with the U.S. ambassador, the chief of the navy, and often with the head of state.

Since he dealt with all the chiefs of Navy, I kept him informed of my IANTN activities and issues; he was very interested and supported my initiatives. We also coordinated on issues related to the on-going negotiations between the United States and Panama on turning over the Zone and the canal. I explained to Boyes, "The revision of the Canal Treaty between the U.S. and the Republic of Panama will ... directly concern Navcommsta Balboa.... One issue will be our HF commercial CW operations which handle all canal transit communications traffic...."

In the spring, I paused to assess my projected personal workload for the year. In addition to overseeing and managing Balboa's daily operations, I would play a key role in two international naval conferences; inspect ten IANTN stations; make two visits to our headquarters; complete my command assessment and correct all technical, administrative and management deficiencies prior to Boyes' three-day visit in July.

My major concern was the risk to my command initiatives to improve Balboa's readiness. My three months on travel could result in a lack of continuity—there was no overall game plan for my crew to follow during my absence. They would just have to "wing it" or "muddle through," and I would have to hope for the best, or resort to crises management if things got off track.

I therefore decided to create an annual command management plan— a roadmap—to direct and support my leadership team. We would create our command goals and objectives through strategic and management planning.

Command strategic planning requires the commander's vision for mission accomplishment. The key outputs are a set of mission-based open-ended goals and quantifiable objectives combined with a management plan for successful execution and goal accomplishment.

My vision for Navcommsta Balboa was a unit that excelled in all its tasks with high morale. My priority command goals were top operational readiness through effective leadership, management and administration;

better living conditions for our single enlisted personnel; upgraded working spaces at each site; and enlisted personnel supervisory training.

Our most urgent task was to identify all technical and operational deficiencies in each of our three operating sites and establish performance standards consistent with a high state of readiness.

To accelerate the identification of deficiencies, I chose a tried and true Navy readiness improvement technique: assist visits and inspections by expert, independent organizations. I knew the approach was risky—we could be putting ourselves on report.

On May 15, I wrote to Boyes, "I have requested that Naval Electronics Command conduct an electronics inspection at Balboa ... a comprehensive electronics inspection was last conducted 1968 ... in March-April, a Tactical Communications Monitoring Team ... identified several problem areas we are taking action on.... We do not have all the test equipment necessary to conduct quality monitoring of our new antenna systems and have requested the needed items. Very respectfully."

I assigned management of the whole ball of wax to the XO. We met frequently with each department head and the weekly MIC meeting facilitated a productive exchange of views, with quality input and advice from the officers and chiefs.

The final plan consisted of a list of goals for the entire command with supporting objectives, tasks and resources assigned to each department. Plan status was reviewed at each MIC meeting. I soon began to see signs of spirited competitiveness among the officers and chiefs—pride and professionalism—and the beginnings of real teamwork. These were the stepping-stones to the command climate I wanted to create at Navcommsta Balboa, one that fostered great command achievements, personal excellence, professional pride, and high morale.

Leaders are never satisfied with their unit's routine results; they are always demanding improved individual and team performance. One way to reach and sustain superior levels of individual performance and organizational mission accomplishment—to excel—is by successfully meeting a demanding and unifying challenge, one that is real and tough to overcome. I needed such a challenge for Balboa. I felt that we had the talent to excel, but we needed unity of purpose to reach our full potential.

In the 1970s, Commander, South Atlantic conducted an annual four-month training cruise called Operation Unitas. He led U.S. Navy Task

Force 138—three surface combatants and a submarine—in combined operations with each South American Navy. After departing Puerto Rico, TF 138 would operate down the coast of South America, through the Straits of Magellan, and up the other coast, transiting the Panama Canal—clockwise one year, counterclockwise the next.

The U.S. Task Force entered each host Navy's port and conducted pre-sail meetings to brief the scheduled combined exercises. Dinners, receptions and cultural events were staged by the host (All work and no play makes for dull Sailors). Then the ships would spend several days on the high seas executing the operation order, then return to port for "hot wash-up" reviews and more socializing. It was all very professional and enjoyable and of real value in maintaining readiness and good Navy-to-Navy relations with our South American friends.

The key to Unitas operational success was reliable long haul communication between the ships and shore comm stations. To maintain a continuous HF radio circuit, the assigned frequencies must be shifted throughout the day and night as propagation conditions ("props") in the ionosphere change—"follow the sun." The circuit operators, radio receiver operators, and controllers monitor the circuit's condition and controllers seize a good new frequency before the working frequency deteriorates and the termination fails. The trick is to know when the ionosphere's propagation conditions start to change.

In the Unitas ship-shore-ship communications plan, TF 138 would sortie from Puerto Rico with the flagship's HF circuit termination (term) at Balboa. Near the equator, the TF commander would shift the term to Puerto Rico.

As the TF neared Rio de Janeiro, the commander would shift the term to Rio. After the TF transited the Straits of Magellan and reached the southwest coast of South America near Chile, the term would be shifted back to Balboa. When the task force transited the Panama Canal, the term would be shifted to Puerto Rico. The station term shifts often resulted in communications outages, an anathema to communicators and Unitas.

When I asked my Operations Officer, Lt. Cdr. Bill Bailey, why Unitas support was done in this manner he replied, "Sir, that's the way it's always been done!" More to the point, everyone involved in Unitas communications planning assumed it was the only way it could be done.

In March 1974, Navcommsta Balboa had placed 41 of the Navy's newest and most powerful HF transmitters into operation. New transmitting and receiving antennas were also installed. The predicted maximum distance for a high-frequency "hop" at the new transmitter's peak power was over 4400 miles—about the same distance from Balboa to the Straits of Magellan.

Balboa's routine terminations were of one- or two-week duration. Balboa's termination with the U.S. Coast Guard icebreakers that were operating in Antarctica was about 4400 nautical miles in distance and of 3-4 week duration. While the Unitas and Antarctic terms were not comparable in duration, it appeared to me that it was operationally and technically feasible to terminate the flagship circuit at the maximum distance from Balboa—the Straits of Magellan.

But no naval communications station had ever continuously terminated a ship circumnavigating South America. Nonetheless, I felt that a single, continuous Unitas termination between the TF 138 flagship and Navcommsta Balboa could improve communications reliability for Unitas.

But we would have to do "work-a-rounds" in our watch sections to cover the added workload and our people would have to endure significant stress and fatigue for an extended period.

There was no doubt in my mind—a single comm station termination for the entire Unitas operation would be the ultimate test of Balboa's capabilities and readiness. If we failed, the "business as usual" folks could have the last laugh on me.

I concluded that this was just the challenge I needed for Balboa, so I tasked my operations department's Lt. Cdr. Bailey, Lt. Pillsbury, and Master Chief Radioman Bennett to figure out how Balboa could pull it off.

I understood that we were thinking "outside the box;" and getting the decision-makers at our headquarters, Navcams Norfolk, the task group commander and flagship to agree with our bold proposal would be half the battle. The key player was our operational boss, Captain Burke on the Atlantic Fleet commander's staff, who provided operational tasking to us via Navcams Norfolk.

A week later, my team had cobbled together a technically sound but operationally challenging concept and plan. To ensure that all my officers and chiefs understood the implications of what I wanted NBA to attempt, I had the team do a MIC brief. We had a thorough, spirited discussion about all the factors and hazards involved. Our most experienced communicators weighed in.

After everyone had their say, I announced my decision, "We will go for it!"

Discretion being the better part of valor, I also decided that, before we went charging off on our challenging, possibly heroic venture, we needed extensive preparations at Balboa. We had to solve our logistics problems and obtain sufficient spare parts to keep enough of our new 80-series HF transmitters on the line for the entire cruise. We also had to resolve the high heat and unreliable air conditioning problems in the new HF transmitters building. And there were other issues; we had to get our arms around all of them.

To achieve the highest possible equipment readiness, I had already requested a complete electronics inspection of Summit, Farfan and the Comm Center. Now it would serve to ensure our readiness and establish a reliable foundation for our Unitas concept. And we would request any other inspection or assist visit deemed necessary for our success.

Having set a course to achieve my first goal, I turned command attention to my second priority—to improve Balboa's single enlisted personnel living space habitability. Balboa's modernization projects prior to my arrival were for technical equipment upgrades to improve the station's communications capabilities. Little had been done to modernize the substandard living and working spaces, degrading my people's morale and undermining my retention efforts. The increasing number of women assigned to Balboa also created a need for their additional separate bathroom and berthing facilities.

In April, I outlined my priorities to Boyes, "Although the major communications projects are nearing completion, I plan to submit several new projects aimed at improvements in the bachelor enlisted quarters (BEQs), our communications center, the Farfan galley, and the conversion of some spaces in the receivers building to IANTN training classrooms…. Overall, I intend to maintain a program that will keep up with building maintenance and repair, with the objective of ensuring that Navcommsta Balboa is a safe, attractive place to work and live. Very respectfully." I followed up in May. "Navcommsta Balboa's budget submission for FY 75 includes 41 addendum items, to improve the material readiness of the station, as well as the habitability … consistent with my objective of improving our material readiness, concentrating on mission related items, then personnel support. Very respectfully."

Boyes replied, "We agree on your funding objective of improving the material readiness of the command, concentrating on mission related items, then personnel support. While we cannot promise financial relief in this time of austere budgets, the first step certainly is to document your needs."

It was a pro-forma response; I would have to fight for habitability improvement funds.

Soon after taking command, I held a request mast for a third class radioman (an RM3 petty officer). It was the right of every member of my command to meet with me privately on any personal issue. He protested his supervisor's refusal to permit him to take the annual Navy advancement examination for petty officer second class. After a thorough inquiry I concluded that, at worst, the petty officer, an African American, had been the victim of racial bias, and at best, unfair treatment. I reversed the decision and counseled his leading petty officer, division officer and department head. The radioman passed the exam and was advanced.

On April 15, I published my first command memorandum of policy:

> (It is the policy of the Navy) ... to ensure equality of opportunity and treatment of all service personnel irrespective of race, color, sex, or national origin.... All personnel must be accorded equal opportunity for enlistment, appointment, advancement, professional improvement, promotions, assignments, and retention. Achievement of an atmosphere of equal opportunity is essential to attaining and maintaining a high state of morale, discipline and military effectiveness.... Moreover, equality of opportunity and treatment is, as always, an inherent function of leadership and is therefore the responsibility of all Navy members.

> I firmly and totally support the above policy.... I fully expect the total support of every officer, chief petty officer, leading petty officer, supervisor and other personnel in leadership positions in helping me to carry out both the spirit and intent of the ... policy .... I further expect, from all personnel ... a positive attitude in regard to equal opportunity in order to create and maintain an atmosphere at this command within which the foregoing policy will thrive.

¡El Capitán!

To ensure that my policy was supported by training, I tasked the XO to create a command action plan (CAP) with an assist visit from the Navy Human Resources Center in Norfolk. Their team of officers and senior enlisted spent a week at Balboa and produced excellent recommendations and suggestions, including indicators that would guide our internal assessments of Balboa's human relations climate. We created and implemented an effective CAP and executed its training program for upward mobility and equal opportunity and treatment.

Meanwhile, I discovered another major personnel and operations issue: conditions in our Pan Canal and Public Coast Radio Station, Comle, which was manned almost entirely by Panamanian nationals under the direction and leadership of a Caucasian U.S. civilian.

During my initial site walk-through captain's call, things just didn't feel or look right. My instincts detected an under-current of hostility among the workers. I sensed they felt disrespected by the command, especially their needs for additional operators and improved working conditions. My initial reaction was to request two additional "ceiling points" (civilian job positions).

My hunch was soon confirmed when I received a request from their union for a labor relations meeting to address Comle issues. The Exec, receivers officer and I convened a meeting in late April with the Comle supervisor, the head of the civilian personnel office at the Naval Support Activity, two leaders of the local union, the shop steward/watch supervisor, four Comle watch supervisors and one circuit operator.

We got an earful: cramped working spaces; poor ventilation; old and badly-worn equipment; overworked operators who were given compensatory time rather than overtime pay, which exacerbated the staffing problems; lack of pay increases, promotions or recognition—clearly a failure of leadership and the command.

I was embarrassed and incensed, but I controlled my emotions. I promised the group that I would take action on their complaints. I promptly added the Comle deficiencies to our management plan—and I informed Boyes:

> I have initiated a comprehensive study of our Comle operations with the objective of expanding the working facilities, improving working conditions, and increasing the number of personnel assigned. I had a very fruitful meeting with local labor leaders, at their request,

and I was able to demonstrate ... that we are taking aggressive action. Your message concerning the possibility of providing two additional ceiling points that I requested did much to convince them of the command's sincerity ... it has been several years since a hard look was taken at the operation and manning of our Comle. Very respectfully.

We went on to create a comprehensive upgrade project for a larger work space, modern transmitters, receivers and ancillary equipment, new furnishings, and improved lighting and air conditioning. Headquarters initially deferred, but our persistence paid off, and we also got the two civilian ceiling points. The new facility was inaugurated in June 1976.

My third major goal was to revitalize our enlisted training program. Balboa ran on the energy of youth. The majority of our enlisted men and women were right out of boot camp and basic radioman school.

The Navy had designated duty in the Zone an 18-month hardship tour for single officers and enlisted. The short tours created an increased personnel turnover rate and turbulence in our watch sections; our mid- and top-level petty officers spent lots of time training our first-term sailors. We needed supervisory and leadership training for the petty officers in order to maximize their potential. But this was a real problem because travel funding limitations prevented sending them to Navy schools.

Vern came up with a great solution: use the Pan Canal training school at no cost. The school's courses covered all areas of personnel supervision and management. We sent most of our petty officers and several chiefs. We also initiated a site rotation plan to give each Sailor experience in transmitters, receivers, and technical control.

Later, I went one step further to improve our supervisory training by establishing a one-week in-house Petty Officer Academy, convening quarterly. The faculty was selected from our own personnel plus some from the Naval Station. The XO covered Navy regulations and our chief yeoman taught them how to draft enlisted performance reports, and the curriculum covered other necessary topics. I presented the course-completion certificates. Balboa was the only Commsta with its own Petty Officer Academy.

To deal with the threat of drug and alcohol abuse among our first-term Sailors, the XO organized a comprehensive sports program with teams in tennis, flag football, slow-pitch softball, fast-pitch softball, bowling, and basketball, to compete with other Canal Zone teams.

He created a fun-filled recreation program that included weekend tours in Panama; canal cruise parties featuring great food and beverages with bands and dancing on the Pan Canal double-deck excursion boat; Chagres River canoe races (our daughter Judy was on the winning canoe); and canal fishing trips.

Everyone got involved and Vern even played flag football. I quickly declined his invitation to join in; I could not envision myself blocking a former academy lineman, but I did team with him for our tennis competition.

The success of our sports and recreation programs was exemplified by our many championship teams and Navcommsta Balboa's official designation by the Secretary of the Navy as a Bicentennial Command in 1976.

The programs greatly enhanced our crew morale and practically eliminated drug and alcohol abuse. We proudly flew our official Bicentennial flag at our three sites.

In the early '70s, the headquarters began upgrading some of the Naval Telecommunications System stations to satellites and consolidating, closing or downsizing others. Balboa was not going be upgraded to satellite. It would be relegated to a back-up role to provide "a residual HF capability," which gave rise to persistent rumors that Balboa was on the chopping block. U.S. Naval Communications Station Puerto Rico would be expanded and upgraded with satellite circuits, and many at headquarters thought that Puerto Rico could service our customers.

In March 1974, the first issue related to NBA's downsizing landed on my desk: the headquarters proposed to shut down our fleet center. Boyes wrote, "We would like to have your ideas on Balboa realignment concepts...." I replied, "... I do not think it would be a cost-effective action ... the type of customers we serve ... cannot obtain highly reliable service from other naval communications stations. Furthermore, it has been demonstrated that no other communications station can provide effective long-haul terminations to ships operating south of the equator off the east or west coasts of South America. ... we should keep the fleet center. It is unique and vital ... there should be no reduction in billets here. Very respectfully." Headquarters agreed; we had dodged the first bullet.

In April, the VII Inter-American Naval Conference convened at Mar del Plata, south of Buenos Aires. My principal duty was to coordinate the delegation's text message service, but because of my IANTN responsibilities, I also supported the delegation in plenary and breakout sessions.

My CAT leader Chief Radioman Scarso accompanied me, and I stationed our CAT First Class Radioman Garza in the Argentine Navy communications station to assist them in coordinating the Balboa IANTN circuit.

In anticipation of the Chiefs of Navy Communications Conference in San Diego, I also studied the conference structure and operations. Among other tasks, they prepared and published all conference documents and transcribed the proceedings daily into English, Spanish and Portuguese.

Our Argentine hosts graciously entertained us at an Estancia (ranch) on Argentina's broad, flat plains—the Pampas. Large pieces of Argentine beef were skewered and roasted on long iron spears thrust vertically into the ground near burning logs. Resplendent in their traditional, colorful garb, Gauchos unsheathed their knives and sliced off steaming chunks of roasted meat for our plates. We dined at polished wooden tables laden with delicious traditional dishes and wine in an enormous decorated barn and we were entertained by a band playing beautiful Tango music.

In May 1974, I made my first trip to headquarters and lobbied for additional funds. I succeeded—and gathered vital intelligence. Boyes inspected his communications stations around the world in order to look people in the eye and find out first-hand what was really going on. Since our turn was on the horizon, I tried to find out about his interests and style.

The admiral came to Balboa in mid-July. We had laid on briefings, facility tours, luncheons, select enlisted meetings, calls on the Canal Zone Governor and the CINC, evening social events, and even an early-morning fishing excursion on the Panama Canal (he was an expert fly fisherman).

Boyes arrived at dawn; he was in a grumpy mood due to commercial flight schedule changes and a sleepless trip. He immediately changed our entire schedule, was very critical and kept everyone off-balance during his visits to our three sites.

During our drives between sites, the admiral hammered me about the IANTN, "Where is the requirement? The IANTN doesn't support the fleet. Why the hell should I pay for it? Are you just having fun and games in South America?" He dismissed my tasking from the CNO and the network's value to the Navy's relations with the South American Navies. "Fine, let the CNO pay for it!"

On the end of his second day, he met with all officers and chiefs in the MIC. We were all feeling a bit bruised and on edge. The admiral looked silently around the room. "When I go aboard a ship and walk around, by the time I get to the bridge I have a good feel for the kind of ship I am on. My feeling about Balboa is that this is a smart, shipshape outfit with a proud crew that knows what they are doing. My compliments to all of you!"

But before we could relax he said, "I saved you this year, but you are going to have to show headquarters why we should keep Balboa. We are in a tough, costly transition to satellites, and we have to downsize and reprogram funds. Don't feel sorry for yourselves; everyone is under the gun!" Then he tasked me to create specific mission studies and identify operational requirements that could be transferred to the Army, Air Force, Pan Canal or Puerto Rico, or eliminated.

On Saturday evening, the admiral, Linda, and I attended a dinner party in his honor at the quarters of his good friends, Rear Admiral Blount and his wife. During cocktails, General Rosson, the U.S. commander in chief, Southern Command, also headquartered in the Zone, confronted me about the IANTN, "During my visit last week, the Chilean Navy chief of communications gave me hell about lack of the U.S. Navy's support for the IANTN. He said they need more equipment." I replied, "Excuse me General, let me get Admiral Boyes; he needs to hear this!" I then explained to both the status of Chile's IANTN station.

The U.S. Navy had delivered all equipment called for in the agreement, and now the Chilean Navy wanted satellite capability for their IANTN station, which was not planned or agreed upon by the U.S. Satisfied with my explanation, Rosson turned to Boyes and told him that the IANTN was "the best program the U.S. military had going in South America" because it was linked to the Navy chiefs, who were the most influential leaders in their respective nations. In Ecuador and Chile, the admirals were members of the ruling juntas, and in Argentina, Admiral Emilio Massera (who I had briefed on the IANTN) was head of the junta. Boyes never again badgered me about my IANTN activities; he supported my IANTN activities.

During our drive to the airport early the next morning, I reviewed the tasking I had received from the Admiral. I gave him some fact sheets about our initiatives and other pertinent info about Balboa that I thought he would be interested in. He was very complimentary about our enlisted re-enlistment rates, which were above NTS and Navy averages, "These are the very best I have seen in the NTS—send a story to the Navy Times!" (Balboa was at the top or near on all NTS and even Navy overall retention rates during my entire tour.)

Later, while waiting for his flight, I left him alone in the VIP room and chatted with his Navy aide to get his take on the admiral's visit. He told me, "The admiral really liked your goals and objectives for Balboa; it's the best thing you showed him. He had been concerned that you were spending too much time in South America and not minding the helm at Balboa!"

On July 23, Boyes acknowledged my earlier trip report on Chile and he added a penned note, "Frank: You are a great naval officer. Don't let tired, grouchy, early-morning rear admirals dampen your fine and dynamic spirit."

Feeling great, I focused again on our Unitas initiative. We had coordinated with Captain Burke and Navcams Norfolk and gotten them on board, and coordinated with the key Unitas TF 138 players, who were skeptical, but did not object. We thought we had a go.

In late July, I sent a message to the task force commander, Rear Admiral Dave Emerson and his flagship USS *Belknap*, Navcommsta Puerto Rico and Navcommunit Rio confirming our intent to proceed with Balboa's single-termination communications concept for Unitas.

Knowing that reliable HF communications were critical to his success, Emerson was not inclined to let Balboa experiment with his task force's lifeline. In fact, he hit the overhead and sent a high-precedence message to Boyes and Burke blasting our single-termination concept.

A huge flap erupted. Messages flew back and forth, followed by telephone calls from me and my team to Captain Burke, Cams Norfolk, the flagship, Emerson's chief of staff, OPNAV, and the headquarters. It required a major coordination effort over several days to get everyone calmed down and back on board.

The fleet states its communications requirements to the Navcams, but the Navcams have the last word in how to satisfy them. Our initiative was saved by Captain Burke, who directed Navcams Norfolk to assign the *Belknap* termination to Navcommsta Balboa for the entire Unitas cruise and to shift to Rio or Puerto Rico only if necessary. Headquarters sent us frequency prediction tables to cover the entire task force track around South America.

To enhance our support to *Belknap*—and further assuage Rear Admiral Emerson's concerns—I provided his flagship with an RM2 controller for their entire cruise and dispatched Receivers Officer CWO2 Foster and Operations Chief Bennett to Roosevelt Roads, Puerto Rico, to coordinate with Emerson's staff and brief USS *Belknap*, USS *Bordelon* and USS *Ainsworth* on our Unitas comm plan.

And I wrote to Boyes, "I wish to apologize for my message to Rear Admiral Emerson concerning *Belknap*'s termination. I realize now that it was open to misinterpretation, and the whole matter should have been referred to you...."

I concluded, "We are striving to develop a competitive spirit at Balboa… make it an All Hands effort and pull together...."

Boyes replied, "Dear Frank, Far better to show initiative than do nothing. Don't fret. We admire your interest and drive. Next time, a quick phone call to advise of your approach would be useful. We enjoyed our visit to your station. It was a pleasure to be with all of you. Charge, Tiger. Smile. Anybody who gets 4 hits out of 10 is batting better than Hank Aaron and Babe Ruth. Warm regards."

On August 6, I published an All Hands letter concerning Unitas XV:

> .... The cruise will last four months, steaming all the way around South America, through the Straights of Magellan and back to the Canal in November. Three U.S. Navy ships and a submarine will operate with the Navies of Argentina, Brazil, Colombia, Chile, Peru, Paraguay, Uruguay and Venezuela.... We have conducted extensive preparations.... What remains to be done? Quite simply, the day-to-day efforts, 24 hours a day, seven days a week for the next four months by each watch section to maintain the best possible communications with *Belknap* ... this will not be a simple task. It has never been done before ... I have a high degree of confidence that we can do it. Our equipment

is ready. We have a good "game plan," and I know that the personnel talent is here at NBA. Maintaining a reliable HF termination with *Belknap* continuously for four months will be a real challenge to all of us.... So let's give it our best efforts. That is all I ask.

On August 10, I wrote to Captain Burke, "The *Belknap* termination is going smoothly. The real test comes near the end of August when the task force rounds the corner of South America and heads towards Rio. Our "main battery" is in good shape here...."

In August, the admiral wrote, "On your studies on VLF, Comle and the IANTN please send me copies as well as the staff. Let me also know about fixing up the enlisted messes at Farfan and Summit.

During Boyes' visit, Lt. Bob Reardon had given him a strong pitch on our dining facility improvement needs and proceeded to "put the arm" on the admiral for additional funds for new steam tables and salad bars at Farfan. Boyes allocated $5000 on the spot from his contingency funds. Bob was like that—never afraid to ask flag officers for help.

I assigned the communications officer, Lt. Seth Pillsbury, to draft the communications studies, tutoring him on the format and content. An intelligent and very capable officer with a keen, analytical mind, Seth was a good writer and understood what I wanted. We all enjoyed his dry, sardonic New England humor. His study, research, analysis, extensive coordination, and hard work in creating the studies made Seth an expert on Balboa and the Naval Telecommunications System structure and capabilities. He was promoted to Lt. Cdr. in 1976 and became the operations officer when Bailey departed.

We tackled the VLF system study first. In September, I reported to Boyes. "Computer Science Corporation completed their inspection of our VLF... finding the material condition of the transmitter below a satisfactory level. If the trend is not reversed the useful lifetime of the transmitter could be as short as three years, and it could suffer a catastrophic failure. A major reason is inadequate funding for the past several years.... " I outlined the actions I had taken to correct the funding shortfall. I also reported the status of our Comle study. Regarding the IANTN study, "We have developed a comprehensive base of information on the IANTN in preparation for the upcoming Communications

Conference "and stated, "I plan to submit the IANTN study to CNO at the end of October. ..."

In September, I departed for San Diego. Lt. Beck and I had a busy time at the Chiefs of Communications Conference, which was chaired by Boyes. It was the first time the IANTN secretariat had participated in a conference. We interacted with all our IANTN associates and they expressed confidence in our leadership and direction. Boyes was very pleased with our conference preparations, proceedings and outcomes, especially regarding the IANTN project status and issues.

The CNO, Admiral Holloway, was also pleased. "It gives me great pleasure to personally commend you for your outstanding performance as Secretary of the IANTN ... for this conference. Your personal efforts ... were professionally done and well received ... many appreciative comments of the delegates. Your businesslike, yet tactful, approach to the many facets of your work with foreign dignitaries is particularly noteworthy.... Well Done."

I returned to Balboa and completed work on the several Balboa mission studies. The CNO approved our proposed 26-week training course in Spanish for the operations and maintenance of the new IANTN equipment. Later, we also justified the need for construction of new training facility office spaces and an expanded secretariat staff with three additional personnel to be provided by other IANTN member navies.

The canal treaty negotiations affected our Comle study. We validated the communications support provided by Comle to Pan Canal as vital to the Canal's operation, and there were no near-term alternatives to Comle's services.

There were two major financial issues: the revenue generated by messages addressed to the port captains for ship transits, and the revenue generated by commercial re-files of messages. The CNO approved the new fees to be paid by Pan Canal to Balboa effective in February 1975. As a reward for our superior study, headquarters allowed us to keep the additional $44K, which I applied to our Comle project and our new supply and fiscal department office.

Meanwhile, our most daunting task, the Unitas term—the big enchilada—was approaching its most critical phase. For almost three months, it had worked like a charm, exceeding our expectations and achieving send-and-receive reliabilities almost like a landline.

Captain John Frank Gamboa, U. S. Navy (Retired)

Our anxiety level peaked the second week in October as the task force began its transit of the restricted waters of the Magellan Straits enroute to its port call in Chile, but as the ships passed through, the termination between Balboa and *Belknap* was maintained at highest quality and without interruption. Our single-termination concept worked just as we had envisioned, planned—and hoped. Undoubtedly, Sarmiento de Gamboa, the 16th century maritime explorer who discovered the passage when he sailed from Spain and around South America to Peru in 1579, was with us in spirit.

I wrote to Boyes, "… NBA succeeded in maintaining a continuous HF termination with the USS *Belknap* … from Puerto Rico, down the east coast of South America, through the Straits of Magellan, and up the west coast of South America…. and we are still terminated. The key to our success was the day-to-day alertness of our controllers both here and on *Belknap*, and our receiver operators … (who) kept right on top of the freqs, and were able to shift rapidly, as required. Overall, we are very pleased with the success of Unitas communications, and I am very proud of Balboa's communicators. Very respectfully."

The Unitas task group arrived at Balboa on November 24 for a four-day port visit. NBA hosted a picnic and cookout for all the task force communicators and electronic maintenance personnel, and my Sailors toured the ships. We held a welcoming reception at Farfan for the admiral, Captain Shultz, the squadron commander (a communicator who was later promoted to rear admiral), the ship captains, and all their radiomen, signalmen and electronics maintenance personnel. I presented Balboa plaques to the admiral and the COs.

A few days later, I received a letter from Rear Admiral Emerson.

> Please accept my personal, sincerest thanks for the outstanding hospitality …. It has been a great pleasure operating with you during the past four months…. Please extend my personal well done to all of your people who made it possible…. The SOLANT communicators and I look forward to continuing operations with you, both for the remainder of Unitas XV and next year on Unitas XVI.

CINCLANTFLT messaged, "The outstanding communications performance during Unitas XV reflects credit on both ends of the termination …. Well Done. Admiral Cousins."

¡El Capitán!

1974 was the most challenging time I had experienced as a naval officer—and the most satisfying. In November 1974, Rear Admiral Boyes was relieved by Rear Admiral Gordon Nagler as CNTC and by Rear Admiral Nivison as DNT at OP 941. Boyes reported on my fitness:

> The accomplishments of Navcommsta Balboa since the assumption of command of CDR Gamboa are numerous and noteworthy ... he corrected a longstanding problem in repair parts.... Initiated a comprehensive upgrade of the station's Public Coast Radio Station facilities ... (and) developed a training facility for the IANTN project, an essential operational and political milestone with our South American neighbors. He has assisted in the planning, organization, preparation and conduct of ... the Fifth Inter-American Conference of Chiefs of Naval Communications ... CDR Gamboa's station has received numerous commendations for comm support from other shore stations, command headquarters, and many fleet units. When weighed objectively, each of CDR Gamboa's accomplishments is commendable. When all are accounted for, his achievements demonstrate his desire and ability to excel in all undertakings.... In his collateral duty as IANTN Secretary, CDR Gamboa has performed far and above what was expected of him. He has distinguished himself as ... a fine diplomat, politically astute, technically skilled and sensitive towards those about him ... Because of this his contemporaries and superiors regard him as an ideal officer and gentleman while his subordinates are always eager to follow his leadership. His station morale is ample evidence of this fact. CDR Gamboa is highly recommended for promotion to the grade of captain.

Although I was deeply immersed in my Balboa initiatives and tasks, my primary career goal—commanding a warship—was never out of mind. After two annual sessions of the commander surface command selection board, I had not been selected for sea command.

In October, I wrote to Admiral Boyes about my concerns, "As we discussed during your visit here in July ... I have not yet been selected for sea command by Bupers.... I will screen one more time, in January 1975... I would greatly appreciate any assistance you may provide. Very respectfully."

Captain John Frank Gamboa, U. S. Navy (Retired)

By then Boyes had been promoted to vice admiral, moved up one level in the Opnav hierarchy, and Rear Admiral Gordon Nagler, his relief, replied to my letter, "This is your last screen before the board and, with your solid record, I am hopeful that you will be selected for command. However, the competition among your year group is very keen and there are few selection opportunities. Therefore, if for some reason you should not screen for command, don't be discouraged but continue to develop your proven subspecialty as the route to attaining captain.... You are doing a fine job in Balboa."

Commander Frank Donovan, president of USNA '59, a tall, popular Irishman with a great sense of humor, was my detailer (and a very successful naval officer who achieved the rank of vice admiral). He told me that my final "look" by the selection board would be even more competitive—only five major ship commands were available for my year group. I had to go the extra mile so Frank advised me to write a personal letter to the president of the board, which was permitted by the Bupers manual. The president had to read it, but he was not required to act upon it. I sent my letter on December 31, 1974, and Donovan personally delivered it to the admiral:

> 1. .... This letter is submitted to the President of the Commander Sea Command Selection Board convening on 14 January 1975.
> 2. I am a naval officer of the line, and my driving goal and ambition is to command a ship of the line. A combatant preferably, but a sea command in any case.
> 3. In my sixteen years of naval service at sea and ashore, three predominant strands have been interwoven in the patterns of my career, which since its inception has been oriented towards command at sea. The three are Surface Warfare, Communications, and International Relations. Each has complemented the other two, but the unifying spirit and theme has always been, and will continue to be, command at sea.
> 4. (I presented a complete summary of my sea tours and related qualifications.)
> 5. Accordingly, command at sea remains my primary goal, for which I consider myself to be fully qualified not only professionally, but morally and physically as well. Therefore, in the best interests of the U.S. Navy and my career, I respectfully request to be

¡El Capitán!

selected for command at sea. Very respectfully, John Frank Gamboa.

The day after the Board approved its slate of selections, Donovan telephoned me, "Congratulations Frank, you got a ship!" He told me that, when the admiral finished reading my letter, he said, "I don't know who else we are going to select, but Frank Gamboa is going to be one of them!"

Elated, I walked home and told Linda. A few days later, I received a letter from Chief of Naval Personnel, Vice Admiral David Bagley. "I am very pleased to inform you that you have been selected for surface commander command…. The board selected those officers it considered best fitted for these positions of great responsibility and your selection reflects credit upon you and your career record. The board was headed by a flag officer with two additional flag officers and six senior surface warfare officers as members. (Ship assignment details)… Please accept my personal congratulations and best wishes for continued success in your future assignments."

On May 1, 1976, the bureau issued my orders to command USS *Fort Fisher* (LSD 40), home ported in San Diego. She was *Pensacola*'s sister ship and only four years in commission—virtually a new ship. I had seen her under construction at Quincy and knew her class better than any other warship. She was an ideal command assignment for me.

Our family life in the Zone was filled with interesting activities. As a boy scout, Jack enjoyed great jungle treks and camping in the dense rain forests. He still loved to search for antique bottles; his favorite discovery was the rare Panama "torpedo." He sluiced and panned for gold in the Chagres River (the canal's primary water source) with his buddies and his favorite high school teacher, Mr. Shaw, who was an expert artifacts collector. Jack was on the school swim team and traveled to meets even in Costa Rica. He also transited the canal as a guest aboard Mimi and Dan Dyer's beautiful yacht *Rabbit*.

Judy was a girl scout and spent all of her spare time riding her first horse, *Principe*. A neighborhood Army wife, Sally Kastl, gave her rides to and from the barn. Sally was a certified farrier and taught Judy about caring for a horse and how to compete in equestrian events.

Captain John Frank Gamboa, U. S. Navy (Retired)

We had wonderful visits from our family. Linda's parents and her Aunt Anne were with us for our second Christmas in the Zone. The next summer, my sister Tina, her husband Jim and their son Mark, a youngster at the Naval Academy, spent two weeks with us. Our sightseeing included a small plane flight to the Cuna Indians' San Blas islands off the east coast of Panama, riding in dugout canoes to visit their villages on nearby small islands, dining on lobsters and sleeping in hammocks inside thatched huts.

In 1975, Linda, Jack, Judy and I flew to Lima, Peru, in a U.S. Air Force C-130 cargo aircraft from Howard AF base in the Zone, crossing over the dazzling snow-capped Andes. In Lima, we were houseguests of Peruvian Navy Captain (later rear admiral) Enrique Petrozi and his wife, Coco, and we toured the famous gold museum and other sights in Lima. We flew to Cusco for the annual festival of the Sun God, and went by train up the mountain to see Machu Picchu.

In the spring of 1975, when my Academy roommate, Cdr. Keith Bunting, was in command of his awesome nuclear-powered ballistic missile submarine, USS *Abraham Lincoln*, he invited Linda, Jack, Judy and me to ride on Lincoln as it transited through the canal.

We made family day trips to nearby beaches and the island of Taboga, and boated with friends to their bohio (thatched hut) camps along the canal, for picnics. We also enjoyed longer trips to Contadora Island, El Valle for carnivál, and a beach cottage at Las Tablas. We thoroughly enjoyed our life and friendships in the Canal Zone, Panama and the IANTN countries.

The Navy's Inspector General Rear Admiral Burton Shepherd visited Balboa in February accompanied by Congressman Alexander from Arkansas, a member of the House Appropriations Committee, and the Master Chief Petty Officer of the Navy. After the visit, Nagler wrote, "Rear Admiral Shepherd upon his return informed me that he was extremely impressed with the fine job you are doing at Balboa. Keep up the good work and I appreciate the effort that you and your people put forth in making the Admiral's visit so successful and educational." This was a great way to start the New Year. My efforts to create a positive command climate were bearing fruit.

Due to drastic reduction in travel funds, I eliminated my Secretariat travel in FY75. To maintain contact with the IANTN station COs, I invited them to visit Balboa for orientation. The Directors from Venezuela and Colombia had very productive visits. The CAT was very busy developing the maintenance and operator training course material—in Spanish.

Because of the long lead-time on construction projects, I front-loaded my fiscal year 1975 annual budget submission with all of Balboa's remaining facility improvement projects, including the remaining modernization of all enlisted working, living and recreational facilities. In early June 1976, we completed 12 new women's barracks rooms at Farfan, and completed the modernization of the Farfan enlisted barracks and the galley, and got new furniture for all site offices. The CAT was very busy developing the maintenance and operator training course material—in Spanish. During my stewardship, I doubled Balboa's overall annual budget and corrected long-standing facility maintenance and habitability deficiencies.

In July 1975, the U.S. Navy downsized its Southern Command, replaced the flag officer with a captain, and drastically reduced the staff. Upon his relinquishment of command in July 1975, Rear Admiral Blount wrote in my fitness report:

> CDR Gamboa is an exceptionally capable officer ... he has exhibited leadership and management abilities of the highest order.... his superb performance is thoroughly documented by laudatory messages and numerous letters of commendation ... Of particular significance is his proven ability to work closely and effectively with Latin American Navies ... facilitated by his fluency in Spanish but, beyond that, he has consistently demonstrated a rare degree of tact, finesse, and organizational ability in working with and gaining the cooperation of foreign naval officers. CDR Gamboa has unlimited potential for satisfying current and future Navy needs in the politico-military area.... He and his wife are a most attractive couple, are active in social, civic and charity affairs, and are truly outstanding representatives of the U.S. Navy abroad. He is recommended without reservation for accelerated promotion and for assignment to positions of increased responsibility.

Navcams Norfolk again assigned the UNITAS flagship termination to Balboa for the duration of the 1975 cruise. We exceeded our 1974 termination reliability performance. We had established a new HF long-haul communications standard in the Atlantic Fleet—and a standard of excellence at NBA.

In November, the Secretary of the Navy approved and funded our project for a permanent training facility on the second floor of the Farfan receivers building. Construction was completed in March 1977, institutionalizing operator and maintenance technical training for the IANTN member navies on U.S. Navy communications-electronics equipment in the Spanish language, the only such technical school in the U.S. Navy at that time.

January 1976 began with our IG inspection (there are only two grades assigned, satisfactory or unsatisfactory). Balboa was judged satisfactory and specifically commended for excellence in "The spirit, enthusiasm, smartness, and appearance of station personnel; exceptionally high level of performance (in six functional areas); and the operational support provided Unitas forces over significantly longer distances than terminations are normally maintained...."

Three days later, Nagler arrived for a two-day visit, accompanied by Captain Burke, our former boss at Atlantic Fleet headquarters. "I was extremely impressed with the overall appearance of your personnel and facilities.... The conditions that your personnel work and live in are some of the finest I have seen any place in the world. The very fine job you have done in the IANTN area is certainly worthy of note. I believe it is one of the finest programs assisting Latin American countries that I have ever seen. You should feel very proud of your accomplishments in this field."

Our UNITAS single termination record performance had a very positive impact on my professional relationship with Captain Burke. During his visit, he told me confidentially that he intended to recommend me for a medal at the end of my tour. Nagler was relieved shortly after his Balboa visit, and I served for only four months under his relief. I never received a medal for my performance in command of Balboa. I assumed that "it slipped through the crack."

The eighth Inter-American Naval Conference was scheduled for mid-August, hosted by the Brazilian Navy in Rio de Janeiro. As a member of the U.S. Navy delegation, I had to provide a status of the IANTN so I scheduled my final station visits. Linda accompanied me on my trip to

Ecuador, and the American embassy's CDR Stephens and his wife graciously hosted us in their home.

My team and I were standing on a high hill overlooking Quito studying the proposed antenna-farm footprint when I inquired about a broad trail that extended far into the distance in both directions. The Ecuadorian commander proudly replied that it was the royal road that connected the Inca realm, a communication system with royal runners that delivered the emperor's messages to his far-flung empire. We had selected an appropriate communications site.

After our team completed the site survey and reached agreement on the communications equipment upgrade package, the Ecuadorian Navy flew us from Guayaquil to the Galapagos Islands for a fascinating sightseeing day-trip, while Linda and Mrs. Stephens toured and shopped in Guayaquil. Linda and I also went to the Otavalo Fair near Quito where hand-woven Alpaca wool articles are sold by indigenous Ecuadorians.

After our return to Balboa, I received the following letter:

> My thanks for the Naval Communications Station Balboa plaque. It will serve as a handsome reminder of your pleasant and productive visit to Ecuador. It is a source of no little personal satisfaction to me that the IANTN is finally back on track here, and I appreciate very much the part you and your colleagues played in getting it there. With best wishes, Robert Brewster, United States Ambassador to Ecuador.

In the Dominican Republic for the inauguration of their IANTN station, I delivered remarks in Spanish and was a guest at their Armed Forces Day ceremony presided over by their President Juaquin Balaguer. He thanked me warmly for my assistance to the Dominican Navy.

In Bogota, we drove to a Colombian Army post in the countryside to inspect a proposed antenna site on a hill located on the post. When we came out of the post commander's office, I had expected to board a Land Rover. But the colonel smiled and said, "There is no road to the site. The only way to the hill top is on horseback!" Wayne and my IANTN operations chief Richardson looked at me with wide grins and quickly mounted their beautiful, spirited, chestnut-colored horses. I gave them a hard, knowing stare, smiled, lowered the chinstrap on my cap, and got on my mount as if I knew what I was doing. I hadn't been on horseback since my Lone Pine ride into the Sierras in 1952.

Captain John Frank Gamboa, U. S. Navy (Retired)

Smartly attired in my service dress blue uniform, I followed the colonel, drawing stares from soldiers as we trotted through the post. We galloped across a field, frightening me out of my wits, and climbed up a long, rugged, thickly overgrown trail to the proposed location, which afforded a beautiful view of the valley and the Army camp below. We all agreed that it was an ideal antenna site.

That evening at dinner with our Colombian hosts, I joked to my team that conducting site surveys on horseback wasn't mentioned in our job descriptions. The next day we flew to Cartagena to inspect the new transmitter facility. The Colombians hosted a dinner party at the historic and beautiful Spanish 17th century harbor fortifications.

In August of 1975, I was tasked by Rear Admiral Nagler to submit recommendations on the downsizing of Navcommsta Balboa. We had worked hard to accomplish its vital Navy mission in a superior manner and to improve every facet of the station. Navcommsta Balboa was successful and proud, with high morale.

Now I had to determine how to dismantle it. It was a joyless task. But the end of my tour was less than a year away, and I did not want to pass the buck to my successor, so I addressed the issue with my leadership team. Several weeks later, we submitted a comprehensive study with recommendations for eliminating selected operational functions and facility reductions.

As luck would have it, the ax fell on April Fool's Day, 1976. Navcommsta Balboa was re-designated as a residual station. Our fleet center itinerant ship/shore circuits were placed on 24-hour standby; our termination requirements were reduced to 3 from 4; and Navcams Norfolk was directed to assign the bulk of fleet terminations to Navcommsta Puerto Rico. HF transmitters at Summit were reduced to 38 from 72, with the excess transmitters to be removed and shipped stateside. Balboa's staffing was reduced by one lieutenant and 34 enlisted billets through attrition. In May, a headquarters team arrived at Balboa to coordinate all actions required by our various study recommendations. We had settled Balboa's future.

As I ascended the line officer profession, I observed my superiors' leadership styles and their impact and influence on the officers and enlisted under their charge. My intent was to enhance the leadership

227

training I had received at the Naval Academy. I also read articles on leadership and discovered that many authors performed intellectual and verbal contortions in defining leadership. Their common theme: line officers are not managers, and it is an insult to be called an administrator. A line officer is a leader—end of discussion. To me that meant that, by merely issuing orders to his officers, the CO's desired excellence in operations, management and administration would occur naturally, just like the dawn of a new day or the going down of the sun.

Well, in my command activities at Balboa I had followed a different path. To improve and maintain the command's readiness, I had overhauled the organization's operational, managerial and administrative functions and corrected its habitability, which required my own thorough grounding in leadership principles, management approaches and administrative skills.

I concluded that the seeming contradictions between leadership, management and administration are nonsense—these functional domains are complementary,

Leadership begins with a person's willingness to take charge of a group and accept total authority, responsibility and accountability for its performance, conduct and welfare.

Leadership was the vital human force that connected all the dots in Balboa's organization and created unity. Management was the approach that we used to create and maintain order; and our administrative skills ensured the command's effective and efficient operation.

First we created motivation—leadership. Next we planned our work—management. And then we worked at effectively executing our plan—administration.

The degree of involvement by a commanding officer in the details of his organization's operations and inner workings depends to a large extent on the abilities and skills of his executive officer, department heads and junior officers—and in Balboa's case, the quality of the warrant officers and chiefs. A senior flag officer is supported by a very experienced staff of expert assistants led by other savvy flag officers and senior captains—many years of professional know-how. The admiral can therefore focus his attention primarily on formulating strategy and tactics to accomplish his mission.

But in an organization like Navcommsta Balboa, the commanding officer's personnel mission is to develop his officers, warrant officers, and chiefs, challenging and training them by precept and example, thereby establishing his unit's standards of performance. He must engage his leadership team on a broad scale of activity in order to determine their abilities, evaluate their strengths and weaknesses, and gauge their potential. But the CO must also guard against "micro-management," taking care not to stifle his officers' initiative. A constant balancing act between broad guidance and detailed specificity, and a fine touch, are necessary.

At Balboa, I firmly believed that leadership was the key to achieving excellence in every functional domain of my organization—operations, management and administration. The directed human energy within Balboa's people—the individual motivation, desire, and energy—was created at each level of authority within my command through dedicated and inspirational leadership by me and my leadership team. It was the vital catalyst in the daily work performed at my level and the XO's, the department heads', the division officers', the chiefs' and the work center and watch section supervisors.' The combined force of our individual and collective leadership produced our desired results.

The CO who is not involved in—or even worse, disdains—the operational, managerial and administrative details of his command is not professional. Organizational ineffectiveness, poor crew morale and low command readiness will surely follow in his wake. In due course, his command will suffer a major mission failure. The only remedy is the commanding officer's relief for cause.

In June 1976 while I was in Washington, Linda flew to San Diego and purchased a house in Rancho Bernardo, a suburb in the rolling hills of North County. To get Jack and Judy into our new home before school started, she, Jack and Judy departed Panama on July 27.

Linda had taken art courses in the local college and two weeks before departing for San Diego, she renewed her saloon artist credentials by teaming with her art professor and good friend, Imogene Cookson, to paint a large seascape mural on a wall in the officers' club. Because of my participation in the naval conference in Rio de Janeiro in August, I could not depart Balboa until the first week in September. I moved into the BOQ.

In July, RADM Nagler was relieved. He made the following assessment of my Balboa performance:

¡El Capitán!

> CDR Gamboa continues to perform ... in a truly outstanding manner. His many and important collateral duties have also been performed in an exceptionally outstanding manner.... He has strengthened (the respect and cooperation) that IANTN navies have toward the United States and the U. S. Navy ... provided superb communications support services to the fleet ... maintained exceptionally high morale ... unequivocally qualified for accelerated promotion to captain. He is one of the head and shoulders officers who are the top proven sub-specialists in the communications community.

In August, I flew with the Vice CNO, Admiral Shear, and the other members of his delegation to the naval conference in Rio de Janeiro. The Navy chiefs approved our proposal for an expanded secretariat staffed with officers from the other IANTN member navies. Peru drew the Lt. Cdr. slot and Colombia and the Dominican Republic each drew a lieutenant billet. The officers reported to the secretariat in early 1977.

United States Naval Communications Station Balboa's talented, dedicated and loyal Navy and civilian personnel enabled me to shoulder the burdens of command and enjoy a challenging, exciting and fulfilling tour of duty. I learned how to lead and manage a large organization, to challenge its crew, to organize and plan for success, to effectively utilize all the resources at my disposal, and to excel in achieving a high level of command readiness. Departing my first Navy command assignment, I felt confident about assuming my first command of a warship.

My travels in Mexico, Central America, Panama, the Dominican Republic and South America acquainted me with these vibrant nations and their beautiful peoples, rich cultures and proud heritages. And my secretary duties improved my Spanish language proficiency. (The Brazilians always insisted that Gamboa is a Portuguese name; a Rio suburb is named Gamboa. They would first address me in Portuguese. Unfortunately, I do not speak the language.)

My work in the Inter American Naval Conferences and the IANTN gave me an understanding of our Navy-to-Navy relations and an appreciation of their great respect and friendship for the United States.

In 1976, Bupers selected me as a proven political-military sub-specialist. I was already a proven communications sub-specialist, so I had earned a rare double sub-specialist designation.

Captain John Frank Gamboa, U. S. Navy (Retired)

At my *despedida* luncheon, Navcommsta Balboa's officers, chiefs and civilians presented me with a handsome plank of polished, reddish-brown Panamanian wood beautifully decorated with two colorful, hand-painted Panamanian cultural icons; the memento is inscribed "The epitome of leadership is to command with professionalism, dedication, and concern for your people."

I relinquished command on September 3, 1976, to Cdr. Pete Crumpacker, USNA '59 and a 17th company-mate, in a ceremony on the lawn in front of Balboa's headquarters building.

Because of the large number of Panamanians and many South and Central American military attaches in attendance, and my Panamanian crewmembers, I delivered part of my remarks in Spanish. I concluded in English with the following:

> To the officers, men and women of United States Naval Communication Station Balboa, you are the finest in all the United States Navy, and second to none in any ranks. Together, we have accomplished much. At times, it has been difficult, and it was often necessary for you to exert that extra effort you so unselfishly gave.
>
> Why did we try so much? Admiral Rickover's comments on the purpose of a profession will explain:
>
> "The deepest joy in life is to be creative. To find an undeveloped situation, to see the possibilities, to decide upon a course of action, and then devote the whole of one's resources to carrying it out, even if it means battling against the stream of contemporary opinion, is a satisfaction in comparison with which superficial pleasures are trivial. But to create you must care."
>
> I know that you will continue to excel….To each of you, my heartfelt thanks and sincere Well Done!

En route to *Fort Fisher*, I stopped in Jacksonville, Florida, for a reunion with Cdr. John McCain, who was then in command of VA 174, the east coast replacement air group for the A-7 attack aircraft. He and his wife, Carol, hosted me at a dinner party in their home with members of John's staff and their wives.

With his irrepressible humor, John described some of his horrific experiences in North Vietnam captivity, and told us how he was inspired and sustained by his fellow POWs.

231

¡El Capitán!

Seven years after my departure from Balboa, on September 30, 1983, Navcommsta Balboa signaled to the U.S. Fleets and the IANTN:

> This last message transmitted from NAVCOMMSTA Balboa marks the end of 79 years of communications to fleet units in the two oceans and being a member of the Naval Telecommunications family. We stand relieved. This is NBA signing off.

Later, the IANTN mission, functions, and CAT were transferred from Farfan to Navcommsta Puerto Rico. The network was then converted to satellite circuits.

The secretariat is now a component of the U.S. Naval Forces Southern Command located in Mayport, Florida.

The IANTN has expanded to 17 countries, including its newest members Guatemala, Honduras, México, Nicaragua and Panama.

Ranch Hands Wiedemann, Pittenger, Larson and me toasting Alice, Pete's bride, August 1958. (Personal collection)

Destroyer Sailor. USS *Putnam*, March 1960, Sixth Fleet, Mediterranean. (Personal collection)

¡El Capitán!

Linda, Jack, Judy and me,
Alexandria, Virginia 1969.
(Personal collection)

Frederick, Tina, Bea, me,
Erlinda and Mosey, Las
Vegas, April 1972. (Personal
collection)

234

Captain John Frank Gamboa, U. S. Navy (Retired)

La Salle quarterdeck honors to Emperor Haile Selassie I, Conquering Lion of Judah, with Rear Admiral Hanks, Captain Crosby, U.S. Consul and me, Massawa, Ethiopia, February 1973.

Naval Communications Station Balboa Commanding Officer and his Lady at Panama Canal Zone Communicators Ball, fall 1975. (Personal collection)

Lt. Wayne Beck and me at Bogota, Colombia, for IANTN antenna site survey, March 1976. (Personal collection)

Relinquishment of command, Navcommsta Balboa, September 1976. (US Navy photo)

Part IV

Command at Sea

Eight Years Before The Mast

Chapter Eight

★★★★★★★

Ships in the harbor are safe, but that isn't what ships are made for.

—Benjamin Franklin

USS *Fort Fisher* (LSD 40) was commissioned in 1972. Her name honored the Union Navy's amphibious assault and capture of the Confederacy's largest earthwork fortification, constructed by Confederate Colonel Charles Fisher on the banks of North Carolina's Cape Fear River. In late October 1976, *Fort Fisher* entered Todd Shipyard at San Pedro, California, for her first regular overhaul. I reported aboard on November 29, and on Friday December 3, I assumed command:

> To the officers and men of *Fort Fisher*, I am extremely proud and happy to assume command of this magnificent ship. You have earned a highly regarded reputation in the Pacific Fleet. In the days ahead, we will work together to maintain it....
>
> To Commander, Amphibious Squadron Five, I assure you that, as the newest member of your squadron, *Fort Fisher* will meet and exceed your high standards of excellence.
>
> To our guests here on *Fort Fisher* today for the first time, I welcome you and extend a standing invitation to visit our ship after we get out of overhaul.
>
> To my friends from Lone Pine, I appreciate your long trip to be here today. But I wonder who you left in charge back home!
>
> To my mother, my wife and my family, thank you!

At the reception Linda, Jack, Judy and I celebrated with Mom, all my brothers and sisters and their spouses and children, relatives, Lone Pine friends and other guests. Enriqueta was first to sign my guest book. She added a comment: "Captain's Mother!"

In the years prior to taking command of *Fort Fisher*, occasionally I would envision myself in the fleet commanding a powerful warship. With sturdy decks beneath my feet and a fresh sea breeze in my face, I stood on her bridge and scanned the horizon with my long glass as I sailed my swift combatant on urgent, even dangerous fleet missions—an inspiring image.

Reality was quite different. *Fort Fisher* was dry-docked and resting high and dry on keel blocks, surrounded by huge mobile cranes and noisy industrial facilities. Her guns and much of her machinery and electronics had been removed and were scattered throughout the shipyard and other places for repair. My ship was totally inoperative. Before I could sail her, I would have to put her back together again—if I could find all the pieces.

Living and working conditions aboard the ship were stressful. Shipyard workers were in practically every space, cutting holes in decks and bulkheads for machinery removal. It was noisy, smoky, dusty and hazardous; safety and cleanliness were a constant concern. And she was only partially habitable—crewmembers would have to live in barracks at the Long Beach Naval Station for several weeks. Married men had to commute the 100-plus miles to San Diego for weekends at home. I carpooled with my operations officer, Lt. Cdr. Bev Daly.

I met with the officers, then chiefs and first class petty officers; my captain's call was next with each division. Chief Master at Arms Capitano escorted me to my enlisted meetings. Over a cup of coffee in my cabin prior to my first division call, I sensed he had something to say so I asked him how the crew was doing. He came out with it, "Captain, there is no spirit of cooperation or harmony in this ship!" Some departments, especially Deck and Engineering, were outwardly hostile to each other. I decided to let my men ventilate to me about their concerns before I began telling them my desires.

My opportunity came soon enough. During my meeting with M Division (Engineering department's propulsion machinery personnel), a young fireman stood up and in a very sarcastic tone of voice asked me, "Captain, what are you going to do for the engineers?" A murmur rippled through the division and several other firemen nearly gasped aloud at his temerity. Smiling, I replied, "Why don't you tell me what you want me to do?" That opened the floodgates. Many of their machinery repair requests hadn't been approved or even submitted. They needed help on their large ship's force work package. They faced long days and weeks of hard work—they wanted me to cut them some slack. And they signaled an unspoken message to me—they felt ignored and unappreciated.

After listening to all their concerns, I promised to get them all the help that I could. Then I talked about my policy of teamwork and cooperation between all divisions. All hands in *Fort Fisher* had to lay-back (pull) together. I expected everyone to be a good shipmate.

As we walked back to my cabin, Chief Capitano was quick to say, "Captain that Sailor is not a trouble maker. He's a good kid." I nodded, "Chief, they all are!"

Following up with my chief engineer and Supships, I got many of their machinery work requests switched from the engineers to the contractor, including the labor-intensive bilges preservation and painting in both main propulsion spaces.

In early February, I heard some "scuttlebutt" (gossip) that there was friction between the engineers and the deck force. I summoned the chief engineer, Lt. Hank Carde, and the first lieutenant, Bruce O'Neil. As they stood at attention in my cabin, I told them,

> I have heard enough about friction between your respective departments. We are all shipmates and I expect full cooperation from all hands. You are hereby directed to take whatever measures are necessary to put a stop to this bullshit. I am holding you both accountable. If I hear any more about it, I will consider it your failure in leadership and it will reflect negatively in your fitness reports. Do I make myself clear? That is all!

A few weeks later, the Deck department duty section was installing a new wire rope on the port crane after working hours. They had only a few men available. As they were attempting to spool the cable, somehow it got out of hand and fell down into the well deck in a "bird caged" (tangled) pile. They needed help to retrieve and spool the heavy cable for testing the next day.

Without any hesitation, the engineering duty officer mustered everybody in his duty section and led them down to the well deck. Side by side, the engineers and deck seamen manhandled the wire rope all the way back up both vehicle ramps and onto the super deck (the deck space forward of the flight deck). Together, they installed it on the crane spool.

The next morning at officers' call, the first lieutenant publicly thanked the chief engineer. Sometimes a captain's best option is to demand a specific outcome.

Later, I asked Chief Capitano how things were going. With a big smile he replied, "Captain, there is so damn much harmony in this ship it almost makes me nauseous!" Well, at least my Sailors weren't jumping ship.

A ship's overhaul planning begins several months prior to its arrival at the shipyard. It is inspected by the ship's company, shore maintenance organizations, potential overhaul contractors, and Supships. The overhaul consists of hull, machinery, electronics and other equipment repair jobs— "the work package"—which is scoped through several "work-definition" conferences. Supships develops a cost and time estimate for each job. The Type desk designates a job for contractor accomplishment, assigns it to ship's force, defers it for post-overhaul, or rejects the job, usually for budgetary reason or time constraints.

Much negotiating takes place between the ship, the Type desk, and Supships, a time-consuming but remarkably effective process. The squadron commander and the amphibious group commander play a vital ship-support role. The final work package is awarded to a commercial shipyard on a competitive contract basis. When the ship enters the yard and the overhaul commences, things begin to happen pretty fast,

Fort Fisher's spare parts were offloaded to a warehouse, to be inspected and counted to ensure their conformance to the equipment they were intended for, and that the correct allowance (number) was in each bin. The storerooms had to be preserved and painted.

In dry dock, the hull paint was sandblasted off and a new coat of primer was sprayed on. Then anti-fouling paint (to prevent barnacles and other sea-growth) was applied to the underwater hull, and Navy haze gray above her black-painted waterline.

Dry-docking revealed corrosion damage to both stern shaft tubes. The tubes extend about 20 feet from the underwater hull and hold the shafts that connect the main engines to the screws. The repairs required a two-month extension of the overhaul, but the extra time broke the logjam of pending work requests. We screened 90 additional jobs (the final overhaul package included 350 shipyard jobs at a cost of over seven million dollars).

My department heads and I were then able to develop our three critical goals: complete a successful overhaul with no further delays; accomplish all underway training and workup for deployment; and sail with Phibron Five on September 13, 1977, for a seven and a half-month deployment with the Seventh Fleet.

Ships coming out of overhaul normally have twelve to eighteen months of training, maintenance, preparations and workup before deployment; we were going to have less than three months. In my initial face-to-face conversation with my boss, Commodore Harry Jenkins, his first comment was, "Frank, don't be late getting out of overhaul!"

Also bearing on our overhaul was "an opportune lift" for a huge quantity of earth-moving and construction equipment—the largest post-Vietnam sealift—to Eniwetok Atoll in the Marshall Islands. The equipment was needed for the U.S. government to fulfill its treaty obligation to remove the entire island's atomic test-contaminated top layer of soil and restore the atoll's habitability for the indigenous population (the contaminated soil was to be entombed in concrete on the bottom of the lagoon).

Two LSDs were scheduled for the lift—*Fort Fisher* and *Mount Vernon*—plus three other ships in our eight-ship squadron. The equipment would be loaded in San Diego and Pearl Harbor and delivered enroute to the Far East.

If *Fort Fisher* could not deploy on time, a huge amphibious group heave-around would ensue and a wet well from another squadron would be jerked around and drastically short-cycled to replace my ship.

Crew turnover further complicated the situation. Prior to deployment, over half the crew would be transferred to new duty stations or leave the Navy, and many replacements would report straight from boot camp. To mold its new teams, *Fort Fisher* would have to conduct two weeks of underway refresher training followed by two weeks of amphibious refresher training. We would also be subjected to many pre-deployment inspections and assist visits by the type and squadron commanders, the Navy's way of preparing ships for extended overseas operations.

In the early 1970's, the Navy experienced several disastrous ship propulsion-space material casualties and fires at sea due to equipment failures and personnel errors. In response, CNO Admiral Elmo Zumwalt had created a ship's engineering and propulsion plant personnel training program with a heavy emphasis on casualty control and equipment and systems maintenance. Before a ship in overhaul could light off its main propulsion plants, it had to pass the Engineering Light-Off Examination (LOE), which focused on equipment and systems readiness and personnel knowledge of systems and casualty control procedures.

But the 800 lb. gorilla was the Operational Propulsion Plant Examination (OPPE) conducted by the Fleet Propulsion Examining Board (PEB). The OPPE focused on propulsion plant readiness, personnel performance in watch stations and propulsion plant watch team casualty control and firefighting. Before it could deploy, a ship had to pass its OPPE.

Faced with these challenges—and no flexibility in a highly compressed schedule—I would have to maximize my overhaul management involvement and exert a full measure of leadership.

The overhaul was a complex management task involving six organizations: *Fort Fisher* (the customer); the amphibious group commander and the squadron commander (the ship's owners); the type commander (the bursar); Todd Shipyards Los Angeles Division (the contractor) and Supships Long Beach (the overhaul technical and financial manager). The common, unifying goal was to restore the ship to its best condition within available resources and time.

As commanding officer, I had to ensure the smooth, effective meshing of these organizations. But first, I had to reorganize *Fort Fisher*'s overhaul management team and approach. The chief engineer had been assigned as overhaul manager (OM), but the main task facing the engineering department was to prepare for and pass the LOE in the shipyard, and then prepare for and pass the OPPE after overhaul. Both of these critical milestones required extensive planning, preparation, and training.

I reassigned the OM job to the operations officer, a former destroyer chief engineer, and the ship's force overhaul management system coordinator job to the CIC officer, who would be responsible for tracking progress on all ship's force jobs. He had prior experience in the system.

I then established a sequence of weekly meetings with the overhaul management teams: ship's force on Tuesdays, Todd on Wednesdays, Supships on Thursdays, and LOE meetings on Fridays. Quality control would be achieved by ensuring that each job was done in accordance with its technical specifications. Each department head would manage their respective repair jobs. I would oversee everything and manage by exception. (I never had to override a department head, but more than a few jobs received my special attention.)

Communication is the essence of relationships. To facilitate my control of the overhaul, I set out to develop a professional, collegial link with the head of each organization involved and their key assistants. I had coffee in my cabin every day with Lou Loring, Todd's ship superintendent. An ex-Navy master chief boiler repair technician, Lou knew ships and understood Sailors. He was highly competent and loved his job. Nothing that affected our overhaul escaped his notice. We quickly established a great working relationship based on mutual respect and trust.

I tasked the Cheng and the OM to create an LOE briefing, which we used to facilitate scheduling and coordination of all LOE-related jobs. Todd added an assistant ship's superintendent, Bob Castro, to supervise all LOE-related work.

I had our shipboard work centers track each job to identify problems that might cause delays; and the officers, chiefs, and leading petty officers visited the shipyard repair shops to track machinery repairs and observe tests of repaired items scheduled for re-installation.

I toured Todd's shipyard facilities and met with shop foremen and craftsmen who were repairing my ship. We established 16 coffee messes throughout the ship for the crew and shipyard workers, to facilitate communication—and scuttlebutt.

Once I had my arms around the overhaul management, I began my weekly routine of visiting division work centers and have a look-see at what my Sailors and the shipwrights were working on, which also ensured that department heads did the same. They or their division officers or chiefs were always present (the XO scheduled my tour in the POD). One morning I inspected the ship's laundry and dry cleaning facility. Waiting for me was a second-class petty officer. He told me all the problems he and his men had endured in Westpac trying to keep the laundry in operation. And the washers and dryers were flimsy, unreliable and had poor spare parts support availability. The machine shop had to fabricate several parts. He described the situation to me in a Sailor's unmistakable technical terminology, "Captain, these washers and dryers are a piece of shit. We need new ones!" But we had only requested their overhaul.

I immediately summoned the chief engineer and the supply officer, who verified the petty officer's account. I directed that new dryers and washers be obtained and that any other laundry and dry cleaning equipment that was unreliable be replaced with top of the line equipment.

Supships approved; it turned out that replacements were quicker and less costly than repairs.

Several weeks later, the "A Gang" (Auxiliaries division) gathered with enthusiasm and gratitude to welcome the arrival of new washers, dryers and dry-cleaning equipment. Easing my crew's workload became one of my top command priorities.

Three weeks after taking command, I launched "The Fleet Sailor," our ship's newspaper to be published every 4-6 weeks by our public affairs officer Lt. j.g. Pat Johnson and journalist, JOSN Johnson (no relation). The newspaper's name was selected from a list of crew suggestions. I also decided to keep a personal journal. On January 5, 1977, I made my first entry:

> I have been in command of *Fort Fisher* a month and three days. My impressions of the ship range from optimism in the potential of the crew to dismay ... in the internal administration and management.... I have attacked all the "hygiene" factors because so very little has been done for the crew.... My captain's calls uncovered many breakdowns in leadership, management and administration. I've started familygrams and a ship's newspaper to keep the families and crew informed. I cut back the work hours on Fridays to get people on the road home earlier ... (held) a Christmas party in the mess decks ... lots of enthusiasm.... I took a look at the number of men on restriction and the length of time they had served (some as many as 60 days!) and rescinded the remaining 5-6 days in three cases to let them know that good behavior is rewarded.... I have such a long way to go! ... I have to ensure that we learn to communicate, and that we respect one another.

The squadron commodore—my immediate superior in command (ISIC)—Captain Harry Jenkins, a naval aviator, had endured six years as a POW in North Vietnam. He was gregarious, and had a great sense of humor. At a dinner party in our home, when asked what things he missed most when he was a POW, he thoughtfully replied, "A cold place to put my beer and a warm place to put my hands! And chocolate cake!" He loved the four-layer one that Linda baked and served for dessert. On January 27, I reported our overhaul status:

> In general, progress is satisfactory ... biggest bottleneck ... is processing of the relatively large package of supplementary jobs ... created a heavy workload on Supships planning, design and contracting offices. CDR Stanley and I met with Supships on 9 December to prioritize the jobs, but due to the stern tube job resolution ... these were not awarded until last week....
>
> The stern tube jobs (and) the underwater hull repair job are going well.... If Todd achieves a successful realignment check next week on the stern tubes, they will proceed with undocking on 22 Feb ... re-dock us on 15 March for installation of remaining sea ballast valves, bounce the ship once (to reposition the keel blocks) for completion of the underwater hull preservation, then undock us on 25 March. Todd is nearing completion of work on major engineering equipment and re-installation has commenced. The four ship service generators were re-installed last week.
>
> ... (In our) overhaul management ... excellent communication and cooperation and our shipboard overhaul organization is meshing effectively with Todd and Supships Long Beach.... For the LOE, we have ensured ... that Todd got off to a fast start.... In summary, Commodore, things are going about as well as can be expected at this point in the overhaul.... Very respectfully.

I scheduled San Diego Human Resources Development Center to conduct a human resources availability (HRAV) to assess individual crewmember's attitudes about their treatment aboard *Fort Fisher*, and to identify all shipboard leadership, management and administrative deficiencies. Our HRAV began with a detailed confidential written survey of the crew, a snapshot of attitudes and perceptions about the command—their opinions of work and life in *Fort Fisher*. I inserted additional questions that reflected my concern for morale, crew welfare and administrative efficiency.

After the Center's analysis and our assessment of the survey responses, we conducted a weeklong workshop at the Long Beach Naval Station to create a command action plan (CAP), guided by expert facilitators from the Center.

Captain John Frank Gamboa, U. S. Navy (Retired)

My fundamental desire was to create an efficient ship's work schedule; opportunities for ship's company professional development through on and off the ship training; programs for personnel recognition; prompt crew receipt of pay raises and promotions; nourishing and appetizing meals; well-maintained, clean and sanitary berthing and bathroom facilities; good laundry and dry cleaning services; efficient processing of personal requests; time off for personal and family needs; a good library; and a dynamic ship's company welfare and recreation program.

The CAP would be my roadmap for creating my desired command climate.

Our first initiatives were the creation of Sailor of the month and supervisor of the quarter programs to highlight superior enlisted crewmember professional performance. The XO, Cdr. John Harms, a strong leader and an expert manager and administrator, coordinated with the department heads on CAP implementation, and it was featured in "The Fleet Sailor" and my familygrams. By the end of the year I had created a separate executive department (it had been combined with the navigation department), 12 new personnel support directives—and a positive command climate.

To create fun and recreation for the ship's company, I tasked two junior officers to organize and conduct an after-work intramural sports program. They created an eight-team slow-pitch softball league and tournament made up of division teams. I required that the officers, chiefs and petty officers play on their respective division's team (to build division spirit and teamwork—men who play together will work well together).

We also organized an intramural bowling league with 12 teams (the wardroom and chiefs mess formed their own teams). We created *Fort Fisher* volleyball and basketball teams to compete with other ships. The ship's welfare and recreation fund paid for the division team t-shirts and ball caps embroidered with team names and logos, shirts for the bowling teams, complete uniforms for the ship's teams and trophies for all champion teams.

The XO and I attended most of the division softball games, and we joined the wardroom team in the bowling league. The intramural sports program created great ship's unity and spirit, improved crew morale and lowered alcohol and drug abuse practically to zero.

¡El Capitán!

Warship management includes a large number of Navy-mandated administrative, maintenance, training, and personnel programs and requires a well-coordinated effort by the wardroom and the chiefs' mess to stay on top of things. Because of our compressed pre-deployment workup schedule, we couldn't let anything "slip through the crack."

Confident that my Balboa management approach could be successfully implemented in *Fort Fisher*, in February, I added some management structure to the normal ship's company organization in order to get "hands on" involvement. I created the commanding officer's management conference including the XO, heads of department, and other officer or enlisted personnel for specific agenda items. My intent was to assess command policies, focusing on effective use of human, financial, and material resources. A major objective was to ensure the efficient day-to-day operation of the ship.

Olive White, a ship interior decorator with an excellent reputation for enhancing the décor of Navy shipboard living spaces, visited the ship and asked me, "Captain, what are you doing to improve the décor and habitability of the wardroom, the chiefs' mess, the first class lounge and the enlisted dining facility? And the barber shop, the library and the crew's lounge?" She had inspected the spaces with my supply officer, Lt. Lon Eastlund.

Impressed by her imaginative ideas and enthusiasm, after checking with Supships and discussing the matter with the XO and department heads, I initiated a ship's habitability improvement project and put Eastlund in charge. Olive and he developed plans to upgrade selected living and working spaces, including the installation of privacy curtains on each enlisted man's bunk.

The total project would cost $200,000 and I was concerned about the overhaul funding. We had pressed the Type desk very hard to approve our 90 additional machinery repair jobs; we were nearing the funding limit for our overhaul; and the Type desk had to reserve funds for post-overhaul re-work. I was also worried about timing. Requesting new work well into the overhaul was a hard sell.

Feeling that I would have to expend another "silver bullet," I decided to personally hand-carry the package to our Type desk officer in San Diego. "You have spent over seven million dollars on hull and machinery, but not a single penny for upgrading the ship's habitability. I want this for my crew. They deserve it!" Cdr. Stanley smiled as he accepted the package, "I am always willing to support what a skipper wants for his crew!"

Stanley knew we had done first-things first and we were making excellent progress. By working hard on our ship, we had gained his trust and confidence the old-fashioned way—we earned it.

Olive's team worked their magic and the habitability project fostered ship's pride and morale. The crew appreciated the privacy curtains on their bunks, especially when they had worked all night and rated "late-sleepers." On its bulkheads, the enlisted dining facility's hand-painted Civil War historical murals of *Fort Fisher* battle scenes became our showplace.

Two weeks before our LOE, we were visited by Rear Admiral Richard Paddock, the new eastern Pacific amphibious group commander. My department heads and I briefed him on our overhaul schedule, issues and concerns, then he toured the ship. He complimented me on our progress and the appearance of the ship and crew, "It's great to see a ship that knows what's going on in its overhaul!"

To prepare for getting underway for the first time in almost eight months, we conducted a two-day "fast cruise." In this simulated sea trial, a ship lights-off the main propulsion plants and steams and operates all ship systems while made fast (moored) to the pier. We manned all underway watch stations, conducted training and verified all the ship's bills. On May 23, the night before my first day at sea as captain, I wrote in my journal:

> Well, here we are on the eve of sea trials. Incredible. And today we unveiled our mess decks paintings. How fast the weeks have passed. How full my time and attention have been. We passed LOE …. It was exciting—the teamwork, the hanging in there together, the comradeship, the decision-making and the problem solving … our prize was the habitability package…. I could characterize the overhaul in one word—teamwork…. My crew is anxious to leave the yard and get on to San Diego and Westpac…. This period has been tough on the married personnel. My kids and Linda have suffered. It's been strenuous for me…. I

pray all goes well tomorrow and that God watches over my ship, my crew, and my passengers.

Having found all the pieces and reassembled my ship, we got underway on May 24 and sailed out of Long Beach harbor to conduct sea trials. Todd and Supships riders conducted many machinery and system tests and a successful full-power trial ending with a "crash-back" and rudder tests. We checked out the radar, navigation and communication systems. I wrote the evening prayer and delivered it on the ship's One MC.

> Almighty God, on this our first night at sea in this year, we pause to give thanks to you for your countless blessings bestowed upon each of us, to give thanks for your guidance through our many days and weeks at work on our ship, and to give thanks for our success. Watch over us each day and take care of our loved ones. Give us courage and strength to do our duty to our country, our families, and our shipmates. Amen

The next morning we anchored in the harbor and brought Commodore Jenkins aboard in my gig. He toured the entire ship, observed the test of our ballast system, well-deck flooding and de-ballasting.

On Friday morning, May 27, I conducted my first personnel inspection and awards ceremony, praising my crew for their outstanding performance, and honoring our first Sailor of the month and our first supervisor of the quarter (Operations Specialist 2 Rusty Hopp). I presented ship's plaques to Cdr. George Nyman, assistant Supships Long Beach, Lou Loring, Bob Castro and the Todd Shipyard general manager.

The manager presented me with a framed copy of *The Laws of the Navy* by Ronald A. Hopwood, inscribed, "Commemorating the combined effort and teamwork during first overhaul."

Because of testimony I had heard at captain's mast from the accused, the witnesses, and the chain of command; the negative crew feedback from my captain's calls; and my assessment of *Fort Fisher*'s command climate, I concluded that the leadership performance of the wardroom, the chief's mess, and the first class was still not up to my standards. I particularly detested the officers' and chiefs' use of the phrase "dirt bag" when referring to a problem Sailor.

Captain John Frank Gamboa, U. S. Navy (Retired)

To make my ethical, moral, leadership and professional behavior standards and my expectations for the conduct of ship's company leaders crystal clear, on June 2, I published a memorandum of policy:

1. Subject: Professional Conduct by Officers, Chief Petty Officers and First Class Petty Officers.

2. Purpose: To promulgate rules governing the professional conduct of *Fort Fisher*'s officers, chief petty officers, and first class petty officers in their day-to-day working relationships with each other, and with personnel assigned or reporting to them.

3. Discussion. Command climate is the sum of all shipboard human interactions, both formal and informal. The formal, professional climate must always be supportive of good order and discipline, and morale. The professional conduct of the officers, chief petty officers and first class petty officers sets the tone for the whole ship, directly influencing the attitude, morale and motivation of the lower ratings. Furthermore, the conduct— specifically the leadership, management and supervisory actions— of the officers, chiefs, and first class must be generally consistent on a ship-wide basis in order to enhance command unity, strengthen the chain of command, and support crew morale. Accordingly, the following rules shall be observed by all officers, chiefs, and first class petty officers. For simplification, they are grouped into two categories: Do and Don't.

DO
a. Treat each person with courtesy and respect.
b. Treat each person equitably regardless of race, ethnicity, color or religion.
c. Address each person by his name. Use rank/rate as appropriate.
d. Be positive in your thinking and in your conversations.
e. Enjoy your work. Be enthusiastic.
f. Regulate the work of each person working for you. Determine a start and a completion time. Allow time for coffee/soft drink/head call breaks. Consider other interruptions.
g. Insure that each person working for you knows and understands what he is supposed to accomplish.

251

h. Strive to build the confidence of each person working for you.

i. Strive to build a bond of mutual trust with each person you work for, each person you work with, and each person who works for you.

j. Take time to counsel each person working for you. If he is doing well, tell him so. If you see shortcomings emerging, or he is not measuring up to your expectations, tell him so, and early on so that he has the opportunity to take appropriate corrective action.

k. Be observant. Know what is going on among the people who are working for you.

l. Get feedback. Keep the loop closed.

m. Use common sense.

n. Be available.

o. Keep your word.

p. Do something considerate each day for each person working for you.

DON'T

a. <u>Don't</u> use first names between officers and chiefs, or between officers and E-6 and below.

b. <u>Don't</u> use first names between chiefs and E-6 and below.

c. <u>Never</u> say anything derogatory about an officer, chief or first class petty officer in public, especially in front of juniors.

d. <u>Never</u> use derogatory names or phrases when addressing a person, even if meant in jest.

e. <u>Never</u> threaten a person. Tell him what you want and expect from him.

f. <u>Never</u> attempt to get revenge. You can't get even.

g. <u>Never</u> allow illegal or wrongful conduct by juniors, onboard or ashore, to go without admonishment or some type of corrective action.

h. <u>Don't</u> permit obscene/vulgar language in public, especially on or in the vicinity of the quarterdeck.

i. <u>Never</u> let a person think you have given up hope in him.

> 4. .... Heads of departments will indoctrinate all officers, chiefs, and first class petty officers within their departments on the above rules, and ensure compliance. Heads of departments will furnish a personal copy of this memorandum to each newly reported officer, chief, or first class petty officer in their respective department....

It was my policy to personally interview each departing crewmember and each newcomer. I personally handed a copy of the Do and Don't memo to each new officer, chief and first class petty officer, ensuring they understood my policy. With departing personnel, I would ask, "If you were to be ordered back to *Fort Fisher*, what would you like to be different here?" I advised new crewmembers that their personal goal should be to excel. I always received valuable feedback from these discussions. And I soon began to see clear indications that the dos and don'ts were being carried out.

In the final two weeks of our overhaul, we conducted another sea trial, completed our antenna radiation patterns, and checked out our ballasting system one more time. On June 9, the eve of our departure, I turned to my journal:

> This is our last night ... we are winding up in great shape.... We put a sign over the side this morning, "Viva Todd, Supships and Pacord! Adios. Thank you from all Fishermen." The yard took a picture of it with all their leading men on the ship. I went up and said a few words of thanks to them. Tough to talk. I'm tired, and get emotional easily. Lou Loring said some nice words too.... Lots of good feeling all around ... a lot going through my mind.... There were days when I was awfully discouraged, and times when it seemed like there was no end to it all.... But I kept my sense of humor and kept things in perspective ... maintained excellent communications....That made a huge difference in the long run ... ensured that my crew treated the contractor and Supships personnel with courtesy.... My officers are doing well handling the ship, and the crew is coming along nicely. So, all's well that ends well. It will be nice to be home in San Diego. Over one fourth of my command tour is over. It was a memorable experience and I am happy about it.

¡El Capitán!

We departed Todd Shipyard Friday afternoon, June 10, seventeen days ahead of schedule (the only ship that completed an overhaul ahead of schedule during my time in the amphibious force). *Fort Fisher* arrived in San Diego on Saturday morning, warmly welcomed on our pier by Commodore Jenkins and happy families.

Fort Fisher had less than three months to workup for deployment with Seventh Fleet. Our first major event was the OPPE. After two weeks in port conducting administrative inspections and training preparations, we got under way for two weeks of engineering casualty control training. For a variety of reasons, the engineering watch sections did not do well. We also suffered several equipment casualties that disrupted the drills. We needed more time to prepare and train. I requested a month's delay in the OPPE.

Rear Admiral Paddock summoned me to his office. Scowling, he growled, "What's wrong with your ship, Captain?" I replied, "Nothing, sir!" He glared at me, "Well, why aren't you ready for your OPPE next week?" Through a tightened jaw I replied, "We simply need more time, sir!" I briefed him on our progress, problems, and what we were doing to correct them. After a few more questions, he granted the extension and dismissed me. I departed his office and returned to my ship, knowing that not even a silver bullet would help our situation.

Fort Fisher remained in port for three weeks conducting preparations for the OPPE and, accomplishing 17 pre-deployment inspections, (we failed one but quickly corrected the deficiencies and passed the re-exam).

On July 27, we were ready to depart San Diego for the Seal Beach Naval Ammunition Depot, adjacent to San Pedro, to load our magazines for refresher training, which would begin the following Monday. I delayed until 1300 due to heavy fog, and then proceeded in limited visibility, but the fog closed to almost zero visibility as we approached the harbor breakwater. When the fog lifted, the ship was on the starboard edge of the channel and I had to take the conn to maneuver around a buoy. After eight months in overhaul, my watch officers and the bridge and CIC navigation teams were in need of training. *Fort Fisher's* readiness for operations at sea was sub-par.

That evening as we steamed toward Seal Beach, we encountered intermittent fog so I was on the bridge past midnight. About 0100 the fog lifted and visibility improved to about five miles and I finally went to bed in my sea cabin. As the ship entered the Long Beach shipping channel, the OOD called to advise me that the fog was closing in again and visibility was dropping. I ordered him to slow the ship to 10 knots.

I was quickly getting out of bed when I felt the deck shudder. I was on the bridge moments later. The OOD reported he had turned sharply to starboard to avoid a buoy. At 0546, *Fort Fisher* had struck an orange spherical marker buoy, one of several forming a perimeter about four thousand yards from an oil drilling rig situated about a mile on the port side of the shipping channel. I ordered, "all engines stop, rudder amidships!"

Visibility was about 5000 yards. The drilling rig lights were visible, but the ship was not standing into danger. There were no other ships in the vicinity. I directed the damage control assistant, who was on watch in main control, to check all spaces for internal flooding. I directed the navigator to fix the ship's position and the Ops boss to prepare a message report. The XO took custody of the quartermaster's notebook and all logs and charts on the bridge and in CIC, and the main control throttle logs.

The DCA reported no flooding so we checked both main engines at slow revolutions. The starboard screw was clear, but the port screw appeared to be fouled so we locked the port shaft. After verifying the ship's position, we continued towards Seal Beach at 10 knots rung up on the starboard main engine. I then transmitted a high-precedence message informing my chain of command.

The fog lifted at sunrise and visibility improved to about five miles. After coordinating with Seal Beach, we proceeded to an anchorage and ballasted the ship to create a starboard list down by the bow, which exposed the port screw tips slightly above water. The Cheng, DCA and one of our designated rescue swimmers embarked in the gig, inspected the port screw and discovered a wire rope wrapped several turns around the port shaft between the stern tube struts and the screw, and an orange and white spherical metal buoy suspended from the wire rope.

Long Beach Naval Shipyard sent divers to conduct an external underwater hull inspection. On the port screw, they discovered that two of the five blades were curled over and chewed up. There were superficial scrapes on the tail shaft where the wire rope had wrapped around. There were no other signs of underwater hull, screw or rudder damage. After coordinating with the shipyard and the divers, I directed the divers to remove the wire rope, unfouling the shaft. Tests of the port engine were normal so I proceeded to the depot and moored to the pier.

Commodore Jenkins appointed Captain Edward Buchanon, USN, commanding officer of USS *Mobile* (LKA-115), our squadron sister ship, to conduct a formal one-officer JAG investigation. He came aboard in the afternoon while we were loading ammunition and collected documents, conducted several preliminary interviews and departed before we left Seal Beach. We got underway with shipyard technicians on board and conducted engine vibration tests at various speeds on both engines, detecting no damage to the propulsion machinery. Their report recommended that the port screw be replaced at some time in the future to eliminate screw cavitation noise. I wrote in my journal:

> I am the subject of an official investigation into the circumstances surrounding a collision by *Fort Fisher* with a marker buoy near the end of the approach channel to Long Beach.... The ship was proceeding at 11.5 knots when the fog closed in. The OOD called me but did not tell me he was having navigation difficulties. I ... felt the ship shudder.... We didn't need this. It will be a hard lesson for me. I know that I will be reprimanded, maybe relieved. God only knows. I feel responsible, and I regret the strain and anguish this will cause my young officers. They are doing just great, and I am proud of them. I love my ship, I love the Navy, and I love my country. The sea is very unforgiving. Eternal vigilance is the price of safety. I lapsed for a moment, and almost had a tragedy. I thank God no one was injured, and that my ship was not seriously damaged. I ... regret that I did not do better. My men deserved more.

The investigation would run its course regardless of my concerns, so I focused on our refresher training. It was my first opportunity to conn the ship in a variety of seamanship evolutions, which I always enjoyed, especially going alongside an oiler in daytime and at night. After a full day of drilling at sea, we would return to San Diego harbor after sunset and anchor near the fleet training group headquarters to prepare for the next day.

Under my supervision, each OOD and JOOD learned get the ship underway and to anchor; I was able to evaluate their respective shiphandling and seamanship skills. The daily channel transits trained our Special Sea and Anchor Detail, especially our bridge and CIC piloting and navigation teams. I dealt aggressively with all our training issues and the ship's company made excellent progress; we completed our training in good shape.

The following Monday, we began two weeks of amphibious refresher training anchored off Imperial Beach, San Diego, and underway off Camp Pendleton. Our training was interrupted on the second day by a storm, which forced us to remain anchored overnight.

I had discovered that writing in my journal cleared my mind and helped me focus on my anxieties and concerns, permitting me to deal with them as objectively as possible. It also helped me to think straight, maintain a balanced perspective, keep an even strain on my emotions and maintain a positive mental attitude. At 0030 August 17 in my sea cabin, I wrote,

> Tropical storm Doreen ... changed our plans. I decided to stay here rather than go out into ... rough weather, rain, low visibility, and possibly high winds.... We are lit off and on 10-minute standby. ... will get higher later in the night.... Into Phibreftra two days now.... We did well in Reftra considering the limited amount of time we had to prepare.... CIC & NAV much improved. Repair parties satisfactory ... all guns fired ... Deck force did very well.... No time to rest on our laurels.

I was worried about my family, especially our finances. After living overseas for four years, it was difficult for us to adjust to the high cost of living and mortgage payments in San Diego. Then burglars broke into our home in the middle of the night while I was at sea. Our new puppy barked and woke Linda up. She called the police and the burglars fled, leaving all our doors wide open.

> Hard to make the mental transition from one place to the next. The weekends are a blur. I try to enjoy my family and be enjoyable, but it's hard to do. Lots of tension. The break-in to our house—the same morning that I hit the buoy—frightened Linda and the kids terribly; they can't feel safe when I'm gone now. Need to improve security and lighting, intercom. So much to do

and so little time…. My 44th birthday came and went. Small but nice celebration with my wife, kids and my niece Kim at home. I thoroughly enjoyed. I don't know how I got so old.

My journal reflected *Fort Fisher*'s readiness and the personal impact of my efforts to improve it,

> My morale is not too good…. Crew morale is hard to judge…. Lots of major pieces of equipment going down…. Lately the command job does not seem much fun to me. Lots of problems and there seems to be no overall improvement in readiness…. Lots of unauthorized absences. Evidence of drug abuse and drinking problems on the increase. The buoy collision investigation is coming to an end. Not pleasant. Probably will get a reprimand. For sure the navigator & the OOD. But I will not bend. I won't give in. I won't yield to self-pity and remorse. I will see this through—all of it and more.

The storm passed and we resumed amphibious training, which was conducted in condition One Alfa (amphibious operations stations) and focused on wet-well operations with landing craft and boats, "Boats to the rail! Away all boats!" The training developed our teams—debarkation control, ballast control, well deck control, CIC, bridge, and signal bridge. We practiced precision anchoring. We launched and recovered landing craft and loaded and unloaded them; and simultaneously landed and fueled, loaded, unloaded and launched helos. The boat officers learned to assemble boat waves near the ship and lead them down the boat lane to the beach in an organized, controlled manner. We also learned how to launch the Marines' amphibious landing vehicle tractors (LVT—also AAV; which carry a squad of fully armed Marines) from our well deck while we were underway. Late at night on August 23, anchored overnight off Coronado, I turned to my journal.

> Our final week of Phibreftra … doing well … teams have learned fast, and so have the boat officers. This week has been rough because the MTT is on board trying to get the engineers ready for OPPE. The schedule—all year—has been rough. It's beginning to show in the officers, chiefs and senior POs. The

families are depressed, I'm sure. After being up in Long Beach for eight months, it is no easy thing to go through this training and then deploy right after. I wonder if it was all worth it—the effort to get out of the Yard early, the hard push on all the training and inspections, the very long hours all year, and the constant concern about the OPPE ... [If we had been delayed in overhaul] we would be transferred to Phibron Three. That didn't seem like a good thing ... to the commodore, and to me, it seemed like a failure. So we pushed, worked, and tried everything possible, and we got out almost three weeks early. I've been very concerned about what would happen if we failed to pass the OPPE. Would we not deploy? Would we sail late? The

As I was writing the last sentence, there was a knock on my sea cabin door. My communications center messenger greeted me, "Good evening, Captain" and handed me a high-precedence message from the commander in chief, Pacific Fleet. The admiral had delayed our OPPE. We would do it during our transit to Pearl Harbor with our squadron!

The fleet commander's reasons for the change were our state of preparation and the limited time available before our deployment. This most welcome change gave us a few extra days to prepare for deployment.

Stunned but elated, I closed my journal—I never completed the last sentence—and routed the message to the XO and department heads.

Receipt of the admiral's message when I was so discouraged was the most amazing coincidence. For the first time in many weeks, I slept well.

The ship's company, especially the engineers, felt a huge sense of relief. We finished our amphibious training in excellent shape and returned to San Diego on Friday afternoon, August 26, and began 17 days of POM (prepare for overseas movement; 30 days was the norm). It was a busy time, but I granted everyone as much leave as possible.

Fort Fisher was moved "cold-iron" alongside a tender and salvage divers successfully replaced the damaged port screw. We then moored stern to the sea wall, lowered our stern gate and commenced loading the equipment for Eniwetok—40 large wheeled items (cement mixers, dump trucks, back hoes, water trucks, a complete cement plant, jeeps, graders, bulldozers) and pallets of cement.

¡El Capitán!

I spent as much time as I could with my family. Linda had resolved our budget issues by getting a job at NCR Corporation near our home in Rancho Bernardo. I took a few days of leave and Linda and I joined my siblings and their spouses in Las Vegas for a fun weekend.

On September 12, the day before the squadron's sortie, Commodore Jenkins awarded me an official letter of instruction (LOI) concerning *Fort Fisher*'s buoy collision. The navigator and the CIC officer each received a letter of caution and the OOD a letter of reprimand (subsequently, the type commander reduced the reprimand to a non-punitive letter of caution, restoring the officer's career.)

The investigation's principal findings were that the OOD and the CIC watch officer had been deficient in maintaining an accurate ship's navigation plot and that coordination between the bridge and CIC was inadequate. The oil-drilling rig and its ring of marker buoys had been incorrectly plotted on the navigation chart on the bridge and in CIC. And there were other findings. (There is an old fleet saying, "A collision at sea can ruin your entire day!") My LOI, written in traditional fleet terminology, was precisely factual and to the point:

> .... The report documents numerous errors and omissions in the routine performance of duties by personnel in CIC, navigation and on-duty watches. These errors and omissions involve such non-conformance with ship's directives, improper qualification of watch standers, and inadequate internal distribution of navigational information, inadequate internal communication and demonstrated lack of supervision as to raise serious doubt as to the overall state of readiness of USS *Fort Fisher*.
>
> 2. You are directed to:
>> a.   Conduct a general review of *Fort Fisher* directives dealing with training and operational matters to ensure their compliance with policy guidance of higher authority.
>> b.   Take such action as necessary to ensure shipboard training and operations are conducted in accordance with published directives.
>> c.   Review the qualifications of all watch officers, watch supervisors, and withdraw designators where qualification requirements have not been met.

d. Immediately establish proper communication and coordination between the bridge and CIC and ensure the full exchange of information necessary in order that they be mutually supporting.

3. You will report actions undertaken, completed, and planned by letter directly to Commander Amphibious Squadron Five on 15 October 1977 with a final summary letter on 15 December 1977.

4. This letter is addressed to you as an instructional measure and does not become a part of your official record. While it is not necessary to point out your responsibility for all that concerns your ship, you are reminded that failure to identify shortcomings, as contributed to this collision, and to institute remedial action places your ship and all therein in jeopardy. Commander Amphibious Squadron Five trusts the instructional benefits you have received from this experience will cause you to become a more proficient naval officer....

I quickly corrected the procedural deficiencies, but they were not the critical issue. The substandard performance of duty by me, the OOD, the navigator, and the CIC watch officer was the main contributing factor in the collision. Because there was periodic low visibility and my watch teams were not up to par, I should have stationed the operations officer— our most experienced naval officer next to the XO and me—on the bridge as command duty officer before I turned in (even though he was not on the watch bill), or even the XO, adding an extra margin of safety. I had failed to act in a prudent and vigilant manner.

The incident changed my approach in assessing my ship's readiness. I became more focused and observant when supervising my watch officers and my bridge and CIC teams (but not excessively so). I employed my officers with greater effectiveness. I learned to pace myself so that fatigue would not impair my judgment. Because of the experience, I did become "a more proficient naval officer." But the pain never went away.

With the PEB embarked, *Fort Fisher* sailed out of San Diego with Phibron Five. That night I made my first journal entry of the cruise, "… Saying goodbye to Linda, Jack and Judy & family was hard … I pray they will be safe, secure and happy until I return. Seven and one-half months seems like such a long time. But if the days are as full as these past ten months, then it will all be over before we realize it. The PEB is on board and tomorrow we start the OPPE. At last. It's been a long time in coming, and my engineers and I are rather tired of preparing. I pray it goes well. They deserve to pass." I also wrote about other matters weighing on my mind:

> My command is rather ragged right now. I pushed harder than I ever have, and the strain is showing on my officers and men and all the families. I'm a little weary and somewhat discouraged too. But we deployed on time. So our goal was achieved. We aimed at this date back in Feb. in the … shipyard…. There were times when I had serious doubts. Even now, I don't know if I was right. No one else seems to recognize what we achieved. No praise from [superiors in the chain]. The buoy collision investigation ended … one more price I paid for pushing ahead. I can correct all the shortcomings we have … the personal wounds will take time to heal….

I also focused on the deployment, "I am resolved to make this cruise interesting, safe, successful, and fun for everyone. I will not spare myself in the effort. … God bless each one of us in the days ahead."

The next morning we began our OPPE, but due to the watch teams' poor performance and actual engineering machinery casualties, the drills did not go well, and the trend was negative. The afternoon of the second day, Captain Ulrich, head of the PEB, informed me that we had failed and I promptly informed my chain.

We would have preferred a different outcome, but after many weeks of anticipation and preparation, it was a relief to have tried; we had learned and improved a great deal. *Fort Fisher*'s fate would be decided after our arrival at Pearl Harbor, where Ulrich would give CINCPACFLT a face-to-face assessment.

Being at sea, operating with our squadron, and steaming toward Hawaii lifted everyone's spirits. The crew was relieved to be underway and on the first leg of our deployment.

We focused on preparing for another crack at the OPPE. The PEB conducted a thorough inspection of the main propulsion spaces and helped our engineers identify and document the equipment and casualty control procedural deficiencies. We submitted over 40 high-priority repair requests to fleet maintenance and repair facilities in Pearl Harbor.

With the XO, department heads and the PEB, I reviewed the status of the propulsion plants, our state of engineering watch team training, and our employment schedule. We needed one week in port to correct all the material deficiencies and revise several watch team casualty-control procedures. When the propulsion plants were ready, we would require one week of engineering drills at sea.

We arrived at Pearl Harbor on Monday, September 19. On the pier were about a dozen shipyard and tender officers and technicians ready to ship-check all our repair requests. I was mooring the ship when the port services duty officer on the pier passed word to me that I had a phone call from Rear Admiral Paddock. I left the XO in charge to complete the mooring and as soon as the brow was in place,

I went to the phone on the pier. The admiral asked, "Captain, can you maintain morale?" I replied, "Yes, sir!" Paddock said, "Good. I am sending you a chief boiler technician and a third class boiler technician to beef up your watch sections. You will have two weeks to get ready to re-take the OPPE. Then you will sail independently to Eniwetok and the Philippines. Keep me informed." I replied, "Aye, Aye sir. Thank you!"

Captain Ulrich went to Makalapa Hill and briefed Admiral Tom Hayward, Commander in Chief, Pacific Fleet. The admiral approved the OPPE re-exam schedule and directed that *Fort Fisher* receive top-priority repair support from the Pearl Harbor Naval Shipyard, the tenders, and other shore maintenance facilities—*Fort Fisher* had a blank check.

That afternoon I joined Commodore Jenkins and our seven other ship captains for a call on the admiral. After traditional amenities, Hayward turned to me and asked, "Captain Gamboa, should we put a mailbox on the pier for *Fort Fisher*?" I replied, "No sir, that won't be necessary!" My fellow skippers smiled understandingly at my being in the hot seat. Several had been through their own OPPE ordeals.

Over the next three days, I called on the shipyard commander, the COs of the tender, the shore maintenance facility, the naval station and the supply center. I valued the opportunity to discuss my ship's situation. Although it had placed my ship in a difficult situation, the fleet would spare no effort in helping us prepare for our OPPE. I thanked them for their support and gave each a presentation photograph of *Fort Fisher*.

¡El Capitán!

Meanwhile, the rest of the squadron embarked a Marine amphibious unit (MAU) a reinforced infantry battalion of 1200 Marines and their helos, vehicles, weapons, ammunition, equipment and supplies. I met with Commodore Jenkins to brief him on my plan of action to correct all engineering deficiencies, train at sea, pass the OPPE, transit the Pacific and join-up with his squadron in Westpac. He approved my plan and sternly directed that I fix my engineering problems and keep them fixed.

That evening I hosted the commodore at dinner in my cabin. Although I was feeling a bit down, I had absolutely no intention of throwing in the towel. Even so, I had to face reality: I was already operating under a letter of instruction. If we failed again I would surely be relieved for cause.

After we sat down to eat, I said, "Commodore, I have given *Fort Fisher* my best shot. If we don't pass the OPPE, then you will have to get someone else in here to sail this ship to Westpac. I doubt it will be me." With calm deliberateness, Jenkins placed his silverware on his plate and looked hard at me. "Frank, I don't want to hear that kind of talk from you. I expect you to pass your OPPE and join my squadron on station in Seventh Fleet. Do you understand me?" I replied, "Yes, sir." He changed the subject and we had an enjoyable evening. Never again did I ever harbor any doubts about my ability to command.

The next morning I held an All Hands on the signal bridge and briefed the crew on our new schedule, our plan to pass the OPPE, and our voyage to Eniwetok and the Philippines. I told them what I expected of them. Then we watched our squadron sister ships stand out of the harbor and sail away. We felt very left out—and very alone.

When I moored *Fort Fisher* in Pearl Harbor, I had been in command over ten months. We had endured great pressures and significant stress but we had worked successfully through many difficult issues and situations. Throughout, I had managed to keep my cool and channeled my occasional anger in constructive ways; I refrained from venting my frustrations on my officers. I did not throw temper tantrums or behave like "a screamer."

Well, for every captain there is always a first time.

In the afternoon of our fourth day in port, I returned to the ship from an official call. As I headed to my cabin, one of my first class ship's servicemen met me at the ladder leading to the passageway to my cabin.

Captain John Frank Gamboa, U. S. Navy (Retired)

He asked me if I was aware that the ship's laundry was down—the prized new washers and dryers could not operate because of low steam pressure. The crew had not had clean laundry for over three days and the situation was getting worse. He had talked to the A Gang, but they were unable fix the problem. I thanked him and said I would look into the matter.

I summoned the XO and asked if he was aware of the laundry situation. He was not. I talked to the Cheng. He was unaware of the crew's lack of clean laundry, but was aware of the low pier steam pressure—*Fort Fisher* was in "cold iron" status receiving shore steam from the pier. To get adequate steam pressure, we needed a donkey boiler, but he had been unable to get one. I told him I would get him a donkey boiler.

I phoned the port services duty officer and explained our situation. He investigated and called back to say that he could not get any more pier steam pressure due to the number of ships on-line on our pier, and that his only available donkey boiler was inoperative. I directed him to inform his CO of our situation, and that I needed adequate shore steam pressure for my ship as soon as possible. I intended to find out what it meant to have the CINC's top repair priority in Pearl Harbor.

The port services duty officer tackled the problem aggressively and soon had shipyard technicians working on the donkey boiler. In subsequent phone calls I learned more than I ever wanted to know about donkey boilers and delivery of shore steam; by midnight *Fort Fisher*'s laundry was back in operation. The laundry crew worked all night to catch up.

The next morning as I was reading my message traffic and having a cup of coffee at my desk, I began to feel a simmering anger. The officers were unaware of our Sailors' needs—or worse, unconcerned. They were not taking care of their men. I summoned the XO, "Assemble all officers in the wardroom immediately!"

I entered and lined the division officers up against a bulkhead. Then I walked the line, pausing face-to-face in front of each, asking if they knew the status of their men's laundry. Each replied, "No sir!" except for CWO3 Dave Miles, my superb DCA. He knew. Then, in excruciating detail, I explained the crew's laundry situation, including the impact on the crew, and the steps I had taken to correct it. They listened at attention, silent and wide-eyed. They had never seen me on a rant.

I then told all the officers that their leadership was unsatisfactory. I told them what I expected of them.

Then I faced the XO and ordered, "All officers are hereby restricted to the limits of this ship" and then I added, "until the Arizona gets underway!" I crumpled a message from the commodore that I had read to them prior to my tirade and hurled it to the deck as I stormed out of the wardroom.

Later that day, I again summoned the XO to my cabin and directed that, on a daily rotating basis, he designate a division laundry duty officer to report to me on the operational status of the laundry, the number of bags of laundry done the previous day, and the number of bags of soiled laundry in each division.

I went ashore only on official business while I had all officers "in hack." On the morning of the third day of their restriction, the XO came to me and recommended that I lift the wardroom's restriction—I had made my point. I conceded, but I continued the daily laundry reporting until we departed Pearl.

And I directed that each division officer, with his division, visit the Arizona Memorial in liberty uniform during normal working hours, as scheduled by the XO. All divisions including the engineers toured the memorial. I was accompanied by the XO and department heads. It was my first visit to that hallowed site, as it was for most of my men—a solemn remembrance.

We completed all repairs and preparations, got underway to a local operating area for engineering casualty control drills. The commodore had detailed our sister ship *Mount Vernon*'s engineering casualty control training team, headed by Ensign Bill Fox, to supervise each drill (afterwards they flew to the Philippines to rejoin their ship). I consulted frequently with the Cheng and Fox on our watch sections' progress.

After six days, the watch teams had achieved all training objectives. Everyone needed some rest and spirit-boosting recreation so I stopped the ship in the op-area, flooded the well deck and had a great swim call for all hands. To the crew's delight, fitted out with fins and snorkel, and mask, I dove in first to check for sharks, along with one of my best non-rated seamen (Smitty, our superb LCVP coxswain).

That night I wrote in my journal, "So, at last I see the possibilities of this … command coming together…. What a long and difficult journey it has been. But, as BM2 Hunter told me, 'God never gives us anything we can't handle.' ...I don't know why God has tested me so. I hope he is with me in the days ahead."

On Monday, October 3, returning to port late in the afternoon, I sent a one-word message to my chain of command: "Ready."

While at Pearl, I periodically phoned Linda to keep her apprised—and to receive her encouragement. After our new schedule was approved, I asked her to come to Hawaii to be with me for the OPPE. I needed her there for moral support. I also wanted her to be able to personally relate to the other wives and dependents a first-hand account of *Fort Fisher*'s situation. She arrived on Tuesday evening on the same flight as my new Executive Officer, Cdr. Gene Bailey. Several other wives came with Linda and many stayed in the base visiting officers' quarters.

Sometime earlier, I had mentioned to my Bos'n how much Linda loved "McNamara's Lace," a Sailor's marlinspike fancywork tasseled lace (like macramé) created from duck canvas. She had admired it on several ships and considered it to be a sign of the crew's pride. As a surprise to me, my deck divisions had created enough lace to trim the entire quarterdeck awning. Linda was thrilled to see it.

I knew that CINCPACFLT's decisions to have *Fort Fisher* conduct our OPPE en-route to Hawaii and to support our re-exam had saved my command, so on Wednesday afternoon, October 5, I called on Admiral Hayward. I had Linda join me, the only time she ever accompanied me on an official call. I thanked him for delaying the OPPE and told him that I was confident we would pass. I presented him a picture of *Fort Fisher*. He was very gracious and wished me well in the OPPE and our deployment. In response to Linda's question, the admiral told her that the ship's Seventh Fleet deployment would not be extended because of its OPPE-related delay in Pearl Harbor. She thanked him and told him that she would reassure the crew's families.

By happy coincidence, as we were waiting to see the admiral, my academy roommate Cdr. Jack Dittrick arrived in the admiral's office on business from the Pentagon. That evening, after his visit to my ship, the three of us enjoyed a great dinner together under the stars, with lots of laughter and reminiscing.

Fort Fisher got underway at 1000 on Thursday with the PEB on board. The OPPE re-exam lasted two days. We returned to port Friday evening. As we approached our berth, I spotted Linda on the pier. She yelled, "Did you pass?" With great joy, I shouted, "Yes!" After we moored, she and the other wives came aboard carrying a huge, beautiful floral lei they had made from colored tissue paper while we were conducting the OPPE. Together, we draped it around the quarterdeck brow. Then I assembled all the engineers aft of the signal bridge for a critique by Captain Ulrich and the PEB. He was very complimentary and wished us well in Seventh Fleet.

When the ship had won the "E" in 1976, the crew proudly claimed that *Fort Fisher* was "the four-oh, (4.0, best) ship in the Navy," and painted a white dot on the ship's starboard side stern hull number, LSD 40, changing the 40 to 4.0. The hull had been repainted in the shipyard, and the number replaced without the dot. One day on the bridge, one of my deck sailors told me that the absence of the dot was undoubtedly one reason why we were having problems with the OPPE.

After the PEB departed the ship, I donned blue coveralls and walked to the starboard side of the stern. As pre-arranged with the first lieutenant I was lowered over the side on a side cleaner's stage (a wooden plank hanging from lines), down to the ship's hull number. Then they lowered a paintbrush, a dot stencil and a can of white paint. I painted a large white dot making it 4.0. A crowd of my sailors watching from the pier cheered me on. Linda, who was on the flight deck looking down, watched nervously. She had not been forewarned.

Linda had reserved base picnic areas while we were conducting the OPPE so every division enjoyed a picnic over the weekend paid for by our welfare and recreation fund.

On Sunday evening, she and I hosted Vice Admiral and Mrs. Sam Gravely, Commander, Third Fleet, for a tour of the ship and dinner in my cabin with Gene Bailey [Gene, an African American, was personally acquainted with the Admiral, having also grown up in Richmond, Virginia] and John Harms. The Admiral wrote me the following letter:

Dear Captain Gamboa,

This is to thank you most sincerely for an outstanding visit and dinner on your fine ship. My wife and I thoroughly enjoyed the entire evening.

I was indeed impressed with the cleanliness of your ship and with the smartness exhibited by all of the personnel that I met. Needless to say your Mess Managers are superb as dinner was outstanding. All in all you have got an outstanding ship.

Here's hoping you have a most pleasant WESTPAC and that you will be returning this way soon.
My regards to your Exec.
Again, thank you.

We victualed *Fort Fisher*, topped off her fuel tanks and supplies, and completed preparations for our trans-Pacific voyage.

On Tuesday, October 11, after embarking two U.S. Army LARCs, huge four-wheeled amphibious landing craft with tires taller than a man, and a warping tug (an LCM-8 modified as a pusher boat); we transited the channel in the late afternoon, departed the Hawaiian Islands and sailed into a beautiful sunset. And the crew and I were awestruck by the view of the lava pouring into the sea from the Kilauea volcano, as we sailed past. After shaping course for Eniwetok, I walked to the stern with Bev Daly and the XO and in a traditional Hawaiian aloha, we tossed the beautiful ship's lei into our wake.

I wrote the evening prayer and delivered it over the ship's One MC on the first night of our voyage,

> Oh God, as we depart Pearl Harbor and set course for Eniwetok, we ask your special blessing upon this ship and its company. Your ocean is so vast, and the sea and wind are in your hands. We give thanks for the many blessings we have received. We ask for your care of our loved ones. Help us always to do our duty to our country, our ship and our shipmates. Amen.

It is a simple fact of life. To be successful in a warship a naval surface warfare officer must enjoy being at sea. As I climbed my career ladder, I came to enjoy being at sea. Sailing the oceans was exciting. I preferred good weather and calm seas, but storms and rough seas added an exhilarating—albeit sometimes frightening—dimension. Overall, I was inspired by the sublime beauty of the sea and the sky, and the sheer awesomeness of it all.

Thanks to her large fuel capacity, *Fort Fisher* had "long legs" and could steam for long distances without refueling. The fleet commander made an exception to Pacific Fleet policy that ships would not sail independently across the Pacific, and directed *Fort Fisher* to proceed unaccompanied to Subic Bay, Philippines, from Pearl Harbor, with a 24-

hour stop for cargo off-load at Eniwetok Atoll. My ship would sail across the ocean alone.

I relished the nautical and navigation challenge. To conserve fuel and hours on each boiler, whose firesides had to be cleaned every 2000 hours of steaming, we sailed with one boiler on line except when in restricted waters or foul weather. We cruised at 14 knots for 17 days and saw no other ship until we sighted a merchantman the day before we entered the Philippines' San Bernardino Straits.

Fort Fisher's passage to Eniwetok was a sailor's delight. We sailed on a calm, deep-blue ocean rippled by gentle breezes beneath an almost cloudless sky with a clear horizon. The rosy pink dawns, bright sunny days, and spectacular sunsets inspired us. At night, we gazed at a celestial dome adorned with twinkling stars, bright planets and familiar constellations.

This was just what my crew and I needed—a busy, yet calm, quiet and relaxed time to refresh our minds, restore our spirits, and prepare for the operational challenges we would face in Seventh Fleet. Having been severely tested and blessed with success, we felt our confidence and pride return.

At sea on October 13, the Navy's birthday, I assembled the crew aft of the signal bridge, where the ocean view was best. I thanked everyone for their outstanding performance in getting the ship and themselves ready for deployment and told them that I was very proud of them. I singled out the engineers for their OPPE success.

I talked about the importance of the Navy and why America's fleet was needed in the western Pacific to defend our vital interests in the Far East. I explained the nature of our mission in Seventh Fleet and the operational challenges ahead.

I told them what I expected of them in terms of individual and team performance in our daily shipboard life and during amphibious operations. I discussed conduct ashore during our visits to foreign ports, emphasizing that we were representing our country and our Navy as guests of our allies when we visited their countries. I told them to use the "buddy system" while on liberty for their personal safety, to stay out of trouble, and to enjoy themselves.

Then I re-enlisted one of our petty officers. Despite our demanding schedule, *Fort Fisher* led the squadron in first-term and career retention throughout my tour, and was near the top in the Pacific Fleet surface force.

After my remarks, the first class petty officers surprised me with "the Medal of the Daring Dot" for my hull-number painting bravery. Then the deck divisions made me an honorary side cleaner and presented me a plaque embellished with McNamara's lace and a side-cleaner's stage. Afterwards, I joined in group pictures with the wardroom, the chiefs, and the first class on the signal bridge.

That night I wrote my first deployment Familygram. "... On Thursday, we celebrated our Navy's 202nd birthday in a unique way. Each division organized a display ... everyone toured ... throughout the day, learning how we operate *Fort Fisher*, a Sailor's show-and-tell organized by the leading petty officers. Our celebration ended with a cake-cutting after a magnificent dinner for everyone prepared by *Fort Fisher*'s outstanding food service division."

I also discussed our accomplishments in getting ready for deployment and our forthcoming Westpac operations:

> .... I wish to conclude this first Westpac Familygram by recognizing the superb efforts of Fort Fishermen.... By the luck of the draw, *Fort Fisher* was tasked to accomplish a great deal in minimum time, otherwise it would have been necessary to shift her to Phibron Three and replace her, with great disruption to the squadrons and ships concerned....
>
> To the everlasting credit of the officers, chiefs and men of *Fort Fisher*, they did what had to be done, with superb professionalism, in keeping with the finest traditions of the United States Navy. The men with families could not have accomplished their tasks without the loyal support and understanding of their wives and children. To each of you I express my deepest gratitude and thanks.
>
> I am confident that *Fort Fisher* will have a successful cruise, doing whatever is required of us, in a manner that will bring credit to our country, our Navy, our ship, and all Fort Fishermen and families.....
>
> I thank you for your support. Keep the mail coming!

On October 16, upon crossing the longitude that separates the Third Fleet and the Seventh Fleet operating areas. *Fort Fisher* chopped to Commander, Seventh Fleet. "Welcome aboard. ARG Bravo operations will be both demanding and rewarding, and will present opportunities to perform a variety of mission roles. Stay ready. Glad to have you join us. VADM Robert B. Baldwin, USN." I replied, "Wilco your 170216Z Oct 77. We are proud to join the first team. We will do our best."

My outstanding navigator, Lt. Bo James, and my top-notch leading quartermaster, Chief King, worked diligently to keep us on our track to Eniwetok with accurate morning and evening celestial fixes, sun lines, and loran and omega fixes. (The chief told me that, because the atoll was so small, some ships had actually missed it!) Thanks to their professionalism, we made radar landfall one minute ahead of our track.

Approaching the entrance to the lagoon, we encountered heavy rainsqualls, strong wind gusts and low visibility. The OOD and the navigation team were unsure of our position and tension was building on the bridge. My journal entry describes the situation:

> We arrived here at 0700, but due to rain, low clouds, and wind/sea conditions, we delayed entering the lagoon. I was overseeing the navigation plot as we started in, and after several poor fixes, it became apparent that we didn't have a good fix, and neither did CIC. With no hesitation, I ordered the OOD to reverse course and we proceeded back out to sea so we could get the navigation team, CIC, and the OOD … coordinated. The rain and wind increased in intensity…. We proceeded approximately two and a half miles, and then came about on a new track leading directly north into the channel. This time both the navigation and CIC teams were well coordinated, the OOD had a good grasp of the situation, and everyone calmed down and went about their business in a professional manner. The rain lessened, visibility lifted, and we were able to get visual sightings…. The channel transit and anchoring proceeded smoothly…. Afterwards, LT James and Chief King thanked me. Amazing what calm, decisive action can do for a ship!

After we coordinated with the officer-in-charge and the U.S. joint task force commander, an Air Force colonel civil engineer, our deck divisions began unlashing and offloading the cargo into LCM-8s and LCUs with both cranes and through the well deck. That evening I wrote in my journal,

Captain John Frank Gamboa, U. S. Navy (Retired)

I feel mentally better since … the OPPE…. My speech to all hands on 21 September was the turning point in my tour. I became the captain. Making hard decisions easily. Speaking plainly and forcefully to my men. Spelling out my basic philosophy as a naval officer, and giving moral conviction to my policies and beliefs. Linda's visit was all that I hoped it would be…. What a marvelous human being….

I called on the colonel, who explained the project and took me on a tour of part of the atoll with John Harms and Gene Bailey while the off-loading was in progress. I could not get over Eniwetok's stark isolation. I took a photo and sent it to my Lone Pine friend, Bill Bauer, who had been there on a successful amphibious assault in WW II.

The next day we hosted the colonel and key members of his staff at a luncheon in my cabin and the wardroom. In the early afternoon, we weighed anchor, departed the lagoon and shaped course to the San Bernardino Straits.

At Eniwetok, I wrote in my journal, "I remain concerned about the weather. Hope no typhoon develops along our track." Well, on the day we arrived, U.S. Navy Weather Center Guam reported that a "quasi-stationary cyclonic circulation" had formed south of our trans-Pacific navigational track about two days ahead of our PIM, and was heading north and would intersect our track. If it stalled, we would be on a collision course. I felt very relieved when it kept moving and crossed before we departed the atoll.

But my concerns had provoked the great Pacific's powerful weather gods. At dusk, the sky turned overcast and gray, the following winds freshened and the seas became confused. Neither the sunset nor the celestial dome was visible—foreboding signs. And then we received our first tailored weather forecast from the Guam fleet weather center predicting weather along our intended track,

> A quasi-stationary cyclonic circulation centered at 09N 172E is producing a northeast to easterly wind flow over your area. A cyclonic circulation centered at 15.1 N 146 E is moving toward the north at 6 knots. A tropical cyclone formation alert has been issued…. 24 hour forecast commencing 200600Z along your track … Wind becoming southeasterly 12 to 18 knots with higher gusts vicinity thunderstorms

273

becoming south to southwesterly after mid period. Seas southeasterly 06 to 09 feet becoming south to southwesterly 07 to 10 feet after mid period.

As I studied the navigator's plot of the center's location, predicted track and proximity to us, I had an ominous feeling—The Pacific Ocean was going to show us an aspect of her nature quite different from our halcyon days sailing from Hawaii to Eniwetok.

Borrowing from Samuel Johnson's "Nothing concentrates the mind like a hanging," nothing concentrates a mariner's mind like a storm at sea. After going over the situation with the navigator and the Ops boss, I convened a meeting with the XO and department heads in my cabin, discussed the possibility of sailing in the vicinity of a typhoon, and directed that the ship be secured for heavy weather. Then I went to the bridge.

Throughout the day, each department head reported on his department's status. The navigator went over our track and movement report and how often we would report our own weather to the Guam fleet weather center. The Ops boss discussed possible impact on our speed of advance and schedule. The Cheng gave me the status of our propulsion plants, fuel, and options to ballast selected tanks to compensate for fuel consumption and minimize the ship's pitch and roll. We discussed when to bring our second boiler on line.

The supply officer went over his plan for meal service in rough seas. The leading hospital corpsman would keep an eye on crewmembers for *mal de mer*. The first lieutenant reported the status of topside spaces and weather decks, and plans to secure the two landing craft and the gig in their cradles and the warping tug in the well deck.

Afterwards, the XO and I reviewed our situation and preparations and discussed possible changes to our daily routine to relax the work schedule and stand down non-watch standers to minimize crew fatigue.

Fort Fisher's high bow and freeboard increased her roll in strong winds. In order to minimize seasickness and prevent things from breaking loose within the ship, I would need to adjust ship's course and speed to minimize pitch and roll. We could not risk a man overboard, so I directed the first lieutenant to be prepared to lash down all hatches and doors leading to weather decks and post warnings against going out (Sailors are naturally curious).

Captain John Frank Gamboa, U. S. Navy (Retired)

By the next day we were experiencing gusts of wind over 35 knots and the building seas were causing the ship's moderate pitching and rolling. I moved the stern lookout to the signal bridge and had all main deck hatches and doors lashed; I passed the word that the crew was allowed to come to the pilothouse for "sightseeing," but few came.

I did my best to display a calm demeanor and sense of humor, in hopes of reducing everyone's stress level (including mine). And we continued watching the barometer and kept a weather eye on the seas, sky and wind. Guam generated weather reports to us twice a day and more frequently as the storm developed and the situation dictated. Their next warning said "… a tropical cyclone formation … is possible within 120 NM … within the next 12 to 24 hours.…" Twelve hours later Guam reported, "…. Winds becoming westerly 12 to 18 knots with higher gusts vicinity thunderstorms. Seas southwest 05 to 07 feet."

Several hours later, I reported to Guam, "Barometer commenced dropping rapidly at about 211100Z. Winds and seas appear to indicate origin from location other than tropical depression 17. Barometer has stabilized and commenced rising at 212030Z. Low reached was 1021 MBS at 212010Z. Seas of 10 feet are significantly higher than … forecast.… Gusts of up to 42 knots.…"

We now had head winds and the ship began plunging into the waves. I sent a report to Guam and my chain of command, "Barometer resumed dropping at 220100Z. Seas still building, winds increasing. Originator slowed to 13 knots … to reduce pitching/rolling. Ship riding well. Surface radar picture shows heavy cloud and rain concentration 35 nm radius. No cyclone activity noted."

Guam responded, "Tropical depression 17 was located near 17.N 147.3E moving north at 05 knots with max winds of 30 knots gusting to 40 knots. Westerly flow into the storm continues to dominate your weather.… Latest satellite data depicts numerous cloud bands with embedded thunderstorms extending some 500 nm within southeast quadrant about Tropical Center 17. Hazardous weather noted your message believed to be associated with this activity. Will continue to monitor your situation closely. Your alertness appreciated."

The next weather forecast increased our tension level. "Tropical Storm Ivy warning #5 upgraded from Tropical Depression 17.… Based on eye fixed at center located near 17.3 N 145.5E at 220250Z by aircraft accurate within 35 nm. Center moving toward the west at 05 knots. …

275

max sustained winds 40 knots near center with gusts to 50 knots 300 nm southwest quadrant.... Latest METSAT data verifies westward movement.... Latest aircraft data indicates Ivy moving westward. Heavy thunderstorm activity extending outward 700 nm in southeast quadrant..."

Fort Fisher was in Ivy's southeast quadrant and experiencing high and increasing winds and the storm was moving westward. "Oh, great! Maybe she'll just hang in there with us all the way to the Philippines!"

The next weather forecast reflected higher winds and seas. I sent a message to the weather center and my chain of command, "Seas continue to build. Have adjusted course to 265 to reduce pitch and roll." That got more attention. I received a message from Commander, Seventh Fleet and a similar message from Commander, Task Force 76, our amphibious boss, "Possible Hazardous Weather. Info received from fleet weather center Guam via weather broadcast indicates USS *Fort Fisher* 220300Z posit 12.1 N 147.7 E with winds 25 to 45 knots on outer fringe of Tropical Storm IVY." We also received another message from the weather center, "Your continued alertness and timely observations of this developing storm are greatly appreciated." We were eager to help.

The ever increasing pitching and rolling were very wearing and the incessant thunder and bolts of lightning were frightening, especially at night, lighting up the storm clouds and the bridge. We were now taking green water over the bow and experiencing wind gusts of almost 60 knots. I decided it was time to get the hell out of Ivy's southeastern quadrant. Subic and the Marines could wait. I informed my chain of command and others:

> .... Intentions. Alter course to 200 degrees true [from 265] at 221000Z to clear 30-knot wind circle. Current winds 240 degrees true at 25 knots with gusts to 50 knots, seas 10 to 12 feet from 240 degrees true....
>
> Remarks. ... Ship is located at edge of southeast quadrant, almost 300 nm south of Ivy's center. Accordingly ... have diverted to southwest to clear the 30-knot wind area. Ship is riding well with slight pitching and 5-10 degree roll. Fuel 63%. Both boilers on the line, plant split. Have ballasted ballast tanks to compensate for fuel expenditure.... MOVREP changes to follow. Ship's position as of 221000Z Oct 77 is 11-55.7N/146-14.7 E. Next report 221600Z Oct 77.

Several hours later, I reported on our continued diversion to the south-southwest, "Ship movement: course 200 T speed 11 knots. Intentions. Remain on present course and speed until about 222000Z, then alter course to 270, weather permitting. Current weather: Winds 240 T at 27 knots, seas 240 T, 10 feet, 07 seconds. Skies overcast with 20% celestial dome clear. Some stars becoming visible. Barometer 29.61 inches erratic climb/fall...."

Twelve hours after heading south, I altered course to starboard to 280 degrees true and increased speed to 12 knots. We were sailing into 28-knot winds, but the seas had subsided to about 6 feet with swells of about 10 feet and the sky was beginning to clear. About eight hours later at 230620Z Oct 77, I reported, "Ship movement: course 289 speed 14 knots. Intentions. Remain on present course and speed until 232000Z, then alter course and speed for entrance San Bernardino Straits en route Subic Bay...."

We had been in the storm more than four days without a good navigational fix, using DR (deduced or ded reckoning) to estimate our position. When we finally got a reliable fix on October 24, we were 10 miles from our estimated position. We felt thankful for the great expanse of sea room along our track.

Ivy continued her westerly-northwesterly movement, and then she actually looped and was headed right back at us! On October 24, she was upgraded to a full-fledged typhoon. Fortunately, she turned away again and posed no danger to us.

We had paid our dues to the mighty Pacific Ocean and sailed through her fury safe and sound. It was the worst storm at sea I ever experienced.

On October 26, the anniversary of the historic WW II battle of Leyte Gulf, the largest sea battle in naval history, *Fort Fisher* sailed across the Philippine Sea, transited the Straits and entered the Sibuyan Sea.

One of my Sailors developed acute appendicitis so we quickly arranged for a U.S. Air Force medical evacuation helo from Clark Air Force Base, near Subic. Seaman Marlin Mathews was on board the helo by 0630 the morning of October 27 and in surgery at the U.S. Naval Hospital later that same day. He recovered and returned to the ship in December during our return visit to Subic.

I had increased speed to close the helo rendezvous point so we arrived at Subic in the morning of that same day. By then our schedule had changed again, canceling our four-day port visit and limiting our stay just long enough to offload the warping tug, embark two LCM-8 landing craft for our Seventh Fleet operations, and load over 40 pallets of provisions, supplies and spare parts. To our great enjoyment, we also received many sacks of mail. Cdr. Gene Bailey relieved as XO and John Harms departed before we sailed.

We got underway for Mindoro to embark a Marine unit that had been training there. The next morning in the South China Sea, we conducted our first Seventh Fleet underway refueling, topping off our fuel tanks for the first time since Pearl Harbor. We arrived at our destination in the afternoon, anchored, ballasted down and began earning our pay in Seventh Fleet.

Rear Admiral Richard Morris, Commander, Seventh Fleet Amphibious Force and Commander, Task Force Seventy Six (TF 76), had his headquarters at White Beach, Okinawa. One squadron of seven or eight amphibious ships was always deployed from San Diego to TF 76. The squadron was divided into two four-ship task groups, Amphibious Ready Group (ARG) Alfa, and ARG Bravo. Alfa always operated as a unit and conducted amphibious assault exercises to maintain battle readiness. Bravo, nicknamed "the greater gator freighters," was usually employed as independent ships in "lifting" (transporting) Marine units stationed at Okinawa to and from training areas in Japan, the Republic of South Korea, and the Philippines. *Fort Fisher* was assigned to Bravo.

On October 28, we embarked the 9th Marines Engineering Battalion Detachment One, their equipment and supplies at Mindoro beach, which had a huge impact on our crew—the ship's population doubled, mess lines were twice as long; the consumption of food and water and the laundry load increased significantly. The Marines provided enlisted personnel to help in the messes and laundry and they cleaned their own living spaces. The Marines had a Navy doctor and a Navy chaplain, so my crew also benefited from their services.

To facilitate the embarkation, an advance party of about a dozen Marines headed by an officer embarked ahead of time. To achieve a smooth and trouble-free integration of the embarking Marine unit and the ship's company, detailed planning and leadership are required by both organizations. A positive, cooperative attitude and a strong sense of teamwork must prevail in both units. The Sailors have to accommodate the Marines in a professional manner and the Marines have to treat the ship's company with respect.

We assembled the embarking Marine unit on the flight deck and I welcomed them aboard. The XO and department heads briefed them on our schedule, shipboard daily routine, and safety. Then the XO met with the CO of embarked troops to establish efficient working relationships between ship's company and Marines.

We arrived at White Beach, Okinawa, and off-loaded the engineers and embarked a Marine artillery company for a lift to Inchon, South Korea. I called on the CTF 76 staff; the admiral was on travel, but I enjoyed visiting with my classmate, Bob Phillips, the intelligence officer.

On November 5, we departed in company with *Denver* and arrived at Inchon, South Korea, on the afternoon of November 7, the site of General MacArthur's historic amphibious landing during the Korean War. We enjoyed a two-day port visit and tours in Inchon and Seoul, and I made a nostalgic visit to the Eighth Army Officers' Club with Gene Bailey. The next day I called on the Inchon mayor and the Korean Naval Sector commander, hosted several Korean naval officers at lunch in my cabin and the wardroom and gave them a tour of the ship.

We then sailed to Busan, South Korea, for a four-day port visit. I called on the mayor and the 2nd Korean Navy Sector commander, a commodore (one star flag officer). I also hosted him and several of his staff captains for lunch in my cabin, and several Korean Navy junior officers in the wardroom, then a ship tour. I enjoyed doing my part in maintaining good relations with our important allies.

And I responded to a letter from Rear Admiral Paddock:

> Greetings from Busan. ... Our first two operational commitments are behind us, accomplished in a safe, professional manner, so we feel almost at home here in Task Force Seventy Six. Our first exercise will be in early December in Busan/Pohang with BLT 2/9 and the ROK Navy and Marines. After that, we will be on par with the rest of Phibron Five in terms of exercise experience in TF 76.... We are happy to be here, and morale is excellent.... Our engineering plant reliability has been outstanding.... We are on station with Seventh Fleet after an arduous year, carrying out our mission with a great feeling of pride in our successful effort to deploy with Phibron Five.
>
> I wish to reiterate my sincere personal thanks for your ... support of *Fort Fisher* ... particularly during our OPPE effort in Hawaii.

¡El Capitán!

> My best wishes to you and Mrs. Paddock for a Happy Thanksgiving. Very respectfully.

I also submitted a report to Commodore Jenkins about *Fort Fisher*'s engineering plant readiness, operations, personnel, conduct ashore, morale, and our performance in ARG Bravo. I discussed my crew's performance in accomplishing a very compressed workup and deploying on time, concluding with a personal note, "I wish to express my deepest personal gratitude to you for your counsel, guidance, and support to me throughout this trying year. I shall never forget that, in my most anxious moments, your treatment of me was always inspirational and supportive. Very respectfully."

We arrived at Yokosuka, Japan, on November 19 for the first two-week upkeep period of our deployment. We caught up on repairs and maintenance, but also had time for my crew to relax and enjoy some good liberty and sight-seeing. Yokosuka was homeport for USS *Blue Ridge*, the Seventh Fleet commander's flagship, and I called on Vice Admiral Baldwin. We had a good discussion and he complimented me on our OPPE and *Fort Fisher*'s readiness.

Despite the fact we were now involved in Seventh Fleet amphibious operations, I continued to work on my goal of improving petty officer leadership in *Fort Fisher*. On November 22, we inaugurated a Petty Officer Academy adapted from the model I had created at Balboa, a five-day leadership course for newly-selected third class petty officers and second and third class who needed additional leadership training. My implementing memo stated the purpose:

> The majority of the problems encountered in the efficient operation of the ship can be attributed to deficiencies in leadership. The ship has neither the time nor the manpower to send all petty officers onboard to the fleet leadership and management school, which is primarily for training E-6 and above.... *Fort Fisher*'s Petty Officer Academy is aimed at developing leadership skills of E-5's, E-4's and in particular, E-4 selectees. The goal is to achieve 100 percent attendance....

Our Petty Officer Academy committee and the XO tapped into our wealth of shipboard talent and selected a faculty composed of outstanding chiefs, first class petty officers, and two officers. Students were excused from routine duty and attended class in their dress uniform to distinguish them from the rest of the crew, and to emphasize grooming and smart military appearance.

I addressed the petty officers at the beginning of the class and again when I presented their graduation certificates. At his request, I placed our outstanding chief career counselor in charge of the academy. It was a great source of crew pride and became our primary retention tool.

Word got around the fleet and several ships requested implementation documents. The academy was one of my most productive and satisfying shipboard initiatives. It demonstrated respect for my Sailors by helping them develop professionally and advance in the Navy.

On November 26, I received the following message from Vice Admiral St. George, Commander Naval Surface Force Pacific in San Diego, with copy to my Seventh Fleet chain of command:

"Personal for Commanders and Commanding Officer. The following is the partial text of a letter received by CINCPACFLT from the mother of a *Fort Fisher* crewmember:

> This is to advise you that your commanding officer of the USS *Fort Fisher* is driving his men to the point of despair. He is emotionally unstable, and unreasonable. Any records he may have reported in which he has achieved new records of efficiency were all done at the backbreaking and spirit-breaking expense of his men. The men are stabbing and beating up on each other because their commanding officer has pushed them to the point where they are like animals turning on one another. We have received a most discouraging description of hell on board the *Fort Fisher*. Our son has been in the Navy 6 years. He has always been a good sailor, taking pride in his work and doing it well. He has been on other ships; but never have we received these kinds of letters from him before. What is going on? Please, Sir, I beg you. Investigate this situation immediately. Ask the men in such a way that they can give you the facts without jeopardizing their standing with the Captain.'

Request provide info NLT 9 DEC 77 on which to base a reply to above correspondence."

¡El Capitán!

While we were in Pearl Harbor, two of our seamen had gotten into an altercation on board ship after returning from liberty. One stabbed the other with a pocketknife. The victim was hospitalized ashore and the assailant was incarcerated in the Naval Station brig awaiting a Uniform Code of Military Justice Article 32 (like a grand jury). Both sailors remained at the Pearl Harbor Naval Station when we departed for Eniwetok. I responded:

> 1. Ref. B reported a stabbing incident that took place on board *Fort Fisher* ... in Pearl Harbor. Incident was investigated by COMNAVSURFGRU MIDPAC and findings confirm ... that stabbing was primarily attributable to alcohol.... Incident took place at a time when the ship's company was working hard to prepare for OPPE re-exam, and ... an increase in the normal stress and tension of shipboard life.... The incident had an unsettling effect on the crew. The chain of command dealt with the incident and the after-effects on the crew in a prompt, straightforward manner, disseminating factual information in the ship's daily newspaper, and through discussions of the incident by dept. heads/division officers....
> 2. (details about our operational tempo and future schedule)
> 3. .... Without question, this has been a tough year for *Fort Fisher* crewmembers and families, but my perception is that my officers and men feel proud of what the ship has accomplished.... Throughout this year my policies have been aimed at balancing ... the requirements of the ship's schedule with the needs and the welfare of my officers and men and their families, consistent with good order and discipline. My own assessment of ref. A is that it was written in response to an emotional letter from a crewmember.... However, in view of the personal allegations against the commanding officer ... I respectfully request that an independent assessment of *Fort Fisher*'s good order and discipline and morale be conducted on board *Fort Fisher* at the earliest opportunity by someone senior to me in the chain. Very respectfully.

When it rains, it pours. Later that same week I received yet another adverse inquiry about my ship—a message concerning a Congressional letter on a petition submitted to Arizona Congressional Representative

Udall by a former *Fort Fisher* enlisted crewmember. After completing Navy boot camp, he had been assigned to electrician's mate school and advanced to third class petty officer, selected for nuclear power training and assigned to an amphibious ship in San Diego pending the start of his schooling. He then had an unauthorized absence, which resulted in his reduction in rate. Soon thereafter, he was sent ashore for one year of humanitarian leave. Then he was assigned to *Fort Fisher* in 1975 and was on board during our overhaul. He was angry because his request for a training course ashore was denied. The ship had no requirement for the particular training he had requested, and based on his record, he was undeserving.

His petition, which he circulated only within the engineering department, was a general complaint about the workload in the department and the treatment of the engineers. He was discharged from the Navy at the end of his enlistment before our deployment.

I tasked the XO to conduct an investigation on the petition assisted by the Yokosuka Naval Station legal office. Very soon, it became clear that the petition was without merit. Only about half of the individuals who signed the petition were still on board (22 enlisted, all non-rated), and most claimed they could not recall why they signed it (one fireman had actually signed it "by direction"). All agreed that the workload and working conditions cited in the petition were long past and they had no complaints about current conditions in the ship.

The two letters were a great distraction to me and the XO as we prepared for our first major amphibious exercise. Despite accomplishing a nearly impossible workup and deploying on schedule, I now had to defend my performance in command. There seemed to be no end to the after effects of our pre-deployment ordeal. As I reflected on my command, a timeless bit of wisdom came to mind: "Be careful what you wish for—you might get it." Even so, I addressed the issues with factual objectivity, rebutting the personal attacks on my command and my performance.

The letters were quite a blow to my morale, but as I worked the issues and rebutted the personal criticism, my attitude hardened. One night as I paced in my cabin and pondered the letters, I said to myself, "Damn the letters—and screw them all. I have done my best. If my superiors don't like the way I am commanding my ship, they are more than welcome to fire my ass!" I walked over to the XO's cabin, "Come on, Gene, let's knock-off ship's work and go to the O'Club and have a drink on me!"

On December 3, 1974, we departed for Numazu, Japan, to join up with *Denver* and *Mobile* and embark Marine elements for our first amphibious exercise in Seventh Fleet, to be conducted at Pohang, South Korea, which opens to the Sea of Japan. Prior to departing Yokosuka, we took an LCU into the well to get the Marines' tanks ashore; we already had two LCM-8s for transporting trucks, light vehicles and cargo. That night I wrote in my journal,

> One year in command. Glad to be at sea. Our upkeep was successful and the engineers cleaned the boilers. No slack. But I hope we're over the hump. I'm going to make sure in Singapore. Well, still trying to undo the after effects of the schedule. Answering a Congressional on the engineers. I'll have to keep trying in that area. Don't feel too 'up' tonight. Tired. Lonely. A little weary. Wish there was an escape to refresh myself. The responsibility just keeps pressing down all the time. I don't think I want to command at sea again. There are other ways to live. I've given this way a lot.

This was the emotional low point of my tour as commanding officer of *Fort Fisher*. I dealt with the anger and the pain and restored my morale by focusing on our amphibious exercise tasks and by working hard at my job with my officers and my chiefs, who always inspired me and lifted my spirits. And by trying very hard not to feel sorry for myself.

The next morning at anchor offshore of Numazu, we enjoyed a spectacular view of Mt. Fuji while ARG Bravo embarked the Second Battalion Landing Team, Ninth Regiment (BLT 2/9), about 320 men. *Fort Fisher* embarked Golf Company, 160 infantry officers and men, including a mortar platoon and weapons platoon; Echo Battery, 2nd Battalion 12th Marines, 122 officers and men with six 105 mm howitzers and a forward observer unit; and a tank platoon with 40 officers and men and five M-60 tanks. My ship was loaded to capacity.

Rear Admiral Morris, the exercise amphibious task force commander, was embarked in *Denver* with his staff. He came aboard *Fort Fisher* while we were anchored and embarking the Marines. In my cabin, we got acquainted and talked about the two adverse letters, and then I escorted him about my ship. He talked with the officers, chiefs and sailors. We returned to my cabin and had lunch with the XO and department heads.

Upon return to his flagship, the admiral sent me a message, copy to Commodore Jenkins,

> I thoroughly enjoyed my luncheon aboard your fine ship. It was like a breath of fresh air to see a ship as clean and well cared for as *Fort Fisher*. There is evidence, from the top to the bottom and at all levels of management, that a spirit of dedication, unity and loyalty pervades your every endeavor. Pass my sincere appreciation to all hands who contributed to making my visit aboard *Fort Fisher* so pleasant.

The commodore's follow-up personal message to me said, "Reference message noted with pleasure. Glad to see you are riding well."

The next day Morris sent the following message to Vice Admiral St. George, copy to Paddock and Jenkins, proposing a Pacific Fleet Commander response to the Sailor's mother:

> Dear Mrs. ...
>
> This is in response to your letter, which describes a discouraging report from your son, stationed aboard USS *Fort Fisher*, suggesting that a heavy workload and unreasonable demands by the commanding officer were in some way responsible for an unfortunate incident in which one crewmember was stabbed by another during an altercation. A thorough investigation indicates that the reported incident was the result of overindulgence in alcohol on the part of the assailant and was in no way related to working conditions aboard ship ....
>
> All Navy ships go through a particularly arduous workup in preparation for a deployment to the western Pacific.... The Navy takes no shortcuts in this process because the safety of the young men assigned to our ships is a paramount concern, particularly during peacetime operations. The commanding officer of *Fort Fisher* has been repeatedly evaluated by his superiors as demonstrating genuine and compassionate concern for the welfare of his men. That concern had to be balanced against the absolute requirement to make his ship ready and safe for a long and demanding deployment. What your son perhaps perceived as unusual demands were simply those necessary to make his ship ready for deployment.

¡El Capitán!

USS *Fort Fisher* has performed extremely well since arriving in the western Pacific. While the first portion of her deployment was particularly eventful, the latter stages will permit crewmembers to enjoy visits to some of the most exotic and desirable ports in the western Pacific.

I am confident that the crew of *Fort Fisher*, proud of what they have accomplished, has settled into the routine of a Westpac deployment designed to balance amphibious exercises, time to perform necessary work, training and maintenance and a series of truly fascinating port visits before they return to their loved ones. Your expression of concern is appreciated. I hope this letter and future letters from your son will reassure you that all is now well with this fine U.S. Navy ship.

Jenkins provided me with the name and address of the woman who wrote the letter. There was no crewmember aboard whose last name or home address matched hers. I thought the letter, which focused intense scrutiny on my command performance, might have been a hoax, but my hunch was irrelevant—my entire chain of command weighed in and I felt the impact deeply.

RADM Morris also sent the following message to Vice Admiral St. George concerning the Congressional inquiry, "I concur with the remarks of C.O. *Fort Fisher*. Originator visited *Fort Fisher* on 5 December, discussed the matter with the commanding officer, toured the ship and had an opportunity to visit and talk with a number of crewmembers including many in the engineering department. I was impressed by both the material conditions on *Fort Fisher* and the crew's pride and spirit."

I never received any more questions or comments from my chain of command about either letter. Or any other nasty letters about my performance.

During our transit to Numazu, I received an urgent message from the U.S. Naval Hospital at Yokosuka that a mole, which had been excised from Lt. Cdr. Bev Daly's face, was a malignant melanoma, and that he needed medical attention as soon as possible. We immediately arranged a helo medevac and he departed at dawn on December 6, arriving at Balboa Naval Hospital in San Diego two days later for extensive facial surgery followed by shore duty for rehabilitation. It was a shock to the wardroom; I was very saddened to lose him—an outstanding naval officer of sterling character and great potential. He made a full recovery and went on to complete 20 years of service in the Navy. I assigned the Navigator additional duties as operations officer until Bupers could send his replacement.

On December 6, ARG Bravo proceeded to Busan, South Korea, from Numazu through the Japanese Inland Sea and the Straits of Shimonoseki to participate in combined amphibious exercise SSANG YONG VII/BLTEX 1-78, which included the ROK Navy and Marine Corps. After our arrival, I accompanied RADM Morris and three of my sister ship captains to calls on the mayor, the naval sector commander, and the Marine Corps base commanding general.

The pre-exercise briefing was held aboard *Denver*. The U.S. and ROK amphibious task forces then sailed to Pohang to conduct a rehearsal. *Fort Fisher* was the primary control ship (PCS) for both the U.S. and ROK Navy assault waves, a new tactical concept to be validated by us. Several ROK Navy and Marine Corps liaison officers were aboard during the exercise to assist us with communications with the ROK ships, boats and LVT waves. RADM Morris assigned Lt. Cdr. Jim Hough, his assistant Ops officer, to me for the duration of the exercise (to replace Bev Daly). Jim had been *Fort Fisher*'s commissioning first lieutenant. He was a great help to me and the XO, and most enjoyable company for the wardroom.

The assault was conducted at dawn, with *Fort Fisher* leading the way to the assault force anchorages before dawn. The USS *Kitty Hawk* carrier strike group provided pre-and post-invasion air support. The lead LVT and helo waves each touching down on time and the Korean LVT waves also hit the beach at H-Hour.

Fort Fisher was at condition 1A, ballasted down with water in the dock for a good part of the first day. For the next two days, we remained anchored while we conducted logistic support operations for the Marines as they conducted tactical engagements ashore in the exercise terrain. The first lieutenant and his assistants were stationed on an open deck at the end of the port wing wall to control well-deck operations. I was at debarkation control on our flying bridge (above the pilot house) monitoring the assault and observing the XO and Ops boss as they directed shipboard operations including launching and recovering landing craft, dispatching equipment and supplies (serials) for the troops ashore, launching, recovering and fueling helos, and handling medical casualties from the battles ashore.

On December 14, the Marines commenced a tactical withdrawal from the beachhead. We welcomed them back at about 2200 for hot showers and a galley serving steak and eggs, a great boost to troop morale. They had subsisted ashore on C-rations in cold weather for three days and nights. The next day, I was a guest of RADM Morris at a luncheon aboard his flagship. The chief of staff, the flag lieutenant and the flag secretary joined us. The admiral told me that *Fort Fisher* was the best amphib they had seen during his tour.

After the exercise ended, we were detached to proceed to Singapore with a brief stop at Subic to offload a causeway and warping tug. Barbour County was in company and I was the OTC. A Russian Krivak class destroyer that had been observing our exercise tagged along about 3000 yards astern for about an hour, and then she turned away and headed north, probably to Vladivostok.

We received a message from the admiral: "I was most impressed with your conduct of exercise SSANG YONG VII/BLTEX 1-78. After a shaky first rehearsal, you rolled up your sleeves, proceeded to correct your mistakes, and executed a classic assault. This most impressive landing provided our visiting newsmen a fine example of how it should be done. My compliments to all who contributed to this first-class operation."

The next morning we rendezvoused with USS *White Plains*, a Seventh Fleet logistics force ship, and conducted a replenishment of much-needed fresh and frozen provisions and supplies.

Fort Fisher would spend another Christmas away from homeport and I was determined to make it as enjoyable as possible for my crew and embarked Marines. I had the XO, department heads and the CO embarked troops create a program in which Santa would visit the ship before we arrived at Singapore.

The supply officer requisitioned 650 Christmas stockings from the Subic supply center and hard candy, candy canes, fruit, nuts and other goodies for the stockings. The supply center responded that they had no stockings; but then they got creative and contracted with two dozen women in a Philippine church group, who hand-made them.

Our embarked chaplain, Lt. Cdr. Paul Williams, and our PACE instructor, Professor Bob Hobbs, who had brought a portable organ on the cruise, organized a choir. (Bob taught a college literature course on board for about 50 crewmembers.) A working party was organized with each division and Marine unit sending helpers to the galley all day to help bake hundreds of cookies. When it was discovered that more cookie cutters were needed to keep up with the workflow, our machine shop Sailors fabricated them. Stuffing 650 Christmas stockings was a big task, but was readily accomplished in two days by an eight-man working party of Sailors and Marines in my in-port cabin while enjoying music from their "boom boxes."

On Thursday, December 22, the festivities began with a great steak cookout on the flight deck. After dinner, everyone gathered on the holiday-decorated mezzanine deck—complete with a trimmed and lighted Christmas tree—to enjoy eggnog, apple cider, freshly baked cookies and ice cream. Our combined officer and enlisted choir of about 30 ship's company and Marines entertained with traditional Christmas carols. The XO and I joined the choir as "walk-ons."

Santa's helo made a safe landing on the flight deck, where he boarded a "mule" (Marine all-terrain vehicle) with his Marine and Sailor elves, and then drove down the vehicle ramp to the mezzanine where they were greeted with great enthusiasm. Santa and his elves gave everyone a Christmas stocking, including those on watch stations.

We arrived at Singapore the next day. Our sister ships *Mobile* and *Barbour County* were also visiting Singapore for the holidays. The XO established a half-day work schedule, my first opportunity to cut the crew some slack since taking command. We organized daily city tours with buses from the ship to downtown Singapore.

Tragically, the first night in port one of our Sailors died from cardiac arrest while he was on liberty. The XO coordinated the details for the body's return to America and an all-hands memorial service on the flight deck two days after Christmas. The New Zealand forces in Singapore provided a bugler to play taps. I went to the airport for the departure of the casket with one of the deceased Sailor's shipmates, who escorted him home.

I called on the commander of New Zealand forces in Singapore, a brigadier. The New Zealand forces officers held a reception for the *Fort Fisher* wardroom and Marine officers our second night in port. I also called on the U.S. Navy liaison office, to coordinate our logistical requirements, including several engineering repairs. With time to relax,

¡El Capitán!

Gene, Bo and I attended a Christmas Eve party at the home of the U.S. Navy liaison officer, a very enjoyable affair that included several U.S. businessmen and U.S. Air Force officers and their wives. Then Gene and I got rooms in a hotel and spent two days swimming, dining and relaxing. The officers joined us at the bar on New Year's Eve.

We held a ship open house for about 2000 New Zealand Army troops and their dependents. Our Marines displayed their light weapons on the flight deck. I hosted the general and his wife for lunch in my cabin. We wound up our port visit with a personnel inspection and award ceremony—the first of our deployment. The COs of our embarked Marine Corps elements paid me the singular honor of inviting me to inspect their troops, paraded in the dock.

Commanding a ship requires great teamwork between the captain and his wife, especially during deployments. Linda provided my command superb support. She kept in touch with the wardroom wives, hearing their problems and concerns, socializing with them, and maintaining their morale. Linda coordinated with the ship's ombudsman concerning issues among the enlisted wives and families. She attended Rear Admiral Paddock's meetings with the deployed skippers' wives and ombudsmen. She organized a Christmas party for all the ship's dependent families and children and created a video for the ship with messages from the dependents during the event, with help from one of the amphibious ships in port (*Monticello*). She also stayed in touch and socialized with the commodore's wife and the wives of the other squadron ship captains.

In addition to caring for Jack and Judy and guiding their schoolwork and activities, she managed the household and periodic car and house maintenance problems; and she had a full-time job. Her letters sustained my morale:

> Sweetheart, I found this card and it's for you. I am not sad, though—I feel a sense of great adventure, vicariously, having you out there at last. The ship is in good condition and your command holds great promise. I think now you will find the great thrill of your first command at sea to be the exciting and satisfying experience you've waited for so long and the genuine pleasure you deserve. I feel good about it now and I know you do, too. Get the E's! We're fine. We're not sad, but we do miss you and want

to know <u>everything</u> you're doing. Loved your Navy Birthday letter. Keep the spirit soaring! Kisses. Linda

I wrote to her on New Year's Eve:

Sweetheart! And so a tumultuous year comes to an end. Quietly. I breathe a genuine sigh of relief, and I am sure you will do the same. It demanded so much from both of us. Well, I <u>do</u> have a feeling of satisfaction with respect to *Fort Fisher*. I hope you will enjoy it with me, as everything that I was able to do I could not have done without the sure knowledge of your love, understanding, and support. Thank you, Honey. I love you.

The Congressional inquiry and the letter from the 'concerned mother' will be surprises to you. Well, these are problems that I dealt with that I felt there was no need to concern you. Now that I am safely beyond them, I look upon them as part of the price we paid for the success we achieved. (I'm surprised I didn't get irate letters from wives!)

I have my sights set on a good year in 1978. I honestly believe that *Fort Fisher* has the potential now to be a great ship. We are pretty good, but we could be <u>great</u>. What is a great ship? I don't know. But I have a desire to create one, and my officers and crew have the potential.

Essentially, I want to create a high standard of excellence, and do <u>everything</u> a Navy ship is supposed to, and do it well. And have an efficiently administered ship, with top-notch management of resources. I want to develop the full potential of every officer and Sailor, and truly make life enjoyable, interesting and rewarding for them. I sincerely believe that Sailors have more fun if they are taught to work well.

Of course, my ship will always be clean. And my quarterdeck will always be the finest in the squadron and embellished with more McNamara's Lace than any other ship in the Navy because it will always give me secret pleasure in knowing that it pleases you.

Happy New Year, Dearest Love. I will be thinking of you.

¡El Capitán!

Yet it is impossible to compensate for each another's absence. Linda's letter enclosed the following poem:

> Miss you, miss you, miss you, everything I do
> Echoes with the laughter, and the voice of you.
> You're in every corner, every turn and twist,
> Every old familiar spot whispers how you're missed.
>
> Miss you, miss you, miss you, everywhere I go
> There are poignant memories dancing in a row.
> Silhouette and shadow of your form and face
> Substance and reality everywhere displace.
>
> Oh, I miss you, miss you.
> There's a strange, sad silence mid the busy whirl,
> Just as tho' the ordinary, daily things I do
> Wait with me, expectant for a word from you.
> (David Cary "Thoughts of Life")

In late December, we received several messages concerning three young American citizens who had been overtaken at sea on their yacht off the coast of Vietnam and incarcerated by the communist government on October 12, 1977. They were held *incommunicado*. The U.S. had no diplomatic relations with Vietnam so America knew very little about their status. I was busy with command matters and didn't pay particular attention to the incident, but I felt intuitively that it had the potential to become a significant international issue for the U.S.

On January 5, 1978, the day before our departure from Singapore, the following appeared in the AP news service: "The State Department quotes the Vietnam government as saying three Americans held in Saigon since October will be released soon. The three—crewmembers of a yacht reportedly seized in Vietnamese waters—were to have been let go before the first of the year. No details of their continued detention or their reported impending release are known."

I got an uneasy feeling as I read this. *Barbour County, Fort Fisher* and *Mobile* would be sailing together near Vietnam about the same time as the yacht's possible release. Our destination was Okinawa to off-load our embarked Marines. The other ships were bound for Subic Bay. The next morning we departed port.

Shortly thereafter, my hunch became a real possibility. The Seventh Fleet commander signaled to his task group commanders: "… In view of uncertainty of Brillig release and … her movements, request P-3 (patrol aircraft) be kept on alert standby.… Adjust track of ARG Bravo ships to pass near the Vung Tau area and be prepared to divert one ship to stand by to provide surface assistance as needed."

Immediately, RADM Morris directed *Mobile* to position itself and *Fort Fisher* off the coast of Vung Tau, and to detach *Barbour County* to proceed to its next port. I sent a personal message to *Mobile's* skipper, Captain Buchanan, "Have reviewed … our potential SAR (search and rescue) effort and am organizing to render all possible assistance in event Brillig is released and sighted.… (with) my twin screw/twin rudder maneuverability (could) bring Brillig up to my stern gate for assistance, sea/wind permitting. We could probably bring her into our well deck and transport her if required. Just thinking. Very respectfully." *Mobile* responded, "Planning and preparations … demonstrate professionalism always noted *Fort Fisher*. Search plans good, however, need to be adjusted considering new guidance received regarding off-shore islands."

Mobile then sent a message to Captain Bob Klee, our boss, "If directed to divert one ship to provide surface assistance, intentions are to utilize *Fort Fisher*. Stern gate capability will allow sail boat to approach and tie up without damage. If required … can take Brillig in wet-well … air search radar also opts for this assignment." I convened a department head meeting including the Marine CO of troops to discuss our readiness to locate yacht Brillig and render assistance. Shortly thereafter, RADM Morris directed *Fort Fisher* to remain near Vung Tau and *Mobile* to proceed to her next port.

Because the U.S. government had no diplomatic relations with the Vietnamese government, the status of the incarcerated Americans and our operations near Vietnam's coast created concern in the U.S. military and diplomatic establishments' leadership, including the secretary of state, the American ambassador to Paris, several U.S. ambassadors in the Far East, the secretary of defense, the national military command center, the Joint Chiefs of Staff, CINCPAC, CINCPACFLT, the CNO, the Commandant of the Marine Corps, every task force commander in the Seventh Fleet, and even the White House. *Fort Fisher* was definitely in the limelight.

¡El Capitán!

On January 7, we arrived at our designated operating area and started a visual and radar search at 12 knots. As directed, I remained beyond 25 nautical miles from the coast of Vietnam and Vietnam-claimed islands. We saw merchant ships and commercial aircraft, but no yacht or Vietnamese naval craft or fishing boats. We investigated each radar contact to positively identify them as other than Brillig.

I submitted a situation report (Sitrep) every 24 hours to Seventh Fleet commanders and many other authorities in the Pacific and in Washington, D.C.; we were ready to take advisory control of U.S. Navy P-3 patrol aircraft from Cubi Point Naval Air Station (adjacent to Subic Bay) for aerial searches. We began to receive intelligence and other reports concerning our operation region. The following message really got our attention:

> HYDROPAC 41/78 (GEN)
> Mariners are advised that hostile acts, which continue between Cambodia and Vietnam could at any time spill over into the contiguous sea areas, resulting in harassment and/or capture of vessels in these areas. Thus, all mariners in the general area of Cambodia and Vietnam are advised to maintain a close watch for such activities. In addition, special warning 45, issued 12 May 1975, is herein repeated for the information of all mariners. Special warning no. 45: … Shipping is advised until further notice to remain more than 35 nautical miles off the coast of Cambodia and more than 20 nautical miles off the coast of Vietnam and off-lying islands. Recent incidents have been reported of firing on, stopping and detention of ships within waters claimed by Cambodia, particularly in vicinity of Poulo Wai Island. This warning in no way should be considered as United States recognition of Cambodian or Vietnamese territorial sea claims or derogation of the right of innocent passage for United States flag vessels, or derogation of the freedom of the high seas.

I immediately convened a SAR Team meeting (XO, department heads, CO Marine troops, and others) to assess our defensive capabilities and posture and determine how we could or should respond if we were fired upon by ships, boats or aircraft—Vietnamese or Cambodian. *Fort Fisher* was not bristling with guns and armament. All we had were three 3-inch twin gun mounts.

Captain John Frank Gamboa, U. S. Navy (Retired)

But we did have a wealth of Marine Corps firepower embarked. The SAR team got very creative and developed a new *Fort Fisher* defensive capability consisting of designated Marine machine gun emplacements around the ship's weather decks manned by Marines. My hull technicians quickly welded the necessary gun mounts. I stationed a Marine sharpshooter on the bridge under my personal control. I then sent the following message to Captain Bob Klee, Commander, ARG Bravo, copy to RADM Morse and Commodore Jenkins:

Brillig SAR Ops

    1. I have exercised at Condition I at day and night on 9 Jan. All three gun mounts are operational, but local control only as all fire control equipment was removed during overhaul. Have no star shells or other night illumination ammo aboard....

    2. To improve defensive fire posture, I have mounted five 50-caliber machine guns in following locations: vacant Mt. 32 gun tub; port and stbd 03 levels, port and stbd stern wing walls. Additionally, have M-60 machine gun teams assigned to foc'sle, port and stbd boat decks and helo deck, and bridge. All 50-caliber and M-60 rifle teams are controlled by me on the bridge through CO troops on the bridge, who has sound-powered phone comm. to each gun team O-in-C. Each team manned by Marines headed by a Marine officer. Flak vests have been issued to all topside Condition I personnel and Marine fire teams.

    3. All [formatted messages] are addressed with pre-cut tapes.... Photo teams have been designated for still and movie pics....

    4. Overall material readiness.

        A. Engineering plant excellent....

        B. Electronics. Excellent....

        C. Provisions. ... have provisions for approx. three weeks wholesome meals.

        D. Brillig matters. Weather continues unsuitable for yachting ...

Klee responded, "External appearance of ship should not reveal additional precautionary measures which could be incorrectly interpreted as provocative should encounter with SRV military, merchant or fishing unit occur." I assured Bob, "All machine guns are stowed in ready service magazines so that external appearance of ship does not reveal additional precautionary measures. Additionally, surface contacts are not closed unless absolutely required to determine positively that contact is not Brillig. Contacts tracking in excess of 10 knots … are not closed at all. All personnel manning Condition III gun mount are out of sight."

Nonetheless, to ensure that we had good command and control and safety procedures for my newly created ship-defense capability, we periodically drilled our Marine fire teams at dawn and dusk when no ships or aircraft were within visual or radar range. We also test-fired all the weapons and exercised the ammo reload teams and prepared sickbay to receive casualties. We issued night observation devices to all lookouts and trained them. We also conducted training for our bridge lookouts and signal bridge watch on what kind of vessel we were searching for, and added sky lookouts to the daytime watches for possible air attacks.

We had Rules of Engagement (ROE) regarding how we could respond if fired upon by Cambodian or Vietnamese boats, ships or aircraft. RADM Morris conducted ROE exercises with us, posing different scenarios that had us being fired upon. We had to reply promptly and describe how we would respond. These exercises were of great help to us in thinking rapidly, effectively and within the ROE about our possible courses of action.

So far as anyone knew, Brillig was still in communist hands in Saigon. My January 9 Sitrep: "Orig. has sighted no Vietnamese naval activity or Vietnamese fishing vessels. Several non-communist merchant vessels sighted and identified … several … commercial aircraft. All radar contacts being investigated until positively identified to be other than yacht Brillig." On January 10, I reported sighting "two fishing vessels, nationality unknown. Believed to be Vietnamese …." Then we got our first hard news on Brillig:

> Bangkok, Jan 10 (AFP). The American yacht Brillig, which was taken into custody by the Vietnamese Navy on October 12 off Vung Tau, left Vietnam on Friday (6 January) for Singapore. This was learned today from a source close to the delegation headed by Vice-Premier Nguyen Duy Trinh on an official visit to Thailand. Before leaving, the crew of the boat was fined several thousand dollars for drug trafficking, the source said, and that over 600 kilograms of marijuana was seized from the yacht. The American crew of three—two youths and a girl—did not pay the fine but signed an acknowledgement of indebtedness before they

were permitted to depart. Meanwhile, the U.S. Embassy in Singapore said the yacht had not left Vietnam due to bad weather.

We also received a message that added a little more zip to our daily readiness drills and what-if "skull sessions" on the bridge, "Gateway City (merchant ship) firing. Master Gateway City contacted in Hong Kong 6 January. Master reports Gateway City was at posit 07-50 N, 104-24 E proceeding south at 15 knots when incident occurred. Boat firing did not appear to be a military craft, no pennant number seen. Initial open fire range was one mile. Automatic weapon(s) described as light hand-held. Master was not close enough to be hit but intent was to warn rather than harm…. Master considers incident closed."

That night I wrote in my journal. "Much to think about and prepare for. But my officers and men are confident, eager and ready. I pray for courage, wisdom and guidance from God, who has always sustained me in my hour of need. Whatever happens, I hope my actions cause no embarrassment to our country or our Navy, and that they are in the best interests of our detained citizens and our country."

On January 11, my Sitrep Five included the following, "Fishing vessel sighted yesterday at anchor; sighted again today in same posit 07-58N, 105-22.4 E. Vessel appeared to have one whip antenna mounted on deckhouse and at least five personnel on board. Have shifted patrol track east into what is considered by originator better intercept position if yacht Brillig proceeds to Singapore. Desire to stay well clear of above-mentioned vessel in view of possibility it is attempting to keep orig. under surveillance." We did not see that fishing vessel again. We received more hard news.

> Hanoi VNA 12 January. The yacht Brillig and its crew of three Americans sailed from the port of Vung Tau today (January 12). The crew—Anne Dellenbaugh, Charles Affel and Leland Dickerman—arrested for violating territorial waters … were … permitted by local Vietnamese authorities to leave Ho Chi Minh City for Vung Tau, at 1300 hours on January 12 … however, bad weather prevented Brillig from putting to sea until today."

My original tasking was to remain on station until January 13, but this message caused RADM Morris to urgently signal me, "Intelligence indicates that Brillig is underway. Carry out original mission [to find

Brillig and render assistance]." I quickly replied, "WILCO." Navy patrol aircraft were also alerted by Seventh Fleet, "Launch ready alert SAR aircraft to be on station at first light on 13 Jan in area south of Vung Tau. Establish comm. with USS *Fort Fisher* and advise you are commencing search. Maintain normal CPA distances from Vietnam landmass and islands." We established voice communications when the P-3 arrived on station, and I submitted Sitrep Seven reflecting our search activities.

The next message from Commander, Seventh Fleet forwarded an alerting cable from the secretary of state,

> Vietnamese in Paris have now told us yacht Brillig and crew again conducted from Saigon to coast on 12 January. Vietnamese said that at 2:00 a.m. local time, January 13, yacht would reach point (unspecified) at which it will be released. It is not clear to Vietnamese in Paris whether yacht will actually leave its escort at 2:00 a.m. 13 January or wait at release point until dawn. Christopher.

I sent a message to my patrol aircraft commander. "Orig. recommends two P-3s on station for maximum detection probability.... Orig. considers Singapore most likely port of call for Brillig due to being down wind/down seas, and proximity. Brunei next most probable destination due to being original destination, and proximity." On January 12, CINCPAC rep. Subic Bay sent the following:

> Have been advised by ... an amateur radio operator that he was in contact with yacht Brillig via a Guam ham operator. Brillig advised that their position at the time was 8-22N, 107-35E on course 200 degrees making good 100 miles per day en route to Singapore in 4 to 5 days ... Brillig has a radar reflector in the rigging and one running light in the masthead and they are transmitting on amateur radio frequency 14320 kHz upper side band.

Immediately, Commander, Seventh Fleet signaled *Fort Fisher*, "... Request you intercept, ascertain status and confirm destination and ETA. For CTG 72.3. Provide air search support to *Fort Fisher* along PIM as required."

I replied, "WILCO. Proceeding to intercept yacht Brillig based on posit given. ETA rdvu about 140230H." Two days earlier, I had moved our patrol to the eastern sector of our search area. We had assumed

Brillig's destination would be Singapore after her release and deduced her intended track—most likely, she would sail east of Con Son Island. Our assumptions proved valid and our estimate of her track and speed were correct. Brillig was about 75 nm from us. We shaped course to intercept and increased speed to 18 knots.

Four hours later at 131850Z Jan 78 (0150 January 14 local), we found her. There was a fresh breeze, but the seas were only 2-3 feet; the sky was overcast and the moonless night was very dark. Our starboard lookout, Seaman Stephen Cook, sighted Brillig's masthead light 15 degrees off our starboard bow, 13,000 yards ahead.

We directed our signal lights at our holiday colors (large U.S. flag) flying high on our mast so they could identify us as an American ship. When we were within 1000 yards, we illuminated the yacht to verify it was Brillig. Then we launched our gig with the XO, Cheng and First Lieutenant aboard to approach her and establish communications.

We knew that the three Americans, having been captured once before on the high seas and having just been released after three months in captivity, would be very frightened and just want us to go away and leave them alone. That was exactly how they responded to the XO (who was using a loud hailer—a battery-powered megaphone). Nonetheless, my task was to ascertain their status.

Despite Brillig crew's reticence, I was determined to get them on board *Fort Fisher*, verify their medical condition, determine their mental state, and inform their families that they were aboard my ship. I also had to determine the seaworthiness of their yacht and provide assistance as needed.

While we negotiated with the yacht, I sent a flash-precedence (the highest message precedence in the military) OPREP-3 Pinnacle (critical) message to the national military command center in Washington, D.C. copy to everyone in the loop (The only Pinnacle and flash-precedence message I ever transmitted in the Navy), "....Yacht Brillig sighted. Assistance party alongside yacht. Brillig states all crewmembers healthy. Boat is in good condition and is seaworthy. Amplifying info to follow."

Meanwhile, the XO turned on his considerable charm and just kept talking persuasively—and relayed my offer of steak and eggs for breakfast. After a few minutes, Charles Affel agreed to come aboard our gig to answer specific questions about their status. He soon calmed down. We repeated our breakfast offer and to send telegrams to their families.

¡El Capitán!

Affel replied, "OK, we'll come aboard and yes, we would like to have steak and eggs!" Deal! Affel returned to Brillig and the gig returned to the ship to wait until daylight.

Our gig with the XO on board returned to the yacht at 0700 and brought the skipper, Cornelia "Cricket" Dellenbaugh, and crewmember Leland Dickerman aboard ship for breakfast in my cabin with me, the XO, department heads and CO Marine troops. Charles Affel remained aboard the yacht 500 yards away. Excellent Navy chow—juicy steaks, eggs cooked to order, orange juice, freshly-baked biscuits with butter and jelly, fresh fruit and steaming hot coffee—soon had its intended effect. They relaxed and began describing their harrowing ordeal: three months in captivity including two months in solitary confinement with no contact with each other—but no physical abuse or torture.

After breakfast, they sent telegrams to their families and visited the ship's store, selecting personal items (soap, toothpaste, toothbrushes, shampoo, etc.) which I personally paid for. They accepted our offer of hot baths in my cabin while their clothes were laundered. Cornelia also agreed that we could bring Charles Affel aboard for breakfast and station Ensign Mark Borchers aboard Brillig for security (my Deck divisions quickly fabricated a canvas sea anchor to keep her from drifting away from us).

Coordinated by the Ops boss and the Supply Officer, Cornellia and Leland compiled a list of navigation charts and supplies: a new navigation wrist watch, fresh water, flashlights and batteries, and food including milk, bread, steaks, canned soda, pastries, boxes of C-rations, ice, and a complete medical kit. We also gave them recent news periodicals, and paperbacks from the ship's library. They were eager for news of America.

By then the Brillig crew was happy to be aboard *Fort Fisher*. They toured the ship, chatting with crewmembers and Marines, thoroughly enjoying their freedom and the opportunity to talk with their fellow Americans. They agreed to stay for lunch and to be debriefed by Lt. Carde, who had spent a tour of duty as an intelligence analyst in Washington, D.C. They described how they were taken into custody and how they were treated in captivity.

Brillig was sailing from Pattaya, Thailand, enroute to Brunei, Borneo. According to their celestial navigation fixes, Brillig was 50 miles from the Vietnamese coast when they were taken into custody by three armed fishing boats. They were towed to Vung Tau. According to Dellenbaugh, the unarmed yacht surrendered after warning shots were fired by the Vietnamese boats. All three crewmembers concurred that the Vietnamese "took great care" handling them and their possessions enroute to their place of detention in Ho Chi Minh City. They reassured them and convinced them that they would eventually be released ... they were not at any time mistreated but in fact were better treated and better fed than most of the other detainees in their facility. ... kept in separate cells and not allowed contact with each other until 22 December, they received several letters from home and after being reunited, they were allowed to do maintenance on their boat. On 6 January, Brillig was released for the first time and allowed to sail south to Vung Tau. They were at sea and making slow headway when a large merchant ship came close to them. When they waved it away, the Vietnamese interpreted it as a distress signal and they were escorted back up the Saigon River. Brillig was released on 13 January when the Vietnamese felt that the weather was good enough for her transit....

Then it was time to let them go and be on our way. I presented Cornelia, Charles and Leland with *Fort Fisher* t-shirts and welcome aboard brochures, and they returned to Brillig. We observed them rig sails and get underway. With a long farewell blast on the ship's whistle, we rang up a full bell (full speed) and shaped course for Okinawa.

I transmitted Sitrep Eleven. ".... All crew members returned to yacht Brillig at 1345 H and Brillig is underway for Singapore, ETA pm 18 - 20 Jan 78. Brillig sailing before the wind on course 195 with main and double headsail rig full and bye. Originator underway enroute Okinawa at 1500H..."

We stood down from Condition III readiness. With relief, but some reluctance, we dismantled our superb Marine Corps fire teams and restowed all weapons and ammunition. We had been on our search and assist mission for one week. We missed our much-desired visit to Hong Kong with no opportunity to re-schedule.

On January 14, we received the following message: "The quick professional response to rapidly changing tasking in the Brillig SAR effort provided evidence that Seventh Fleet is flexible and ready. Well Done. Vice Admiral R.B. Baldwin."

¡El Capitán!

That night I wrote in my journal, "I'm happy for my officers and men. They worked hard and deserved this success. So did our Marines.... We ... did it well, so we are sailing to Okinawa feeling like we can do anything.... Well, a rescue mission in the world spotlight, and carried off very neatly. Professionally. I hope it was a credit to the U.S. Navy. Quite a way to start 1978. Only God knows why."...

On January 16, we received a message from our boss, RADM Morris: "To the entire *Fort Fisher* and Marine Corps team, WELL DONE." On January 25, the secretary of state sent the following via the commander in chief, Pacific,

> Appreciation for Assistance. With the American yacht Brillig finally berthed in Singapore, I would like to thank you for the work you and the men and women in your command did to locate and assist the Brillig and crew on its departure from Vietnam. The captain and the crew of the *Fort Fisher* deserve special commendation for their generosity and sensitivity toward the three Americans. The crews of the aircraft who helped to locate the yacht also deserve recognition. We salute you all for completing this mission as professionally as usual but with added and timely doses of humor and humanity. Warm regards, Christopher.

A message from the commander in chief, Pacific said, "Please pass on to all hands CINCPAC's appreciation for job well done." Then commander in chief, Pacific Fleet signaled, "The hallmark of Seventh Fleet has always been the rapid, professional response to an ever-changing environment. Well Done. T. B. Hayward, Admiral, U.S. Navy."

We maintained radio contact twice daily with Brillig until she arrived safely in Singapore on January 20. The P-3 aircraft relocated her every day and communicated with her by voice radio and with Brillig's permission even made a couple of low passes to take aerial photos.

The yacht was met in port by U.S. State Department representatives as well as the news media. Cornelia publicly thanked the U.S. Navy for its assistance. After three weeks repairing their boat and resting, the Brillig crew departed Singapore and continued on their voyage to the Indian Ocean and then home to America.

The story of Brillig's detention and release by the Vietnamese, and her interception and assistance by *Fort Fisher*, was released to the media by the Navy chief of information and appeared on national TV and many

Captain John Frank Gamboa, U. S. Navy (Retired)

American and foreign newspapers, which is how Linda, Jack and Judy and the ship's families learned of our Brillig affair. We were proud of our "15 minutes of fame."

We off-loaded the Marines and equipment at White Beach, and then we sailed up the coast about 20 miles and anchored off shore near their base to land their tanks on the base beach. The Marines invited me to ride ashore on our LCU with the first tank and drive it, which I then drove—under the tank commander's close supervision—along the beach and over a few dunes. Then we sailed to Subic Bay.

During our Brillig affair, the rest of Phibron Five was in Subic for a change of command. Captain David G. Ramsey relieved Captain Harry Jenkins on January 19. Jenkins evaluated my yearlong performance:

> Quiet, meticulous, talented administrator. Detailed planning and close monitoring of progress responsible for completing overhaul 17 days early. Successfully completed all pre-deployment training in only three months. Supported Eniwetok project with largest lift ever carried by amphibs. Unusual and outsized equipment presented unique problems but were handled without damage or personnel injury. Has made significant improvement in material reliability through a well-planned, well-managed program. Extremely sensitive to personnel welfare and needs. Actively seeks improvement in human resources management through viable human relations program, training and interpersonal communications. This made possible an accelerated workup to deployment without impact on morale. Personal appearance and conduct above reproach. A fine officer. Highly recommended for major command and accelerated promotion. During recent independent SAR mission to locate and aid yacht detained by Vietnam, demonstrated outstanding foresight in planning and conduct of an extremely successful mission, in an area where a mistake would have been most embarrassing to the U.S. Government.

We arrived in Subic on January 23 for two weeks of maintenance and upkeep, and we were greeted by our new commodore. I welcomed Captain Ramsey aboard, immediately feeling a rapport with him as we saluted and shook hands. He was a fellow "black shoe." I invited him to tour my ship and talk to my wardroom and chiefs' mess, which he did the following week.

¡El Capitán!

Ramsey shifted *Fort Fisher* to ARG Alfa from ARG Bravo for the remainder of our deployment. We traded places with *Duluth*; she embarked a Navy helicopter mine countermeasures squadron as part of Exercise Team Spirit. Our new role was secondary control ship, a backup to USS *Mount Vernon* (LSD 39) our class sister ship.

The commodore hosted a luncheon aboard his flagship *Tripoli* for all the squadron skippers. I had not been with them since our call on Admiral Hayward five months earlier. Ramsey talked about his basic policies and spelled out his operational philosophy, his standards and expectations. He also alerted us to his penchant for good ship handling and seamanship.

While at Subic, I had the great pleasure of entertaining my brother-in-law Eino Lehtio, his wife Susan, and their three marvelous sons, Marty, William and Jacob, at dinner in my cabin after touring them about the ship. Eino. An Air Force communications technician, was stationed at Clark Air Force Base, near Subic. On another evening, I hosted Cdr. Larry Gressens and his lovely wife Sherry, good friends from our tour in the Canal Zone; they were stationed at Subic.

And I held a captain's mast. Standing before me were four of my deck seamen who had gotten a little too rambunctious ashore and even insubordinate to their superiors aboard ship. I slapped them with three days confinement on reduced rations—bread and water. Their punishment was actually advantageous to them—they lost no money and would still have some remaining days of liberty in Olongapo. Even though I was all heart, I am not sure my Sailors saw their punishment in the same light. They did their confinement in the Naval Station brig run by the Marines, not exactly a church social. They shaped up right away. I had no more mast cases in Subic.

The first time I awarded one of my Sailors three days in the brig on bread and water was in San Diego. We were at sea and I was extremely busy, but on the second day of his confinement, accompanied by my chief master at arms, I took time to check on him in his cell. I chatted with the Sailor as I took in his austere surroundings. The only reading material he was allowed was a Bible, if desired. Distractedly, I asked, "Well, are you getting enough to eat?" He gave me a very puzzled look, but before he could answer the chief interjected, "Yes sir, Captain. He's getting all the bread and water he wants." I replied, "Oh. Very good! Thank you, chief!"

Captain John Frank Gamboa, U. S. Navy (Retired)

While at Subic, I received the following letter:

> Dear Captain Gamboa and the Crew of the *Fort Fisher*,
>
> Many thanks for such a warm welcome to the free world. All the friendly smiling American faces and the great food went a long way towards helping us feel alive again. We appreciate all the efforts of you and your crew to find us, waits for us, and gives us a wonderful celebration of our freedom. Special thanks to the cooks for the two best meals I have ever had. You certainly deserve the best-mess award.
>
> After we left you we had one of our best-ever sails on to Singapore. The wind went down to force 3-4 and it was a very comfortable broad reach all the way. We thoroughly enjoyed your delicious steaks for breakfast and dinner three days in a row. The new watch eliminated any worries about navigation and even the flu barely dimmed our appreciation of good food and beautiful sailing.
>
> I hope you had a successful voyage to Okinawa and points beyond and that this letter finds you and all the crew well. We will remember your hospitality each time we open a can of C-rations on our trip back home. We will be leaving Singapore for Seychelles and Africa in two weeks or so.
>
> Thank you again, on behalf of all the crew of yacht Brillig.
>
> Sincerely,
> Cornelia Dellenbaugh, Chief Engineer.

I took time at Subic to promulgate my command goals for 1978, which I designed to focus "… attention and action by each department organizationally, and all hands individually, on the specific things that we wish to accomplish during calendar year 1978…. Objectives within each goal are quantifiable and measurable. By giving visibility to our goals, we can create unity of purpose and greater ship's spirit. If each individual … knows and understands what the command is trying to achieve, then he can better understand and see the value of his personal contribution …" Here are the ten goals:

1. To operate *Fort Fisher* in a safe manner, with no serious personnel injuries or deaths.
2. To meet every operational commitment in a professional, seamanlike manner.

305

3. To maintain *Fort Fisher* in the highest possible state of equipment readiness within resources available.
4. To maintain a high level of morale within *Fort Fisher* at every level of rank and rate.
5. To ensure equal opportunity and fair treatment for every person serving on board *Fort Fisher*.
6. To achieve maximum professional growth in each person serving on board *Fort Fisher*.
7. To achieve a 60% first-term and a 90% career reenlistment.
8. To maintain *Fort Fisher* in a high state of cleanliness, sanitation, and material preservation.
9. To contribute to a good public image for the U.S. Navy.
10. To be the best ship in Amphibious Squadron Five.

My chief engineer, Lt. Hank Carde, was relieved by Lt. Bob Bovey while we were in Subic. I regretted losing Carde, an outstanding officer who had borne the brunt of the overhaul workload and the OPPE ordeal. He cast off our bow line from the pier as we waved farewell and got underway on February 8 with Marine BLT 2/3 embarked. We transited the Straits of Taiwan to join up with ARG Alfa.

Before departing Subic, we received a very pleasant surprise. Seventh Fleet's Rock Band "The Orient Express," who styled their music after the Bee Gees, embarked and sailed with us to Numazu. Their seven musicians led by a chief staged a concert on the flight deck after we got underway, then played for the crew in the mess decks and when we went alongside for refueling. The band was a great morale enhancer. We were the only Gator so honored during our squadron's deployment.

ARG Alfa and Bravo began staging Marine units in Korea for Exercise Team Spirit. We proceeded in company to Numazu to deliver the Marines for their cold-weather training at Camp Fuji, in two feet of snow. It took over 18 hours to offload their 400 pallets of cold weather gear, blankets, tents and rations all in freezing weather. We departed Numazu the next day and sailed to Okinawa to embark Marine Communications Squadron Eighteen and Marine Air Control Squadron Four, with 18 officers and 300 enlisted. We arrived on February 17, and spent 36 hours embarking personnel and stowing over 200 equipment vans and vehicles on the helo, super, mezzanine and the well decks, in cold rain, hail and wind. We rotated the Deck force on stations and kept them going with lots of hot chocolate, coffee and sandwiches. Then we departed for Pohang, encountering more foul weather along the way.

The next morning we joined up with USS *White Plains* to receive much-needed provisions. Because our flight deck was loaded with Marine equipment, we had to rig our seldom-used forecastle replenishment station, which exposed Deck personnel to even more cold wind and made the shiphandling and cargo transfer much more difficult and dangerous.

Because he was a superb ship handler, I assigned the conn to my XO, Cdr. Gene Bailey, spelled by Lt. James, my best junior officer shiphandler. We went alongside starboard side to *White Plains*, in 15-20 knots winds and rough seas. Two hours later, we completed the evolution and broke away. I received a message from the commodore,

> The captain of *White Plains* has just told me that *Fort Fisher's* seamanship alongside and cargo handling, under adverse sea and weather conditions, are the best he has seen since he has been replenishing Seventh Fleet ships over one year. Well Done!

That evening I wrote in my journal, "Our unrep with *White Plains* was the toughest I have ever done. Rough seas. Made a 20-degree course change while alongside. Received 47 pallets in two hours. .... *Mount Vernon* collided with *White Plains* as she made her approach on *WP's* stbd side ... seriously damaging her own accommodation ladder, port whip antennas and flight deck netting, ... (and) *WP's* stbd flight deck netting. God!"

We arrived at Pohang the next day. Waiting on the pier was Lt. Mike Cordasco, my new operations officer. We disembarked the Marines, another dawn to dusk non-stop evolution. Most of the vans were airlifted off our flight deck by deafeningly loud CH-53 Echo heavy-lift helos. The next morning ARG Alfa sailed to Yokosuka for two days in port. Afterwards, we would sail to Numazu, re-embark the Marines and lift them to Korea for Team Spirit.

During our transits between ports, ARG Alfa steamed in formation with the flagship in the center and a ship stationed on either side of the flagship's bow and one astern, 1000 yards separation between the ships and the guide. The formation base speed was 12 knots; at slower speeds, a ship can be slow and sluggish in maneuvering. Our maneuvering speed was 17 knots.

The commodore would exercise the ARG at tactics for about two hours in the morning in a column, a line abreast, or in an echelon left or right. Ramsey had high seamanship standards and would verbally blast a ship by voice radio for not maneuvering smartly.

In daylight, Ramsey maneuvered by either signal flags or voice radio. The ships quickly learned to keep an alert signal bridge. The trick was to maintain one signalman with a long-glass constantly viewing the flagship's signal halyards.

When "signal in the air!" was sounded by the signalman, the other signalmen would spring into action, snapping matching signal flags onto our halyards as fast as the commodore's signal bridge was bending on signal flags out of their flag bags.

When they understood the signal and were ready to execute, the ships "two-blocked" their flag hoists [hoisted to the top of the yardarm]. Then the flagship rapidly hauled down its signal, the ships followed suit, and everyone commenced the maneuver.

If a ship was slow in two-blocking their hoists—delaying execution—the commodore would summon the captain by radio and yell in his finest Virginia accent, "Do y'all have anyone manning yoah signal bridge?" to the amusement of the other captains.

At night Ramsey used the ships' yardarm blinkers (a white light on each end of the highest mast yardarm) to signal course and speed changes. It was all very nautical and great sport. My watch officers enjoyed these basic ship evolutions and learning by doing.

After tactics, the commodore would detach the ships to proceed on independent ship exercise (ISE). Each ship would "do its own thing" sailing independently while remaining within visual signaling distance from the flagship. On signal, we would rejoin the flagship in our night steaming formation. Prior to entering port, the commodore would form the ships into a column with the flagship in the lead and the other ships in order of seniority. Rank hath its privileges (RHIP).

We liked steaming with the commodore. My bridge watch teams and I quickly adapted to operating with our sister ships—and learning their personalities and characteristics. "She's pretty sharp and always on station." "You can't tell which way she will turn!" "Those guys are a hazard to navigation!" It was all much more interesting and exciting than

Captain John Frank Gamboa, U. S. Navy (Retired)

independent steaming, even though I had to spend even more time on the bridge—and pay more attention.

But ship formation tactical maneuvers are also risky business; one—or more—ships may misunderstand the signal or commit an error in executing, thereby increasing the risk of collision. And maneuvering ships at night increases the risks.

On March 8, ARG Alfa was steaming in the Sea of Japan enroute to Pohang from Numazu. After our morning tactics, the commodore detached the ships for ISE. That evening, the commodore's night intentions stipulated that ships would continue ISE throughout the night and rejoin at 0500 in column formation with *Fort Fisher* in station two astern of *Tripoli* and ahead of *Mount Vernon*. *Barbour County* was tail-end Charlie. This was our normal column station sequence.

In my night orders, I directed the OOD to remain 4000 to 6000 yards on the port beam of the flagship on parallel course and same speed, and that I be awakened at 0445. Once on the bridge, I intended to be on station at 0500 as directed in the night intentions, which I noted did not state "on signal."

I got to the bridge about 10 minutes before 0500 and had some strong black coffee as I oriented myself to the tactical situation and the dark, moonless night. We were at 4000 yards range on the port beam of the flagship. *Tripoli* was on course 300 and speed 10 knots. I noted that *Mount Vernon* and *Barbour County* were almost in their respective formation stations.

I directed the OOD to come right and proceed to station two astern of *Tripoli* at 17 knots. As I was closing the formation, the commodore signaled by voice radio for the ships to form column, but with *Fort Fisher* now assigned to the van, station one, instead of station two! All ships immediately questioned the signal. I continued closing to station two in the formation.

Suddenly, the commodore signaled an immediate course change to a new base course of 221, a seventy-nine degree turn to port. *Tripoli* started turning left to the new base course—heading directly toward us. Puzzled by the sudden course change, I hesitated.

Then I noticed that *Tripoli* was rapidly closing *Fort Fisher*, with constant bearing on our starboard side, CBDR. I directed the OOD to come left to the new base course and proceed to station one.

309

¡El Capitán!

Range to *Tripoli* was now 800 yards and closing fast, so I increased our rate of turn by directing left full rudder. *Tripoli* was now at 600 yards on our starboard beam and still closing with steady bearing. She loomed huge—her red hangar deck lights glowing very bright. I backed the port engine one third to further increase my rate of turn to port.

Tripoli sounded five blasts on her ship whistle—the maritime signal for danger—and radioed, "My rudder is right full!"

The commodore radioed, "*Fort Fisher*! Interrogative your intentions!"

I responded, "I'm coming left to course 221!"

He replied, "Very well!"

Tripoli drew ahead of us and her range opened.

I steadied up on base course 221, speed 12 knots. Then the other ships fell in astern of *Fort Fisher* in column formation in signaled order.

It had all happened so fast.

I sent a personal flashing light message to the captain of the *Tripoli*, copy to the commodore, "My apologies for embarrassing you. We were proceeding to station two at 17 knots, when signal changed our station to station one. Our turn to port was too slow."

Later, I learned that the staff watch officer and the flagship OOD did not understand my movements. Both assumed that no ship would take station until the commodore signaled and executed "Form One."

Our near collision frightened my entire bridge team—and me. We estimated that *Tripoli* had closed to within 400 yards—maybe less. After a decent interval, I reviewed the incident with the OOD, JOOD and CIC watch officer, discussing what had transpired and ensured they understood how we had stood into danger and why I took the actions that I did.

We were detached to proceed independently into Pohang harbor to our assigned anchorage. After dropping the hook, I went to *Tripoli* in my gig and apologized to the captain. He related to me that, on another occasion before *Fort Fisher* joined the ARG, *Mount Vernon* was stationed broad on *Tripoli*'s starboard bow. When directed to take station astern of the flagship, *Mount Vernon* had turned LEFT instead of RIGHT and had endangered *Tripoli*, who was forced to turn hard left to avoid a collision. It had also happened at night.

Captain John Frank Gamboa, U. S. Navy (Retired)

The captain looked at me and joked, "Operating with you guys is like dropping a bunch of bee bees on a glass table—I never know where the hell you're going!"

I left his cabin and walked down the corridor to pay my respects to the commodore, mentally and emotionally prepared to receive a chewing out. But Ramsey didn't mention the incident except to say that we all needed to stay alert. I agreed. That night I wrote in my journal,

> …. Danger passed as we steadied on new course and *Tripoli* drew ahead of us, range opening. The commodore came out with a new signal, increased base speed to 12 knots, and we proceeded safely to station. He then apologized to the ships for putting out a signal changing the sequence order, and for forming up at less than 12 knots. Then he said that ships will always join from abaft the beam, adding "I will hang the next CO who points the bow of his ship at another ship in this squadron."

Our dangerous situation was created by several factors. First, the commodore's night intentions message did not state that we would form up "on signal" as he normally specified. I interpreted his message literally and was maneuvering to be on station by 0500. I could have questioned the night intentions, but being the new guy in the group, I did not feel comfortable questioning the commodore.

The second factor was the new sequence of ships—different from the night intentions and not our normal sequence. This confused all ships; everyone radioed, "Interrogative order of ships!" which delayed execution and further complicated the situation. Meanwhile, I was already maneuvering to take station two.

The third complicating factor was the sudden course change, which turned *Tripoli* sharply left toward *Fort Fisher*. The staff watch officer had not taken into account the new base course to enter port. When he was prompted by the ship's navigator, the staff watch officer signaled an immediate course change to remain on track. I should have come to the new course immediately—as did the flagship.

When the new course was signaled, the form one signal had still not been executed. So I was still proceeding to station two. Due to the sudden course change, *Tripoli* immediately turned to port, coming right at me,

311

which created a CBDR – a dreaded "constant bearing, decreasing range" situation.

But what compounded the confusion between *Fort Fisher* and *Tripoli* and on the staff was my violation of fleet doctrine: <u>never anticipate</u> when maneuvering in a group of ships; <u>only</u> maneuver after the event has been signaled and executed—regardless of any "intentions" message. I had anticipated the column form up without signal.

This was the closest I ever came to a collision with another ship—the only time I ever heard five blasts sounded on a ship's whistle or had to maneuver my ship *in extremis*. One time was one too many.

Team Spirit was our longest and most challenging operation. The assault was pre-dawn so we would approach the objective area and anchor at "oh-dark thirty." We participated in pre-exercise briefings on the flagship and then proceeded to sea for a rehearsal at nearby Tok Sok Ri, the amphibious objective area (AOA), but the rehearsal was delayed twenty-four hours due to high winds and rough seas.

Mount Vernon was the Primary Control Ship and *Fort Fisher* was secondary, so we had to closely monitor her operations and be prepared to take over in case of a PCS casualty (simulated or real), and take control of all the boats and monitor helo operations within the AOA. We provided our LCM 6 as a medical boat and our LCVP as a press boat with media reporters and photographers embarked.

While at sea after the rehearsal and prior to the assault, the task group refueled from USNS *Navasota*. When we were alongside, her captain called me on the phone and distance line between our two bridges and said, "You guys have real class. Everything is going very smooth and nice! Thanks for not straining my rig!" I passed the compliment to my deck force, engineers and the bridge team.

D-Day was the 12th. We went to general quarters at 0230 hours, then "Boats to the rail!" as we approached our anchorage (the boats are lifted out of their cradles and lowered to the deck edge for crew boarding). We set condition One Alfa (1A) at 0330. Then we anchored and "Away all boats!" (boats are lowered to the water and cast off). H-hour was delayed until 0530 due to a man-overboard from one of the LVT's; fortunately he was wearing a lifejacket and was safely recovered in the dark.

As often happens in all amphibious exercises, there were real equipment casualties. "The Day's News," our ship's daily newspaper, reported, "Repair Division has been kept busy … working on the stern gate marriage blocks, which had to be refurbished because of extensive use … the port boat deck cradle was broken while the LCM-6 was being launched. The cradle had to be cut off and bent back to shape then welded back on. HTFN Miner and HT1 Ewing completed the job before the rehearsal was over."

After D-Day we conducted training in underway launches of ROK LVTs from our well deck, part of our Navy-to-Navy training. Later, we proceeded to sea and joined up with the USNS *Passumpsic* for a night refueling, the first of our deployment. It was a cold, clear, star-lit night with a quarter-moon. The replenishment course was down-wind in a following sea with moderate swells in 18 knot wind, 38 degrees, which made the alongside ship handling and the Deck personnel's work even more difficult. I assigned the conn to the XO for the entire evolution while I kept a watchful eye. Two hours later, we broke away and returned to our amphibious exercise anchorage. *Passumpsic* signaled "Well Done."

The topside refueling team was pretty miserable after two hours in the frigid night air, so I did what any right-minded, salty skipper would do—I "spliced the main brace" on the mess decks (offered a shot of "medicinal whiskey") to each member of the topside fueling detail to help them thaw out. The chief master at arms and my corpsmen were amazed at how many crewmen we had in that detail—almost half the crew showed up for a shot of team spirits.

At anchor the next day, we conducted training for Korean Marines in wet-net debarkation. Four infantry companies, almost 1000 men, came aboard through the well deck on our LCM-8s. They filed up the vehicle ramps to the port and starboard boat deck debarkation stations. With the LCM-8s alongside, the troops went over the side and climbed down rope nets into the landing craft like GIs and Marines in WW II (since the introduction of helos, wet-net debarkation into landing craft has been a back-up method of getting troops ashore).

On March 16, we received a message from Commodore Ramsey,

> As Team Spirit '78 draws to a close … well done for long hours of sustained performance in cold, windy climate. For our control men at debark stations and deck seamen and airmen on each ship—well done under the same weather conditions and hours, and for keeping men

and material moving. For all who supported them—well done for long hours, attention to duty and a successful planning/execution of the classic amphibious assault.

Phibron Five departed Pohang on March 18 en route to Numazu. We would transit the Straits of Shimonoseki for the fourth and last time. That evening I wrote,

> .... The crew and ship performed superbly ... as I expected they would ... an incredibly busy 12 days. We had cold, rough weather ... but my crew was warmly dressed in the cold weather clothing we purchased prior to departing San Diego.... We launched and received so many boats and landed and launched so many helos I long ago lost count. Same for ... helo fueling. All our boats worked ... minor casualties quickly restored. We damaged the ship and the boats a little ... fixed what we had to, fast. We were up before dawn ... to bed late at night ... up early again and do the next event. ... my crew worked hard, did their best, and maintained their sense of humor.... Morale is excellent ... now that we are homeward bound. It is a fine crew, better than I ever dreamed. Respectful, cooperative, spirited, hardworking, loyal, and dedicated. I feel tired and emotionally drained. But mostly I'm proud of what we did together. There is no finer record by any ship in PACFLT.

We arrived at Yokosuka on March 22 for 13 days of maintenance and upkeep, our final such event in Westpac and the last opportunity to prepare the ship for our three-week homeward-bound voyage. We did inspections, repairs, maintenance, sports, our final personnel inspection and awards ceremony, and enjoyed great liberty. Everyone was in a good mood with a spring in their step.

On April 3 after morning quarters, I held an All Hands Aft on the flight deck.

> This afternoon we will get underway for a port visit we have all been waiting for a long time. Our Westpac is drawing to a close.... we will have steamed 27,915 nautical miles ... more than once around the globe ... and we still have Numazu, Pearl and San Diego to go.....[summary of all our Westpac events and evolutions]...

314

Captain John Frank Gamboa, U. S. Navy (Retired)

Well, how did *Fort Fisher* do? What is the result of all this human effort?

We have the best record of any ship in the squadron, in ARG Alfa and ARG Bravo. Our guns shoot every time. Our engineering plant is the most reliable. We never hurt a Sailor or a Marine, nor damaged or lost a single piece of equipment that we carried. We met every commitment, and when we were called upon suddenly to divert, find and assist Brillig, we did it with exceptional performance, right before the entire national military command structure. Our conduct ashore is exemplary. No one comes close to our intramural sports program. *Fort Fisher* leads the squadron in retention. No ship communicates as well. We feed better than any other ship, and we are known for our cleanliness and smart, ship-shape appearance.

In a word, you have excelled. As a ship's company, you are second to none in the Pacific Fleet. The skipper of *Navasota* said it all: "You guys have real class!"

So, we start our voyage home with a feeling of accomplishment and satisfaction.

I want to thank each of you—the officers, the chiefs, the first class, all petty officers and all non-rated for your hard work and your loyal, dedicated performance of duty.

I am very proud of you.

Well Done!

Now, let's go home!

We anchored in the harbor, ballasted down and embarked our LCU and our two LCM-8s. Then we sailed into the shipping channel, joined up with ARG Alfa, transited overnight to Numazu, and off-loaded the Marines for the last time. After ARG Bravo's join-up, the squadron shaped course to Wake Island to rendezvous on the morning of April 10 with Phibron Seven and pass the baton to the new guys. Then we were on our way to Pearl Harbor.

Fleet tradition calls for commanders to send laudatory messages to their units upon completion of deployment.

As we complete our 1977-78 Westpac Deployment, I commend you on a fine effort devoted to peace and understanding. That we can return home as scheduled is the best proof of a successful deployment. The world and especially our own country remain uninvolved in total

315

war because of the sacrifices you make each day. I share with you the pleasure of reunion with your families and those important in your life. Enjoy those moments fully. You deserve them. In summary and to paraphrase: Freedom has a special meaning for those who have sacrificed for it that the protected can never know. Well Done. Commodore Ramsey.

RADM Morris: As Phibron Five departs for reunions with loved ones, the crews of your ships can reflect with pride on a most demanding and eventful deployment. (Our amphibious exercises) and the brilliant Brillig SAR should provide a store of sea stories that will stand you in good stead 'til you steam this way again. Well Done."

And the fleet commanders sent similar praise.

We arrived in Hawaii on the morning of April17, disembarked the MAU, victualed and fueled, and embarked a dozen sons of crewmembers for their "Tiger cruise" to San Diego. Our son, Jack, was among them and we had a happy reunion. I looked forward to doing a "show and tell" for him about my ship and my life at sea. Jack was on the bridge as we got underway and transited the channel. It felt great to have him at my side and to explain how we operated *Fort Fisher*.

With his innate curiosity, Jack was all over the ship and took part in every Tiger activity we had scheduled. He slept in my in-port cabin. I wrote in my journal, "My first day at sea with my son on board. He seems happy, and interested … having fun and I am enjoying his company." The Tigers fired our guns and observed a high-line transfer of personnel between *Fort Fisher* and *Denver*. Jack explored the ship from stem to stern and from the signal bridge to the shaft alleys (unauthorized). He enjoyed shooting stars and sun lines with the navigation team.

At dinner in my cabin, I asked Jack what he thought about being at sea in a Navy ship. "Dad, I can see why you love your life. It is fascinating and really great fun." I then asked him the logical follow-up, "Would you be interested in going to the Naval Academy and becoming a naval officer?" Looking me straight in the eye, he said, "Dad, I think I would rather be a National Geographic photographer."

He went on to study Fine Arts at UCSD and created a great rock band there. A "right" and "left" brain individual, he has deep interests and extensive knowledge in literature, music, and mechanics. He is a gifted

316

artist, has published poetry and a novel, and he has rebuilt three Volkswagens. An interesting, entertaining conversationalist, he is a boon companion. Jack blessed Linda and me in 1992 with Emma, our bright, beautiful granddaughter.

Fort Fisher steamed ahead of the squadron to Del Mar north of San Diego to off-load the Marine tanks and load four LVT retrievers. On April 26, the last night of our deployment, I wrote in my journal:

> Well. Anchored 1.5 miles off the coast of beautiful Southern California! Lovely weather. Leave at midnight to join up with the squadron and enter port. All is in readiness. It ends at last. <u>So</u> many days. So much activity. So much excitement. So much sadness and loneliness. Danger. Good weather and bad. Sorrow and laughter. Tears and joy. Depression and elation. So much happened. We were tested so hard. Life seemed unfair at times. But life is beautiful. My greatest desire was to do it all safely, professionally, and to the best of my ability. I am deeply proud of my ship, my officers, my sailors, and myself. I am proud too of Linda for her courage, support, love, and encouragement. My Jack and Judy too. In a few hours, I will be with them, hugging them close and beginning a new life. It will be a joy to see them all again, and my mother and brothers and sisters and in-laws. I love them all. I thank God for all his blessings, and for seeing me through these many, many days.

We joined up with the squadron at 0600 on April 27 and steamed into San Diego harbor at 0900 on a beautiful, sunny day. The crews of all the ships proudly manned the rails in sparkling white uniforms. We anchored, ballasted down, "kicked out" the LVT retrievers and the LCU and the two LCM-8s for the amphibious base at Coronado, de-ballasted and proceeded to our pier.

Waiting there for us were all our families with balloons and lots of welcome-home signs and a Navy band playing great music. The Sailors were home from the sea. We waved and cheered at their happy, smiling faces. Only a Navy man and his family can understand the joy that we all felt.

"Moored! Shift colors! The Officer of the Deck is shifting his watch from the bridge to the quarterdeck! Liberty Call!"

¡El Capitán!

Fort Fisher remained in port for 45 days, allowing maximum leave for the crew. I made the happy transition to being at home. While on deployment, I had accepted an invitation from the principal of Lone Pine Union High School to deliver the commencement address for the 58th graduating class. I coordinated with his administrative assistant, my good friend Pauline Aigner. I worked on the speech while steaming to San Diego. Linda, our kids and Mom accompanied me to Lone Pine.

I delivered the commencement address on June 8, 27 years after my own graduation. Many friends were in the audience, including my Annapolis classmate Glen Harper, who was rector of the Lone Pine Episcopal Church. I talked about the Navy, *Fort Fisher*'s Seventh Fleet deployment, the Brillig affair and the meaning of freedom. I concluded with the following:

> You have many things going for you. You are endowed with common sense, knowledge of right and wrong, excellent intelligence, and you are citizens of the most generous, compassionate, wealthy, dynamic, and above all, free country that this planet has ever known. I would add one other important thing in your favor. You were fortunate enough to have lived in Lone Pine, a community with great pride, spirit, and a heart as big as the Sierras and above all, a profound sense of duty to its children. That spirit will inspire you in the days ahead.

Fort Fisher got underway on June 13 for training operations with the squadron in the local op-area. Per my request, two weeks later we sailed alone to Mazatlan, Mexico, my heritage visit in honor of my parents, grandparents and ancestors. Linda and several other wives flew there to meet us. On the way there, I had to tell my ship's company that *Fort Fisher* was going to transfer to Phibron Seven in the fall and commence workup for another Westpac, sailing on March 1, 1979, just ten months after returning from our recent deployment. Commodore Ramsey had selected us to take the place of *Thomaston*. *Fort Fisher*'s time in at home port was going to be cut short because *Thomaston* was not able to complete her overhaul on time.

I called on the mayor and the Mexican Naval District admiral. Visiting with the admiral, I inquired about my distant cousin in the Mexican Navy, Commander Jose Martín Avitia Herrera. The admiral knew him personally and placed a telephone call to his office at the Naval

Captain John Frank Gamboa, U. S. Navy (Retired)

Headquarters in Mexico City. Martín and I agreed to meet when my ship visited Mexico in the future.

Linda and I then called on His Excellency Miguel Garcia, the bishop of Mazatlan and my cousin, also meeting his brother Trinidad, the monsignor. They were born and raised in El Rincon, Durango, Dad's neighboring village. They were among his closest childhood friends and their brother had married one of his sisters. In 1960, the bishop had made a special trip to San Jose de la Boca to renew Mom and Dad's wedding vows in the village church.

I presented the bishop with a ship's plaque. I requested that he grant a special blessing for *Fort Fisher* and he graciously invited us into his private chapel for his prayer. Later that day, Linda and I hosted a luncheon in my cabin for the admiral, the American consul, the monsignor and the mayor's representative. That afternoon a reporter and cameraman from the local TV station came aboard and interviewed me in Spanish for their evening news.

Back in San Diego, Linda and I hosted a dependents' cruise in July for over 150 guests. To provide a real amphibious flavor, we brought most of them aboard in two LCM 8s with the ship ballasted down while anchored in the harbor. Jack and Judy and their friends, Mom, my siblings and their spouses and children and many friends joined us. When all were aboard, we transited the channel and sailed on blue water, then came back and anchored off Coronado to enjoy a plentiful and delicious cookout on the flight deck.

Because of her reputation as a sharp crew and smart, clean ship, *Fort Fisher* was twice selected as Navy visit ship at Broadway pier in downtown San Diego. (The admiral's aide told me that the admiral would send VIPs on short-notice visits to only two of his ships: England and *Fort Fisher*.) We hosted hundreds of men, women and children for tours.

While we were visit ship in August, Linda and I hosted a dinner party in my cabin for Mom, Leco and Evelyn, and our Lone Pine family doctor, George Schultz and his wife Hazel. We also had a reunion with my classmate Captain Chuck Larson and his lovely wife Sally when we hosted them aboard at lunch, together with our friend, retired RADM Eugene Farrell. Chuck was in command of Submarine Development Group One at Ballast Point. We also did a great weekend in Las Vegas with the Larsons.

319

¡El Capitán!

In August, we began a three-month PRAV in San Diego. Concurrently, we accomplished administrative and maintenance inspections in preparation for deployment to Westpac.

Passing the ship's material maintenance management (3M) inspection was one of our most difficult challenges. It covered maintenance requirements for each piece of machinery, electronics, equipment, and each boat in the ship. Department heads schedule their respective maintenance requirements and maintained quality control through accurate documentation and their personal "spot checks," which are reviewed during inspections.

To help the XO (the 3M program manager), I personally did at least three spot checks weekly during the PRAV. The department heads selected the maintenance item and the XO ensured that departments sampled good samples of their respective 3M system requirements.

I would not play "gotcha." I wanted everyone to look good. My spot checks were scheduled in the Plan of the Week and in the Plan of the Day. My Sailors took pride in preparing and doing their "show and tell" with the captain and I enjoyed learning more about my ship and my Sailors. My officers and chiefs appreciated my "command attention." *Fort Fisher* earned one of the top 3M inspection grades in the Pacific Fleet surface force.

With only four months remaining in command, I thought about my future. I would be in the zone for promotion to captain in the spring of 1979. My successful shore and sea command tours made me feel confident of promotion so my desire was to get a captain's sea command as soon as possible.

But after five years in command, I felt that my family and I needed a break from the demanding responsibility. I considered War College or the CNO staff, but these options would require that we leave San Diego in Jack's senior year. After discussions with Linda, I requested a shore tour in San Diego to avoid uprooting my family.

On a Saturday morning the first week in October, I attended a change of command aboard the Mobile. Walking to the ceremonial area, I encountered Rear Admiral Paddock, who asked, "Have you heard from Bupers?" Surprised, I replied, "No, sir!" Smiling, he said, "You will!" and then proceeded on his way with no further word.

Captain John Frank Gamboa, U. S. Navy (Retired)

On the following Monday, I was at my desk when I received a phone call from my detailer, who cheerfully informed me that, per Paddock's direction, I would "cross-deck" (no break in sea duty) in February 1979 to the USS *Tarawa* (LHA 1) for duty as executive officer (her first blackshoe XO). Along with *Fort Fisher*, she would sail on her first deployment to Seventh Fleet on March 1, 1979, as flagship for Phibron Seven.

Shocked, I stood up and looked out my porthole. There she was, moored to the pier next over from ours. She was huge. My first sensation was a feeling of excitement, which rapidly changed to apprehension. I hadn't known when I broke the news to my crew, that I would also deploy ten months after my previous cruise. The needs of the Navy would again override my plans. In the words of John Lennon, "Life is what happens to you while you're busy making other plans."

Linda and I discussed my orders, especially the hardships of another extended family separation, but we would remain in San Diego. I would have a key role in the first deployment of a new LHA. After talking it over, we just accepted our fate. For me, *Tarawa* was a bridge we had to cross on the way to my next sea command.

Paddock also selected *Denver*'s Captain Bob Klee as the commanding officer. I wrote in my journal, "*Tarawa* is a mixed blessing. I am concerned about Linda and the kids. I have no doubt that I can improve that ship and support Bob Klee better than any other naval officer around right now. But it will cost in terms of my time for my family...."

I would relinquish command of *Fort Fisher* on December 22, report to *Tarawa* on January 8, and get the ship through two weeks of refresher training and two weeks of amphibious refresher training. Klee would take command in February. So Bob got some slack, not me. RHIP.

I turned my attention to winding up my final weeks in command of *Fort Fisher*. We got underway on October 19 and began our workup for deployment with our new squadron, Phibron Seven. The training went well except our engineering drills for the OPPE. After much effort to get the engineering watch teams up to speed, I concluded that the new chief engineer was technically unqualified. His was a gross mal-assignment by Bupers; he had never had an engineering tour and he was deficient in leadership. I relieved him and made the operations officer, a former chief engineer, the new Cheng. He got the engineers back on track in short order. After discussions with Bupers, I agreed to keep the former cheng as operations officer. They could not assign a replacement prior to the ship's deployment.

The second week in December, we published the last edition of the ship's newspaper under my command. I wrote for the Fleet Sailor,

> .... It has been a very full ... successful year and we can all look forward to a happy Christmas holiday period with families and friends knowing that *Fort Fisher* met all its commitments with professionalism.... I wish to express my ... gratitude to each of you for your superb performance, support and loyalty.... I have enjoyed my days on *Fort Fisher* ... I wish each of you every success and happiness. Good luck and God speed to a 4.0 crew and a 4.0 ship.

On December 13, I turned to my journal, ".... my last night at sea in *Fort Fisher*.... We joined up with *Taluga* in thick fog and refueled.... At 1300 a helo took the ship's picture and did touch and go's.... noise measurement in the morning off San Clemente Islands, then re-arm from *Mount Hood* ... expect to arrive in port at 1900.... Lots of "cleaning up" & putting things in order ... fitreps, speech, etc. Wow. No slack right to the end. Had a final dinner with the wardroom tonight. No formalities or speeches. Just light and enjoyable."

The next afternoon I wrote, "At sea, enroute to San Diego. Well, we did it all ... finishing two hours early.... Then joined up with *Mount Hood*, receiving nine pallets of ammo.... The weather was beautiful and the crew performed superbly, as it always does.... I'm very proud of them. They do everything so well. I leave this ship in good shape.... So, I wind up my sea tour in good fashion. We will arrive in port at 1930 a day early, a nice reward for my crew.... I have enjoyed my days in command. I did my best. I treated my men honestly and fairly. I love my wife, my children, my mother, my family and my country."

My last week in *Fort Fisher* was very busy as I prepared to relinquish command. At 1817 December 21, after writing my farewell remarks, I wrote my final journal entry, "This has been a most hectic week ... commodore's and the command turnover inspections. Had a dependents' Christmas party too! Overall, it was all that I expected of a command at sea tour—and then some! I have no regrets. I hope I can rest now and enjoy my wife and family. Thank you, God, for looking after me so much. Finis."

Captain John Frank Gamboa, U. S. Navy (Retired)

At 1400 on December 22 on a beautiful afternoon with ship's company assembled on the flight deck, and Mom, Linda, Jack, Judy, my siblings and their spouses, nephews and nieces, friends, all crew members, their families, and other guests present, I relinquished turned over command to Cdr. Kenneth Barry. Commodore Ramsey delivered most complimentary remarks about *Fort Fisher* and my performance. A proud Virginian born in Richmond, he attributed part of my success to the fact that his wife Nancy and my Linda were both from Danville, Virginia, and my XO Gene Bailey was also from Virginia. Ramsey evaluated my performance in a very laudatory manner, highly recommending me for promotion to captain and for selection to a major sea command.

At home a few days later, I received a letter from commander, naval surface force, Pacific Fleet. The text is etched on a brass plate mounted on a wooden plaque decorated with a Navy Command at Sea insignia. Here is the entire document:

Dear Captain Gamboa,

Command at sea is a personal responsibility without parallel in the modern world. There is no other position calling for the maturity, sound judgment and eternal vigilance that has been required of you daily during your tour as commanding officer, USS *Fort Fisher* (LSD 40). In no endeavor other than command of ships do the character and example of a leader play such a role that shapes the individual lives, the welfare and mission accomplishment of the team. The authority of the commanding officer at sea is as nearly absolute as possible, in a Navy of free men serving in defense of their freedom.

The reward of successful defense of our Nation makes it all worthwhile. It is truly a sacred duty and a sacred honor. Successful completion of your tour in command is witness of your proven record of dedication and professionalism. You stand among those select few who know well the awesome responsibility of command at sea. I am proud to have served with you as a member of the Naval Surface Force, U.S. Pacific Fleet.

You have my sincere best wishes and my utmost confidence that you will continue to serve our country well. Good luck and Godspeed.

¡El Capitán!

Warm regards,
W.R. St. George,
Vice Admiral, U.S. Navy

Linda and I read the admiral's letter together. Then we enjoyed a champagne toast to *Fort Fisher*—and to each other.

Chapter Nine

★ ★ ★ ★ ★ ★ ★

I would like to think that I am smarter today than I was yesterday.

—Abraham Lincoln

I reported aboard USS *Tarawa* (LHA 1) on Monday, January 8, 1979, and we got underway for a week of training in the local op area. Four days later, I relieved the incumbent, feeling proud to be second in command of the Navy's newest and magnificent amphibious assault ship.

Tarawa was the lead ship in a new class of five helicopter carrier general purpose amphibious assault ships, named in honor of the hard-fought WWII amphibious landing on the Japanese-occupied island of *Tarawa*, the first victory in Admiral Nimitz' central Pacific campaign. She was as big as a WW II fast aircraft carrier; the LHA's flight deck is 810 feet long with two aircraft elevators. Her cavernous dock has an automated cargo-handling system and is enclosed by a huge stern gate. Forward is a spacious two-deck vehicle storage area.

LHAs are one deck higher than an attack aircraft carrier and have a high freeboard. A bow thruster helps in mooring. The ships are powered by two huge steam boilers, the largest ever fabricated for Navy ships, and two main engines equipped with throttles controlled automatically from the bridge with a top speed of 23 knots. The ships have excellent medical and dental facilities including four operating rooms, a complete laboratory, and up to a 300-bed capacity by using adjacent troop spaces.

The ship's company includes 60 officers and 800 enlisted. The *Tarawa*'s troop embarkation capacity is huge: a marine amphibious unit (MAU) commander and staff; a reinforced infantry battalion landing team (BLT) with light weapons, ammunition, materiel, a logistic support unit and supplies, three Marine helicopter squadrons, and a detachment of vertical takeoff jet aircraft. LHAs are a quantum increase in amphibious warfare capability compared to the smaller LPH class helicopter carrier that I had sailed with in Phibron Five.

The rank and seniority of the department heads and their assistants—and know-how—was much higher than in *La Salle*, Balboa and *Fort Fisher*, so my leadership and management goal was to utilize the wardroom's experience with optimum effectiveness. My first priority was to successfully accomplish four weeks of general and amphibious refresher training. I directed well deck operations from the debarkation control center, adjacent to flight deck control center, facilitating my coordination of both operations.

The ship had a closed-circuit television system and broadcasting studio that we used to keep the crew informed and brief them on training results and progress, which became a hit with the crew and fostered ship's spirit. I used the system throughout Westpac for a daily evening news report and special events.

Back in port, I then coordinated the embarkation of Commander, Amphibious Squadron Seven and his staff. (My classmate and good friend, Commander Phil Given, was the commodore's chief staff officer). Klee assumed command on February 9.

On March 1, *Tarawa* sailed with Phibron Seven for Westpac, stopping in Pearl to embark the 37th MAU. Several high-ranking flag and general officers visited *Tarawa*, including Vice Admiral Trost, Deputy CINCPACFLT (later CNO). I coordinated their ship tours led by the captain and the commodore, developing a tour template that came into good use during Westpac for more than 40 VIP visits. Everyone wanted to see the fleet's new "Super Gator."

Upon sortie from Pearl, *Tarawa*'s total embarked population was over 200 officers and 2600 enlisted. To coordinate the shipboard daily routine, I worked one-on-one with each department head and their officers, holding department head meetings only as dictated by our schedule and extraordinary events. I also worked to establish excellent relations with our embarked Marine unit leaders and their staffs.

My daily routine was fast-paced with many activities sandwiched between morning officers' call and eight o'clock reports. There was always someone in my office on business. I also had the daily batch of messages and correspondence that required my personal attention. I delegated as much as possible and depended on my executive department staff to coordinate my daily routine. The Plan of the Day was drafted by our outstanding ship's secretary, Lt.j.g. Jerry Hart. The personnel officer, Lt.j.g. Craig Green, was also a great help to me.

I conducted daily berthing and messing inspections to maintain cleanliness and sanitation and to keep my finger on the pulse of the crew and the Marines. I enjoyed developing teamwork and spirit with generous doses of humor. By the time we chopped to Seventh Fleet, I was comfortable as XO and enjoying my job.

Tarawa's deployment included port visits to Manila (cut short by an emergency sortie to avoid a typhoon), Subic Bay, Singapore, Thailand, Hong Kong, Okinawa, and South Korea. We participated in four amphibious exercises culminating with Exercise Fortress Gale in Korea, the largest amphibious exercise in Westpac since the end of hostilities in Vietnam. We exercised *Tarawa*'s considerable amphibious assault capabilities and smoothed out our internal procedures and coordination with the commodore and the MAU. Our Westpac was very successful and demonstrated the powerful capabilities of an LHA

Even so, our most unique challenge during the deployment had nothing to do with amphibious warfare. On May 8, *Tarawa* was anchored at Pattaya Beach, Thailand, for liberty and recreation. That afternoon the Navy frigate USS *Robert E. Peary* arrived, carrying 443 Vietnamese refugees the ship had rescued from a sinking boat in the Gulf of Thailand. Smaller than a destroyer, her weather decks were overflowing with humanity. *Tarawa* was directed to remain at Pattaya, take all refugees aboard, and provide them food, medical care and shelter until they could be processed by the U.N. Refugee Commission and accepted by Thailand.

I convened a department head meeting to allocate roles and responsibilities for supporting our guests. The combat cargo unit and the Marine logistic support unit organized the refugee embarkation, support and security, including assignment of a Marine enlisted escort for each family. Deck department and Assault Craft Unit One transported the refugees to the ship. The supply officer created a tailored menu and a separate meal schedule for them. Our two doctors and medical staff evaluated each refugee's medical condition. The chaplain coordinated a fund-drive for personal health and welfare items for the refugees.

The U.N. Refugee Agency and the U.S. Embassy coordinated arrangements with the Thailand government to transfer the men, women and children ashore as soon as their documentation was completed and facilities were ready. We set up a registration center in our well deck, organizing the refugees into seated rows. Those who spoke English served as interpreters. Sick Bay treated refugees with dysentery, skin rashes, sunburn, and other ailments resulting from poor nutrition and exposure.

A 300-bed enlisted Marine berthing compartment was evacuated for our guests. The Marines were scattered throughout the ship to every available empty bunk. Clean linen and blankets were provided and soap, towels, washcloths and personal hygiene items were distributed to each family.

Accompanied by a Vietnamese interpreter and the chief master at arms, I inspected the berthing compartment on the first night. The children had all been fed, bathed and bedded down on the bottom bunks, with the smallest ones lined up several per bed, crowded but happy with full stomachs and smiling faces. The women had washed clothes in the showers and the wet garments were hung all over the compartment on clothes lines strung up by the Marines. The scene resembled a huge camp out. The next day all the children were given new underclothes, t-shirts, shorts, sandals, and toys purchased ashore with the funds donated by our crew and the Marines.

The third morning they were aboard, one of the women suddenly went into labor and one of our hospital corpsman delivered a healthy baby girl in the berthing compartment. It all happened too fast to get her to Sick Bay. Her parents named her Grace *Tarawa* Tran (the family eventually settled in Pennsylvania). Our daily TV news program featured several English-speaking refugees who described their experiences in leaving their homeland, thanked everyone and kept us posted on the new arrival—mother and baby were doing fine.

On the fifth day, the U.N. Refugee Agency and the government of Thailand were ready to receive the refugees ashore. We assembled them in the well deck and transported them to the beach by LCM-8s. Then we got underway for Subic Bay for two weeks of upkeep.

Bob Klee wrote in his Familygram, "For all of us this unexpected task provided a unique opportunity to exercise *Tarawa*'s extensive capability for providing humanitarian assistance on very short notice. The entire crew and embarked Marines responded in superb fashion, demonstrating great flexibility and ingenuity, as well as traditional American generosity and compassion. We can all be proud of what we accomplished as a team."

On June 8, *Tarawa* was pierside in Subic Bay when Rear Admiral Ramsey, Commander, Amphibious Group Eastern Pacific, called to inform me that I was on the captain promotion list. He also called Linda. Later, Ramsey wrote to me and said "Which ship shall I earmark for you?"

To celebrate, and to ease another long separation, Linda flew out to join me in the Philippines with a group of other *Tarawa* wives, including the captain's wife, Valerie. Linda and I enjoyed traveling to Manila, Bagio and Subic, and then she flew with the other wives to Hong Kong to meet us for our next port visit. We enjoyed the shopping, dining and ambiance of that beautiful city.

At the end of the deployment, Vice Admiral Foley, Commander, Seventh Fleet, awarded me a Navy Commendation Medal, "For meritorious achievement in the performance of outstanding service as Executive Officer, USS *Tarawa* (LHA 1) during the first LHA deployment to the Western Pacific...." It was my first Navy medal.

In November 1979, I screened for a major sea command. My detailer told me that several LPDs were available in San Diego and asked me what I would like to do. I could go ashore first; however, my intuition was to seize the moment. I talked with Linda and she reluctantly agreed that I should accept another sea command assignment. We strongly desired a ship home ported in San Diego and one that would not deploy for at least a year.

The bureau responded with an ideal assignment, USS *Vancouver* (LPD 2); she would accomplish a nine-month overhaul in San Diego and not deploy for a Westpac until January 1983 with Phibron Three. That would be after I relinquished command. I would enjoy my entire tour in homeport. My detachment from *Tarawa* was set for August 1980.

I would assume command in February 1981 after attending the 17-week Senior Officer Ship Material Readiness Course (SOSMRC) for prospective steam ship commanding officers at the Navy's training facility in Idaho Falls, Idaho. The course was required initially for prospective commanding officers of carriers, cruisers and destroyers, all participants in the OPPE program; the amphibious steam ships began participating in 1976. Even so, when Bupers issued my orders to command *Fort Fisher*, I was exempted from SOSMRC due to *Fort Fisher*'s overhaul and projected deployment schedule. Instead, I was assigned to the school of hard knocks—I would learn all about LOEs and OPPEs by accomplishing them while in command.

¡El Capitán!

On April 30, 1980, I was frocked to the rank of captain. In June, Captain Dwight D. Timm, a naval aviator, assumed command of *Tarawa*. Klee's fitness report recommended me for "command of an LHA or a major communications station ashore." He became Rear Admiral Ramsey's chief of staff and subsequently was selected for commodore, a one-star flag rank. He then commanded Seventh Fleet's Amphibious Task Force 76 in Okinawa.

On Friday, August 29, 1980 in San Diego, I was relieved by Cdr. Richard Schuerger. The wardroom lined up in the hanger bay and I walked the line, shaking hands with each officer and saying farewell to my shipmates. Having accomplished the mission Rear Admiral Paddock had assigned to me—to manage *Tarawa*'s transition to fleet operations and her first deployment—I departed her quarterdeck with a feeling of pride and satisfaction.

In October, I reported to SOSMRC, which was headed by my friend and classmate Captain Pete Hekman. (Pete went on to be Commander, Naval Sea Systems Command as a vice admiral.) There were 15 other captains and 8 commanders in my class. Four captains had orders to command destroyer squadrons and one a service squadron (logistic ships); eleven of us would command ships; and one was going to be XO of an aircraft carrier. The commanders all had orders to command either a destroyer or a frigate.

I became good friends with Captain Jeff Dennis, USNA '57, who was also slated to command an LPD in San Diego. It was the most seasoned, savvy, professional, prestigious and fun group of naval officers I was ever associated with.

The SOSMRC mission was to teach the safe operation of Navy ship steam propulsion plants at the command level: personnel training in engineering casualty control, preparation and training for LOEs and OPPEs, engineering systems maintenance programs, and management of a ship overhaul.

The excellent ship engineering plant management tools that I acquired in SOSMRC reinforced the lessons I had learned the hard way in *Fort Fisher*. It was not a lightweight "gentleman's course," but we had time to socialize and explore Idaho on weekends. It was winter so most of the class turned to skiing. After enduring lots of physical pain and considerable loss of dignity, I learned to ski, an activity we enjoyed with Jack and Judy when they were teenagers. Linda and I still enjoy skiing.

A major benefit of the SOSMRC course was my extended break from the pressures of over eight consecutive years in command and second in command. My stay in Idaho Falls afforded me an opportunity to rest, refresh, reflect and strategize about my next ship command. It felt like a sabbatical.

Confident that I had developed an understanding of warships, command principles and fleet amphibious operations, I had lots of ideas and enthusiasm about how to achieve command excellence in *Vancouver*. This would be my last time as a warship captain; I wanted give it my best shot and do it right. I could hope for a sequential sea command—the top fleet assignment for line captains—either an amphibious squadron or an LHA for those in the fleet amphibious force, but it would be a long shot.

USS *Vancouver* (LPD 2) was the second ship of the Raleigh class landing personnel dock, very similar to LSDs. They had a larger flight deck (two helo spots versus one for LSDs), and almost three times the troop-carrying capacity. Built in the New York Naval Shipyard at Brooklyn, she was launched on September 15, 1962. She was 522 feet long (the class is about 40 feet shorter than *Fort Fisher* but the later LPD 4 class were longer) with a 100 foot beam, 20 foot draft, a fully-loaded displacement of 13,600 tons and a maximum speed of 21 knots. She was commissioned on May 11, 1963, with a ship's company of 466 personnel including 26 officers. She could embark 800 combat-ready Marines.

During her initial deployment with Seventh Fleet in 1964, *Vancouver* participated in the first amphibious assault of the Vietnam conflict and was a key member of the first Seventh Fleet Amphibious Ready Group, earning 13 combat ribbons and stars in frequent Westpacs. The "Van Can Do" was the premier LPD in the Pacific Fleet.

I assumed command on February 11, 1981, in San Diego. My relieving inspections confirmed what I had anticipated. The19 year old ship had "signs of the sea showing plain." The comprehensive nine-month overhaul work package was valued at $22.5 million. I added my requirements for refurbishment of all living, berthing, messing and work center spaces, especially the replacement of all damaged office furniture and re-tiling of decks in all living and working spaces.

On February 23, *Vancouver* entered the shipyard and I implemented my *Fort Fisher* overhaul management organization and approach. My goals were similar to those in *Fort Fisher*: to complete on time in the best possible material condition through quality work in all contractor and ship's force jobs.

The overhaul work package was over three times the size and cost of *Fort Fisher*'s, but the critical difference was time. Nine months was sufficient to complete on schedule if I stayed on top of the effort and we had no extraordinary work growth. Post-overhaul, I would have not three, but 14 months, to prepare her for deployment. And maintaining crew morale would be much easier—we would be in homeport. I even took Linda on a tour of the dry dock—hardhat, rubber boots and all—to see *Vancouver* from the bottom up.

During the overhaul, I developed *Vancouver*'s pre-deployment workup schedule. In addition to refresher training, amphibious refresher training, pre-deployment inspections and POM, we would conduct two minesweeping exercises with embarked mine sweeping unit commanders, an LPD's secondary mission. After nine months in overhaul, my crew would need some recreation, so I included port visits to Mazatlan, Mexico, and San Francisco.

A ship captain's inspirational leadership and personal charisma can go a long way toward motivating a crew to do well in all their tasks, but excellence cannot be achieved solely by emotional exhortations and heart-felt appeals for dedicated crew efforts. To excel requires intelligent and thorough command planning, preparation and training supported by a solid foundation of good leadership, effective management and efficient administration.

And a unifying challenge that requires total crew involvement is mandatory. My shore and ship command experience taught me that such a challenge had to be very relevant to the mission.

At Balboa, the challenge of a Unitas single HF radio circuit termination around South America had mobilized the entire command and our success had resulted in high station readiness and morale.

In *Fort Fisher*, our dual challenges of early overhaul completion and deployment with Phibron Five enabled us to complete overhaul 17 days ahead of schedule and successfully accomplish all pre-deployment requirements in one-fourth the usual time.

So I began my search for a suitable challenge for *Vancouver*'s crew. First, I assessed the potential of my ship's company. *Vancouver*'s wardroom experience level was significantly higher than *Fort Fisher*'s; most of my department heads were Lt. Cdrs. The chiefs were professional and strong leaders. Crew experience level and morale were good. And we had an ideal employment schedule after overhaul. I felt confident that we had the potential and conditions necessary to excel.

All that was needed was the right challenge. As I thought about it, I reflected on all my warship tours, refresher training in particular because it required total ship's company involvement. The most difficult event in refresher training is to rapidly and correctly set damage control conditions throughout the ship—conditions Yoke and Zebra. In condition Yoke, the ship is opened up to permit access to most compartments and spaces in order to facilitate maintenance, repair and ship's routine. Condition Yoke is the normal damage control condition at sea. In condition Zebra, the ship is buttoned up for maximum watertight integrity to prevent or contain battle damage, flooding and fires. Condition Zebra is set at general quarters when a ship prepares for battle or has an emergency such as a fire, a collision or grounding. To properly set these conditions, the watertight doors and hatches and other damage control fixtures in each compartment must be in top operating condition and the crew has to be properly trained.

During a ship's first day of refresher training, the fleet training group riders check the crew's setting of Yoke and Zebra ship-wide, and about four other times thereafter while the ship is in training. Failure is the norm in the setting of these damage control conditions, especially the first, second or even the third time that Yoke and Zebra are set and checked—and some ships never get it right. It was the most difficult and frustrating requirement in all my refresher training experience.

As I stewed about this Reftra requirement, Eureka! The challenge came to me in a flash of inspiration—we would pass every checked setting of Yoke and Zebra in refresher training! A well-coordinated preparation effort during overhaul would be required from all hands. Our success in damage control in Reftra would create top damage control readiness and unify my crew.

Brimming with confidence and enthusiasm, I announced my decision at our next weekly overhaul meeting. I noticed that several officers and chiefs frowned and shook their heads in dismay, which further convinced me that I had found the right challenge.

¡El Capitán!

A couple of days later as I was walking about the ship on a look see, I encountered the DCA, who told me that many hatches and scuttles throughout the ship were warped and could not be properly closed, "Captain, if you want to pass Yoke and Zebra we are going to have to repair or replace them!" I responded, "Well, let's fix the ones we can fix and replace the ones we can't repair!" He warned, "It's going to take a lot of money and a lot of work."

About a week after my exchange with the DCA, I was standing in the middle of the flight deck talking with the ship's overhaul superintendent and the Cheng. My new hull technician chief petty officer approached us. One week prior, he had reported on board from Fleet Training Group in San Diego. With a salute, the chief got right to the point, "Captain, I hear you want to pass Yoke and Zebra every time in Reftra!" I replied, "That's right, chief! Do you know how to do it?" He said, "Yes sir. But my hull techs need to replace all our warped hatches and scuttles and to repair other hatchways and damage control fittings." With that, he handed me a requisition and said, "The ship's welding machines. Ours don't work! I need two new ones!"

The Cheng, Lt. Cdr. Chuck Carroll, cleared his throat and glared at the chief. I asked Chuck "Is that right?" He replied, "Sir, I have a very tight budget." I said, "OK, here's the deal, you pay for one and I pay for one. Let's get them!" We shook hands and I signed the requisition. Then I asked the chief what else we had to do to achieve our goal. The Cheng interjected that he would task the DCA and the chief to develop a plan and brief it at the next overhaul meeting.

Many ships create a "DC Tiger Team" to run around the ship checking damage control readiness and repairing all of the DC fittings in need. I refused to allow that approach. Each division would be responsible for its own DC readiness.

The DCA's DC readiness plan led to new initiatives in each division and innovative organization and training of each division's damage control petty officers and repair parties. Each duty section had to conduct a damage control inspection of seven compartments after working hours using the compartment damage control 3M maintenance card. The CDO turned in the inspection forms to the DCA at the next morning quarters. The DCA assigned corrective action that day to respective divisions or to his own hull technicians if necessary. Each department head reported the status of their DC discrepancies at our weekly overhaul meetings.

Captain John Frank Gamboa, U. S. Navy (Retired)

I knew that leadership was the key so I directed the department heads to assign a chief in each of their divisions to be the division damage control (DC) petty officer. The chiefs could designate as many assistants as they needed. I also sent two lieutenants, junior grade, and four ensigns to a six-week DC repair party leader training course in San Francisco (they would be the repair party leaders in our GQ team).

The initiative created a lot of new repair work and damage control awareness throughout ship's company. The DCA and his division replaced over 20 hatches, scuttles, compartment ladders and joiner doors and divisions replaced all worn ladder steps in their spaces. R Division—equipped with two shiny new welding machines—repaired many other hatches, hatchways and damage control fittings. By the end of overhaul, we had achieved top-notch DC material readiness and had set the stage for excellence in refresher training.

I also focused on improving the habitability of crew living and working spaces, and replacement of all broken and damaged file cabinets, bookshelves, desks and chairs. Every berthing space was renovated and damaged bunks were replaced. Rusty privacy partitions in the heads were replaced with new ones made of stainless steel. Long Beach Naval Shipyard fabricated new tables, benches, locker doors and air conditioning and heating ducts for many troop spaces. By the end of the overhaul all crew and troop berthing areas were in like-new condition.

A ship's captain uses a variety of techniques for communicating with his crew and over time determines what works best for him. I enjoyed face-to-face talks with my men, deriving much of my energy and inspiration from our interactions and getting a good feel for their morale and spirit. I especially enjoyed developing real challenges for my crew through well-defined goals. But it was not enough just to promulgate them through the chain of command. I preferred to explain them to my leadership team face to face.

To differentiate from the XO's department head meetings, I created a command management council to help shape my command policies, goals, and objectives. I convened this forum every two or three weeks (more often if needed), especially during the overhaul when I was developing a command action plan and creating my desired command climate. When I finished hammering out my desired policy and implementation road map, I would convene a meeting of all officers, chiefs and leading first class petty officers—the command's composite leadership team—in the wardroom for a command information brief.

Commander Gary Uhlenkott, my outstanding executive officer, "warmed up" the group with his list of housekeeping items that needed their attention such as crew uniforms, personal grooming and appearance, berthing inspections, processing of personal request chits, policies on personnel time-off and leave. When the XO was ready, I would join the group.

The great benefit to me in this approach was that I was able to look all my leaders in the eye and tell them where I wanted to go, spell out the difficulties we would face and the results that I expected them to achieve. They quickly learned to ask questions and give me their gut reactions— vital feedback that clarified my thinking and injected common sense into my initiatives. Our dialogue forced me to reduce my lofty visions to discrete tasks and actions that could be understood and supported on the deck plates. In the process, I strengthened an informed chain of command in *Vancouver*.

But the main value of the management council and the information brief is that they helped me to create a command climate of harmony, teamwork and a desire to excel, thereby sowing the seeds of our success.

One of the great professional pleasures of being a ship's captain is to have your own gig. In the amphibious force, a ship's boats are considered to be an expression of the parent ship's seamanship, smartness—and pride. Some ships rarely used their gigs, so they were embarrassingly unreliable. I planned to use my gig as much as possible and ensure that I could always rely on mine; so during our overhaul, *Vancouver*'s gig and all our other boats were offloaded, completely refurbished and the enginemen and coxswains were sent to school.

While I was attending SOSMRC, our son Jack spent some time with me in Idaho and Linda rented out our Rancho Bernardo house and moved into Navy housing on Ballast Point Submarine Base. (Our neighbors were submariners, and my classmate John Vick and his wife Judy moved in next door when we were both squadron commanders.)

Linda was studying for a Business degree at National University and also working there as an academic counselor, and it would be more convenient to her classes and her job. We enjoyed the spacious, historic home (the Army built the houses when Ballast Point was a coastal defense site prior to WW II).

We especially enjoyed the awesome harbor view. The shipping channel was just a few hundred yards from our house, and when *Vancouver* transited the channel outbound and sailed past our quarters, I would signal Linda with two blasts on the ship's steam whistle. When I returned to port and blew the whistle as we sailed back in, she would get in the car and head for the pier in time to meet the ship and bring me home.

After the gig had been refurbished, each morning during the overhaul and afterwards when the ship was in port, I would drive to the Admiral Kidd Officers' Club at Point Loma, park my car, walk down to the boat landing and board my waiting gig. The coxswain would have a thermos of hot black coffee and a fresh pastry for me from our ship's bakery. The boat officer would give me a packet containing all messages received overnight, the Plan of the Day, and the San Diego newspaper. We would cruise the channel for the 20-minute ride to the ship. At the end of working hours, the gig would return me to the boat landing. This was our daily routine in bright sunshine or gray skies, in fair weather or foul.

The first day I was scheduled to depart the ship in the gig, the Cheng took it for a test run and a fuel line ruptured. Our lifeboat had to go to his rescue. He was embarrassed and it never happened again.

We maintained a backup boat afloat that we also used for other ship needs. The gig and boat were inspected daily by the chief engineman or LPO or the A division officer, and by a deck officer or chief bos'n mate or LPO. The quarterdeck kept an eye on the boats made up to our rigged boat boom. The gig crew stood no watches and wore their sparkling whites with pride. All the ensigns and several of the j.g.'s became qualified boat officers. The overall result was high gig and boat readiness and smartness in *Vancouver*.

On November 8, we completed our overhaul on time. Prior to departing the shipyard, I reviewed *Vancouver*'s needs for repairs that were not accomplished during the overhaul for a variety of technical or funding reasons. Aware of the immense technical know-how and industrial skills of navy repair ships, I requested and received two-month maintenance availability with the repair ship USS *Ajax*, and a follow-on availability specifically to support our OPPE.

¡El Capitán!

Maximum ease of worker access between a repair ship and its customer ship ensures efficiency and mutual support—and eliminates lots of hassle. This can best be achieved by mooring alongside the repair ship. Usually only destroyers do this. *Vancouver* was starboard side to *Ajax* for three weeks in January.

In addition to many vital machinery repairs, *Ajax* also took care of all of our officers' annual physicals, crew dental examinations, and a variety of other medical services, saving a great deal of time and ensuring the health of my crew.

During overhaul, *Vancouver* was assigned administratively to squadrons just returned from deployment. She was in Phibron One when I assumed command, then near the end of our overhaul, we transferred to Phibron Five. On January 1, 1982, we transferred to Phibron Three, our permanent home and deployment squadron. My fitness report by my first two commodores follow.

> Comphibron One: Captain Gamboa's performance ... has been superlative in every respect ... (he) has maintained complete control of the overhaul while also insisting on keeping his ship safe and clean.... Chain of command communication is excellent.... Captain Gamboa pursues a rigorous retention effort.... His fine sense of leadership, professionalism, and innovation coupled with his calm approach to problem solving leave no doubt that *Vancouver* will perform well when she returns to the operating fleet. I strongly recommend him for accelerated promotion and future command of an LHA or an amphibious squadron.

> Comphibron Five: Captain Gamboa is an aggressive, totally dedicated and superbly competent officer who has demonstrated superior abilities as commanding officer ... his ship completed an extensive overhaul on time.... an officer of exceptional value to the Navy ... strongly recommended for a sequential command and early selection to flag rank.

In January 1982, Vice Admiral Baggett, Commander, Naval Surface Forces Pacific, requested that I represent his force by hosting a visit of Vice Admiral R.L. Walters, Deputy Chief of Naval Operations, Surface Warfare.

Captain John Frank Gamboa, U. S. Navy (Retired)

It was a sincere pleasure to lunch aboard USS *Vancouver* (LPD 2) last week.... I was particularly delighted to ... make the Surface Warfare Qualification presentations to your three young officers. That ceremony and the outstanding "first impressions" made by your chief petty officers serve well to demonstrate the reason behind your successful retention program. There is no doubt that Pride and Professionalism are thriving in *Vancouver*....

Again, many thanks for your most gracious hospitality and all the best wishes to you and your men for continued success.... The *Vancouver* book ends have made a splendid addition to my office here at the Pentagon and I thank you for that most thoughtful gesture.

The bookends, decorated with McNamara's lace and the ship's seal, were created by my Deck divisions from damaged wing wall oak batter boards in the ship's dock that were replaced during overhaul. Batter boards prevent damage to the wall's steel plating by landing craft during wet well operations. I presented sets to VIPs on special occasions and a set embellishes my desk.

In January, I called on Commander, Fleet Training Group with the Ops boss to request assist visits for *Vancouver*. Because our refresher training was not scheduled until April—first we had to pass our OPPE—we arranged for training assists to prepare our bridge, navigation and CIC watch teams for at-sea operations after nine months pier side (we created an FTG pilot program); lessons learned from my *Fort Fisher* post-overhaul buoy collision trauma. FTG also helped make each department fully aware of Reftra requirements.

We passed the OPPE in mid-February. The following week, we sailed to Mazatlan, Mexico, for an enjoyable three-day port visit in company with the USS *Niagara Falls*, conducting valuable training during three days en route and three days homeward bound. We invited Navy League guests, a Marine Corps band for entertainment, and 150 Marines from Camp Pendleton to share in our enjoyment, and to build good relations with our future shipmates. We all enjoyed the port visit and band concerts on the flight deck and in the city plaza.

Vancouver went on to excel in Reftra. Commander Fleet Training Group signaled,

As a result of superlative performance demonstrated throughout refresher training, USS *Vancouver* has been outchopped early from training as of 021200 T April 82. *Vancouver* has demonstrated the readiness, leadership and team performance which provides every confidence that the ship is fully ready for advanced operations....*Vancouver* has provided a standard for planning and execution of training readiness which is worthy of emulation. WELL DONE!

Our amphibious group commander commented, "I have followed your Reftra closely and note with special pleasure your early release. WELL DONE to All Hands.... Your professionalism and obvious pride marks you as one of our finest Gators. Keep Charging. RADM Walsh sends." We were the only amphibious ship to be released early in Reftra in all the time I was in the Pacific Fleet amphibious force.

Commander, Training Command Pacific and the Commander, Fleet Training Group wanted to know how we did it. I responded:

.... Approach consisted of ... aggressive pursuit of three long-range goals: a successful overhaul; identification of individual and team training and school requirements; identification of material deficiencies, coupled with a development of crew awareness of importance of damage control readiness.... No Damage Control Tiger Teams were employed. Each department was responsible for their own spaces except that discrepancies beyond damage control petty officer capabilities were corrected by R Division ....

Command focus on goals was maintained through weekly Command Management Council, Planning Board for Training, and weekly Command Information Briefs for all officers, chiefs, and E-6s.... Long range planning, steady pursuit of high state of material readiness and training, and a good mixture of crew enthusiasm, hard work and a desire to excel made the end result possible.... Our goal of passing Yoke and Zebra every time in Reftra paid the highest dividends in all hands involvement, cooperation, teamwork, and enthusiasm; we passed 5 for 5 in Yoke and 4 for 5 in Zebra. The 'spill over effects' into all other areas of training was most beneficial.

We went on to excel in two weeks of amphibious refresher training, earning the top grade—excellent. Our Insurv inspection results were also outstanding, reversing the ship's aging trend. In July, *Vancouver* was tasked to accomplish a second OPPE by the Pacific Fleet's Propulsion

Examining Board as we transitioned into the regular fleet OPPE cycle, and we passed. At that time, we were the only ship in the Navy to pass two OPPEs within five months.

An irksome characteristic of *Vancouver*'s bridge was the lack of platforms on the bridge wings for the conning officer or pilot to see the sides and stern of the ship when alongside underway or when mooring the ship. It was an LPD 1 class deficiency and there was an existing ship class alteration, but it was designated for ship's force accomplishment. The Type desk rejected my request for the alteration during overhaul.

When we returned to sea, my officers addressed the issue again. After my thorough study and look see, I approved a project proposal by the navigator and the DCA for ship's force accomplishment with some technical assistance by ship waterfront maintenance facilities during our two-week upkeep period following completion of all refresher training.

After delivery of several sheets of steel plating, the DCA and his chief hull technician supervised a week of cutting and fabrication on the flight deck by our hull technicians—using our two new welding machines. The platforms were installed with two cranes, one to rig them in place and one to hold the welders (we did one side, and then we turned the ship around and did the other).

At the insistence of the project team, when the job was complete, I welded my initials and the date on the deck of the starboard platform—and "G-Alt." The repair division presented me with a rating patch making me an honorary hull technician. When we returned to sea, the harbor pilots really appreciated the platforms, which improved the ship conning safety. They were totally amazed that the ship had built them. My crew and I were very proud of our G-Alt. We had re-established Van-Can-Do's rightful place on the waterfront as the best ship in the Pacific Fleet.

A big social event for the wardroom was the annual Gator Ball dinner dance. All my officers who were not on duty, and their wives, joined Linda and me for this gala event. Everyone enjoyed a delicious dinner, excellent wine and a great dance band.

Linda and I were on the dance floor when Rear Admiral Bill Walsh approached us. "Frank, have you thought about your next assignment?" Before I could reply, he said, "I want you to be one of my squadron commanders!" Without thinking, I blurted out, "But sir, I want to command an LHA!" Walsh replied, "You have already done that. I need you to be one of my commodores!"

Suddenly realizing what he had said, I quickly replied, "Aye Aye sir, thank you! I am honored!" After shaking hands, and in a mild state of shock, Linda and I went to Rear Admiral Ramsey's table and excitedly told him the news. "I know! Congratulations!"

With the end of my command tour on the horizon, Linda and I decided it was time for a special treat for the officers and their ladies: we would host a series of shipboard dinner parties in my cabin, which had been completely refurbished by Olive White during the overhaul.

We organized the dinners with 10 guests per event. Linda and I would meet them at the Broadway pier boat landing. As we cruised in the gig to the ship, we would enjoy a glass of wine (legal in a gig but not aboard a Navy ship) or soft drinks, with hors d'oeuvres prepared by Linda.

Beginning on the quarterdeck, we would take our guests on a tour with a display of the flight deck repair locker and damage control gear with the flight deck petty officer displaying his night helo operations lighted coveralls; then to the mess decks and galley where the duty cooks explained how meals were prepared and served; then down a ladder to the well deck where deck seamen demonstrated operation of the water barriers and an articulated fork lift would drive up the vehicle ramp with a pallet of cargo; then to the bow where the Bos'n Mates described how the anchors were dropped and housed.

Thoroughly enjoying themselves, our guests asked questions and took lots of pictures. Then we continued on to my cabin, which Linda decorated with fresh flowers, often roses from our garden.

After enjoying a sumptuous dinner, we would lead our guests up to the pilothouse for coffee and dessert. The duty quartermasters would display the harbor charts and demonstrate the various navigation and piloting instruments on the bridge; the duty operations specialists displayed the radars in CIC; and the duty signalmen demonstrated the yardarm blinkers and night vision devices. All my Sailors took pride in their "show and tell."

We departed the ship at 2200 in the gig and offered liqueurs as we cruised under the stars back to the boat landing, viewing the awesome lighted curve of the Coronado Bridge and San Diego's beautiful harbor.

All the officers and their wives or guests were hosted in this manner. We enjoyed the events so much that we also hosted my mother, my brothers and sisters, their spouses, and several nephews and nieces, and our neighbors and other friends.

It was a particular pleasure to have Mom aboard for an evening after all the times I had phoned her the night before going out to sea to ask for her *"bendicion." "Si mijo, con todo mi corazon!"* Our daughter Judy invited her National University library co-workers, and our son Jack included his best friends, Jens Haerter and Steve Lucas.

One particularly enjoyable evening we hosted a wardroom dinner for RADM Dave Ramsey and Captain Jim Hayes, former *Vancouver* COs, and their wives and Cdr. Wirt Fladd, a *Vancouver* XO (and my future chief staff officer), and his wife. (When Linda and I picked up the admiral and Nancy in my gig at Coronado, the first thing the admiral did was to open the cowling and inspect the engine.) Upon seeing the refurbished captain's cabin, with fresh McNamara's lace curtains at the windows, Ramsey turned to me, and said "Frank, you have gilded the lily!"

As is customary in the fleet, the wardroom hosted a hail and farewell party for Linda and me and to welcome the prospective commanding officer and his wife. I thanked the officers and wives for their loyal support and friendship during our tour. Linda's comments are the most insightful and relevant I ever heard regarding the role of the captain's wife:

> Thank you Gary and Margaret for the party. This officers' wives' group is unique. Each of the women in it is one of a kind— that is to say, we have an independent, headstrong bunch of people here. Margaret and I have not had an easy time trying to keep up the energy and interest in a wives' group while the ship has been in port ... Not to mention the times it was supposed to be out but they worked so fast and came home early. Unheard of!
>
> ... A Navy wife tends to maximize her time with her man more than any civilian could ever relate to. At least a smart one does—so a wives' group function is considered secondary, something to do when there is no husband at home. But we keep pushing the wives' functions when the guys are in. Some people wonder why.
>
> We need to know each other well. We need to break through the barriers and know each other on a day-to-day basis, so that

when things are good we have fun together, but also so that when things aren't right—when help is needed—we know how to give it to one another.

Maybe the ship has been out for a couple of months and the time has begun to drag. A wife might become unreasonably despondent over routine problems—the car battery, the dryer belt, the kids' grades, maybe she is sick and needs help. Maybe she has to go for surgery and she's afraid. Maybe she is drinking too much—or taking too many tranquilizers. Maybe her child is in serious trouble.

The real purpose for pushing wives' activities when the ship is in is so that we have each other to rely on when the ship is out. It doesn't happen automatically when the tugs push the ship out into the channel.

By now, the officers' wives are on their way to closeness and rapport, and none of them have lost their freedom or individuality because of it—that is always the unspoken apprehension among young Navy wives and their husbands.

I would like to ask the officers to help me in the numbered days we have remaining before deployment to speak to the enlisted men who work for you and encourage them to send their wives to the enlisted wives' meetings. They will need each other—to get information, and to get help when they need it and to give help to others when they are able….God bless you all. Thank you.

Because of my prior sea and shore command experience, my *Vancouver* tour of duty was relatively stress-free. My ship's nine-month overhaul in San Diego permitted me to spend more time at home and it made life much more enjoyable for Linda, Jack and Judy—and me.

I greatly benefited from all my hard-earned lessons from my *Fort Fisher* command; I had more know-how and I was wiser. As a result, I was a better overhaul manager and achieved the optimum benefit from the resources at my disposal. And I had sufficient time to plan and execute *Vancouver*'s schedule post-overhaul and did a better job of prioritizing events and my command attention. This made me more effective in motivating and training my officers and crew.

Captain John Frank Gamboa, U. S. Navy (Retired)

Fortunately, I did not have to deal with major overhaul or training issues, or a drastically compressed workup period in preparing *Vancouver* for her deployment. Although it was not easy—command never is— Linda and I thoroughly enjoyed my command of the Van Can Do. I was ready for my squadron commander responsibilities.

In recognition of their superior performance, on the day before I relinquished command I awarded Navy Commendation Medals to three junior officers, the warrant officer DCA, and 14 chief petty officers, over half the chiefs' mess. They were the best wardroom and chiefs' mess I served with in my career. My final report of fitness reflected my ship's performance:

> This period for Captain Gamboa and USS *Vancouver* is filled with a number of continuing successes. *Vancouver* completed a successful mine countermeasure exercise wherein the ship served as flagship for ComMineRon Five. Two important inspections were passed with flying colors. Overall ship performance in a 3-M inspection was 90%, one of the highest grades recorded in the force.... By all measures, Captain Gamboa has completed a highly successful tour in command at sea with superior readiness, morale and retention the hallmarks of his ship. I have the highest confidence in Captain Gamboa and that he will continue to make significant contributions to the viability of amphibious warfare in his new capacity as amphibious squadron commander. Upon completion of this tour of duty, Captain Gamboa will surely be eminently qualified for promotion to the grade of commodore and is so recommended.

I was awarded the Meritorious Service Medal by Admiral Foley, Commander in Chief, U.S. Pacific Fleet, with a citation that reflected my fitness report.

In San Diego on October 5, 1983, I was relieved by Captain Eugene Pellerin, a helicopter aviator. Here are the highlights of my remarks:

> I have been responsible for the condition of this ship and the conduct and performance of this crew since I assumed command 601 days ago before many of you here today....*Vancouver* is a ready ship.... Now it took a bit of effort to get where we are today, and there are more than a few local commands and civilian industrial firms that,

345

without their outstanding help and support, *Vancouver* would not be in her present condition....

There are many more things that we did, but ... I will only tell you that this ship's company has excelled as no other I have ever known. Not once did they falter or fail to rise to the occasion during operations or repairs, conducting training evolutions at sea in day or night, in good weather and foul, whether they were tired or full of energy....

To my mother, Linda, Jack and Judy: thank you for your love and total support. To *Vancouver* men ...you have my deepest appreciation for your loyalty and dedication to duty. I wish you every success.... I will now read my orders:

When relieved of duties as commanding officer of United States Ship *Vancouver* (LPD 2), consider yourself detached, proceed to whatever port in which Commander Amphibious Squadron Three may be, and report to him for duty as his relief.

Chapter Ten

★ ★ ★ ★ ★ ★ ★

To do great things is difficult, but to command great things is more difficult.

—Friedrich Nietzsche

Thinking about my new duty assignment, I recalled my early years as a junior officer aboard destroyers where I first witnessed the strong, dynamic leadership of squadron commanders—the commodores. Highly respected Navy captains and veterans of WW II, their chests were adorned with medals and campaign ribbons earned in violently contested sea battles, mostly against the Japanese Navy in the Pacific theatre. They spoke with salty directness, strode the decks with a confidant swagger and wore their caps—glistening with "scrambled-eggs" (heavy gold braid on the visor)—at a slight starboard tilt. These crusty officers of the line exuded a powerful command presence and, if the situation warranted, they could be fiercely tough sons of bitches. I knew that I was not of their battle-hardened mold, but I would attempt to emulate their leadership.

I assumed command on November 9, 1982. I did not command the warships in my squadron; I commanded their commanding officers. Mindful of the Pacific Fleet amphibious force's illustrious legacy, I was proud to be the commodore of Amphibious Squadron Three, to see my broad command pennant flying from my flagship's mast, and to hear the quarterdeck ring four bells on the One MC and announce "Phibron Three: Arriving!"

My squadron consisted of seven amphibious warships:, USS *New Orleans* (LPH 11), my flagship; USS *Barbour County* (LST 1195), USS *Denver* (LPD 9), USS *Durham* (LKA 114), USS *Monticello* (LSD 35), USS *Schenectady* (LST 1185) and USS *Vancouver* (LPD 2).

Shortly after I broke my pennant, *Monticello's* deployment was unexpectedly cancelled due to extensive material problems and other readiness deficiencies. She was removed from Phibron Three without replacement, reducing my squadron to six ships and only two wet wells.

My staff consisted of 18 officers and 45 enlisted men, headed by a commander who was the chief staff officer (CSO) and three other commanders: the operations officer, the officer in charge (O-in-C) of a tactical air control squadron (Tacron), and a chaplain. There were three lieutenant commanders, three lieutenants, a warrant officer and a Marine Corps captain combat cargo officer. My enlisted men included a chief signalman, chief radioman, chief operations specialists, Marine gunnery sergeant, quartermasters, radiomen, yeomen, and mess specialists. When deployed, my staff was augmented with a full Tacron, a Navy Seal team, a beach master unit, and an assault craft unit with two LCUs and four LCM-8s.

Almost before I could I unpack my sea bag, I was in command of an amphibious task force (ATF) in a major fleet exercise. Four days after assuming command, I sortied Phibron Three and three other amphibious ships to join Kernel Usher 83-1, a Rim of the Pacific (Rimpac) Third Fleet exercise with the *Coral Sea* carrier battle group, a surface action group, a logistic support group, and my ATF. The frigate USS *Ramsey* was assigned to my task group to provide anti-submarine protection.

The battle lines were drawn between Orange and Blue forces and we engaged in simulated air, surface, and anti-submarine battles all the way to Hawaii, where our amphibious assault landing would be conducted.

Sailing on my first amphibious assault operation as Commander, Amphibious Task Force (CATF, "catiff"), I studied the operation order developed by my predecessor; with my staff, I went over each phase of the exercise.

In *Fort Fisher* I had learned the role of the primary control ship in directing the landing craft and Marine amphibious vehicle assault waves to the beach (Marine amphibious vehicles were initially designated LVT's (Landing Vehicles, Tracked) and were commonly referred to by Marines as "Amtracs." In 1984, Marines re-designated LVT's as AAV's (Assault Amphibious Vehicles). The Marine Corps is currently in the midst of the developing the next generation of amphibious vehicles to be designated EFV's (Expeditionary Fighting Vehicle).

I also learned the role of the landing ship tank (LST) in conducting sea-borne launches of Marine amphibious vehicles. In *Tarawa*, I learned the basics of the air assault phases and the general operations and tactics of amphibious warfare. Now I would control the ATF and supporting task groups, and in close coordination with the Marine commander, landing force (CLF, "cliff"), conduct the entire seaborne phase of an amphibious assault.

Captain John Frank Gamboa, U. S. Navy (Retired)

Navies have been conducting amphibious warfare (invasions, assaults, raids) from the sea for more than two millennia. In 490 BCE, a Persian fleet of 600 ships landed an army of 22,000 men on the beaches of the Bay of Marathon near Athens.[1] In the 20th Century, the purpose of amphibious warfare was to land, on hostile shores, an armed force of size and firepower sufficient to establish a secure a beachhead, and then conduct a rapid build-up of armor, artillery, other arms and enough additional troops to vanquish the defending forces and seize their territory. In the 21st Century, its purpose remains the same. It is the most complex of all naval operations.

The U.S. Navy and Marine Corps developed their amphibious warfare concepts, ships, weapons and tactics in the 1930s, and then battle-tested and refined them during WW II in hard-fought amphibious assaults against Japanese-held islands during Admiral Nimitz' Central Pacific campaign and General MacArthur's concurrent Southwest Pacific campaign. These battles validated amphibious warfare strategy, tactics, weapons and materiel as did the amphibious invasions in North Africa, the Mediterranean, and of course, the most famous of all, Normandy.

During WW II, The Navy designed and constructed various classes of amphibious ships including LSDs, landing ship tanks (LST), troop transports (APA), cargo ships (AKA), command ships (AGC), and a variety of landing craft. The Marine Corps developed its amphibious vehicles to transport infantry units from amphibious ships to the shore and once ashore, to serve as fighting vehicles to transport infantry units to their objectives.

The LST was designed to launch Marine amphibious vehicles at sea approximately 2000 yards from the beach. LSTs also landed armor, artillery and wheeled or tracked vehicles by grounding the ship's bow directly onto the beach and opening their huge bow doors for cargo egress. Later LST designs incorporated huge floating causeways that were lashed onto both sides of the ship's hull and "splashed" (launched) near the beach, permitting vehicles to drive over them to the beach from the LST.

After WW II, the Navy and Marine Corps developed helicopters and tactics for vertical envelopment of the objectives, which landed troops and weapons inland beyond the beachhead. This required conversion of Navy WWII light carriers into helicopter assault ships (LPH class) with Marine troop and weapons embarkation capacity. In the 1960s, a new

349

class of LPHs was designed from the keel up as an amphibious task force helicopter carrier and CATF flagship. Helicopters required the addition of a helicopter flight deck (helo "spots") on all other amphibious ships.

LPDs were also designed and launched in the 1960s, expanding the amphibious task force wet well and troop transport capabilities. Their two helo-spot flight deck increased the capability and lethality of vertical envelopment tactics. The development of Marine vertical take-off attack aircraft (Harrier) and large heavy-lift helos (CH-53E) in the 1970s led to the design and construction of much larger and more capable general purpose helicopter amphibious assault ships (LHA class) in the 1970s and the very similar LHD class in the 1980s.

Planning for an amphibious assault begins with an Initiating Directive (ID) issued by the fleet commander jointly to the commanders who are assigned the mission and are responsible for the assault planning, implementation and execution: the Navy Commander, Amphibious Task Force (CATF) and the Marine Corps (or Army) Commander, Landing Force (CLF).

CATF develops the ship composition of the amphibious task force and supporting naval task forces plan and the plan for movement to amphibious objective area (AOA).

CLF develops the composition for the landing plan, which includes all elements of troops, helos, amphibious vehicles, armor, artillery, other weapons, and logistics.

With close collaboration and coordination, CATF and CLF develop the operation plans and orders for a successful mission.

Supporting task forces include carriers for aircraft bombing, rocket attacks, and close air support before, during, and after the assault; and surface combatants for shore bombardment on enemy hard targets and troop concentrations with gun, missile and rocket fire as directed by the CATF's tactical air control squadron and combined arms control center. The carriers also provide combat air patrols to protect the amphibious task force.

Submarines land SEAL and Marine reconnaissance units to conduct pre-assault tasks. The fleet logistic train supports the ATF, carriers and surface combatants.

All naval task forces report to CATF for assignment and execution of their amphibious assault tasks.

Captain John Frank Gamboa, U. S. Navy (Retired)

Since WW II, the amphibious landing date is called D-Day. The launching of the assault is coordinated by two key milestones: H-Hour, the time of beach touchdown by the first wave of Marine amphibious assault vehicles, and L-Hour, the time of landing of the first wave of Marine helicopter-borne troops.

Synchronization by timelines coordinates all aspects of the assault. Each phase is timed to the minute, including the task force's arrival in the AOA; commencement of pre-assault bombardment of shore targets by aircraft and combatant ships; loading of troops into amphibious vehicles and helos; launching of amphibious vehicles and helos; and launching of landing craft and wave control boats and the Navy beach guard units that control all landing and movement of armor, artillery, wheel and track vehicles, troops, other personnel, and logistics, and the return of personnel casualties to ships.

Because of its complexity, each amphibious landing is preceded by a full-scale rehearsal in order to validate every phase and facet of the initial landings and time lines. In combat, the rehearsal is conducted far removed from the actual objective area to preserve tactical surprise, but for peacetime training exercises the actual objective area is usually used for both the rehearsal and assault.

At a pre-sail conference, the CATF and the CLF conduct combined briefings on the assault rehearsal. All ship captains and Marine element commanders and their key staff officers and enlisted men participate and iron out any last-minute changes. A post-rehearsal meeting is held to resolve problems. The task force then gets underway and proceeds to the AOA.

The key preliminary decisions for launching the assault are the confirmation of D-Day, usually by CATF and CLF, but sometimes by higher authority. In either case, CATF and CLF jointly confirm L-Hour and H-Hour.

Weather is a primary consideration in amphibious operations. The Normandy landing was originally scheduled on June 4, 1944, but a sudden, violent channel storm that generated high winds, turbulent seas and limited visibility had made the entire operation unsafe, so General Eisenhower delayed the invasion until the storm passed or moderated.

On June 5 at his SHAEF Headquarters in England, Eisenhower met with his staff to consider the possible confirmation of June 6 as D-Day for the invasion. His meteorologists had reported a possible break in the storm on the 6th for a couple of days. Even so, it was still a dicey situation.

But the General fully realized that the huge invasion force could not be held ready on station indefinitely. At the conclusion of the briefing, he looked silently around the room for a few moments. Then Ike made his historic decision, "Okay, let's go!

As Rimpac forces closed the Hawaiian Islands a tropical depression developed southwest of Hawaii. Two days later, the depression was upgraded to a tropical storm. The day before we entered Pearl Harbor, it was upgraded to Hurricane Iwa. We arrived at Pearl Harbor on the evening of November 21.

At my commanding officers' luncheon the next day, I discussed the possibility of an emergency sortie and placed all my ships on four-hour standby, pending my weather briefing at 0730 the next morning. We began embarkation of the MAU and scheduled a possible emergency fly-off of all the Marine helos (flown aboard the day before at sea) back to their hangers at the Marine Corps air base at Kaneohe, where they could be sheltered. I called on the base commander, the supply depot commander, Commander Third Fleet and Commander, Naval Surface Group Mid-Pacific, who was Senior Officer Present Afloat (SOPA), to inform them of my intentions regarding the hurricane, and to ensure that my ships would receive priority logistic support.

On November 23, my staff weather brief left no doubt that Iwa was going to come close to—or make a direct hit on—Pearl Harbor. I ordered my commanding officers to halt the embarkation of Marines, fly off the helos, and sortie.

I telephoned Vice Admiral Bill Lawrence, Commander Third Fleet (whose chief of staff was my good friend and classmate, Captain Taylor Keith), and Rear Admiral Rorie, to inform them of my decisions. As SOPA, Rorie had started preparations to sortie the rest of the ships, or secure them to their piers.

Vancouver got underway and transited the channel, followed by *New Orleans*, *Schenectady* and *Ramsey*. The channel course led us directly into Iwa's dangerous semi-circle with heavy seas and almost 50-knot winds. It was a very close-run thing. After the *Ramsey* transited, SOPA closed the channel and ordered all other ships to remain in port and secure for heavy weather.

Captain John Frank Gamboa, U. S. Navy (Retired)

We headed eastward through the Kauai channel to position my ships in the lee of the island chain. We had 30-40 knot winds and 10-15 foot seas, but conditions moderated in the lee during the evening as the hurricane tracked north by northeast.

At dawn, we altered course to starboard, rounded Molokai and headed back to Pearl in bright, clear skies and relatively moderate seas. *Schenectady* had lost a boat boom, the only damage to my ships.

Durham had not gotten underway due to lack of tugs and pilots prior to the channel closing, and she was held safely by two tugs pushing her against the pier during the height of the storm. *Mount Vernon* had not completed repairs to one of her boilers.

Hurricane Iwa made a direct hit on Kauai, causing major damage, flooding and a loss of power, only the third hurricane to strike the Hawaiian Islands in their recorded history.

We entered port in the afternoon, resumed embarkation of the Marines and reconfigured our amphibious assault, shortening it by two days. We got underway late the next day and conducted a rehearsal and backload.

On D-Day we conducted the air portion of the assault, but cancelled the beach surface assault due to high surf conditions. We accomplished all close air-support tasks with the *Coral Sea* air wing, bombing and strafing targets on Kahoolawe.

We also conducted shore bombardment call-for-fire missions with several destroyers, frigates and cruisers, thoroughly exercising my Tacron that was skillfully led by Cdr. Glen Jacob. They put tons of ordnance on a variety of shore targets, thoroughly training our Combined Arms Coordination Center.

RADM McCarthy, the Carrier Battle Group commander, visited my flagship by helo during the fireworks. VADM Lawrence also flew out to see how the exercise was going. My squadron and the MAU acquitted themselves well in our first major fleet operation.

My ships, my staff and I—the new team—had been through a successful shakedown. But we also had some screw ups. Steaming back to San Diego, I reviewed our performance with my staff, focusing on our decision-making processes and staff coordination procedures. Overall, I felt that my staff and ships had performed well, and I told them so. I was confident that we could become a great team. Everyone just needed to know my heading and expectations.

To clear away the barriers to my staff's optimum effectiveness, the Human Resources Development Center conducted a one-day staff workshop in San Diego to address staff roles and responsibilities and improve our internal communications and staffing procedures. The center conducted one-on-one private interviews with me and each staff member to identify staff and squadron issues and concerns, which were summarized for me and the CSO.

Then we designed a workshop agenda on staff operations. This facilitated quick development of teamwork, rapidly ramped up our readiness for fleet operations, and cleared the decks for creation of my policies and standards. Fundamentally, we would be mission-oriented, professional and successful—and have fun doing it.

On January 21, 1983, Phibron Three would deploy to Westpac for seven months. Fourteen months after our return we would again deploy to Seventh Fleet. After Rimpac, Rear Admiral Bill Walsh, my boss, gave me a "heads up:" Pacific Fleet flag officer discussions were on-going concerning the need to deploy an ATF to Westpac in 1984 in company with a Carrier Battle Group "just like we did in WW II."

The ATF's deployment date would conform to the battle group's deployment date, not the other way around.

Accordingly, Phibron Three would be short-cycled and have only 10.5 months between deployments. Since I would have no voice in the decision, I put this tantalizing bit of news aside and turned to my immediate task—to prepare my squadron for deployment in less than six weeks.

Prior to Rimpac several of my ships had experienced significant material problems that required my personal intervention. Our pre-deployment workup and POM period continued to be problematic, riddled with emergent ship repairs and ship administrative and technical system deficiencies. It became very obvious to me—and to higher authority—that Phibron Three staff and ships had not prepared well for deployment.

In January, my squadron's readiness took another serious hit—a major material casualty to one of *New Orleans*' two emergency diesel generators. After several failed repair attempts, the decision was made to replace the generator, requiring a 10-day delay in our deployment; and in turn, Phibron 5, the deployed squadron, was extended 10 days in Westpac. Not a good omen and not a good way for the new guys to join Seventh Fleet.

We sortied on January 30, 1983. Because of our delay, we lost our much-needed maintenance period at Subic following our trans-Pacific voyage. Instead, after a brief stop at Subic to victual and top off fuel, we would proceed directly to Team Spirit, the major exercise of our deployment.

In the 1970s-'80s, the Pacific Fleet amphibious force and Pacific Fleet Marine Force (FMF) deployed a MAU to Seventh Fleet consisting of one reinforced battalion landing team with three infantry companies, an artillery battery, a tank company, supporting light weapons, a logistic unit, and three helo squadrons (about 1800 Marines). The landing plan called for simultaneous touchdown of one infantry company on the assault beach by amphibious assault vehicles and one infantry company on an objective area beyond the beach by helicopters. The third infantry company would be held in reserve in the ATF, to be landed as dictated by the tactical situation ashore.

The key to a successful amphibious assault is the rapid buildup of combat power ashore. The buildup speed depends on the ATF's ship composition, especially the number of wet-well ships.

In my era, the typical deployed eight-ship squadron was organized in two amphibious ready groups (ARGs): ARG Alfa, the Seventh Fleet amphibious ready group, included a helicopter carrier, two wet wells, and an LST with the Marine Amphibious Unit embarked. ARG Bravo, whose mission was to provide lifts for Marine elements to Seventh Fleet training sites, consisted of two wet wells, an LKA and an LST.

To compensate for the loss of *Monticello*, I shifted *Durham* to ARG Alfa. She had just returned from two years in the reserve fleet and an extensive overhaul. More than half her crew was new to the ship, with minimal at-sea time and no recent amphibious squadron operations experience.

The loss of *Monticello* and *Durham*'s capabilities and readiness imposed major constraints on ARG Alfa's capability for rapid buildup of combat power ashore.

LKAs carried 15 landing craft, including four LCM-8s. These single-screw cargo ships first had to anchor and then off-load their boats by winched cargo booms, a slow, hazardous evolution, even more so in darkness or foul weather. And *Durham*'s aluminum-hulled "8-boats" were more susceptible to damage than steel-hulled boats, especially when carrying tanks.

Because of her relatively short length (the LPD 4 class hull was about 50 feet longer), *Vancouver* was limited in the number of tanks and landing craft that could be carried simultaneously so one tank was parked aboard the LCU in the well, and the other four were parked on the well deck forward of the LCU.

Wheeled vehicles and various serial-numbered items (serials; ammo, rations, water, etc.) were stowed forward of the well deck. Overall, the well deck stowage was a tight fit with no wiggle room.

Despite these constraints, we had to accomplish our mission. Thanks to my staff's extensive amphibious warfare experience and operational know-how, we came up with a "work around" for the ship assault plan and the Marines' landing plan that would optimize our amphibious assault capabilities and the speed of combat power buildup in the objective area—pre-H-hour transfers.

The basic idea was to accomplish the pre-H-Hour transfer of tanks and units two hours before H-hour (which was usually at dawn). All pre-H-Hour transfers would therefore occur at "oh dark thirty." Here is the whole enchilada.

ARG Alfa would approach the AOA pre-dawn at 18 knots with all the ships darkened. *Vancouver* would slow, ballast down and launch the LCU underway with its single tank. *Vancouver* would then anchor one hundred yards to seaward from the right flank of the boat lane line of departure (LOD), the beginning of a 2000-yard boat lane to the beach.

At the same time, *Durham* would anchor one hundred yards seaward on the left flank of the LOD and lower all of her boats into the water. When waterborne, they would report to *Vancouver*.

Vancouver, still ballasted down, would take two of the LCM-8 boats lashed together side by side, "married," into her flooded dock, and then deballast sufficient to ground the boats on the well deck. One tank would be loaded into each boat, and then *Vancouver* would ballast down, launch the boats, and repeat the evolution with another two married 8-boats, resulting in a total of five tanks afloat and ready to proceed to the beach on schedule.

Durham's LCM-6 and LCVP boats would embark the beach master unit and the medical team from *Vancouver*; a second LCM-6 would be used as a salvage boat to assist in clearing any boats that had broached on the beach.

As primary control ship, *Vancouver* would organize all the landing craft into boat waves in waiting circles off her bow and stern within infrared light signaling distance. When all was in readiness, she would dispatch the boat circles to the LOD, where they would form waves and proceed to the beach according to the assault plan time lines for touchdown at H-Hour.

Every option in an amphibious assault has a cost. Our landing plan scheme (pre-H-Hour transfers) compromised tactical surprise. The ARG was made vulnerable to shore fire and air attacks for two hours longer, and the requirements for air and surface protection were extended.

The complexity of our assault plan dictated the need for full-scale rehearsals over and above those in our scheduled Seventh Fleet exercises. Practice makes perfect.

On February 9, 1983, the morning we departed Pearl Harbor for Westpac, we conducted the first test of our landing plan at Barking Sands Beach in Kauai. That night I described the results in my journal:

> Well, it was quite a day. Reveille at 0430. Skinny T (*Schenectady*) started the day by wrapping her holding tank (sewage) shore transfer hose around her starboard screw, delaying her ... one hour. *Denver* was delayed due to engineering plant repairs; finally underway about 1100 ... lousy communications, atrocious boating, two beached boats, two inoperative amphibious assault vehicles on the beach after landing, one that couldn't go forward and had to be towed to the LST... by another amphibious assault vehicle in rough seas ... rough weather ... frontal system ... increased the winds to 30 knots and kicked up the seas.... So many problems that it was hard to keep them sorted out. Wirt went to *Vancouver* and I went to *Durham* (by helo).... *Durham* ... boats are awful. They need practice. No one hurt ... (but) one man from an eight boat washed overboard in the surf and picked up by

¡El Capitán!

New Orleans' helo. A super job. As a result of six-hour delay … we are in a caravan dash to the chop line. But we will make it.

Each night when my squadron was at sea I sent a "CATF Intentions" message to all ships. After completing our landing plan rehearsal and backload, I sent,

> CATF Intentions/Comments…. Analysis of today's exercise reveals need to direct increased command attention to radio equipment, boat handling in the well deck, boat control in the AOA and command and control procedures in general. Each ship will conduct a thorough critique of today's events and submit comments…. I expect each ship to concentrate on training en route to chop line. We are not ready for Team Spirit. Amplifying directives to follow. Nonetheless, it's good to be heading west. Gamboa sends.

We joined up at sea with Phibron Five on the morning of February 12. The CSO and I flew to USS *Belleau Wood* (LHA 5) for breakfast and our turnover briefing with Commodore Harry Gimber and his CSO. The rest of my staff officers did the same with their counterparts. The permanently deployed MAU commander, a Marine Corps colonel and his staff, shifted from *Belleau Wood* to *New Orleans* and our embarked reinforced BLT reported to the MAU commander. After we "took the baton," we shaped course for the San Bernardino Strait.

I transmitted a CATF Intentions message to my ships: "Welcome to the Seventh Fleet…. Heads up and heads high. Do your best and we will leave Westpac with a record to be proud of. I am proud of your efforts to date, and confident of your future success…. Gamboa sends."

Soon after the MAU commander embarked, we discussed our ship mix and landing plan. We agreed to practice as often as possible, naming our rehearsals "Landex;" each one required about four hours to execute, not counting all the preparations.

When we entered Subic Bay or Okinawa, we conducted a Landex at Zambales Green Beach and White Beach respectively, both H- and L-Hours. After completing the backload, we would enter port and go on well-earned liberty, joking that if it was easy, anyone could be a Gator.

Amphibious squadron ship commanding officers are of different warfare communities. My flagship CO was a captain helicopter pilot.

Captain John Frank Gamboa, U. S. Navy (Retired)

Durham's was a captain attack aircraft pilot. *Vancouver*'s was a captain helicopter pilot. *Denver*'s was a captain diesel submariner (USNA '57, one year senior to me—the only "Trade School" CO in my squadron). My two LST COs were naval surface warfare commanders. All my skippers were on their first tour as ship commanding officers.

Ship captains inherently desire to control their command's operations and destiny. Conversely, commodores have to lead their captains toward a common goal. This fleet state of affairs creates dynamic tension between a commodore and his captains. My goal was to convert this vital human energy—the struggle for power and control—into synergy among my ships and staff. The game would turn on the quality of my leadership, my staff's amphibious warfare expertise, and the professionalism of my captains.

Regardless of the differing ranks, warfare specialties, levels of experience and backgrounds, I needed to create and maintain a viable command relationship with each CO in order to achieve the highest possible state of squadron readiness. We had to relate and communicate effectively and understand each other.

I tried to instill confidence by issuing my directives, tasking, orders and guidance in a clear, professional, straightforward and timely manner. My intent was to treat my captains with courtesy and respect, never to berate, browbeat, or intimidate. But their perception of my command style may have differed from mine.

To facilitate command relationships, I hosted group luncheons in my cabin during each in-port period for all COs and my CSO. We talked squadron business and got to know each other. The captains reciprocated my hospitality by inviting me and the CSO to lunch with them and their officers. In addition to specifically scheduled pre-exercise briefings, and inspections, I usually had one-on-one meetings with the COs aboard their ships, permitting me to see their ships and crews and assess their command climate first hand. Recalling how I disliked being "fetched," I rarely summoned a CO to my flagship to resolve an issue. But if necessary, I did.

My principal interactions with my ship captains occurred during squadron operations at sea, where we were always in constant motion—a very dynamic state, requiring my close attention in every phase and facet.

Our communications were almost always within the context of operational tasks. I achieved command and control by tactical signals executed by my staff underway watch officers through voice radio, signal flags, and yardarm blinker lights, as well as text-messages transmitted by radio circuits and signal lights. My letters were mainly on administrative matters such as inspections and reports.

If my ships screwed up or were not performing to my satisfaction, I would send the offending CO a brief, direct personal message. This trait became a point of humor within my staff. "Yes sir, Commodore, send him a personal!" (At our last staff meeting, my chief signalman presented me with a thick binder containing copies of all my 1984 "personals," a treasured memento.)

Every commodore has a unique command style. In Seventh Fleet, we participated in Exercise Team Spirit, the first amphibious operation of our deployment. My ships were not at their best in the early stages. I sent a personal to the commanding officers:

> Team Spirit Success
> 1. Our mutual goal is to achieve a totally successful Team Spirit exercise ... teamwork requires constant two-way communications.
> 2. Specifically, I expect an acknowledgement from you when I have called a matter to your attention....
> 3. ... I have experienced ... difficulty in maneuvering the formation due to poor communications....
> 4. ... The daily air plan is a complicated evolution to execute under ideal weather and comms...
> 5. .... Stay on top of the situation. Gamboa sends.

In all my actions to create and maintain positive command relationships, I fully understood the need to promptly establish my squadron's performance standards and correct all shortcomings. Getting there was not always all sweetness and light. I sent the following message to one of my captains whose ship was in a planned restricted availability (PRAV, primarily contractor repair work), and was not measuring up:

> Visit Impressions
> 1. The following are my impressions of your command gained from your briefing and ship tour....
> 2. No department head discussed ship's force work.... Deck plate questions to crewmembers left the impression that a

prioritized ship's force work list is not in being.... Your chiefs were not in evidence, nor were your officers. I ... expected to see them along your tour route....

3.   Overall, your sailors have an unkempt appearance, need haircuts and shaves, and are lacking in military courtesy. They answer seniors with "yeah/no." Your Exec is un-aggressive, especially in areas of crew appearance and ship's cleanliness, particularly in crew's heads and berthing areas.

4.   You are hereby directed to conduct a personnel inspection at morning quarters in working uniform. Emphasis will be given to haircuts and facial hair.

5.   Overall, I am increasingly concerned about the seeming lack of enthusiasm and spirit in (your ship). While I fully understand and appreciate the disruption and impact caused by the contractors on your ship's routine, and the disruption of your habitability, I expect you to maintain firm control of your command, and maintain high standards of crew performance, appearance, military bearing and courtesy, and high standards of cleanliness and sanitation.

6.   I will visit your ship on ... I expect to find improvement in all areas discussed above....

But it was more enjoyable to compliment my COs:

Personal for Captain Greenhoe and CDR Anthanson (ARG Bravo was in the Philippines) from Commodore Gamboa
Exercise Tangent Flash

1.   The success of the SOG in executing Exercise TANGENT FLASH with professionalism, élan, and obvious pride is a fitting climax to the superb efforts that you have both expended since departure San Diego ... you have continued to challenge and develop your crews and wardrooms not only in the conduct of amphibious operations, but ... during upkeeps. The conduct of your men ashore reflects the outstanding sense of discipline and responsibility that you have instilled ... WELL DONE.

2.   FYI, Western Australia liberty is as good as advertised—or better. Eat your heart out.

3.   Warm regards, Frank

361

¡El Capitán!

It was important that I observed the COs in a variety of situations and kept tabs on their status—especially their ship's morale. Whenever operations, weather and time permitted, I would fly on my helo to each ship, or go by gig if we were anchored, and spend a couple of hours with the captain and his officers and chiefs, and to give his ship a look-see. During amphibious operations the CSO and I usually visited the ships independently, but on occasion we would go together. I wrote in my journal:

> Went aboard *Barbour County* to watch her … disembark vehicles over her bow ramp and observed operations on the beach … inspected the Marines' defense perimeter. Flew back to the flagship for lunch with Captain Miller and staff (7th Fleet)…. Lots of praise from the Seventh Fleet observers. Flew ashore with Commodore Klee and talked to the Korean Navy salvage coordinator (two Korean Navy LSTs had broached on the beach). Bob and I took an LCM-8 ride off the beach and then transferred at sea to *Vancouver*'s boat for a ride to Beaufort to see the CO and ensure he understood his role in the salvage ops. Then back to the beach to talk with the ROK Navy admiral. Coordinated lift of two pumps to their LST. Flew back home.

I tried to stay on top or ahead of the situation. I paid attention to my units' morale and spirit and made every effort to foster and sustain viable cooperation and harmony between my ships and our embarked Marines.

My modus operandi facilitated my development of objective evaluations of each commanding officer's fitness—leadership, character and performance in command. And I enjoyed my command relationships.

When Phibron Three sortied for Westpac, there was no official word on our next Westpac, but after our stop in Hawaii to load the Marines and for briefings at CINCPACFLT headquarters, there was no doubt in our minds that we would be short-cycled between deployments and deploy with a carrier battle group in May 1984. My ships would have significantly less time for preparation and workup, compounding the inherent difficulties in achieving pre-deployment workups and readiness.

To prioritize allocation of vital shore maintenance and training services for deploying ships, the carrier battle group (which included surface combatants and a nuclear submarine) and the amphibious squadron deployments to Westpac were always offset by several months. With deployments coinciding, the demand for services by the increased number of ships would be very competitive, even contentious.

My experience in working up *Fort Fisher*, *Tarawa* and *Vancouver* taught me the importance of advanced planning and aggressive execution. Some activities can be conducted simultaneously, but not major events such as OPPEs, PRAVs and Reftra. These requirements must be scheduled sequentially and with time to prepare—and allow for "do overs." Overall, because of significantly less time available, a well-planned and executed squadron effort would be required to achieve high readiness and deploy on time.

Since each CO was responsible for his own ship's readiness, I could simply say to my skippers, "We are sailing for Westpac on May 30, 1984. I expect you to be ready. Keep me informed!" Then I could fly my absentee pennant from my flagship's signal halyard, work at lowering my golf handicap, enjoy doing whatever else commodores do, and let my CSO run the show. What a fun job and great life that would be!

Well, that was neither my leadership style nor my modus operandi. In the event we were not ready to sail on time, I wanted to know why— and how to get back on track. So I chose my other option—my staff and I were going to be visible and involved. The issue was how.

As soon as my ships were hull-down on the horizon and heading west from the Hawaiian Islands, I held a staff meeting to discuss the situation and our preparations for our next deployment.

I saw the issue mainly in terms of a fight for services and resources to support a very success-oriented schedule for each ship. We had to create opportunities for our ships to excel and preclude crisis management— knowing full well there would be crises. I defined success as all ships in Phibron Three enjoying a 30-day POM and sailing on time with top readiness. To succeed, the staff and ships had to "lay back together."

My basic approach was to assess each ship and determine its pre-deployment readiness requirements including their ship's company personnel replacements. (The personnel replacements due to crew rotation would be difficult across the squadron; each command had to be aggressive in filling their vacancies.)

Based on our assessment, my staff and I would prioritize each ship's workup events and their services and resource needs and then develop their workup schedule in coordination with all ships, the group and type commanders, and the shore repair, maintenance and training organizations.

I was blessed with two superb key assistants: Commander Wirt Fladd, chief staff officer, and Commander Ed Kline, operations officer. Wirt had four ship commands under his belt and wore a Silver Star for a successful at-sea combat engagement with a North Vietnamese arms running trawler off the coast of Vietnam. Ed had a successful sea command. They were intelligent, aggressive, dedicated, highly professional and collegial naval officers; I thoroughly enjoyed our respective associations.

And they were very conscious of my commanding officers' prerogatives, so they pushed back, "Commodore, why are we trying to tell the skippers how to suck eggs?" I countered, "We're not. I assume they know how. We are simply going to provide the eggs!" When all was said and done, I sent a personal message to my captains as we sailed toward the chop line:

> Westpac '84 Workup Game Plan
>
> 1. In view of Phibron Three's ten-month turn-around for our next Westpac (May '84-Dec '84), it is necessary to lay the groundwork now for the critical events, and develop a game plan that will get all ships ready (all inspections and training completed by April 30, '84) with the greatest benefit (readiness), and the minimum of schedule compression and crisis management. I am sure you will all agree there has got to be a better way than the workup you went through to start this Westpac.
> 2. (In several paragraphs I outlined my top-down planning approach and bottom-up ship roles, the ships' major pre-deployment requirements and schedule planning guidance)
> 3. I realize that thinking about the next time around while we are just beginning to enjoy the fruits of our recent arduous efforts may cause some painful flashbacks, and seems premature, but you all understand how quickly the fun passes and this profession turns back into a job rather than an adventure! Warm regards. Gamboa sends.

My staff did a superb job assessing each ship's readiness and coordinating their re-deployment workup requirements. By developing the ships' proposed schedules and resolving issues in a helpful spirit, we established a good dialogue and created mutual trust and confidence with each ship—the essence of teamwork. In the process, my staff became expert on all ship and squadron maintenance, training and inspection requirements within their areas of responsibility.

Vice Admiral Harry Schrader, USNA '55, a surface warfare nuclear-trained officer and forceful leader, had been commander, naval surface force Pacific (in San Diego) a short time when I assumed command. His primary mission was to support the Pacific Fleet surface ships with people, spare parts, maintenance and repairs, training, and funding.

On March 23, I messaged RADM Walsh, RADM Ramsey (then Vice Admiral Schrader's Deputy), and my classmate and good friend Captain Marty Hill, commander, ship repair facility San Diego, outlining our proposed pre-deployment workup schedules for each ship in Phibron Three. I concluded,

> (I request) a PRAV Planning/Work Definition Conference be held on board *New Orleans*, *Durham*, *Vancouver*, and *Barbour County* at Sasebo, Japan, the second week in June and on board *Denver* and *Schenectady* in Yokosuka, Japan, the third week. Informal discussions with Captain Hill [Supships San Diego]... indicated ... support for early PRAVs and the PRAV planning team visits to Phibron Three ships during current Westpac. Request your support of the foregoing. Unless otherwise directed, I will broach the subject with Vice Admiral Schrader if the opportunity avails during his visit to the ARG in Hong Kong....Very respectfully.

After stopping at Makalapa Hill to seal the deal with Admiral Foley on Phibron Three's shortened turnaround, Schrader flew to Westpac from Hawaii to visit his deployed ships and commodores. Ramsey forwarded my message proposal to him. Walsh was on travel, so his chief of staff, Captain Jim Hayes, responded, ..."[your message] reminded me that ... policy will now permit OPPE's while enroute home port from a deployment if all other scheduling obstacles can be surmounted. Such scheduling, if possible, might help with your tight turn-around. If you are interested in going for such a plan, our schedulers will work with you to try to make it fit. Just let us know what you want and we will give it a try. Best regards, Jim."

¡El Capitán!

Hayes had discerned my underlying concern. The OPPEs were the long pole in the tent, requiring several weeks of preparation and training workup in port and at sea and usually required an extension for training, maintenance or repairs. If we could somehow overlap some pre-OPPE and other events and activities with our current Westpac operations, we could stretch out the ship schedules and milestones to create some wiggle-room.

But there was no precedent for what I was contemplating—conducting Eastpac ship workup events during our Westpac deployment. While we were operating in Seventh Fleet, we were prohibited from bringing the mobile training teams from Eastpac aboard to prepare for the OPPEs or other work-up events. This was a big no-no, almost a taboo (numbered fleet commanders have their territorial imperatives). Nonetheless, it was important to our squadron's turn-around schedule. The admirals could say no to the overlap, but their yes would be a huge win for my squadron. I decided to put this wild card in play.

The ARG arrived in Hong Kong. I met Schrader at the airport and hosted a luncheon for him with my ARG captains. The next day the admiral's engineering and material officer, operations officer, and scheduler met in my cabin with me, Wirt, Ed, and Lt. Cdr. Phil Kasky, my material officer, to discuss our proposed ship workup schedules. They were up to speed on our message and approach and informed us that the admiral wanted the OPPEs out of the way early on; they quickly agreed to our workup schedule overlap in Westpac and to make the engineering mobile training teams available in Westpac in order to conduct two OPPEs enroute home.

Schrader's staff also agreed to fund all six PRAV planning conferences and 3-M inspections in Subic and Japan. And they assured us that Schrader would get all the other Pacific Fleet admirals on board. Bingo!

We moved up our OPPEs and scheduled two between Pearl Harbor and San Diego, leaving only two for San Diego in September. (Only our four steam ships conducted OPPEs. The LSTs, which had diesel engine propulsion, were not yet in the OPPE program.)

That night I attended a dinner party honoring Schrader, hosted by the U.S. Naval Attaché in Hong Kong. At the end of the party I positioned myself near the exit. I wanted to look the admiral in the eye and take a full measure of his commitment to support my squadron's short-cycled turn-around schedule.

The admiral gripped my left arm, "Frank, you are doing a great job and having a wonderful cruise. I told Admiral Foley that Phibron Three has a new regime and new leadership…. We are going to show everyone that Phibron Three can be ready. I want you to ask for whatever you need. Come in with a message to me. Don't hesitate to ask. Keep charging!" I thanked him and pledged my very best efforts as we shook hands.

Upon returning to his headquarters, Schrader sent the following personal message to pertinent Seventh Fleet task force commanders,

> CincPacFlt has directed a ten plus month turn-around of Phibron Three in order to include an amphib scenario in RIMPAC 84. This abbreviated inter-deployment cycle will require some front-loading … Discussions with Frank Gamboa in Westpac indicate opportunities exist for … material assessments, MTT training and possibly even one OPPE prior to OUTCHOP. Frank will soon be providing [all concerned] with OPPE planning data and your support is solicited in order to develop an orderly workup sked for Phibron Three…. [He added] I recognize the undesirability of conducting admin events in Eastpac ships when forward deployed…. Frank will be working toward the accomplishment of at least two or three OPPEs … during the Jun/July 83 return transit. Warm regards."

I selected *Durham* and *Vancouver* as the first amphibious force ships ever to attempt an OPPE while returning from deployment. I also decided that trying to conduct *Denver*'s in Westpac was too high-risk—over the top—crowding our schedule and pushing our luck beyond reasonable limits. All the flags concurred. It was time to tell Linda what I was up to:

> Hi Honey. I am developing a plan for preparing the squadron for the next deployment. You may ask, "Why are you working on that?" Well, the squadron is scheduled to deploy again in May of next year … (with less workup time than normal). I am developing a management plan … that will help the ships help themselves…. I'm excited about what I have laid out. It is risky…. But I firmly believe the ships are fully capable of doing it and … by having a challenging and well-planned schedule that we

can all work together on … to everyone's benefit…. A ten-month turn-around isn't easy, but we are going to ease the pain as much as possible…. I firmly believe that, if you set up ships to succeed and help them towards their goals, they will help themselves and they will … succeed beyond all expectations. Our sailors are the greatest heroes we have in the U.S. of A. Just wanted you to know. I love you very much. (Wish me luck!)

There was some back and forth between Vice Admiral Schrader and CINCPACFLT concerning the readiness consequences—intended and unintended—of the decision to combine the forward deployments of a carrier battle group and an amphibious task force. Schrader was adamant about engineering training and maintenance and providing his ships their required support. He looked hard at the role of the group commanders and squadron commanders and was shaking them up. The last section of his personal message to the CINCPACFLT deputy concerning amphibious ship readiness said,

> …the underlying catalyst (in low readiness) has really been the lack of involvement by the chain of command, and notably the squadrons' and group commanders' staffs. A more intensive deck-plate management of training programs and maintenance programs is demanded when institutionally we have not provided them in other ways. In summary, I can and will influence ISIC involvement; better training schedules; and maintenance support…. Beginning with the FY83 Phibron Three inter-deployment cycle, steps are being taken to implement some of the programs we think necessary to improve amphibious ship readiness…. Frank Gamboa is an innovative thinker and doer. Warm regards.

The ARG returned to Subic Bay for two weeks of much-needed maintenance and upkeep. Our main focus was on our next ARG amphibious landing operation, Valiant Usher 83-7AS at Lancelin Beach on the west coast of Australia.

In six previous attempts by other ARGs, no successful surface assault had ever been accomplished there—no amphibious assault vehicles or landing craft had touched down on the beach—primarily due to unfavorable weather and sea conditions.

Captain John Frank Gamboa, U. S. Navy (Retired)

My staff and I reviewed the exercise reports on the previous attempts, the charts and characteristics of the Lancelin operating area, and its weather patterns for that time of the year. My goal was to conduct a successful landing of amphibious assault vehicles and LCM-8s with tanks if possible.

We would visit Fremantle and Perth before and after the exercise, coinciding with Australia's 41st celebration of the WW II Battle of Coral Sea between U.S. and Japanese Navy carrier task forces on May 1, 1942. The U.S. Navy emerged victorious, halting the Japanese drive toward Australia. The celebration of this historic victory is attended by the commander in chief of the Pacific Fleet. Our Lancelin exercise and participation in Coral Sea Week activities would be the major events of our deployment.

On April 17, the ARG sortied from Subic Bay and shaped course to the Indian Ocean and Fremantle via Lombok Strait. We had a pleasant, uneventful passage, sailing under the spectacular Southern Cross. We arrived at Fremantle on April 26 and held a pre-sail briefing aboard *Vancouver*, and then we sortied the next morning and conducted a rehearsal at Lancelin. After the rehearsal we steamed westward overnight, intending to return to the AOA at dawn for our assault D-Day, April 28.

That evening I received an urgent message from *Vancouver*. She was experiencing severe vibrations in her main engines at speeds above five knots, and had lost her pit sword (a metal device that protrudes beneath the hull and measures water depth by sonar).

The CO assumed that the ship had touched ground during the rehearsal and damaged her screws. Internal inspections revealed no hull leaks or other damage. After discussions with the CSO and Ops, I determined the ship was not in danger, and directed her to proceed independently at safe speed back to the AOA and anchor for D-Day operations. As a precaution, I moved her designated anchorage 500 yards to seaward. After the assault waves had touched down, the SEAL team would conduct an underwater inspection of her hull, screws and rudders.

Knowing that the incident would ring alarm bells in every flag bridge in the Pacific Fleet, I made a critical decision: I would not report the incident until I could visually confirm, about 20 hours later, *Vancouver*'s grounding and the extent of damage.

¡El Capitán!

We successfully conducted our Lancelin D-Day assault in ideal weather. Both waves of amphibious assault vehicles touched down on the beach on time, the first ever at Lancelin. The LCM-8's also touched down, but the tanks were not landed because of the steep beach gradient and sand conditions, which would have required laying of steel matting on the beach to get the tanks ashore. The LCM-8s would also be at risk during off-loading and back-loading the tanks.

As soon as the SEALs completed their assault beach tasks, they went to *Vancouver* and conducted an underwater hull inspection and took pictures. I flew to the ship by helo and the SEAL team leader showed me the pictures and briefed me on what they had found: severe damage to both screws, and scrapes and dents on her skeg keel between the screws. In its damaged condition the ship could not sail from Australia back to Subic.

I directed the captain to submit a casualty report and a request for replacement of both screws, and then I returned to *New Orleans* and with the CSO drafted a message to Bob Klee and the world. I appointed *Durham*'s prospective CO (who would relieve in Fremantle) to conduct a one-officer JAG investigation of the grounding.

Two days later commander, Seventh fleet directed Commodore Klee to proceed to *Vancouver* and take charge of the investigation. (In the early 1980s, at the insistence of a particular Congressman who introduced the bill, the Navy reinstated its one-star flag officer rank called Commodore (COMO) to differentiate its one star rank from its two star rank of rear admiral, as had been desired and requested of the congress for years by the other services—which each had a one star rank, brigadier general. The Navy had no choice but to comply, reluctantly. When the Congressman retired, Navy supportive congressmen promptly changed the commodore title to Rear Admiral Lower Half, RDML, and its two-star rank to Rear Admiral Upper half, RADM. Then all was right in America's flag and general officer ranks and inter-service comity was restored.)

I continued the amphibious landing exercise and conducted two days of scheduled—and hard to get—live-fire training ashore for Marine howitzer batteries and attack helos, as well as shore bombardment by *Barbour County* and *Durham*.

Vancouver's grounding and casualty reports requesting two new screws triggered an extensive coordination effort to assess the ship's damage and develop her repair options. The Navy repair facility at Subic Bay immediately dispatched its diver team headed by Commander John Hamilton to the ship to investigate the damage and develop repair recommendations. The Navy supply system located port and starboard replacement screws in Guam.

That evening I wrote in my journal, "…. Both screws damaged and need replacement. Messages and hot-line calls to the world. Investigation underway. Can't really see how this will end, but for now it is pretty bleak all around. *Vamos a ver*. I'll get her fixed…. So, that ends the cruise. From here on its explanations…. I will stick to my guns. We did the best we could. Sorry to see a fine ship and a fine staff hurt."

The Subic repair facility diver team arrived on *Vancouver* while we were at Lanclin and conducted an underwater hull inspection and vibration analysis prior to her return to port. Commander Hamilton agreed that the ship's screws had to be replaced before she could sail from Australia and resume operations.

There were two options: tow her to a dry-dock in Singapore or Subic to replace the screws and repair the hull; or conduct waterborne screw changes in Fremantle, then sail her with the ARG to Subic Bay and dry dock her there for the other repairs. *Denver* would replace her in the ARG.

The fleet admirals and the Australian Navy authorities concurred with my recommendation to conduct a double waterborne screw replacement with *Vancouver* berthed at HMAS Stirling naval base, Fremantle, for the repairs. A team of Australian Navy divers would assist the U.S. Navy diving team.

The U.S. Pacific Air Force command airlifted both large, heavy screws to Subic Bay together with a forklift capable of carrying them into and out of the massive Air Force C-5A Starlifter cargo aircraft. It stopped in Subic for the divers and their tools, equipment and rigging gear, then flew to the RAAF Pierce Airbase, about 50 miles north of Stirling.

Two huge flatbed trucks hauled the screws and rigging gear (95,000 pounds) through the cities of Perth and Fremantle at midnight with police escorts clearing all vehicles and traffic lights for passage of the wide loads, arriving pier side pre-dawn on May 6. The estimated completion date was May 13.

I reconfigured the ships to fit our reduced ARG capabilities, transferring all Marines from *Vancouver* to *Durham*.

¡El Capitán!

Early on the morning of May 1, Commodore Klee arrived, broke his flag in *Vancouver* and commenced his investigation. *New Orleans* and *Barbour County* entered port that afternoon.

On May 3, Admiral Foley and his entourage arrived from Sydney about noon at the Hotel Sheraton in Perth. Klee had arranged for us to meet with him there. During our drive to the hotel, I told Bob that I had brought the Lancelin AOA navigational chart to show the admiral the grounding details.

Bob objected, "The admiral is not going to be interested in that level of detail. We will just give him a quick overview and status and answer his questions!" I forcefully countered, "Foley was one of my navigation instructors at the academy and I worked for him as a sailing instructor during plebe summer after my graduation. I am confident he would be interested in seeing the chart!" After a period of silence, Klee said, "Okay Frank, it's your call."

We waited in the hotel lobby for the admiral. He arrived with his aide, my classmate, Captain Bill Pendley, and they greeted us. The admiral turned to Bill, "Where can we talk?" Bill replied, "How about over here in the cocktail lounge, sir." It was empty and we sat in the four leather lounge chairs around a low square table. I gave the admiral a status on *Vancouver*, the on-going repairs, and my intentions for the ARG until *Vancouver* could rejoin us. Bob presented the status of his investigation. The admiral listened and asked a couple of questions.

After a brief pause, I said, "Admiral, I brought the navigation chart. Would you like to see it?" He leaned forward in his chair, "Yes!" So I spread it out on the table and explained my exercise objectives and duration, the AOA, the boat lane, the beach, the ARG anchorages and disposition in the AOA, the point of grounding, and pertinent navigational features.

Foley examined the chart in silence, and then he turned to Klee, "Well Bob, I am sure you will look carefully at all of this and do what you have to do. Thank you gentlemen." Klee and I departed the hotel and returned to *Vancouver*—in silence.

That evening I attended a reception for Admiral Foley at the Australian Navy's Trafalgar House. Bill Pendley joked, "Frank, don't get too close to me—I don't want to get any coral dust on my shoes!" No matter the circumstances, running a classmate never ceases. We chatted about Foley and I told him about my relationship with him during my plebe summer tour, including his threat to fire me. Bill replied, "Oh yes, Frank, he remembers!"

After the reception I attended a dinner for Admiral and Mrs. Foley hosted by the American Consul. At the end of the evening as Foley was departing, I said. "Admiral, I hope my actions and my ships have not caused you any embarrassment here in Australia." He gripped my arm, "No, of course not, Frank!" As he turned to go, I said, "I wish I had stayed awake more in your navigation class!" Foley turned and looked back at me with hearty laughter.

It is a Navy tradition that official inquiries aboard ship are conducted at a table covered with a green felt cloth. When I commanded *Vancouver*, I refurbished the captain's cabin. I discovered that *Vancouver* did not have a green felt table cover, so I had one made, appropriately bordered with four gold stripes, befitting my rank.

On May 6, I faced Klee across "the long green table" and prepared to deliver my testimony. I could not help reflecting on life's vicissitudes— and its ironies. It was the first use of the beautifully adorned green felt table cover.

In developing my written preliminary statement for the inquiry, I summarized my experience in amphibious warfare including my ship commands, my squadron command philosophy, my demonstrated concerns for safety, my command relationships with the ship COs and CLF, my staff operations and decision-making process, and my specific objectives at Lancelin. Here are excerpts from the 21 pages and 15 attachments of my official statement:

> ... This is a preliminary statement regarding my command decision at Lancelin to place the anchorage for the PCS, USS *Vancouver* (LPD 2) at a distance of 2100 yards from the beach.... safety is always uppermost in my mind. The selection of the beach and anchorages were thoroughly coordinated with the CLF, the CO of the PCS, and the other ships of the ARG. The concept of operations and the boat lane and anchorages were briefed at the pre-sail conference by the CATF and CLF staffs for TG 76.3 and TG 79.4.... I also conducted an informal meeting with all of the ARG ship commanding officers in my cabin, with my CSO in attendance, to go over, once again, the concept of operations ....

In all the foregoing, no commanding officer raised the issue of the location of the anchorages to either me or my staff, nor did any other personnel of the task group, nor did the Australian liaison officers....

I am always acutely aware that each amphibious assault vehicle has 15 combat-equipped Marines embarked in their waterborne transit to the beach, and two waves that totaled 250 souls. They have an extremely poor chance of survival if the vehicle starts to sink.... CATF and CLF must jointly obtain permission from higher authority ... to (launch) more than 3600 yards from the beach, due to the increased ... risk....

In summary, my command decision at Lancelin was a well thought out, coordinated process that had safety as a primary consideration....

In my opinion, the primary reason for *Vancouver*'s reef strike was the inadequacy of the navigational chart in that the recorded depths therein are inaccurate, and the reef that *Vancouver* grounded upon in a ballasted condition is unmarked.

Klee completed taking testimony, hauled down his flag and returned to Okinawa on May 7.

The ARG's nine-day visit to Western Australia during Coral Sea Week was the major social event of the year for Western Australia and my squadron enjoyed the festivities. Despite the burdens of repairing *Vancouver*, reconfiguring the ARG, and preparing for my testimony, I had many protocol and social responsibilities in Perth and Fremantle. I made calls on the Governor of Western Australia, the Lord Mayor of Perth, the Naval Officer in Charge (Western Australia), and the CO of HMAS Stirling naval base.

I attended social events hosted by the Australian American Association, which organized the Coral Sea Week activities, including a "First Night" reception and dinner dance at which Admiral and Mrs. Foley, my ship captains and I were the guests of honor.

We also enjoyed a day at the racetrack featuring a race in which a horse was "named" for each of my ships. The race was televised, including my presentation of a prize to the winning jockey, on live TV.

I participated in *Durham*'s change of command and attended the MAU's change of command. I played a round of golf with my ship captains and Australian naval officers. (I managed not to hit any of the kangaroos on the fairways!) I hosted a luncheon and a dinner aboard my flagship for Australian Navy and civic officials.

And I took time to go back to the Perth Sheraton Hotel. Sitting alone at the table where my memorable face to face with Admiral Foley had occurred, I had a long drink while reflecting on my years since the memorable summer at the academy during my first duty as a new ensign—working for Lieutenant Foley.

On May 9, I sortied *New Orleans*, *Durham* and *Barbour County* to operate at sea near Fremantle while awaiting *Vancouver*'s return. I wrote in my journal, "This week was a rush of events … I'm drained. No word on the inquiry. Australian/American Association activities were incredible with so much genuine friendship. Australia is a great country with great people…. The final event was evensong at St. George's Cathedral … a wonderful way to wrap things up. I thank God for those precious few moments … in His presence."

On May 11, I flew to HMAS Stirling naval base and shifted my pennant to *Vancouver* for her sea trials. *Vancouver* got underway and conducted tests at various speeds and turns ahead and astern with no vibrations or other aberrations in either main engine or rudders. The screw changes were successful. I returned to my flagship by helo and shaped course for Subic Bay through the Sunda Strait, up the west coast of Borneo and through the Palawan Passage.

On May 15, I sent a message to Air Force, Navy, Marine Corps and Australian Navy and Pacific Fleet command authorities involved in repairing *Vancouver*,

> [a description of the situation and events] … on behalf of Vancouvermen and the Sailors and Marines of the Seventh Fleet Amphibious Ready Group, our sincere expression of … appreciation as well as a hearty 'Well Done' for the superb help of all personnel concerned, when help was sorely needed… Captain J.F. Gamboa, USN, Commander Amphibious Squadron Three and Commander Seventh Fleet Amphibious Ready Group sends.

On May 22, the ARG arrived at Subic Bay and we conducted our final Landex. *Vancouver* offloaded all remaining embarked Marines, tanks, vehicles, weapons, ammunition and logistic supplies to *Denver*, then she entered dry dock to repair her skeg keel and hull damage, and remove and reinstall both screws, which had to be "blued" onto the shafts (this couldn't be done underwater).

Together with Phil Kasky, my superb material officer, I participated in *Vancouver*'s repair conference with the Naval Ship Repair Facility. My goal was to ensure that she would be completely restored to top readiness. There was some consideration in Seventh fleet to delay her hull damage repairs until our return to San Diego, but I fought successfully to complete all repairs at Subic—her re-deployment schedule had no slack for dry-docking and repairs. I wanted to bring her home as she had left—in top condition.

The repair facility CO agreed and scheduled round-the-clock industrial work to repair her pit sword and skeg keel, and to complete the installation of her new screws.

My staff and I then conducted ARG ship visits to participate in the PRAV conferences, and do the final planning for *Vancouver*'s and *Durham*'s MTTs and OPPEs. We had succeeded in setting up the required services for our turn-around plan. Nonetheless, with all the additional work involved, I knew there was a human toll on my ships' crews—I was depriving the engineers and other personnel of much-deserved relaxation and recreation ashore. During *Durham*'s PRAV conference the chief engineer—an outstanding young naval officer—said it best, "Commodore, I never thought I would see Eastpac in Westpac." I felt the same way.

Commander, Seventh Fleet's flagship, USS *Blue Ridge*, visited Subic Bay while we were there. I paid a courtesy call on Vice Admiral Jimmy Hogg (USNA '56) and briefed him on the grounding, *Vancouver*'s repairs and the ARG's status. We enjoyed reminiscing about our days together in 17th Company.

I telephoned Linda to let her know how things were going and to talk about matters at home. As always, her moral support was critical to my morale. She was working full-time while studying for her bachelor's in business administration at National University while I was on deployment. She told me in one of her letters said, "Sweetheart, I think I aced my final tonight! I'll let you know…. I was happy to know that *Vancouver* is steaming with your squadron fast as ever. I hope the dry-docking doesn't expose additional damage…. You know best what has to be done, and I'm sure your intuition is right…. You're thinking toward the 10-month turn-around and the long-term good of the ship, the squadron and the Navy. Your right intuition is what makes you great and another man mediocre.... I love you. Only 49 days left! Linda."

In June, Commodore Klee submitted his investigation to Vice Admiral Hogg recommending that no disciplinary action be taken against me or *Vancouver*'s commanding officer. But Vice Admiral Hogg took a harder line and forwarded the investigation to Commander Amphibious Group Eastern Pacific, recommending that *Vancouver*'s commanding officer be charged with hazarding his ship. Hogg also issued me a non-punitive letter of caution:

> It has been established that this grounding was primarily attributable to *Vancouver* failing to navigate through unknown and hazardous waters using an incomplete chart that was so marked. The commanding officer persisted in directing his ship to an anchorage despite a number of factors present to warn him the margin of safety was so extremely narrow as to be unacceptable. Substantial damage was sustained by the ship. While, in the final analysis, commanding officers are ultimately responsible for the safety of their ships, it is apparent from the investigative report that you contributed to the unfavorable circumstances surrounding the grounding. As Commander Amphibious Squadron Three, you assigned the *Vancouver* anchorage. Emphasis was placed by you on close proximity to and safe control of landing craft by stationing the ship near the beach when a vantage point further out would have been adequate to accomplish all operational considerations and at the same time place the ship in a less dangerous location. After the grounding, you failed to aggressively seek additional information in order to file timely, accurate reports despite your being informed of *Vancouver*'s loss of pit sword and vibration problems. It was almost 26 hours before you reported to higher authority that grounding had occurred. Accordingly, you are administratively cautioned pursuant to reference (b) and (c). This letter, while non-punitive in nature and thus not becoming a part of your official record, is addressed to you as a corrective measure.

The amphibious assault exercise had been assigned to ARG Alfa by the Seventh Fleet amphibious task force commander. The AOA chart that we used was the latest one available. Neither in his tasking directive nor in all six previous exercise after-action reports was there any mention or reference to "unknown or hazardous waters" in our anchorage area, nor "an incomplete chart that was so marked."

While it is true that moving the anchorage 500 yards to seaward would have prevented this accident, this opinion is based mainly on 20-20 hindsight and the fact that I anchored her safely in that location after her reef strike.

Not highlighted in the investigation was the very relevant consideration that *Vancouver* was in a fully ballasted condition (much deeper draft at the screws) when she landed precisely on the pinnacle of the reef, straddling it between the screws and maximizing damage to both and the skeg keel. Neither did the report speculate if she would have grounded at normal steaming draft. Because of the nature of amphibious warfare, amphibious ships routinely navigate near the shoreline—and shoal water—carefully.

But I felt that the letter of caution was justified. When I decided to deliberately delay notifying higher authority, I knew that I was violating Navy regulations—and tradition,

After Phibron Three's return to San Diego in July, COMO Boland, commander amphibious group Eastern Pacific, convened a mast on *Vancouver*'s CO. At Boland's request, Australian authorities conducted a hydrographic survey of our Lancelin Beach exercise area and provided him an up-to-date navigational chart for his mast. Their survey confirmed that an uncharted reef with several pinnacles was located at *Vancouver*'s anchorage.

At the mast, I concluded my testimony as follows,

> Sir, this was my operation. I selected the anchorages based on the best information available and after weighing all the navigational and operational factors necessary to conduct a safe landing of LVTs and boat waves on the beach. My commanding officers exercised their best judgment; no commanding officer carelessly hazarded his ship. *Vancouver's* commanding officer took all reasonable precautions in proceeding to his assigned anchorage and in executing the tasks that I assigned to him. His ship struck an uncharted reef in a ballasted condition. If there is any blame to be fixed for this accident, it is mine alone. I accept complete responsibility for the grounding.

Boland dismissed all charges and forwarded his findings up the chain of command, recommending no further disciplinary action against me or the CO. His decision and recommendations were upheld.

The *Vancouver* grounding at Lancelin was the most serious and high-visibility mishap suffered by an amphibious force ship in the Pacific Fleet during my eight years in the force. And it was the cause of the most searing pain that I experienced in my naval career.

I have looked back at my amphibious assault at Lancelin with as much objectivity as I can muster, weighing again my frame of mind, my intentions, my planning, and my execution. Vice Admiral Hogg was right. The grounding would not have occurred had I moved the anchorages to seaward another 500 yards. But that was not what I did.

A couple of years later at a '58 tailgate in Annapolis, I had an opportunity to reminisce with Rear Admiral Bill Pendley about our memorable Perth hotel cocktail lounge meeting with Admiral Foley. I asked Pendley if Foley had ever commented about the grounding.

Bill reflected for a few moments. "Oh yes, now I recall. The admiral said that there is often a tendency among naval officers to push themselves too hard in accomplishing their mission."

Perhaps that is so, but that is also the nature of our profession.

On May 31, the ARG departed Subic and arrived at Okinawa the next day. Phibron One arrived the day after. On *Tarawa* we passed the ARG baton to Captain "Snake" Morris, who was CATF for Exercise VALIANT BLITZ at Okinawa, the second-largest amphibious exercise conducted by Seventh Fleet since WW II. I was in charge of the air assault. My ships preformed expertly. Then *New Orleans* and *Durham* went to Sasebo.

Following her successful sea trails, *Vancouver* resumed operations in ARG Bravo and joined *Denver* and *Barbour County* at Yokosuka. *Schenectady* sailed independently to Guam, and *Ramsey* was in Subic.

USS *Ramsey* (FFG 2) was a single-screw frigate that had been assigned to me after Rimpac for escort across the Pacific due to her relatively low fuel capacity. During our trans-Pacific voyages to and from Westpac one of my steam ships refueled her about every fourth day, both ships gaining valuable experience in rigging and conducting close-in fueling. We continued to operate with her from time to time during our deployment so I adopted her and included Cdr. Mike Clark in my CO luncheons when we were in port together. It was a pleasure to operate with *Ramsey*—a shipshape, heads-up frigate that was always on the mark.

As we prepared for our homeward journey I could not cut anyone any slack. *Denver*, *Barbour County* and *Vancouver* conducted their maintenance and material management system (3-M) inspections and received excellent grades, attesting to their good preparation. We conducted PRAV conferences for *Denver* and *Barbour County*. *New Orleans* accomplished Phase I mobile training for her post-deployment OPPE in San Diego. Having accomplished Phase I, *Durham* and *Vancouver* prepared for Phase II training in engineering casualty control drills enroute to Pearl Harbor.

Whenever I praised my ships and Marines, I first considered our mission and then the character of their performance, pride, and professionalism in fulfilling their loyal commitment to our nation. When ordered on extended overseas deployment—away from their homes and families—they spend countless and often lonely hours carrying out arduous, frequently hazardous tasks.

They don't do it for the money—America could never pay the full value of their dedicated service. They do it because they love their country and are loyal to their oath of service, earning and deserving their fellow citizens' respect and gratitude.

Accordingly, it is a leader's moral obligation to commend performance of duty by those under their command. With great satisfaction I sent the traditional farewell messages:

> To CTF 76: We have enjoyed working for you, and we look back with pride and satisfaction at the challenges afforded us in Team Spirit, Tangent Flash, Valiant Usher, Valiant Blitz, and SOG operations.... Your outstanding support throughout Phibron Three's Westpac '83 made it interesting, challenging and fun all the way.... Adios. Hasta La Vista.

> To the Marines, ... the Gators of Phibron Three extend best wishes to our friends and former shipmates, the Marines of 31 MAU. From Tok-Sok-Ri, to Subic, to Lancelin, we worked together to make all L-and H-hours on time. Our joint achievements and our safety record are a source of great professional pride for us.... Gators Three salute you, and bid you fond Adios, Hasta la Vista, and Semper Fidelis.

Captain John Frank Gamboa, U. S. Navy (Retired)

I sent similar messages to the BLT and Marine helo squadrons.

On June 29, we changed operational control to Third Fleet. In addition to our deployment mission and tasks, the squadron had accomplished all the planning and scheduling and had completed some of the major events for our follow-on deployment, a remarkable achievement by my ships and staff, especially considering the extra burdens imposed by *Vancouver*'s accident and repairs.

Though I had achieved all that I had set out to do, the grounding had cast a pall on me and my squadron. I was fatigued and feeling the strain of being in command, preparing for the deployment, and conducting task force operations 12-14 hours a day, seven days a week, day after day for more than nine months. The seemingly endless efforts had taken their toll. Everyone was weary, as reflected in my journal on our last day with Seventh fleet:

> The cruise was excellent. Ships all operated well.... Superb teamwork with the Marines. We met all commitments. We behaved ourselves in port.... My staff coordinated superbly, better than any staff I have been associated with.... OPPE workups are tough and have added a significant burden and stress on the ships and the COs, especially *Vancouver* and *Durham*.... It has been difficult for me and my family.... I have no regrets that my sea duty is coming to an end....

Working with my staff regenerated my enthusiasm. My spirits were also lifted by watching beautiful sunrises and sunsets each day during my exercise walks on the flight deck. I had my staff watch officer call and advise me on the expected quality of the event. I skipped it if the horizon was too cloudy.

Our toughest challenges—two OPPEs—still lay ahead of us. We had to pay attention, work the problems, and support "The Mighty Bull" (*Durham*) and "the Van-Can-Do." Each suffered engineering casualties while conducting drills, requiring repairs in Pearl.

In April, I had invited my former *Columbus* shipmate, Dr. David Chigos, president and founder of National University, and a captain in the Naval Reserve, to serve on my staff for the last leg of our voyage. David, his wife Ruth, and Linda, were on the pier at Pearl to welcome us. It was a wonderful surprise to see Linda a week sooner than I had expected.

I called on Commander, Naval Surface Group Middle Pacific Rear Admiral Conrad J. Rorie, Vice Admiral Lawrence, Commander Third fleet, and Admiral Foley. I discussed the deployment highlights. During my meeting with Rorie he told me that Foley, Lawrence and he were in agreement that I was the best squadron commander in the Pacific fleet. That really improved my morale!

We departed Pearl Harbor without *Durham*; her engineering repairs delayed her until the next morning. The Propulsion Examination Board started the OPPE in the afternoon and the next day she passed with flying colors. Meanwhile, she had fallen over 300 miles behind the squadron so she rang up a full bell and proceeded at 19 knots for 48 hours to catch up, demonstrating her high engineering readiness.

The PEB's transfer from *Durham* to *Vancouver* required expert flight planning and execution. The Mighty Bull was 60 miles astern of *New Orleans* and *Vancouver* was 120 miles ahead. We flew the PEB in *New Orleans'* helo to the flagship for lunch, and then to *Vancouver* in the afternoon.

After overcoming problems with her boiler feed water chemistry, *Vancouver* began her OPPE on July 12. The following night, I received the best news of the entire deployment: she passed!

I placed a radiotelephone call to Walsh, who was at a dinner party at the Admiral Kidd Officers' Club. I then sent the following message to the squadron, copy to Admirals Schrader, Ramsey and Walsh: "… With *Vancouver's* and *Durham's* successful OPPEs now history, all squadron deployment objectives are successfully accomplished. It was a clean sweep. Accordingly, all units will proudly fly one new broom from their halyards standing into San Diego. Well Done!" And I sent a personal to my captains:

> I wish to express to each of you my great admiration of your superb performance throughout the deployment. You met every challenge with enthusiasm, intelligence, and perseverance. You have established high standards of professionalism in Pacific Fleet's Amphibious Force. Your dedication and loyalty have inspired me. It has been a great personal pleasure and honor, and a real challenge, to operate with such a class group of commanding officers. Thank you for your support, which was exceptional throughout. Have a joyous

homecoming. WELL DONE! Warmest personal regards. Commodore sends.

I also sent a final laudatory message to all my ships and made my final journal entry of the deployment, "*Vancouver* passed her OPPE! Fantastic! What a <u>huge</u> victory for her and the squadron. A clean sweep! Never done before. But my God, what a travail. Nevertheless, our strategy was sound, and we got the help we needed. There was <u>never</u> a better squadron. I'm honored to be their squadron commander. I thank God for all his help and mercy. Foggy tonight, but we just keep pressing on. Had radar landfall at 2000. Called Linda; they will all be on the seawall at Ballast Point waiting for us."

On the morning of July 14 (our wedding anniversary), the squadron sailed proudly into San Diego harbor with all ships parading their crews in sparkling whites—and flying new brooms from their signal halyards. To my knowledge, no Pacific fleet squadron, Gator or DD, ever duplicated Phibron Three's twin OPPE success during homeward voyage from Westpac.

Shortly after our return, RADM Walsh was relieved by COMO Boland. Walsh evaluated my performance:

> Captain Gamboa is my best current squadron commander. He is ready now for flag rank of commodore, and I strongly recommend such selection by the next board to meet. His unsurpassed seamanship, broad warfare knowledge, vast amphibious experience and his enthusiastic, spirited and strong leadership style make him and his squadron second to none and indicate his readiness for positions of flag-level responsibility and authority...
>
> .... (His squadron) enters a ten-month quick turn-around period and then deploys his squadron to the western Pacific again. Of all my squadron commanders, he is best equipped for this difficult task.... Captain Gamboa is a totally superb professional whose dedication, superior warfare and sea-going knowledge make him invaluable to the Navy. He will be a strong and effective leader as a flag officer.... His ranking as 1 of 4 says it all. He is the best of the best in this category of all sequential command captains.

¡El Capitán!

After a happy and restorative period of leave with Linda, Jack and Judy and a family reunion in Las Vegas with Mom and my siblings, I turned my attention to the execution of our ten-month turn-around (TMTA) plan. We had to get off to a good start in the ships' PRAVs and do all jobs right the first time. My staff got into the nitty-gritty of the plan execution, visiting the ships and supporting shore commands to stay on top.

I met with each tender captain and all shore repair and maintenance facility commanding officers to solicit their support for our TMTA. I attended each ship's initial PRAV repair conference to set the tone. My policy was to participate thereafter only if there were issues to resolve and the COs needed my support—but not to do their job for them. My material officer attended every weekly ship's repair conference and facilitated resolution of issues.

At our daily staff meetings, each staff officer briefed from a milestones status board that we devised, which displayed all the ships' scheduled events under their cognizance, color-coded: black, in progress; red, behind schedule; green, complete. Effective leadership and management reduced our stress level and promoted enjoyable teamwork. "Commodore, we have a green board!"

About a week after *Schenectady*'s change of command, I paid a visit to the new CO. Over coffee in his cabin, I asked him for his opinion of our TMTA plan. He said, "Commodore, I think it's great! You have created a roadmap so my departments and I don't have to waste time trying to figure out what we have to do to get ready to deploy. All we have to do is execute. That's the fun part!"

At their request, my staff and I briefed two other amphibious squadron commanders on our approach.

In October, the USS *Alamo* (LSD 33) joined the squadron. They had just completed overhaul and were beginning workup for their OPPE and Reftra. My staff and I met with the new skipper and reviewed the status of his ship. His main concern was that the economizer tube bank in each boiler was not in good shape—they tended to spring leaks. He had tried to get them replaced during overhaul, but the Type commander would not fund the job. We quickly adjusted her schedule to conform to the squadron's milestones.

Captain John Frank Gamboa, U. S. Navy (Retired)

The TMTA included all areas of ship readiness except one. Here is a message that I sent to my good friend and fellow amphibious squadron commodore Captain Jeff Dennis, USNA '57, as he and his Phibron Seven were homeward bound from a Westpac.

> Personal for Commodore Dennis from Gamboa
> Subj: Boats/misc
>
> 1. From discussion with the Chief of Staff and the Commodore, I am made aware that you are deeply into planning your squadron's work-up for the next deployment. So I would like to pass on a "heads up" on an area that my ships did very poorly in preparing for, and that is, boat upkeep/repairs/preps for phibreftra.
>
> 2. Without exception, each ship failed to exercise what I consider long-range planning, proper inspection and preparation, and maintenance in getting ready for phibreftra. No command took advantage of the opportunity to off-load all boats at the end of 30 days leave and upkeep and send them over to the Naval Beach Group for thorough inspection, followed by proper ship's force documentation and submission for outside assistance as necessary. The COs, First Lieutenants and Chengs forgot about/ignored/neglected, etc. (insert derogatory adjective according to your personal style) the boats during PRAVs, and so when the phibreftra readiness inspections rolled around, there were casualties of every nature, flail-ex's, boat swaps, last-minute requisitioning, etc. Overall, a sorry spectacle for Gators.
>
> 3. As you may know, my own plans for getting the squadron ready listed everything a ship has to do. At times I felt like I was robbing my ships of initiative. So, I deliberately left the boats at the COs' discretion, with minimum guidance from me, i.e., "Ensure your boats are ready!" I was wrong to do so, and paid for the error by added work for my staff in laying on MCC/EMA support, and heartburn for me and the COs.
>
> 4. I would suggest that you direct each CO in no uncertain terms to get his boats inspected prior to PRAV and have your N4 shop go for a harbor cruise in each boat.

5. Otherwise, you may expect the usual message report to the Commodore from the Naval Beach Group airing all your ships' boat deficiencies (and others) and your discussion with Como Boland explaining why. Nuff said.

6. Looking forward to seeing you, Jeff. Warmest regards, Frank"

I never had to meet with a repair facility commander to resolve a job issue for my ships. I phoned several to thank them for successful resolution of a tough problem. All except one PRAV were accomplished on schedule. *Barbour County* was the lead ship in the new Pacific Fleet diesel engine OPPE program. Her PRAV problems and OPPE preps caused us to revise her schedule. Because of our advance preparation, the TMTA had flexibility, so there was no adverse impact.

My ships had all passed their OPPEs and had performed superbly in Reftra and amphibious refresher. We were ahead of the power curve. And then in December, Boland announced that *Durham* would be transferred to Phibron One on April 1, '84.

She was my most ready ship and Captain Chuck Barker was my best surface warfare officer. I was frustrated and angry to lose him and his superb ship.

In January 1984, the USS *Mobile* (LKA 115), a fleet reserve ship home ported in Long Beach, joined my squadron after months tied to the pier; she was struggling with engineering problems as she prepared for her OPPE.

After receiving Kasky's assessment of her engineering plant, I called her new commanding officer, Captain Lew Schriefer, USN, a Naval Academy aviator, and told him to get his ship down to San Diego as soon as possible.

Knowing that Sailors will help Sailors, I moored her alongside *Durham* for several days to "cross-pollinate" the crews. Then I met with the *Durham*'s crew and explained why they were leaving the squadron and asked them to help *Mobile* as much as possible. The Mighty Bull's crew responded as I expected; they pitched in to help *Mobile* get up to speed quickly on her OPPE, squadron ops, and what to expect in Seventh fleet.

My CSO and I met with Lew and reviewed his game plan to get ready. Then I held an All Hands Aft to welcome them—and gave them my first challenge. If they worked hard and got their ship ready to steam reliably by March, I would take them with me to Acapulco for four days of liberty. Their morale improved quickly—as did her readiness. She sailed with us to Mexico and performed very well.

The Mexico trips were excellent training—and a good incentive for my ships. We had two group sails ("Con Fritos I" and "Con Fritos II"). Leaving a planning and support unit headed up by Ed Kline ashore at the group headquarters, I embarked with the rest of my staff on *Vancouver* and sortied on February 13 in company with *Schenectady* and *Mobile*. My good friend and yachtsman, Henry Gladstone, was my special guest on *Vancouver*, along with several Navy Leaguers.

With assistance from the Naval Attaché in Mexico City, I made arrangements to meet in Acapulco with my cousin, Captain José Martin Avitia Herrera, who had graduated at the top of his class from the Mexican naval academy at Vera Cruz in 1962. I hosted José and his lovely wife Lorena for lunch aboard *Vancouver* and gave them a tour of the ship. He was the first Mexican Navy midshipman to sail on a U.S. Naval Academy midshipman summer cruise. In 1985, José Martin was deep-selected to Rear Admiral.

Enroute back to San Diego, we received the great news that *Alamo* had passed her OPPE.

At home, Linda was preparing for the wedding of our daughter. It was a beautiful event, but sadly, Linda's father had suffered a mild heart attack the day before and was in the hospital. After the wedding, Judy and her new husband had the limo drive from the church directly to the hospital to visit him in her wedding gown. The reception was lovely and it filled the Admiral Kidd Club and overflowed into a huge tent on the lawn.

Two days later, I was back aboard *New Orleans*, ready to shape course for Acapulco with *Durham*. Linda and her mother, aunt, brother, sister-in-law, and the newly-weds were my guests on board for breakfast before we got under way. Then they drove back to Ballast Point to wave goodbye from the seawall as we exited the channel.

I had invited the Marine Corps band from Camp Pendleton to join us and provide some great music enroute. On our voyage back to San Diego, I recorded my thoughts, "...Con Fritos I & II were ... a superb success, a great boost in training for the ships and a great reward for their hard work. All enjoyed the liberty ... (and) gained an appreciation for Mexico.

The band was magic and their city plaza concert was very well received… With our Marine counterpart staff aboard, we have successfully planned Kernel Usher 84-1A…. We are ahead in the overall planning…." While we were enjoying our port visit, *Mobile* passed her OPPE.

The last phase of the TMTA, was completed on time in great shape. One underway training requirement remained: amphibious Reftra for *Barbour County*.

On April 23, I sortied the squadron for the first time since our return from deployment. It felt good to be back at sea with my ships. *Denver* had remained in port recovering from her Insurv inspection (she passed) and *Barbour County* was completing the last week of her amphibious Reftra, conducting causeway operations and beaching.

The main focus of our squadron ops was Marine helo flight training and touch and goes on each flight deck, and amphibious rehearsals off of Camp Pendleton with the new the '53 Echo Marine heavy lift helos as a tune-up for fleet exercise KERNEL USHER.

At sunset on April 25 as I was sitting down for dinner in my cabin, the communications center passed me an urgent message: *Barbour County* was hard aground, broached starboard-side-to, on Coronado's Silver Strand in San Diego. She had been conducting a beaching exercise, her final amphib Reftra requirement—literally driving the ship's bow onto the beach to disembark vehicles. The weather had deteriorated, the wind and surf picked up, and her stern anchor failed to hold and the surf drove her onto the beach broadside.

After extensive coordination, we stood up a salvage effort. Several tugs and a salvage ship pulled her off the beach at high tide the next evening. She was badly damaged, and in late May, she was removed from my squadron without replacement. She spent six months in a shipyard undergoing $18 M of repairs. She was not operational for over a year. Her grounding occurred a year and two days after *Vancouver*'s grounding at Lancelin.

In the fall of 1983, I was contacted by Vice Admiral Lando Zech, the Chief of Naval Personnel, to request my assistance to the bureau and the Navy recruiting command in their Hispanic recruiting initiatives. The Navy was trying to increase its number of Hispanic officers. I was one of the very few Hispanic line captains in the Navy, and the only one in command. I agreed to help.

In March 1984, I took Jose M. Burrell, Ph.D., superintendent of Santa Cruz Valley Union High School in Eloy, Arizona, to Acapulco aboard *New Orleans*.

In April 1984, I embarked Hispanic newspaper reporters from the Los Angeles' *"20 de Mayo"* to witness the ARG's amphibious training operations at San Clemente Island and Camp Pendleton.

I spoke at Hispanic heritage events in San Diego and Oakland, and I participated in a conference in Albuquerque, New Mexico, hosted by the Association of Naval Services Officers (ANSO), created by Secretary of the Navy Ed Hidalgo to recruit Hispanic officer candidates. I enjoyed my participation in these activities, but I had no desire to be diverted from my duty preference: A tour in OPNAV—either amphibious warfare or communications.

On March 5, 1884, the assistant secretary of the navy (manpower and reserve affairs) received a memorandum from the deputy assistant secretary of defense for equal opportunity and safety policy requesting that the Navy submit three nominations for director of defense military equal opportunity, a military 0-7 billet (flag or general officer) "... responsible for policy development and program oversight relating to equal opportunity for military personnel in the Department of Defense...." The deputy was Hispanic and she desired that a Hispanic naval officer (this was not a stated requirement for the billet) with command experience be nominated for the new position.

Well, it took about a microsecond for chief of naval personnel Bill Lawrence and the CNO Jim Watkins to figure out who they would nominate—they could count on one hand or less the Navy's Hispanic senior line officers with command experience. My detailer (Captain Taylor Keith, classmate and friend) called and told me to report ASAP to the Pentagon for interviews.

I was very upset by this turn of events and not at all fooled by the dazzling prospect of a flag billet, having already served in two joint billets in which I was two ranks junior for the positions, with no effect on my promotion. And I deeply resented being used as a token Hispanic based simply on the personal desires of a novice political appointee.

When I arrived in Washington, I met with Vice Admiral Lawrence to express my objection to the assignment and my professional desires to be assigned to the CNO's staff, but to no avail. He had marching orders for me from the CNO and the Secretary of the Navy. On May 2, I received orders to report to the secretary of defense for duty as his director of military equal opportunity, dooming my last opportunity to serve in OPNAV.

Phibron Three achieved the highest material and operational readiness certifications during my time in the amphibious force. The ships' grades in 3-M systems and medical readiness inspections were the highest ever recorded in the Pacific Fleet naval surface force. All ships enjoyed a one-month POM period free of inspections, training and urgent repairs, permitting crews time off to attend to their personal affairs.

The squadron sailed on May 30. We conducted amphibious exercise Kernel Usher 84-1 off San Clemente and Camp Pendleton, and then we joined forces with two battle groups and the Japanese, Australians, New Zealanders and Canadians and participated in Rimpac-84. We arrived in Pearl Harbor on June 14 for ten days of upkeep and maintenance. Linda flew to Hawaii to enjoy a few days on the beach with me and to plan our move to Washington.

Between June 25 and 28, my squadron successfully conducted amphibious exercises at Kahoolawe and Kauai with two carrier battle groups in support—an abundance of air and surface fire power, and then returned to Pearl to victual and top off fuel. We had achieved all our TMTA and Rimpac requirements.

In spite of our hard-won successes, fate had played—and kept on playing—cruel tricks on Phibron Three. First, we lost *Durham*, my most ready ship. Then came *Barbour County*'s disastrous broaching that removed her from my squadron without replacement. I had six ships.

During the Rimpac amphibious exercise, *Denver* developed a major boiler steam line leak that required an 11-day shipyard repair in Pearl. *Vancouver* developed a severe vibration in her starboard main engine, which sent her to the shipyard for replacement of a damaged steam turbine, a three-week delay.

When the squadron departed for Westpac, I left both ships in the shipyard and sailed with four. Then just as she was completing her repairs, *Vancouver*'s deployment was cancelled and she was sent back to San Diego, the direct result of a new Pacific Fleet policy to significantly reduce Seventh Fleet's amphibious force operational tempo, reducing my squadron to five ships.

On July 2, *Alamo*, *New Orleans*, *Mobile* and *Schenectady* sailed for the chop line in company with the Enterprise battle group. I rendezvoused with Commodore Harry Gimbers's out-chopping squadron and flew to his LHA flagship *Belleau Wood*, commanded by my good friend and former detailer Captain Frank Donovan. We took the baton, embarked the 31 Mau commander and staff, then we rejoined Seventh Fleet. We felt right at home again. We had only been gone ten months.

On July 4, *Alamo* suffered casualties to both of her boilers: leaking economizer tubes (oh yes, the ones the Type commander refused to fund for replacement during overhaul), causing her to go dead in the water and fall 100 miles astern. I sent *Mobile* back to take her under tow if necessary and return her to Pearl Harbor for repairs, but we got a lucky break. *Alamo* had a boiler repairman in her engineering department and he was able to plug all the leaking tubes, permitting her to relight fires and proceed to catch up with *New Orleans*.

I assigned *Schenectady* to continue to Westpac with the carrier group and directed *New Orleans* to proceed independently to Iwo Jima to conduct our first Seventh Fleet exercise. *Alamo* and *Mobile* would join up with us after.

On July 15, we conducted a simulated non-combatant evacuation exercise on Iwo. We then flew all the Marines ashore so they could march up to the summit of Mt. Suribachi, as requested by the BLT commander, Lt. Col. Chuck Krulak (later Commandant of the Marine Corps).

The MAU commander and *New Orleans* skipper accompanied me on calls on the Japanese Navy island commander and the naval air station commander. Afterwards, we toured the island and some of the WW II caves. We ended our tour at the summit of Mt. Suribachi, enjoying a spectacular view of Invasion Beach. *New Orleans* remained at anchor offshore overnight.

The next morning before we got underway for Subic, the ship's captain, the MAU commander, the chaplain and I conducted a memorial service on the flight deck in remembrance of the Sailors and Marines who died capturing Iwo Jima.

¡El Capitán!

New Orleans shaped course for Subic Bay. We overtook *Mobile* and *Alamo* as well as the oiler USNS *Passumpsic* in order to refuel my ships one last time before entering port.

Prior to our sortie from San Diego, COMO Boland had requested a description of our TMTA plan to share with his staff and his other Phibron commanders. We transmitted six different messages, one for each functional area, and a summary message outlining my approach. The TMTA was the most complex—and the toughest—technical and operational challenge of my career. I had to plumb the depths of my shipboard experience in thinking through the issues, structuring my approach, and training my staff, my COs, and their respective wardrooms and CPO messes.

My basic approach was management by goals and objectives. The study and research required to identify, validate and compile all ship and squadron pre-deployment requirements, and to negotiate the best sequence of events with each ship, the group and type commanders and the waterfront maintenance and training commands were hard work for me, my staff and my ships.

No organized, integrated compilation of an amphibious squadron's pre-deployment requirements (560)—in effect a master pre-deployment check-off list—existed prior to Phibron Three's TMTA plan. It was born of dire necessity, the mother of invention.

I thoroughly enjoyed engaging with my staff, my ships, the tenders and repair ships, the waterfront maintenance centers, repair organizations, training units, and the group and force commands involved in this complex enterprise.

My staff and I became smarter and more professional in achieving squadron readiness and making life more enjoyable for all my ships' companies—and their families.

The collegiality and teamwork that I experienced with my staff and my ships' wardrooms and chiefs' messes enriched my life and made me a better naval surface warfare officer and commodore.

On the morning of July 19, I completed my last at-sea staff meeting and went to the bridge to relax in my chair and enjoy a cup of coffee with my staff watch officer. It felt great to be at sea on a beautiful day in company with my ships. As I thought about my last Seventh Fleet operation the next morning—fueling ships at sea—my staff communications officer handed me a high-precedence and specially-encoded message (for my eyes only) from CTF 76:

> ARG Alfa Message Traffic
> (four referenced messages)
> 1. Ref a states you concur on a recommendation from ComSeventhFlt to ComThirdFlt. Ref b implies you non-concur with my direction concerning keeping *Alamo* in Subic for repairs. Ref c states you non-concur with me in handling of Cobra Gold Eagle control. It is inappropriate and presumptive for juniors to concur or non-concur with their seniors. Further, you aired your disagreement in traffic addressed to other commands. Knock it off. You command the task group but I command the task force.
> 2. I understand *Alamo* has contacted SRF Subic to request following additional work be undertaken during forthcoming port visit, unsupported by casualty reports.... Request you follow up and be prepared to brief me on the full extent of *Alamo*'s material problems when I see you. Respectfully, Como. McCaffree.

I folded the message into my pocket, left the bridge, went down to the flight deck and paced alone for about twenty minutes, breathing deeply of the sea air. Then I went to my cabin and drafted my reply to this scathing rebuke—the only one that I ever received as a naval officer:

> ARG Alfa Message Traffic
> A. CTF 76 190500Z Jul 84
> 1. WILCO.
> 2. I have re-read messages cited, and in the cool light of a new day I can see now that my messages were not adequately staffed from the standpoint of your prerogatives, and I sincerely regret the tone. I apologize for any embarrassment or inconvenience I caused you. My intent since my squadron departed San Diego 51 days ago has been to work each problem to the best of my ability in order to provide you a ready squadron, on station, ready to execute your desires and tasking in the best way we can.

3. I take this opportunity to reiterate my fullest loyalty and support to you, Commodore.

4. New subject. In view of the problems reported by *Alamo*, I would like to change our schedule Sunday to start with a briefing and tour aboard *Alamo*. We can then go to *New Orleans* for a briefing on each ship, followed by a brief on Cobra Gold. I will send a message on this for your comment. Overall, I fully support your approach on *Alamo*'s readiness for extended ops.

5. The intent of my recommendations vis-à-vis repairs on economizers is to not commence reconfiguration of the ARG until the repair alternatives are available. In that regard, my plan for reconfiguration is being fleshed out within the ARG. You can appreciate my need to keep the MAU CDR and elements, as well as all my ships, on an even keel throughout the process while minimizing the heartburn. It is most disruptive to the ARG teamwork and landing plan, but we will do it, and smartly, if so directed. Start time must be no later than 1300 Monday in order to sail on time, and all hands will be ready to execute.

6. Meanwhile, for your info, I have overtaken *Alamo* and *Mobile* and have them and *Passumpsic* under my tactical command. We will top off *Mobile* and *New Orleans* in the morning prior to entering port. *Alamo* declined as she is on one boiler while cooling the other for inspection. I'm enjoying my last night at sea with my ships and my last after eight consecutive years at sea. The fun is over too soon.

7. I will meet you at the airport, Commodore. Warm regards and very respectfully, Frank.

This was the most confrontational episode that I ever had with a flag officer. In January 1984, Wirt Fladd had transferred to Bupers. The situation would never have come to pass had he been my CSO. A commodore needs a deputy to protect him from his own aggressiveness—and inflated ego—especially in tense situations or in developing an urgent course of action. Wirt and I had that kind of relationship. His capable relief and I were getting there, but unfortunately, not enough Pacific Ocean had passed beneath my flagship's keel.

Captain John Frank Gamboa, U. S. Navy (Retired)

After replying to the commodore, and to assuage my bruised ego, I drafted and sent my final message to my ships, including *Barbour County* and *Durham*, who were no longer in my squadron:

> Gracias y Adios
>
> 1. For All. As I prepare to haul down my pennant, I want to express my profound admiration and sincere appreciation to you and your officers and men for your outstanding performance during the twenty-one months I have had the honor to be your commodore. Your record of notable achievements in Westpac 83 is unequalled. Your legendary accomplishments ... between Westpacs have established a new standard of excellence in the Amphibious Group.
> 2. For the Mighty Bull *Durham* and *Barbour County*, your sterling performance in Westpac 83 and during workup is remembered with pride, respect, and affection.
> 3. As you take on duties in Seventh Fleet, I am confident that your pride and professionalism will see you through to an outstanding cruise, second to none. Fair winds and following seas.
> 4. For my staff, your hard work, total dedication to duty, unswerving loyalty, and inspirational performance in all your endeavors has made my job a total pleasure. Your professionalism in developing and supporting the squadron's ten month turn-around, and the quality of your planning for amphibious operations has established you as the premier amphibious squadron staff in the Pacific Fleet.
> 5. For all. Farewell, and my sincerest WELL DONE. Commodore Gamboa sends.

The ARG arrived in Subic and I enjoyed a pleasant surprise. The Pacific Stars and Stripes newspaper edition dated July 19, 1984, featured a full-page article with pictures of me and my flagship and my comments on my job as a squadron commander. I had been interviewed before my departure from San Diego, but had thought no more about it.

The commodore arrived the next morning and I accompanied him to *Alamo* to determine her status. Then we went to the flagship for a briefing on the ARG and Exercise COBRA GOLD in Thailand. That night I made my final journal entry before turning in, "McCaffree arrived at 1000 and we had a nice day visiting *Alamo*; briefs in *New Orleans*; and dinner with the CSO, my relief Howard Eldridge, and the COs of *New Orleans*, *Mobile*, *Schenectady* and *Alamo* at the O'Club. A nice way to go. (*Denver* arrived the day after I left.) *Alamo* will stay in Subic to do the economizer repairs and miss Cobra Gold (*Denver* took her place). I hope she joins by Singapore."

Commodore McCaffree's evaluation of my fitness was brief (I served under his command only 12 days). He recommended me for duty in OPNAV as chief of staff in the amphibious warfare division, and for promotion to flag rank. COMO Boland's report of my fitness was top-drawer:

> Captain Gamboa is a splendid naval officer whose dynamic leadership established the highest standards of performance both operationally and materially throughout Amphibious Squadron Three....Illustrative of his significant accomplishments throughout this period include: (listed eight results)...
>
> Captain Gamboa's demonstrated leadership encompasses a wide range of skills.... He is a consummate organizer and negotiator who can bring out the best in the planning process, pull together the resources to support the plan, and finally, bring about favorable results through dedicated training, devoted hard work, and meticulous supervision...
>
> Frank Gamboa is a most resourceful and polished naval officer. He was my best seagoing squadron commander. He has unlimited potential for future growth within the Navy and should be assigned to only the most demanding billets afloat or ashore. He is ready now to assume the responsibilities commensurate with flag rank and should be promoted now.

The underlining was his, and Boland recommended me for a Legion of Merit, but it was downgraded somewhere higher up in the chain to a Meritorious Service Medal,. The medal citation echoed the fitness report.

I relinquished command on July 23 in a traditional ceremony held in *New Orleans*' hangar bay. It was well attended with destroyer, cruiser, carrier and shore station COs, the CVBG rear admiral, and other flag officers, with a reception in the wardroom. COMO McCaffree delivered great remarks—a classic description of our nation's maritime strategy and the role of its naval amphibious forces:

Captain John Frank Gamboa, U. S. Navy (Retired)

.... By virtue of the ocean areas, which separate the United States of America from the markets of the world and from most of our allies, the U.S. has always been a maritime nation. We have understood the importance of sea power to our national survival and the value of strong naval forces to our national objectives. Naval operations enable us to carry the battle to the enemy; hence they are principally offensive in nature. Our maritime strategy emphasizes the offensive capabilities of the Navy and Marine Corps to establish sea control over vital ocean areas and to project power in times of conflict.... Amphibious assault is the most complex of naval operations, with major difficulties and risks but great strategic advantages when executed successfully.....

Amphibious forces are the most uniquely equipped and useful of all naval forces to accomplish a wide variety of tasks. They are capable of conducting major combat operations. They are especially well suited for limited intervention to protect United States' interests overseas and to support beleaguered friendly governments....

The planning and execution of (these tasks) are the responsibility of Commander Amphibious Squadron Three. He must plan, rehearse and conduct each exercise to achieve the greatest benefit to his task group. Each tactical exercise and amphibious landing must be innovative.... Comphibron Three has other responsibilities and concerns as well. He must constantly watch the material condition of his ships and naval support elements and know when and how to turn a deteriorating material situation around....

The officer who now commands Amphibious Squadron Three was recently profiled in the Stars and Stripes. He exemplifies the experienced and exceptional quality naval officer upon whom the Navy bestows special trust and confidence by his assignment to an amphibious squadron command. He is Captain Frank Gamboa, United States Navy. Captain Gamboa is one of the Navy's most experienced and senior amphibious warfare officers. He has commanded Phibron Three with distinction for the past two years.

Captain Gamboa, I congratulate you on your many successes while in command and on the reputation you enjoy within our

¡El Capitán!

Navy. I wish you great success in your challenging duties and new responsibilities in the office of the secretary of defense....

Here are the highlights of my farewell to my squadron and to fleet operations:

Welcome, *bienvenidos*, and thank you for honoring us with your presence today. It means a great deal to Captain Eldredge and me that you chose to attend this very special occasion. Our families could not attend, but we feel very much at home and among special friends here in Subic Bay.... I am particularly glad to see our professional superiors and peers from the Naval Air Force and the Cruisers and Destroyers. I hope this cultural exchange visit with the Seventh Fleet's Navy-Marine Amphibious Force Team will be mutually beneficial.

Thank you for your compliments Commodore McCaffree. I deeply appreciate your being here today....

... I don't want to expound on the number of exercises that we've conducted during the past 21 months because it will make my staff feel they are overworked. Despite what the Stars and Stripes says ... I can't really claim to have advanced the state of the art of amphibious warfare, but I hope I have made a contribution towards its continuity. Therefore, before I read my orders and haul down my pennant, and go ashore after these past eight years of sea duty in the Pacific Fleet, I want to share with you just a few happy memories that I take with me from this, the most challenging and exciting assignment I have ever had.

... I have been privileged to serve with outstanding Commanding Officers and ships. There are none finer in the fleet. Their enthusiastic support kept me and my staff working hard to keep up with them...

Amphibious ships are built to carry Marines. Marines ... can be very intimidating, and I'm glad, because they have to be tough to carry out their mission.... I have been honored to work with you and observe your combat expertise close up.

My staff members are the waterfront experts in their respective areas of responsibilities, and no one does it better than they do, the premier amphibious planners and doers in the fleet,

Captain John Frank Gamboa, U. S. Navy (Retired)

Muchas gracias por todo. You'll have to understand that they had to become bi-lingual.

Coming to Subic is always a happy occasion for me. I was here when my captain promotion came out, and in one of those typically grand romantic gestures that naval officers make from time to time, I called Linda and she flew out to join me here for our celebration. By the time we did Subic, Baguio, Manila and Hong Kong, my captain's promotion pay for the next two years was gone. But we were having fun....

Another memorable experience is the cultural heritage journey that I enjoyed ... sailing my ships to the Mexican Riviera.... And then sailing ... along the same voyage track as my ancestors in their Spanish galleons—this is as far as they came—to these beautiful Philippine Islands where there are many Gamboas. So it is a nice feeling for me to end my voyage here also.

Finally, my wife and children and family and I have farewelled each other in San Diego these past eight years more times than I care to recall. But what I treasure most is that some of the nicest things we've ever said to each other, we said in our letters as we kept in touch across the vast Pacific Ocean. So I remember them this morning and thank them for their constant love and support throughout.

Captain Eldredge, I congratulate you on your assignment and wish you every success and happiness with Amphibious Squadron Three. I will now read my orders....

Captain Pafias, please haul down my pennant.

¡El Capitán!

USS *Fort Fisher* (LSD 40) Pacific Fleet, 1976. (US Navy photo)

Enriqueta and her son aboard *Fort Fisher*, Long Beach, CA, December 3, 1976. (Personal collection)

Captain John Frank Gamboa, U. S. Navy (Retired)

Fort Fisher Wardroom in Western Pacific, Navy birthday, October 13, 1977.
(Personal collection)

Amphibious Squadron Five, WESTPAC September'77- April '78. (US Navy photo)

¡El Capitán!

Fort Fisher and Brillig in South China Sea, January 1978. (US Navy photo)

Presenting *Fort Fisher* plaque to our cousin, Miguel Garcia, the Catholic Bishop of Mazatlan, Mexico, June 1978

Captain John Frank Gamboa, U. S. Navy (Retired)

USS *Tarawa* (LHA 1) 1980. (US Navy photo)

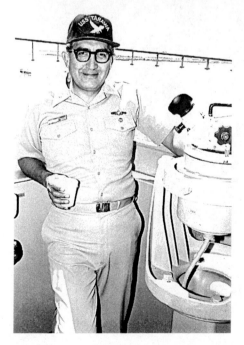

Tarawa Executive Officer, San Diego harbor, May 1980. (Personal collection)

USS *Vancouver* (LPD 2), Pacific Fleet 1981. (US Navy photo)

Vancouver Wardroom and wives at Gator Ball, Coronado, CA. August 1982. (Personal collection)

Captain John Frank Gamboa, U. S. Navy (Retired)

Commodore, Amphibious Squadron Three, November 1982. (US Navy photo)

Seventh Fleet Amphibious Ready Group Alfa, WESTPAC January '82-July '83. (US Navy photo)

¡El Capitán!

MAU Commander, me, VADM Harry Schrader and CO USS *New Orleans*. Hong Kong, April 1983. (US Navy photo)

Capitan de Navio Jose Martin Avitia Herrera, Mexican Navy, his wife Lorena, and me aboard *Vancouver* at Acapulco, Mexico, March 1984. (Personal collection)

Captain John Frank Gamboa, U. S. Navy (Retired)

Iwo Jima memorial service USS *New Orleans* flight deck, July 1984. (US Navy photo)

Relinquishment of squadron command at Subic Bay, Philippine Islands, July 1984. (US Navy photo)

Part V

The Pentagon

In The E-Ring

Chapter Eleven

★ ★ ★ ★ ★ ★ ★

We hold these truths to be self-evident, that all men are created equal.

— Thomas Jefferson

I arrived in San Diego in time to help Linda pack out our household goods for our drive to Virginia. For the first time, we would move to a new duty station without our children. Jack was a freshman in the University of California at San Diego, and Judy was married, working and studying at National University in San Diego. Our nest was empty. At our farewell breakfast in Old Town, Jack did his best to cheer us up, "Well Mom and Dad, just go back there and have fun and grow old together!"

Starting the aging process, we drove straight to Las Vegas and enjoyed the shows and casinos, and visited my sister Erlinda and her husband Jean and their children. Driving again across America the beautiful, we crossed the Great Basin of Nevada and Utah, traversed the Rockies and the continental divide, motored across the Great Plains, toured the Eisenhower presidential library in Abilene, Kansas, then crossed the Mississippi, passed through the Ohio Valley where we visited with Linda's aunt Anne in Thompson. After several days of house hunting in Arlington, Virginia, we moved into a Rosslyn penthouse condo. No kids, no pets – we were living like grown-ups. I would ride the Metro to work.

At long last, I was in the Pentagon, but my office was in the basement and I had no horizon view. The defense military equal opportunity programs office was organizationally in the defense manpower, installations and logistics directorate headed by Assistant Secretary of Defense Larry Korb. I reported to the deputy assistant secretary of defense (DASD) for equal opportunity and safety policy.

My staff included one female Marine Corps colonel, one male Air Force Lt. Col., one male Army captain and an Air Force enlisted female secretary. I was responsible for policy formulation, oversight and coordination of the military departments' equal opportunity programs.

409

I also had oversight of the Defense Equal Opportunity Management Institute (DEOMI) in Melbourne, Florida, which is responsible for training human relations specialists for all defense department component agencies, analyzing armed forces personnel data and statistics, conducting research, and developing unit assessment tools and training initiatives.

Linda had completed her bachelor's and master's degrees, and found herself without a job, no kids at home, and no Navy wives group to fill her days. She decided to volunteer at the second Reagan presidential inaugural committee and she was soon working long hours every day.

After the president's swearing in, she was retained as a member of a small staff to wrap up the inaugural affairs. She was then invited to volunteer in the White House's beautiful old executive office building; her ornate office even had a fireplace.

She worked for Fred Ryan, the president's scheduler. She helped screen charities for distribution of leftover inaugural funds, and co-created two monthly White House newsletters, *White House Highlights* and *Private Sector Initiatives*. Several months later, she was awarded a political appointment at the Veterans Administration in the public affairs office, where she would be working for the director, my classmate and our good friend, Don Jones.

Linda wrote letters for President Reagan's signature and speeches for him to record for veterans associations' conferences; assisted with the annual "National Salute to Hospitalized Veterans," chaired by various movie stars; testified before Congress on the issue of homeless veterans; and created a national VA public affairs training program, which had her traveling around the country.

Linda won an award and a promotion for the best training program design in the federal government. During presidential trips she was often detailed back to the White House to fill in for the news summaries staff, who were traveling with the president. She went on to serve in President George H.W. Bush's administration.

I got acquainted with my key service secretariat and military department counterparts, and learned the issues. I accompanied the DASD to the Naval Academy to discuss the academy's EO program with Superintendent Rear Admiral Chuck Larson.

I also had to design and oversee the construction of a new office in the A ring for the combined civilian and military EO staffs, coordinating with the famed Doc Cook, the Mayor of the Pentagon. My ship construction and overhaul savvy came in very handy. I greatly enjoyed working with Mr. Cook, a former Navy captain.

In April 1985, the DASD resigned. Secretary Korb called me into his office and told me, "Frank, you commanded ships so you can sure as hell do the job of a deputy assistant secretary!" He appointed me as the DASD EO.

I promptly moved into the DASD's oversized office in the exalted "E" ring. My peers in OSD and the service secretariats were three-star generals, flag officers and senate-confirmed presidential appointees. A few days later, I called on Congressman John McCain, explained my new job and asked for his advice. Smiling, he said "Pal, just stay off the front page of the Washington Post!"

I served as an ex-officio member of the defense advisory committee on women in the service (DACOWITS) created by President Harry Truman in 1951. Its 33 members were from academia, corporate America and the public sector, including retirees from the armed forces and congress. I traveled with several DACOWITS members to the Military Academy at West Point and Vandenberg Air Force Base in California to see how women were treated. And with Lt. Col. Wiggins, I traveled to an Army post and an Air Force base in Germany to assess their respective EO programs. These activities helped me determine the scope of my responsibilities and gauge the impact of Defense EO policy within the armed forces.

Soon after my arrival in the Pentagon I discovered a debilitating perception: EO staffs were considered to be "stove-pipe" organizations that served in an advisory capacity rather than as a line organization, as if EO did not fall within the military chain of command. Contributing to this perception was the fact that, in OSD, the military EO staff was not part of the OSD military manpower and personnel directorate headed by a three-star general.

Since its creation by Secretary McNamara in 1963, the EO Office had consisted of the military personnel EO staff and the civilian personnel EO/EEO staff reporting directly to the DASD EO. Neither staff participated effectively in OSD's personnel policy formulation, which reinforced the perception that military EO was purely advisory.

From my perspective, there was no consistent accountability for EO from the office of the secretary of defense down to the ship division level or the company level in Army, Air Force or Marine Corps. I concluded that the McNamara-era EO office was outmoded and ineffective.

Even so, the Navy department was moving to incorporate its EO program into the chain of command through a new initiative called the command-managed EO program, but it needed reinforcement from OSD. I therefore met periodically with the CNO to brief him on how the Navy's EO posture looked from the OSD perspective. In my first meeting with Admiral Watkins, he told me, "Frank, I value your input because my pronouncements to the fleet on EO have a half-life of about three months!"

Through working the issues, I resolved that I would attempt to reorient the entire domain of military EO into the chain of command. Commanding officers simply had to be held accountable for their personnel's equitable and fair treatment.

I thought the first step was to dissolve the DASD EO Office and incorporate its military and civilian EO staffs into the respective military manpower and civilian personnel staffs. But after several futile attempts, I concluded that, in OSD (as well as the president's other cabinet agencies), major changes in organizations and their way of doing things are driven by presidential policies and implemented by political appointees.

In September 1985, Larry Korb resigned and was replaced by Chapman Cox (a Marine Corps Reserve Lt. Col.). In our first meeting, I briefed him on the lay of the land and advised him that military EO was primarily a leadership issue that belonged in the chain of command. I also expressed my opinion of the OSD EO organization: it was organizationally outmoded, mission ineffective and should be dismantled and reconfigured within the respective OSD military and civilian manpower directorates.

Cox agreed with me. And he was very clear about his role and his intentions. "I consider myself to be the secretary of defense's principal EO official and I want do a few things to improve EO in the armed forces!"

Captain John Frank Gamboa, U. S. Navy (Retired)

His first major initiative was to create an EO council consisting of the services' assistant secretaries for personnel. He would chair the council and I would be its executive director. My recommendation to do away with the DASD EO office and incorporate its staff elements into the respective military and civilian manpower staffs fit perfectly with his approach. But we realized we would face entrenched bureaucratic opposition in doing away with the ineffective, albeit relatively high profile DASD EO office.

Several weeks later—after coordinating with his military and civilian personnel deputies and his counterpart service secretariat assistant secretaries—Cox announced his planned EO organizational changes in OSD. I briefed the service assistant secretaries for manpower one-on-one on his initiative and then relayed their reactions to Cox after each of my meetings. We then formulated a change strategy and implementation tasks for abolishing the McNamara-era EO organization and creating the new approach.

To provide political cover for his changes, Cox stipulated—with Deputy Secretary Taft's consent—that I would continue to use the title of deputy assistant secretary for EO, but focus solely on military EO policies and programs. Cox would work with the DASD for civilian personnel on civilian EO and EEO issues. Cox made the Safety Policy office a separate staff element reporting to himself.

We had set the stage for the revitalization of equal opportunity policy and programs in America's armed forces. I felt optimistic.

On February 14, 1986, Cox publicly announced the organizational changes. Just as we anticipated, the federal EO establishment fought back. I did not make the front page of the Washington Post, but I was cited prominently in a highly critical article published on the front page of the Federal Times that named Cox and me as the co-conspirators in the disestablishment of the DASD EO office. The article asserted that our changes would undermine EO policy and programs in the defense establishment; it was viewed as a major setback for EO in the military departments. But Cox and I were undeterred; we just answered the media questions, hunkered down and implemented the changes.

I drafted and coordinated two memoranda to the defense components and staffed the OSD organizational changes. The first was signed on April 9, 1986 by William H. Taft, IV, deputy secretary of defense, "… the office of the assistant secretary of defense for force management and personnel staff elements dealing with equal opportunity policies and programs have been restructured within the civilian and military personnel directorates, respectively. This reorganization will strengthen the equal opportunity policy formulation process, recognizing that the creation and safeguarding of equality of opportunity and treatment are an integral component of personnel management as well as an inherent responsibility of leadership...."

The second memo to the defense components was signed on April 17, 1986, by Chapman Cox: "... This establishes the Defense Equal Opportunity Council ... members are the assistant secretary of defense for reserve affairs (and the military secretariats' assistant secretaries for personnel). ... An executive director will assist me. My intention is to schedule the DoD EO council meetings quarterly, with two civilian and two military agendas yearly. The civilian agenda will include equal employment opportunity issues, as necessary...."

These changes led to the revitalization of defense EO policy and made military EO a leadership and chain of command matter. But it took time to institutionalize these changes; the defense department's bureaucratic processes are slow—and contentious—by nature and design. The respective new department of defense directives for the military equal opportunity program and the civilian equal opportunity and equal employment opportunity program were published a year later in May 1987.

Colonel Harvey Kaplan, USA, director, military EO programs office, who replaced me when I became the DASD EO, and Colonel E.E. "Wig" Wiggins, USAF, commandant of DEOMI—both experts in EO programs and issues—were invaluable in drafting and coordination of the new directives and the development of our new initiatives.

As executive director of the DEOC, I dealt directly with the service secretariat manpower policy-makers, meeting periodically with each of them to coordinate the meeting agendas and minutes. Getting the Army, Navy and Air Force assistant secretaries for personnel on the same page with Assistant Secretary Cox was like loading cats in a wheelbarrow. I quickly learned that dealing with their respective administrative assistants to schedule my meetings with the secretaries and to schedule our council meetings required my best political skills and my most charming manner.

Soon after the reorganization, we launched the first-ever comprehensive baseline review of the defense department's military personnel EO program. We created an OSD working group, with Col. Kaplan as chair, assisted by Col. Wiggins and DEOMI. The working group included representatives from all the service secretariats, military headquarters and major service field agencies for manpower, personnel acquisition, training and EO. The group created 12 review objectives and several joint service subcommittees to create an overall plan of action and milestones.

Our driving goal was to make unit commanders responsible for incorporating EO into their chain of command. Training of each level in the chain down to the noncommissioned officer supervisory level was a key component of the new approach. It required many weeks to coordinate and implement the new policies and the associated training. I got a lot of exercise walking miles of pentagon corridors.

We established a requirement for an annual defense EO conference, a venue for stakeholders to address issues, share what was working well, track program status, and develop consensus on new initiatives. (In the 25 years since Bob McNamara created the program, OSD had never hosted a military EO conference.)

Working hand in hand with Kaplan and Wiggins, and with superb assistance from Annette Sturdevant, an expert organizational development and EO consultant, we convened our first four-day conference at Gettysburg, Pennsylvania, in May 1987, with a most fitting conference theme, "Achieving Equal Opportunity through Effective Leadership." Chapman keynoted the opening plenary session. Lt. Gen. Tony Lukeman, USMC, the deputy assistant secretary for military manpower and personnel policy—and our new military EO boss— chaired the conference. DEOMI experts facilitated eight breakout session workshops. All the services participated, and we welcomed several observers from other federal government agencies.

The initiatives enabled OSD and the services to effectively address one of the most complex personnel issues faced by the armed forces— and one of the most challenging societal issues in America.

I also organized and hosted Pentagon Black History Month observances, including one with Oprah Winfrey and Secretary Caspar Weinberger.

Through my engagement on the issues, and with study and research, I acquired knowledge and understanding sufficient to speak in depth about equal opportunity and treatment in the Military. I represented the

¡El Capitán!

Secretary in several regional EO conferences and Hispanic Heritage Month observances in Washington, D.C. as well as events in California and New Mexico.

My most significant speaking engagement of my Pentagon tour occurred at the Naval Academy on June 11, 1987, in Rickover Hall when I addressed the Naval Academy Military Leadership Conference, the first such conclave ever convened at the Academy (initiated by Superintendent Chuck Larson prior to his departure).

My topic was "Minorities and Women in the U.S. Navy: The Leadership Challenge." The speech reflected my coming to terms intellectually, emotionally and spiritually with the complex subject of EO&T in the armed forces. I discussed OSD's organizational changes and our new EO&T program initiatives. But my main emphasis was on leadership. I began with a somewhat nostalgic remembrance.

> As an alumnus with a perspective of 29 years since my graduation and commissioning as a line ensign, I realize now more than ever how enduring are my early impressions and perceptions of the Academy. I never faced a single challenge or adventure in the fleet, especially in command, that wasn't educationally or philosophically linked to my four years here.
>
> My role today is to provide a dimension concerning minorities and women in the context of naval leadership. I believe that leaders of units of mixed racial, ethnic, and gender composition require specific leadership skills supported by awareness and sensitivity, or insight. Not all leaders possess this insight due to a variety of factors, including their education or general life experience in interpersonal relations. But ... it is my firm belief that the necessary skills, awareness and sensitivity for effective leadership performance in any unit, regardless of demographic makeup or ethnic or cultural diversity, can be acquired by officers and non-commissioned officers.
>
> ... Any discussion concerning minorities and women in organizational life perforce must include the basic issues of equal opportunity and fair treatment... For women, sexual harassment, a form of gender discrimination ... can be central to such issues....
>
> The development and sustainment of a positive human relations climate within an organization depends to a critical degree on good interpersonal communications .... Cultural traits can facilitate or

impede these communications … and unit harmony. Stereotypical thinking … is one of the major impediments to effective communication and is often the basis for personal prejudice and discriminatory behavior….

…. To paraphrase our declaration of independence, "all persons are created equal." … an officer assumes a special obligation when he or she swears to uphold and defend our nation's constitution….

I also talked about the impact of Hispanic cultural and ethnic characteristics, norms, and traits in the armed forces:

… Hispanic Americans fit comfortably within our Navy's culture (especially) our patriotism, valor, and loyalty, and of course, our maritime heritage. We have always been among the first to join ranks in defense of our country. Our tradition of valor under arms is best exemplified by the fact that, among this nation's Congressional Medal of Honor recipients, the highest percentage among ethnic groups is that of Hispanic-Americans….

Our cultural identity and our ethnic pride are two of our most valuable assets. They energize and motivate us as we strive to achieve our personal and professional goals within the mainstream of American life…. Our nation and society thrive on this type of energy. Indeed, they would deteriorate without it.

I completed my tour in the pentagon on July 26, 1987, the longest tour of duty of my career. I was awarded the defense superior service medal:

> Captain John F. Gamboa, United States Navy, distinguished himself by exceptionally superior service as deputy assistant secretary of defense for equal opportunity from April 1985 to July 1987. Through his superb leadership, sensitivity, and insight on issues concerning the effective utilization of women and minorities in the Total Force … developed and guided the implementation of the defense equal opportunity council (DEOC), the restructuring of the civilian and military equal opportunity staff elements … and the initiation of a comprehensive review of military and civilian components … contributed to the overall improvement of the program and renewed emphasis on equal opportunity throughout the Total Force….

¡El Capitán!

By then, Vice Admiral Bill Lawrence had retired from active duty and was serving in the leadership chair at the Naval Academy. Needing to close the loop, I sent him a copy of my award citation and the two new EO directives. Here are highlights from my letter:

> I am departing the secretary of defense staff tomorrow and I'm returning to the Navy on July 31. I am pleased and proud to report that I successfully accomplished the mission that you and Admiral Watkins assigned to me when you sent me to this job. It was truly interesting and challenging. It was not easy, and it was very frustrating at times, but ... I feel that I am a better officer and a better human being for having served here.
>
> I leave with the feeling that the Defense equal opportunity program is on a firm foundation and will evolve from here on in a rational and needs-based manner.... Very respectfully.

I reported to Rear Admiral Arlie Campbell and relieved my classmate, Captain Wes May, for my "twilight tour" as assistant chief of staff for plans and programs and acting deputy commander, Naval Telecommunications Command. I worked on improving the management of the headquarters and program planning for system projects. I joked that I wasn't going to give the Navy the best years of my life – I was getting out after 30!

I retired on April 30, 1988, in a traditional ceremony held in the Navy Chapel in D.C. I was awarded my third meritorious service medal. Linda, Jack, Judy, Enriqueta, Linda's parents, and many classmates and other friends were there. Former Secretary of the Navy Edward Hidalgo and Vice Admiral Bill Lawrence (Ret.) were present. Representing Lone Pine were Midshipman Third Class Jose "Pepe" Cervantes, USNA '90, and Midshipman Fourth Class Chuck Miller, USNA '91.

Vice Admiral Chuck Larson, Commander Second Fleet, flew in his helo from his flagship USS *Mount Whitney* at sea and delivered most complimentary remarks.

Then he joined our classmates Rear Admiral Dick Pittenger, Rear Admiral Ben Montoya, and Captain Chuck Smith, who had graciously formed up as side boys to pipe me over the side.

All secure.

Captain John Frank Gamboa, U. S. Navy (Retired)

First Office of the Secretary of Defense Equal Opportunity Conference, May 1987, Gettysburg, Pennsylvania. Me in center of front row with Col. Kaplan and Col. Wiggins on my left. (OSD photo)

Retirement at Washington Navy Chapel, April 30, 1988. (US Navy photo)

Epilogue

★★★★★★★

... I have fought the good fight. I have finished the course. I have kept the faith.

—2 Timothy 4:7

Keith Bunting, Jack Dittrick, John McCain and I comprised the highest number of '58 roommates who were commissioned as line officers and achieved the rank of captain.

In 1982, John was elected to the U.S. House of Representatives from Arizona and then to the Senate in 1986. We enjoyed our first reunion since graduation when John was the commencement speaker for the USNA Class of 1993.

During John's campaign for the 2000 Republican presidential nomination, Jack and his wife Carolyn, Linda and I and our daughter Judy, and many classmates and wives campaigned for him under the direction of Rick Davis, John Weaver, Christian Ferry and Carla Eudy.

I worked with many of John's fellow POWs, including Ev Alvarez, Bud Day, Orson Swindle, Paul Galanti, Bob Shumaker and many others—The Patriots—and we accompanied John on his famous Straight Talk Express bus to many campaign events.

Our daughter Judy joined the paid campaign staff as coordinator of all volunteers at the headquarters. She did a superb job and accompanied me to New Hampshire on John's campaign plane when he announced for the Republican Presidential nomination.

Our campaign headquarters team for the Veterans' national coalition included my good friends Don Jones, Chuck Larson, Joe McCain, Carl Smith, Tom Barnett, Norm Bednarek, Mike and Eileen Giglio, Cy Kammeier, Stamps and Pat Howard, Lang Sias, Angie Williams, Al Zapanta, Justin Oppman, Jeff Howard and Bryan Alvarez.

In September, 2008, Jack and Carolyn Dittrick, Linda and I, and Bill and Mimi Schramm were at the Republican National Convention with many other friends when John accepted the Republican Party's nomination for president. We all campaigned for him and tried our best to get him elected.

Captain John Frank Gamboa, U. S. Navy (Retired)

Jack earned his economics doctorate while still in the Navy. After retiring, he joined the Mason School of Business faculty at the College of William and Mary as an economics professor and the assistant dean. When Keith retired, he joined Computer Science Corporation and expertly directed development of training programs for ballistic missile submarine crews. Keith passed away in December 2002, and Jack in November 2009.

In 1994, Linda and I created Gamboa International Corporation (GIC), a management consulting firm in Fairfax, Virginia. We supported a department of defense advanced technology program that created alternatives to ozone-depleting substances used in weapon systems and developed Halon-replacement fire suppressants. Dr. Don Dix, director, advanced technology, defense research and engineering, and his primary deputy Paul Piscopo headed this critical initiative. We recruited the program's technical director, Dr. Richard Gann, a distinguished National Institute of Science and Technology fire scientist. He provided superb leadership and world-class expertise for a talented team of scientists from the federal government, private sector and academia in accomplishing the program goals, ensuring Defense compliance with the Montreal Protocol on Ozone-depleting Substances.

GIC also teamed with the U.S. - Mexico Chamber of Commerce and worked with Al Zapanta, Charles Cervantes, Joe and Toni Chapa and Eric Gustafson in creating a million-dollar IADB-funded environmental cleanup program in Leon, Guanajuato, Mexico, a first.

After serving in a destroyer and a nuclear submarine, Pete (Franz) Wiedemann left the Navy as a Lt. Cdr., graduated from Temple University as a doctor of medical dentistry and enjoyed a highly respected practice in Chadds Ford, Pennsylvania.

Dick Pittenger served in destroyers and excelled in anti-submarine warfare. As a rear admiral, he served as the Oceanographer of the Navy. After retiring, Dick headed the marine operations division at Woods Hole Oceanographic Institute, in Massachusetts.

Chuck Larson became the second youngest rear admiral in Navy history, earned four stars, served as commander in chief, Pacific, and then was recalled from retirement by the secretary of the navy to serve a second tour as Naval Academy superintendent, only the second naval officer to do so. He is the first to earn seven Navy Distinguished Service medals. After his second retirement, he was instrumental in the establishment of the Naval Academy Foundation and served as its first president. Chuck is a Naval Academy Distinguished Graduate.

My '58 Mexican-American classmate *y buen amigo* Ben Montoya had an outstanding career in the Navy Civil Engineer Corps. As a rear admiral, he became the first minority officer to serve as the Navy's Chief of Civil Engineers and Command, Naval Facilities Engineering Command. Ben is a Naval Academy Distinguished Graduate.

My nephew Mark Bradley followed in my footsteps and graduated in the USNA Class of 1977. After Les Hewitt and me, six more Lone Pine High School alumni entered the service academies and graduated; four from the Air Force Academy and two more from the Naval Academy; my cousin, Jose "Pepe" Cervantes, USNA '90, and his Lone Pine High classmate, Chuck Miller, USNA '91. No student from Lone Pine High has failed at a service academy. I doubt that any high school in America of comparable size (about 25 seniors per year) can match my hometown's proud record.

After the '58ers in PG school at Monterey created the USNA '58 Class Association in 1964, scores of classmates and wives in Annapolis and in the greater Washington, D.C. area helped to manage the association, sustaining '58's dynamic organizational effectiveness, legendary unity and spirited collegiality. In May 1970, monthly luncheons were organized in the Washington, D.C. area by Warren "Poj" Walters and others and have continued for over 40 years. Classmates in Annapolis, Norfolk, San Diego and San Francisco areas meet periodically for luncheons and other events.

In 1971, Poj and Frank "Pooch" Caldwell and Annapolis-resident classmates helped organize our world-famous '58 tailgates at the Navy-Marine Corps Memorial Stadium and the alumni's largest group of football season ticket holders. Paul Polski served as class president from 1978 to 1993.

In 1994, Gordon Gerson and I were elected president and vice president respectively. Most '58ers and their spouses attend our class five-year reunions, loyally support brigade activities, the Naval Academy and the alumni association, and contribute generously to the foundation, including a substantial legacy gift, living up to our motto, "58 is Great!"

During my junior and mid-grade line officer tours of duty, my career evolved into a single unifying theme—command at sea. For almost thirteen consecutive years, from May 1972 until July 1984, I served as a warship XO, commanded a communications station, commanded a warship, again served as a warship XO, commanded my second warship, and then served as squadron commander. Hauling down my commodore's broad command pennant in Subic Bay brought to an end my over seventeen years of fleet operations.

My ship commands were the fulfillment of my primary goal as a surface warfare officer. Amphibious squadron command was my career capstone, a daunting, exciting duty that totally challenged my leadership, seamanship, management and amphibious warfare planning/execution skills. By then I was at the top of my game, an immensely enjoyable and fulfilling time in my life.

I firmly believe that my successful shore and sea commands and other career achievements are a testament to the education, professional foundation and thorough preparation that I received at the Naval Academy. I believe it is the finest undergraduate institution in the world.

My highest honor and privilege in the Navy was commanding my shipmates—officers, chiefs, Bluejackets and Marines. It was their dedication to duty, skillful task accomplishment and loyalty that enabled me to achieve my goals. I am eternally grateful to them.

My entire period of naval service was accomplished during the Cold War. In due course, I acquired an understanding of the Navy together with an appreciation of its strategic relevance and critical value to the United States' national interests and defense. I am proud that my service contributed to America's security.

Mine was not a typical naval surface warfare officer career. I could have opted for war college or staff duty ashore in between my XO and command tours, but that was neither the hand I was dealt nor my preference. (However, when Bupers informed me in *Tarawa* that I had been selected for senior war college, I excitedly called my detailer and asked about orders to the National War College. He replied, "You can just toss that letter into your circular file. You are not an e-ring ballerina!)

And Linda reminds me that there was a period of time when we moved 19 times in 19 years, including new-construction duty, unaccompanied tours, shipyard overhauls away from homeport, re-home porting, and hardship tours in foreign lands. That doesn't include all those forward deployments.

Among the 900 graduates in the class of 1958, only one naval surface warfare officer below flag rank exceeded and only one equaled my number of command tours, both good friends and distinguished naval officers. Captain Greg Streeter had five sea commands, including twice as a destroyer squadron commodore, and Captain Jack Chrisman commanded four ships, one in each rank from lieutenant to captain.

The Naval Academy had 28,266 graduates through June 1958. I did some research to determine how many Mexican Americans graduated from the "trade school" before me and my three Mexican-American classmates—Ben Montoya, Richard Cordova, and John Pinto. Unfortunately, midshipmen's ethnicity was not recorded until 1977 so it is very difficult to identify Mexican-American graduates prior to us. Based on my discussions and e-mails with the USNA registrar's office and my review of the USNA Alumni Association Register of Alumni, I estimate that the number is less than 20, most after WW II. But I was able to verify that, prior to the 1970s, the vast majority of Naval Academy Hispanic-American graduates were of Puerto Rican origin.

With respect to U.S. Navy warship commanding officers, in my time it was common knowledge within the naval surface warfare officer community that Sam Gravely was the first African American to command a major warship (and the first African-American admiral).

But I never knew or heard of a Mexican-American warship CO prior to me. While serving in the Office of the Secretary of Defense, I tried to identify other Mexican-American naval surface warfare officers who had preceded me in command of a major "blue water" U.S. Navy warship. I was unable to find any; however, more current research by others has identified two Hispanic-American line officers who might have been Mexican Americans: Captain C. Kenneth Ruiz, USNA class of 1943, a distinguished WWII submariner and naval aviator who commanded an aircraft carrier during the Vietnam War; and Captain William P. Rodriquez, USNA class of 1954, a naval surface warfare officer who commanded a minesweeper.

Accordingly, I believe that I was the first Mexican-American naval surface warfare officer in the history of the United States Navy to command a major warship as a commander, the first to command a major warship as a captain, and the first to command a squadron of major warships. I also believe that I was the first to command a U.S. naval communications station as a commander. I welcome any evidence to the contrary.

Captain John Frank Gamboa, U. S. Navy (Retired)

In October 2006, I wrote to the chief of naval operations to validate my claims. Here is his reply:

> Dear Captain Gamboa,
>
> Thank you for your letter regarding verification of historical information about your naval career. After consulting with the Naval Historical Center and reviewing available personnel records, we are unable to answer your specific questions ("Am I the first Mexican-American to command..."). Unfortunately, we did not categorize Hispanic officers with a specific ethnic code for Mexican-American until 1977.
>
> You should be justly proud of the path blazed by your pioneering service and the outstanding accomplishments you achieved during your thirty-year career. Your example is inspiring and proves the point that diversity makes our Navy stronger.
>
> Thank you for your leadership and service to the Navy and our Nation.
>
>
> Sincerely,
> M. G. Mullen,
> Admiral, U.S. Navy
>

It was very difficult to transform myself into a good student and a candidate for the academy, something no other Lone Pine Mexican American had done (or for that matter, very few anywhere else in America in the 1950s or prior). During my four-year effort in high school and junior college overcoming educational, financial, ethnic and cultural barriers to enter Annapolis, and then when I was a midshipman and naval officer, I vanquished my feelings of intellectual and academic inadequacy.

At the Academy I had but six Hispanic-American classmates. In the fleet I was wardroom shipmates with only two Hispanics: Lt. Robert Rivera, a Mexican American aboard *Tarawa*, and Lt. Dave Lopez, a Spanish-American member of my amphibious squadron staff, both superb helo pilots and outstanding naval officers.

When I was Ops officer in *Pensacola* and my good friend and Little Creek Amphibious Base neighbor, Commander Bill Daniels, USNA '54, was XO in Ponce, a newly commissioned LPD, I visited with Bill and toured his magnificent ship. He introduced me to the First Lieutenant Eddie Rivera, a Mexican-American Lieutenant Limited Duty Officer.

¡El Capitán!

"Frank, Eddie wanted to meet you because he had never seen an Ops Mex, only Deck Mexs! And you know what, neither have I!" I responded, "Well, get used to it because I am going to be *La Salle*'s next XO and that will be even greater!" We had a good laugh. Bill retired as a rear admiral. His son Bill and my nephew Mark are USNA '77 classmates.

Having grown up in totally integrated communities in Owens Valley, I felt accepted and comfortable in each of my tours of duty. And despite my distinctive minority status in the Naval Academy and in the Navy, I enjoyed total equality of opportunity and treatment in both institutions, to their ever-lasting credit. I deeply enjoyed my time at the academy and in the fleet and made many non-Hispanic life-long friends. But when I was a junior officer, sometimes when I was enjoying a social situation I felt a loss of my Hispanic cultural identity and joy together with a sense of separateness from my shipmates, even my close friends.

After I left the Navy and went into business in the private sector, I made many friends among Mexican-American professionals, politicians and business owners in Washington, D. C., northern Virginia and elsewhere. During an extended business venture in Mexico I met and worked with federal government environmental officials in Mexico City and state and city officials and business owners in the city of Leon, Guanajuato, including then governor, later president, Vicente Fox (he complimented me on my Spanish). And I joined several Hispanic professional, political and social associations including the U.S.-Mexico Chamber of Commerce, the Hispanic War Veterans of America, the Republican National Hispanic Assembly of Virginia, the Capitol Hill Breakfast Club and the Chorizo Club.

So I have regained and renewed the Hispanic cultural joy that I had longed for as a midshipman and as a naval officer. Happily, I now enjoy my American culture together with the culture of my forebears.

My efforts to cope, adapt and compensate also caused me to experience emotional turmoil about who I was and what I was becoming. I honor my beautiful Mexican heritage, and I am proud of the dynamic Mexican component in our multi-faceted American culture. Even so, my official ethnic designation as a Mexican American arbitrarily truncates my family history and ignores my total lineage and bloodlines, a richly-diversified gene pool—Basque, French, Portuguese, Sonora Yaqui Indian and Spanish.

Captain John Frank Gamboa, U. S. Navy (Retired)

Through the process of creating this memoir, I have resolved my years of confusion and internal conflict concerning my personal identity; a direct consequence of growing up bilingual in America within two sometimes-clashing cultures. I am a multi-cultural American of predominantly Spanish descent.

I never aspired to be a flag officer, believing that such a felicitous promotion was in the hands of fate and God. Even so, after I shipped my oars and came ashore at the Pentagon, I felt that my promotion odds were favorable because almost every annual rear admiral selection board picked one amphibious squadron commander or a captain of an LHA or LHD. But I also knew that my lack of OPNAV duty and all its ramifications was a significant career deficiency. Even though my OSD billet was of flag or general officer rank, I felt that, politically, it carried zero weight in competition with my peers, especially those in the fleet or in OPNAV.

But in reality, my age was the primary barrier to flag selection. I was three years older than most of my contemporaries—the time it took me to enter Annapolis. Due to armed forces officers' mandatory retirement age, the Navy has a bias toward youth in selecting its flag officers.

Several days after the 1986 rear admiral selection list was announced, I attended a Navy League reception in D.C. By chance I had an opportunity to converse with Rear Admiral John "Smoke" Wilson, a firstie from my USNA 17th Company days who had served on the board. As we chatted about the list, he paused, looked me in the eye and told me, "Frank, you had a great career but the actuarial tables caught up with you!"

I take great pride in the fact that three of my Phibron Three officers were promoted to rear admiral: Wirt Fladd, my chief staff officer; Phil Duffy, my flagship captain; and Lew Schrieffer, CO of USS *Mobile* (LKA 115), a flag selection percentage from one amphibious squadron command that far exceeded the norm. And I am very proud that Cdr. Ed Kline, my superb operations officer, was the commissioning CO of USS *Whidbey Island* (LSD 41), the lead ship in the Navy's newest class of wet wells, which carry the Navy's newest landing craft version, the air-cushioned landing craft (LCAC).

¡El Capitán!

In each of my commands I gained confidence from my achievements and I learned from my mistakes. I also benefited by trying to emulate successful warship captains in whose wake I followed. Accordingly, in a spirit of helpfulness to midshipmen, naval officers, naval surface warfare officers and members of the USNA Class of 2008, with whom the Class of 1958 is bonded in our alumni association's "Another Link in the Chain" program for classes separated by 50 years, I wish to pass on what worked for me. The following is a synthesis of my values, my beliefs, and my lessons learned as an American naval officer:

> The foundation of a successful career in naval surface warfare is created through dedicated preparation, application, and energetic work. Begin when you set foot on the decks of your first warship.

> Acquire well-rounded technical knowledge about warships. They are comprised of complex systems. A naval surface warfare officer must know his ship, how to operate it, and how to fight it.

> Develop your shiphandling skills and a seaman's eye, a natural feel and sense of timing for ship's speed, distance traveled and relative motion. It is the naval surface warfare officer's trademark. You will experience countless hours of study, observation and application on the bridge in learning how to expertly conn a ship in every type of fleet operation, in all sea conditions, in every kind of weather, in daylight and darkness. Enjoy your development.

> Learn how to lead and motivate by precept and example, to look after your people and to maintain your ship's habitability. It is home at sea for ship's company. A captain sails his ship only with his crew's assistance. How well he sustains, prepares and leads them will determine his success.

> Learn how to plan and execute. These are the fundamental skills that a naval surface warfare officer must possess in order to lead and manage a unit of people, command a warship, and conduct successful naval operations.

Captain John Frank Gamboa, U. S. Navy (Retired)

Ship's company performance is the key to a warship's optimum readiness. Come to understand the purposes, inner workings and dynamics of each component of this organization.

Develop the ability to create rhythms of productive human activity in the wardroom, the chiefs' mess and all ship's work centers. Learn how to elicit all hands' attention to duty and work. Acquire these skills early on and season them with maturity.

Strive to create excellence in each level of your ship's company—the wardroom, the chiefs' mess, the first class, the petty officers, and the non-rated. Develop their skills and potential. You owe this to them—it is your command responsibility. Reward each according to their contribution.

Choose the right challenges for your command. Every Navy warship has the inherent potential to excel in its mission. With all your might, strive to achieve your command goals. Success builds your crew's professionalism, confidence, unity, pride and morale.

Learn how to lead and manage by goals and objectives, an immensely powerful and highly effective way to mobilize organizations, create great teams, excel in mission accomplishment, and develop human potential. This requires skilled strategic planning and top-level direction coupled with organized, disciplined teamwork. The superior results achieved through this distinctive leadership and management technique will justify your investment in effort, resources and time.

Strive with spirited energy and great dedication to create a viable, proactive command climate in which effective communication and teamwork thrive in all components of your ship's company, with equal opportunity and fair treatment for all hands as the norm. The tenor and tone of a warship's command climate are predictors of its crew performance, especially in critical events and times of great stress. And they convey to the Navy and to the rest of the world what the captain is all about.

¡El Capitán!

Hone and temper your judgment so that you will know how to create excellence without arrogance, and to know the difference between ego and egotism.

Carpe Diem. Seize the moment. Shakespeare said it best in Julius Caesar, Act 4, scene 3:

> There is a tide in the affairs of men
> Which, taken at the flood, leads on to fortune;
> Omitted, all the voyage of their life
> Is bound in shallows and in miseries.
> On such a full sea are we now afloat,
> And we must take the current when it serves,
> Or lose our ventures.

Keep a steady strain. Just as your ship's mooring lines could snap from too much tension, learn to be calm in trying situations, and to enjoy ease and relaxation when you can. Nurture your spirit and sustain your morale through a positive, optimistic attitude.

Hold fast. Condition yourself intellectually, mentally, emotionally, physically and spiritually for the long haul, and especially for your times of testing and trial. Which will come.

Remain true to yourself. Your race, ethnicity, culture and upbringing are not obstacles. They are vital resources; personal wellsprings of great power, strength and value. As you adapt and assimilate in the Navy, retain your personal identity.

Love the sea. If the sheer awesomeness and beauty of the oceans, the sky and the star-filled heavens neither motivate you intellectually nor inspire you spiritually, you are in the wrong profession. Take off your uniform and do something else with your life.

Captain John Frank Gamboa, U. S. Navy (Retired)

Love the Navy. The naval service is very demanding and the fleet may send you in harm's way. You cannot serve with success, satisfaction and pride unless you love the Navy.

Love America. Our marvelous country is the source and the object—the wellspring—of your dedication. It is not possible to command a warship without loving our great nation.

Love your family. The bedrock of a naval officers' success, satisfaction, pride and happiness is a loving spouse—your helpmate and best friend.

In America and in foreign lands, Linda created our home, tended our hearth and shaped our family values. She guided the growth and development of our marvelous children, Jack and Judy, with intelligence, understanding and constant love. In my commands she uplifted the wives' spirits and created unity; she cared for my crews' families with sensitivity and compassion.

She was on the pier when I sailed away, and she was there when I came home from the sea. Always.

She was my anchor to windward throughout my naval career. And she remains the moral compass of my life.

Who can find a virtuous woman?

For her price is far above rubies.

The heart of her husband doth safely trust in her.
—Proverbs 31:10

Roommate reunion, Naval Academy Superintendent's Garden, May 1993.
(Personal collection)

Endnotes

Chapter One

    1. Christopher Langley, Images of America: Lone Pine, Acadia Publishing, San Francisco, CA, 2007,

    2. Text by Mary Austin, photographs by Ansel Adams, *The Land of Little Rain;* (Houghton Mifflin Company Boston; The Riverside Press, Cambridge, 1950.), In 1981, I wrote to Ansel requesting a copy of Junior's photo and invited him to dine on my ship *Vancouver*. In his note, responding to my letter, he declined my invitation due to his poor health, but he sent a signed copy of the photo.

    3. Edited by Liliane De Cock, *Ansel Adams;* (New York Graphic Society; Little, Brown and Company, 1972.)

Chapter Ten

    1. Editors of Time-Life Books, *Time Frame 600-400 BC. A Soaring Spirit;* (Time-Life Books, Inc., Richmond, VA,1987)

Abbreviations and Acronyms

AAV	U.S. Marine Corps amphibious assault vehicle
AOA	Amphibious Objective Area
ATF	Amphibious Task Force
BLT	U.S. Marine Corps Battalion Landing Team
BOS'N	Boatswain's Mate
BUPERS	Bureau of Naval Personnel
CAG	Commander, Air Group
CALS	Communications Area Local Station
CAP	Command Action Plan
CAT	Communications Assistance Team
CATF	Commander Amphibious Task Force
CBDR	Constant bearing, decreasing range
CDR	Commander; also Cdr.
CHOP	Change of operational control
CIC	Combat Information Center
CINC	Commander in Chief
CINCPAC	Commander in Chief, Pacific
CINCPACFLT	Commander in Chief, Pacific Fleet

CHENG	Chief Engineer
CHOP	Change of operational control
CLF	Commander Landing Force
CNO	Chief of Naval Operations
COD	Carrier Onboard Delivery
CO	Commanding Officer
COMSEVENTHLT	Commander, Seventh Fleet
CPO	Chief Petty Officer
CSO	Chief Staff Officer
CVBG	Carrier Battle Group
CVA	Attack Aircraft Carrier
DD	U.S. Navy destroyer
DESRON	Destroyer squadron
DETAILER	Bureau of Naval Personnel official who selects duty assignments for officers
DNT	Director of Naval Telecommunications
DEFCON:	Defense Condition
EXEC	Executive Officer
FITREP	Naval officer's report of fitness; fitness report

FTG	Fleet Training Group
FMF	Fleet Marine Force
PHIBRON	Amphibious Squadron
GQ	Ship's General Quarters
HF	High frequency
HRAV	Human Resources Availability
IANC	Inter-American Naval Conference
IANTN	Inter-American Naval Telecommunications Network
IG	Inspector General;
INSURV	Navy Board of Inspection and Survey;
ISE	Individual ship exercise
ISIC	Immediate Superior in Command
JOOD	Junior Officer of the Deck
JOOW	Junior Officer of the Watch
JCS	Joint Chiefs of Staff
LCM	Amphibious Landing Craft Medium
LCU	Amphibious Landing Craft Utility
LCVP	Amphibious Landing Craft Personnel
LHA	General Purpose Amphibious Assault Ship

LHD	General Purpose Amphibious Assault Ship Dock
LKA	Amphibious Fast Attack Transport Ship
LPH	Amphibious Helicopter Carrier
LPD	Landing Personnel Dock
LPO	Leading Petty Officer
LOE	Light-Off Examination.
LOD	Line of Departure
LSD	Amphibious Landing Ship Dock
LST	Amphibious Landing Ship Tank
LCDR	Lieutenant Commander, also Lt. Cdr.
LT	Lieutenant; also Lt.
LTJG	Lieutenant Junior Grade; also Lt.j.g.
LVT	Amphibious Assault Vehicle; also AMTRAC or AAV
MAU	Marine Amphibious Unit
MIC	Management Information Center
MSC	Military Sealift Command
NAVCAMS	U.S. Naval Communications Area Master Station
NTC	Naval Telecommunications Command

NTS	Naval Telecommunications System
OM	Overhaul Manager
OPNAV	CNO's staff
OOD	Officer of the Deck
OPPE	Operational Propulsion Examination
OPS BOSS	Operations Officer
OSD	Office of the Secretary of Defense
OTC	Officer in Tactical Command
PCO	Prospective Commanding Officer
PEB	Propulsion Examining Board
PHIBREFTRA	Amphibious Refresher Training
PIM	Position and Intended Movement
POD	Plan of the Day
REFTRA	Refresher Training
SECNAV	Secretary of the Navy
SFOMS	Ships Force Overhaul Management System
SHIPALT	Ship Alteration
SOPA	Senior Officer Present Afloat
SUPPO	Supply Officer

SUPSHIPS   Supervisor of Shipbuilding, Conversion and Repair

SWO   Surface Warfare Officer; also Senior Watch
                   Officer

TYCOM   Type Commander

UNREP   Underway Replenishment

WESTPAC   Western Pacific; also a cruise to the Western
                   Pacific

XO   Executive Officer; also Exec

CPSIA information can be obtained at www.ICGtesting.com
Printed in the USA
265782BV00004B/1/P

9 780984 637171